LESBIAN AND GAY STUDIES

Lesbian and Gay Studies

A Critical Introduction

Edited by

Andy Medhurst and Sally R. Munt

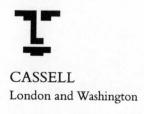

CASSELL
London and Washington

FOR A CATALOGUE OF RELATED TITLES IN OUR SEXUAL POLITICS LIST, PLEASE WRITE TO US AT THE ADDRESS BELOW.

Cassell
Wellington House
125 Strand
London WC2R 0BB

PO Box 605
Herndon
Virginia 20172

First published 1997

British Library Cataloguing-in-Publication Data
A catalogue record for this book is available from the British Library.

ISBN 0-304-33881-8 (hardback)
     0-304-33882-6 (paperback)

Printed and bound in Great Britain by Biddles Ltd, Guildford and King's Lynn

Contents

Contributors

José Arroyo is a lecturer in Film Studies at the Univesity of Warwick. He has published on the films of Pedro Almodóvar and Isaac Julien and has written for *Jump Cut*, *Attitude* and *Sight and Sound*.

Sarah E. Chinn recently received a PhD in English from Columbia University. She has published articles on lesbian and gay studies and American literature. Her book *Blood, Skin, Self: Reading the Body as Evidence* is forthcoming from Cassell.

Joshua Dale is Assistant Professor of English at Tokyo Liberal Arts University. He is currently researching Japanese s/m, and fetish culture and performance.

Jonathan Dollimore is Professor of English in the Humanities Research Centre at the University of Sussex. His books include *Radical Tragedy* and *Sexual Dissidence: Augustine to Wilde, Freud to Foucault*. He is currently engaged in a project on *Death, Desire and Loss in Western Culture*.

Alexander Doty is Associate Professor of Film and Popular Culture at Lehigh University. He has written *Making Things Perfectly Queer: Interpreting Mass Culture* and co-edited *Out in Culture: Gay, Lesbian and Queer Essays on Popular Culture*. He is currently working on a collection of queer readings of classic films.

Lisabeth During teaches philosophy at the University of New South Wales, Sydney.

Richard Dyer is Professor of Film Studies at the University of Warwick. Among his many books are *Stars*, *Now You See It*, *Heavenly Bodies*, *Only Entertainment*, *The Matter of Images* and *White*.

Terri Fealy teaches philosophy at the University of New South Wales, Sydney.

Ben Gove has recently completed his University of Sussex doctoral thesis, 'Cruising Culture: Notions of Promiscuity in Contemporary American Gay Male Writing'. He has written for *Screen* and has taught at Sussex and at Lehigh University.

Laura Gowing is a lecturer in History at the University of Hertfordshire. She is one of the editors of the journal *History Workshop* and is the author of *Domestic Dangers: Women, Words and Sex in Early Modern London*.

Judith Halberstam is Associate Professor of Literature at University of California, San Diego where she teaches classes in queer theory, the novel, film studies and cultural studies. She is the author of *Skin Shows: Gothic Horror and the Technology of Monsters* and co-editor with Ira Livingston of *Posthuman Bodies*. She is currently finishing a book on 'Female Masculinity' and she regularly writes film columns for *Girlfriends* magazine.

Lynda Hart is Associate Professor of English at the University of Pennsylvania and the author of *Fatal Women: Lesbian Sexuality and the Mark of Aggression* and the forthcoming *Between the Body and the Flesh: Performing Sadomasochism*. She has also edited *Making a Spectacle: Feminist Essays on Contemporary Women's Theatre*, co-edited *Acting Out: Feminist Performances*, and published widely in feminist and queer theory, performance studies, and film and cultural studies.

Peter Horne is the co-editor of *Outlooks: Lesbian and Gay Sexualities and Visual Cultures*. He teaches a course in Lesbian and Gay Studies at the University of East London, and is a contributor to *Modern Times: Reflections on a Century of English Modernity*, a volume produced by the members of that university's Department of Cultural Studies.

Christopher Lane is Associate Professor of English and Comparative Literature at the University of Wisconsin, Milwaukee. He is the author of *The Ruling Passion: British Colonial Allegory and the Paradox of Homosexual Desire* and co-editor of the forthcoming *The Psychoanalysis of Race*. He is currently completing *From Man to Man: Psychoanalysis and Victorian Masculinity* for the University of Chicago Press.

Reina Lewis teaches in the Department of Cultural Studies at the University of East London. She is author of *Gendering Orientalism: Race, Femininity and Representation*, co-editor of *Outlooks: Lesbian and Gay Sexualities and Visual Cultures*, and has published widely in Britain and North America on issues of sexuality, gender and culture.

Mary McIntosh taught sociology at the University of Essex for many years. She has written on a variety of topics: 'The Homosexual Role', *The Organisation of Crime*, 'The State and the Oppression of Women', *The Antisocial Family* (with Michèle Barrett), *Sex Exposed: Sexuality and the Pornography Debate* (edited with Lynne Segal). Her current work is on prostitution and public policy. She was active in the Gay Liberation Front and the Women's Liberation Movement and was a founding editor of *Feminist Review*.

Andy Medhurst is a lecturer in Media at the University of Sussex, where he has also taught on the pioneering MA in Sexual Dissidence and Cultural Change since its inception. He has been publishing on issues of sexual identity and contemporary culture since 1982; his latest book is *A National Joke: Popular Comedy and English Cultural Identity*. Also a noted critic, journalist and broadcaster, he has written extensively for *Sight and Sound*, *Gay Times*, *The Wire* and *The Observer*.

Sally R. Munt is the author of *Murder by the Book: Feminism and the Crime Novel* and *Heroic Desire: Lesbian Identity and Cultural Space*. She has edited *New Lesbian Criticism: Literary and Cultural Reading* and *Butch/Femme: Inside Lesbian Gender*.

Vivien Ng is Chair of the Women's Studies Department at the State University of New York at Albany. She is currently writing a book on Chinese feminists in the early twentieth century.

Elspeth Probyn is Associate Professor and Head of Department in Gender and Cultural Studies at the University of Sydney. She is the author of *Sexing the Self: Gendered Positions in Cultural Studies* and *Outside Belongings*, and co-editor of *Sexy Bodies: The Strange Carnalities of Feminism*. She is currently working on the connections between food, sexuality and citizenship.

Jay Prosser is the author of *Second Skins: The Body Narratives of Transsexuality* and has written a number of articles on transgender issues. He lives and works in London.

Vincent Quinn is a lecturer in English at the University of Sussex. He has co-edited a forthcoming issue of *Textual Practice* on eighteenth-century sexualities and is working on a book about male friendship in the eighteenth century. His other research interests include modern Irish drama and theories of biography and letters.

Judith Roof is author of *Reproductions of Reproduction: Imaging Symbolic Change, Come as You Are: Narrative and Sexuality* and *A Lure of Knowledge: Lesbian Sexuality and Theory*. She is Professor of English at the University of Indiana.

Cath Sharrock is a lecturer in the School of English and American Studies at the University of East Anglia. She has published on eighteenth- and nineteenth-century writing by women. Her work on sexuality and the body includes the editing of a special issue of *Paragraph* on sexuality and gender. She has also published articles on paramedical theories of homosexuality in eighteenth-century England and is currently engaged on her next book, *Pathologising Bodies 1660–1800*.

Alan Sinfield is Professor of English at the University of Sussex. Among his many books are *Literature, Politics and Culture in Post-War Britain, Faultlines, Cultural Politics – Queer Reading* and *The Wilde Century*.

Affrica Taylor is a lecturer in the Centre for Indigenous Australian Cultural Studies at the University of Western Sydney, and a doctoral student in Women's Studies at the University of Sydney. She is currently working on the connections between identity, community and place across the relations of sexuality, gender and race.

Nina Wakeford is a lecturer in Sociology at the University of Sheffield. In 1995 she was awarded a three-year ESRC Fellowship to research issues of gender and sexuality in virtual communities. She has published in the fields of sociology, education and technology, and is currently working on a book, *Networks of Desire*.

Simon Watney is Director of the Red Hot AIDS Charitable Trust, a funding agency for international community-based HIV/AIDS education based in London. He has been actively involved in British and international lesbian and gay politics and culture for some twenty-five years. He is the author of *Policing Desire: Pornography, AIDS and the Media*, published by Cassell.

Bonnie Zimmerman is Professor of Women's Studies at San Diego State University. She is author of *The Safe Sea of Women: Lesbian Fiction 1968–1989* and co-editor of *Professions of Desire: Lesbian and Gay Studies in Literature* and *The New Lesbian Studies: Into the 21st Century*. She is currently editing *The Encyclopaedia of Homosexuality, Volume 1: Lesbian Histories and Culture*.

Introduction

Mapping the field

All introductions are constrained by rubrics of justification and flavoured by a pinch of defensiveness. They belong to a genre which is highly predetermined and shaped by unavoidable questions: why did we plan this, how did we execute it, what is its rationale, can it claim to be distinctive? Copious reading of similar collections and their self-conscious, cautiously hedged introductions confirms this; most les/bi/gay/trans/sex anthologies are prefaced by title anxiety. This is an anxiety we share (though size, we feel, is not a problem).

Against the prevailing trend in publishing, we wanted to name this collection *Lesbian and Gay Studies: A Critical Introduction*. Maybe, as a lesbian and a gay man, we just egocentrically as editors wanted to see ourselves reflected in print; maybe it is no more than an effect of identity, or perhaps of our generation (we are both in our late thirties), but not all the contributors to this volume would identify in this way, and it does appear a discourtesy not to display their diversity up front. However, we have our reasons: whilst Queer Theory seems to have superseded Lesbian and Gay Studies nomenclature in the academy, we are disturbed by the elitism which has come to be associated with it, in spite of its originally inclusive political agenda. Both of us grew up as working class, and are suspicious about terminologies and strategies which would – often unintentionally – serve to alienate our home constituencies. 'Queer', from a British perspective, has manifested its own exclusions, and has become a minority discourse institutionalized within academic and performance/art contexts. Queer is unreclaimed by a majority of lesbian and gay men; as a gesture of inclusion, it has remained persistently suspect. Paradoxically, we believe that 'lesbian' and 'gay' have historically appealed across class and racial differences, the terms have a lived inclusiveness despite their unfashionability in certain contemporary intellectual circles. Within the realm of the symbolic (language and representation), the heterogeneity of lesbian and gay life remains largely unarticulated. Practices of representation have attempted to homogenize cultural divergencies into white, middle-class paradigms, but differences are manifold in the way that homosexuals have appropriated these terms. In reality, lesbians and gays have inhabited difference and embraced it. *Lesbian and Gay Studies: A Critical Introduction* is in part an attempt to bring that diversification to the reader. As Joseph Bristow has already pointed out:

> . . . lesbian and gay criticism does not comprise a coherent field. That, as I will argue, is its strength. Because of the alliance it endorses (the potentially controversial 'and' at its centre), it does not stand as one thing alone with fixed demarcations and singular methodological concerns. . . . Surrounding the co-ordinating 'and' between lesbians and gay men . . . are all sorts of anxieties about who has the right to speak for whom, about who is entitled to read and write about another's work, and about how we can, if we choose to do so, together create an area of knowledge about same-sex desires. At no point can we forget that lesbian and gay subcultures contain within them many discrete sexual-political groupings. Both have their separatist constituencies, just as they simultaneously include men and women who work from an understanding that we have more in common with each other than not. (1992, pp. 1–8)

The intention here is not to invite further internecine strife between lesbian, gay, and queer terminologies. As this book clearly shows, all these categories have strategic presence and subjective authenticity for some people. That we can, and do, argue so dynamically about what our sexual identities and practices mean, is indicative of that powerfully assembling 'and', a signal of connection and differentiation. The 'and' is to be constantly negotiated.

Nonetheless, we would not and could not deny that 'lesbian' and 'gay' are far from perfect terms to deploy, not least in the way that they could be seen as adhering to outdated gender binaries. Exclusions become apparent, one such being that concepts like 'lesbian' and 'gay' gesture towards gender-identification, when some would argue that can only reinforce sexual desire as dependent on gender (whether to 'the same' or to 'the opposite'), and that the truly radical proposition then would be to focus on sex/sexual practices alone. The trap of gender might arguably be avoided by a title like *Sexuality: A Critical Introduction*, but such a choice would inevitably, at the level of reception, imply that we focus on heterosexuality; we do, but not centrally.[1] As Bristow also comments, lesbian *and* gay criticism is one outcome of the violence that has been done to us by a heterosexist culture, reducing differences to the same: 'homosexuality is the word we are still too often made to share, even though it is clearly one we have jointly learned to subvert and resist' (1992, p. 3).

Conversely, the current 'add-on' tactic of appending queer/bisexual/transgender to lesbian and gay ironically has the effect of connoting the exclusionary properties of all lists. It is a similarly flawed strategy. Specific lesbian and gay communities have certainly been guilty of discriminatory acts, for example some gay men against women, some lesbians against perverts, and we don't wish to gloss over that, but we see ourselves as contributing towards the manifestation of lesbian and gay as pragmatic interventions and heterogeneous terms. We want to refute the rumour that 'Lesbian and Gay Studies is dead', a comment both whispered to me conspiratorially and declaimed at me victoriously by various faculties over the past year. But Lesbian and Gay Studies is alive, *and* kicking. Whilst some academics are rampantly deconstructing their own precarious hold in academia, we would like to caution that the end of identity is more feasible to some than to others. Claiming a lesbian or gay identity remains a risk – in many senses.

Running parallel to the problem of identity is the concomitant problem of disciplinarity: is there such a thing as Lesbian and Gay *Studies*? There can be no such thing without the lesbian and gay identities and communities that inform it, and are simultaneously constituted by it. Our title is intended to recall the first major textbook of the field, *The Lesbian and Gay Studies Reader*, which claimed, along the lines of Eve Kosofsky Sedgwick's distinction between the universal and minoritizing discourses on homosexuality, that its task was to investigate general, dispersed homosexual *tendencies*, and/or the specific aggregation of particular lesbian and gay *identities*. Abelove, Barale and Halperin asserted that lesbian/gay studies (their phraseology) 'does for sex and sexuality approximately what Women's Studies does for gender' (1993, p. xv). Certainly there are parallels between Lesbian and Gay Studies and Women's Studies, not least in the overt political agendas of each. Feminist thought has had, and continues to have, a founding and trenchant influence on the now abundant academic studies of human sexualities.

Lesbian Studies persists in bestriding a creative and critical bridge between Women's Studies/Feminist Theory and Lesbian and Gay Studies/Queer Theory. Feminist Studies during the 1980s remained somewhat radical on theorizing sexuality, but within the field there was a dull tiredness: it needed a new blade. The parallel expansion of Foucauldian gay male interest in sexuality studies gave Lesbian Studies a prospective suitor. The closetry of Gay Studies within Critical and Cultural Studies mirrored the experience of Lesbian Studies within Women's Studies, and this new partnership, Lesbian and Gay Studies, a marriage characterized by all the uneasy evading of difference generated by any over-expedient union, has become a weird wedlock of alliances which in its limited way can work. Cynics might call it a double-beard, a marriage of convenience in the grand tradition of keeping people quiet so we can get on with consummating our own desires. More positively, it can reflect the genuine allegiances between lesbians and gay men which have been consolidated over the past hundred years, and more recently, in urgent response to the homophobic violence directed at us all since AIDS.

Looking to Lesbian and Gay Studies for a definitive methodology is hopeless; as in any field of worthwhile academic inquiry, multifarious traditions are evident. It is helpful to compare it to another comparative newcomer, that also – not coincidentally – grew out of the 1960s: the (inter) discipline of Cultural Studies, which engages in the ideological analysis of cultural texts. Lesbian and Gay Studies concentrates on the ideological analysis of sex, sexuality, and sexual identity, concepts that can also be understood as texts or discourses. Lesbian and Gay Studies assumes that there is – or could be – a common aim to this, one that could disclose the mechanisms of sexual oppression and identify how those mechanisms intersect and reinforce other matrices of oppression primarily organized around gender, class, or race. There are many conjunctions between Cultural Studies and Lesbian and Gay Studies: both areas are committed to exposing the naturalizing discourses that reinforce commonsense assumptions in daily life, discourses that have oppressive effects. Neither sticks to one preferred methodology over another, but, like an eclectic intellectual guerrilla, utilizes any serviceable means. This expedient unpredictability, rapidly mutating into established and new academic fields, is the ingenious effulgence, and the risk, of Lesbian and Gay Studies. As a faux-discipline, it both desires recognition and abjures it, it invests in academic approval, even as it undermines those same criteria for belonging. Lesbian and Gay Studies is an unstable (sexual) chemistry: that is its strength and its vulnerability.

Lesbian and Gay Studies: A Critical Introduction is a project generated out of its editors' friendship. As a lesbian and a gay man, we have worked with each other and supported each other over the years, both of us further sustained by the affinities and coalitions which form part of an established tradition in British academic life of consonance across identities. In the UK the model for organizing and conceptualizing radical struggles is not the rise of identity in the 1970s, but the old Broad Left imperative of collaboration. We often succeed in alliances where the US fails; to a Brit, the dominant mode of politicizing and writing from the perspectives of different ethnicities, despite its own best-intentioned rhetoric of coalition across identities, gives the impression abroad of an uneasy amalgam of competing interest groups; politics in the USA seem to falter in the face of entrenched and competitive individualisms. In the UK there are fewer of us, and we need to maintain working relations between different political and cultural interests; here these differences become more tacit. (This can be seen positively as dialogic, or negatively as a sell-out, depending on your position. Admittedly, coalitions can require the enforcement of silences 'for the greater good'.)

Many of the academics who facilitated a distinctive Lesbian and Gay Studies in the UK were involved in the Gay Liberation Front in London, Birmingham and Brighton in the early 1970s; men and women such as Richard Dyer, Elizabeth Wilson, Simon Watney, Alan Sinfield, Jeffrey Weeks, Mary McIntosh, and Ken Plummer were members of Gay (and latterly Lesbian) Liberation, and worked throughout the 1970s and 1980s in both the academy and in community publishing to maintain a populist constituency, arguing for an integrationist approach to the study of sexuality. All remained committed to the initial aims of Gay Liberation, consciously associating with other oppressions such as race, class, and gender, making the case for a mutual strategy against all forms of subjugation in the best traditions of the British Left. We need to remember our foundation in a political movement, and not lose 'street theory' to 'straight theory'.[2] Street theory is a sharp, accessible and direct political analysis of what needs to be done; it is intelligent activism. 'Straight theory' erases the lives of lesbians and gay men, not just in content but also in relevance. It rewards us for cutting ourselves off below the neck. We are invited to become talking heads for the bourgeois literati. Alan Sinfield calls on us to refuse an over-professionalized Lesbian and Gay Studies, and conceptualize ourselves, in Gramsci's terms, as 'organic intellectuals' (1994, p. 74) members of political movements agitating for material change, and not necessarily academics.

Lesbian and Gay Studies in the UK relates to its American counterpart in geographically and conceptually hybrid ways. It is a relationship which, in academic and political terms, often appears colonial; there still lingers in post-war British culture the resentful envy that greeted American GIs stationed in Britain in the Second World War: 'They're over-sexed, over-paid and over here'. Yet Lesbian and Gay Studies in Britain has irrefutably benefited from the export of American theory – the 'special relationship' gloated over by Margaret Thatcher and Ronald Reagan has had unforeseen consequences. Certainly there is an energy in US Lesbian and Gay Studies, a willingness to engage, a vibrant, creative and engaged intelligence which this book acknowledges and draws upon in a significant number of chapters by American contributors.

But capitalism ensnares us as the market determines the structure of our field, for example commissioning editors in the UK have one major concern – will it sell in the USA? This rarely works the other way around. We do have our local hegemonies in Lesbian and Gay Studies too, such as the Left-leaning tendencies already mentioned, plus perhaps an over scrupulously policed personal ethics, and an eager cynicism for what is perceived to be some of the stranger Hollywood-like eccentricities which drift over the pond. The Lesbian and Gay Studies culture in the USA (like the broader academic mainstream there) seems much more oriented towards the creation of a star system;[3] as incidents like the saga of the infamous student fanzine *Judy* (dedicated to the enshrining of Judith Butler) have shown, it is best to remember the very human corporeality of even the brightest stars. The 'and' of Lesbian and Gay Studies should remind us against reification; it is an 'and' which always implies we are not alone to judge.

The real relations of struggle, against our well-funded enemies from the Fundamentalist Right and the wider discourses of heterocentrism and homophobia, risk becoming neglected if we place too much emphasis on divisiveness and competition amongst ourselves. There is not the space (nor the inclination) here to propose a defence for Lesbian and Gay Studies, addressed to the homophobic academy that caricatures us as soft, seductive, and corrupting of the rigours of Western Thought, that accuses us of narrow, and politically motivated manipulations; that, in short, falls prey to the very anti-intellectualism it makes the centre of its own attack, as Martha Nussbaum made so brilliantly clear in an article in *The New Republic* (1992, pp. 26–35). But that violence is the mundane and profound backdrop to everything we do. It is because Lesbian and Gay Studies collapses the personal, the political, and the self in its aims, that the academy is inexorably suspicious. Pretensions to objective knowledge still remain powerful persuaders in the economy of academic capital. Homophobic and censorious skirmishes continue to characterize and shadow the workaday existence of queer scholars, but the insights of our own research should assist us in perceiving and rebutting these attacks. Our defence is our intellectual flexibility. Perhaps the coherence of Lesbian and Gay Studies only comes in the politics, in a realm of evolving praxis which is perpetually becoming, rather than here. Politics is what Lesbian and Gay Studies is *for*. In this, Lesbian and Gay Studies is inexorably optimistic.

SALLY R. MUNT

Mapping this book

Sitting down to plan a collection like this begins with a session of delirious speculation – what if we asked Professor X to write about the theory of Y? – that is somewhat akin to the drawing up of party invitations, the selection of a sports team, or the compilation of a cassette of favourite tracks. Inevitably, however, some potential guests are double-booked, some valued players fall prey to last-minute injuries, and some songs just don't fit. Nonetheless, we wouldn't pretend to deny a feeling of editorial pride (two parts elation to one part relief) on surveying this finished product and on noting how closely – despite the inevitable narrative of accidents, emergencies, predictable wranglings and unexpected thrills – it matches our original ideal. What we hoped this book would offer was a genuine introduction: not a collection of essays that already assumed specialized knowledges, but a set of chapters that helped those new to Lesbian and Gay Studies, whether students or the wider public, find their way through the contested, contentious, controversial debates.

Hence our decision to devote the first half of the book to a series of contributions which trace how lesbian and gay perspectives have intervened in and substantially reshaped existing academic disciplines and intellectual agendas. Students of those more familiar fields should in this way gain a clearer vision of what makes lesbian and gay work different and important. The second half of the book builds on the foundations laid in the first: it contains essays which both summarize and develop questions that have been of particular importance within the mobile and elastic boundaries of Lesbian and Gay Studies itself. (In deference to that elasticity, perhaps I should say 'itselves', but I have an abiding distrust of intellectualized neologisms.)

This book, like any book, cannot claim to be comprehensive. Our clutch of disciplines, for example, has evident absences (sociology, anthropology, politics), though many of the concerns of those disciplines do occur in other spaces throughout the book (questions of class, definitions of subculture, strategies for change). While we have not set out to conform to any one ideological paradigm, meaning that you will find conflict in these pages as well as consensus, there are still important voices unrepresented here, most notably those of radical feminism and lesbian separatism. There is also no chapter given over specifically to a discussion of Queer, in all its activist, sub-cultural and theoretical ramifications.[4] Such a chapter was originally picked for our team, but when its author became unavailable we turned initial disappointment into editorial rethink, realizing that not only do discussions of Queer figure substantially throughout the book (in Sarah Chinn's account of gender performativity, Judith Roof's exploration of the queerness of postmodernity, José Arroyo's consideration of New Queer Cinema, to name only three from many), but that to bestow a chapter on Queer might reify it in a way that masked its deep, diverse and disputed impact on the whole range of lesbian and gay lives and thinking.

Many issues reverberate across the book, productively refusing to stay politely behind the demarcations we originally designed for them. Questions of race and ethnicity, for example, are the central focus of Vivien Ng's chapter, but they also feature in many other pieces (Zimmerman, Sinfield, Dyer and Taylor among others). Similarly, the names of key thinkers frequently recur, though one of the strengths of the book's structure is that subtly different versions and evaluations of their work emerge. Radical academics have always wisely distrusted the notion of a single canon of key texts, but in the growth of lesbian and gay thought there are certain unavoidable figures whose work must be negotiated, which is why readers of this book will find copious references to pioneers, figureheads and superstars like Audre Lorde, Adrienne Rich, Monique Wittig, Gayle Rubin, Joan Nestle, Judith Butler, Eve Kosofsky Sedgwick, Jeffrey Weeks, Richard Dyer, Alan Sinfield, Jonathan Dollimore, Simon Watney, Kobena Mercer and Leo Bersani. Some of them contribute their own chapters to this collection, but we have also, to honour another of the early ideals that we have happily managed to sustain, included work by younger, newer critics who may well represent the future of the field(s). (As editors in our late thirties, we find ourselves ambivalently placed, just too young for Gay Liberation and just too old for fully-fledged Queer.) The only individual to receive the ambiguous accolade of his 'own' chapter is Michel Foucault, in recognition of the fact that his work has been, for better or worse, the cornerstone inspiration behind so much of Lesbian and Gay Studies.

As a preamble to the book's contents, let me offer an inevitably partial sketch of its chapters. Part 1, 'Bodies of Knowledge', begins with Affrica Taylor's account of how the academic traditions of Geography have recently begun to take on board 'the ways in which space is sexed and sex is spaced'. Geographical and spatial terms – position, location, terrain, site – have established themselves at the centre (there's another one) of contemporary critical thinking, and Taylor's chapter offers a thoughtful, nuanced exploration of both that general process and a set of more specific case studies that range beyond established disciplinary boundaries to draw on post-colonial theory and Foucauldian perspectives. Geographical and spatial concerns also figure prominently in Nina Wakeford's chapter on 'Cyberqueer', though here the focus is on how the less perceptible spaces of the Internet 'resist an orderly cartography'. Writing with refreshing clarity about an area overly prone to alienating insider jargon, Wakeford provides an introductory guide to the different forms of on-line communication, a reflection on the potentially profound cultural changes they could signal for lesbians and gays, and a reminder that questions of power, hierarchy and homophobia should not be forgotten in the utopian stampede to embrace cyber-life.

To move from the dizzying futurism surveyed by Wakeford to the world of eighteenth-century literature might initially seem a step back towards academic traditionalism, but as Vincent Quinn demonstrates in his chapter on 'Literary Criticism' those binaries no longer have much credibility in today's intellectual context. Quinn raids the Internet for his key case study, a parodic biography of a 'typical' graduate student in critical theory which discloses a great deal about how new methodologies rooted in lesbian and gay theory have been received by the gatekeepers of disciplinary orthodoxy. Through a shrewd and felicitous set of examples, Quinn charts both the impressive successes of queer work in literary criticism (departments of English have frequently been the most congenial home for lesbian and gay academics) and the dangers of a critical practice which neglects its politicized roots in favour of excessive abstraction. Laura Gowing's chapter on 'History' strikes a similar note by underlining the fact that an interest in recovering the lesbian and gay past has a broad sub-cultural and political appeal far wider than the narrow confines of the academy. With a sharply attuned sensitivity to the dangers of anachronism and the problems of definition that beset any attempt to scrutinize the sexual past through the lens of the present, Gowing offers an impressive overview of the ways in which contemporary queer historians have begun to unravel the complexities of understanding the meanings of same-sex desire in different and contradictory historical contexts.

History is also vital, as José Arroyo shows, to lesbian and gay work in Film Studies, where key questions have included 'what were the pioneering gay and lesbian films . . . which directors or actors were homosexual . . . which films from the past . . . had a special significance to past generations of lesbians and gays?' Alongside that work of historical reclamation, Arroyo traces queered perspectives on stereotyping, stardom and pornography, and the ways in which lesbian interventions unsettled the heterosexual presumptions of feminist spectatorship theory. Arroyo is keen to stress the active creativity of lesbian and gay audiences, a point echoed by Alexander Doty and Ben Gove in their study of television and popular music. Studies of the mass media which attend only to textual representations can only, they insist, tell half the story, since it is equally important to examine 'how a marginalized viewer can claim the products of dominant culture as her own'. This stress on queer reading strategies, whether of sitcoms or pop stars, enables us to move beyond the tired binary of 'negative' and 'positive' images. Peter Horne and Reina Lewis' chapter on 'Visual Culture' reiterates the importance of lesbians and gays as interpretative communities, shifting the focus this time to the range of visual texts, from paintings via photography to fashion and style, that have been so important to sexual subcultures. They also evaluate the dilemmas facing artists who are lesbian and gay over whether to embrace or reject the label of lesbian and gay artists (the politics of labelling crop up in many parts of this book) and consider the contributions made by visual discourses to sexual-political activism.

Lisabeth During and Terri Fealy's chapter on 'Philosophy' is not a survey of specifically lesbian and gay work in that discipline, preferring instead to offer an unabashedly partisan account of how certain traditions in European philosophy (Nietzsche, Foucault, Merleau-Ponty, Deleuze, Wittig) might prove useful for radical lesbian and gay thought today. They see power, desire, deviance, difference, perversion and subjectivity as key terms in any queer debate, arguing that an awareness of how particular philosophers have addressed them will facilitate strategies of 'resistance . . . insubordination and . . . transformation'. Foucault is further explored in Elspeth Probyn's chapter, which deftly introduces his enormously influential theories of the social construction of sexuality. Acknowledging how 'daunting' a figure Foucault can seem, Probyn nonetheless demonstrates the continuing relevance of his ideas, revealing for example how the television talk shows hosted by Oprah Winfrey and Ricki Lake operate along entirely Foucauldian lines, and arguing with elegant persuasiveness that Foucault's conceptualizations of desire and identity still have much to offer us as models and methods for social change.

Bonnie Zimmerman's judicious survey of 'Feminism' maps out the different traditions and tensions within feminist thinking, explores the integral role within them of lesbian perspectives, and challenges those postmodern Queer-era writers who have dismissed feminism as a species of outmoded identity politics to answer the question 'if not feminism, then what?'. She also emphasizes the importance of Women's Studies as an institutional base for lesbian theory, enabling such theory to develop, at least until the late 1980s, more rapidly and thoroughly than the comparatively rootless, isolated and disparate work done by gay male academics. Christopher Lane's chapter makes a vigorous case for the usefulness of psychoanalysis for Lesbian and Gay Studies. Refuting what he sees as the caricature of psychoanalytic concepts promulgated by some Queer Theorists, he argues for a re-establishment of Freud as a radical thinker on questions of desire and fantasy. According to Lane, lesbian and gay politics has been too quick to blame Freud for the homophobic excesses of his subsequent interpreters, overlooking in that process the 'erotophilic' and potentially liberatory implications of Freud's own writings. Judith Roof launches an analogous defence of an equally misunderstood intellectual paradigm, postmodernism. She sees the postmodern assault on established conceptual categories as fruitful territory for lesbians and gays committed to a parallel assault on normative versions of sexuality, and counters those who accuse postmodernism of being apolitical with her view that postmodern thinking does not so much abolish political frameworks as ask us to rework them in more flexible ways. For Roof, a queer postmodernism has as its central aim the dethroning of monoliths and the promotion of openness, moves which may signal an end to the categories of sexual identity around which lesbian and gay politics have hitherto cohered.

Many chapters in both halves of this book make use of personal, autobiographical material; Sally Munt's chapter, placed strategically at the book's centre, is a sustained reflection on the political implications, the theoretical complexities and the emotional risks entailed by such a practice.

Lesbian and gay academics, she argues, have a particularly intense stake in this debate, since the raw material of our theorizing is, in a sense, ourselves; what we think and teach and publish 'cannot only be driven just by intellect'. This then brings us into conflict with traditional notions of scholarly dispassion, obliging us to justify our self-referencing in some way. Two of those ways, Munt claims, are twin dead ends – an overly abstracted theorizing of the personal, and an emotive rejection of all theory on the grounds of the greater authenticity of 'pure' experience. She calls for a more integrated approach, a Lesbian and Gay Studies where theory and experience support and draw upon each other, where neither seeks to disqualify either, where our minds and bodies cease to be polarized and strive to be synthesized.

Part 2 of the collection, 'Debates and Dilemmas', begins with Alan Sinfield's chapter 'Identity and Subculture'. For Sinfield, subcultures are crucial because it is there that collective identities are forged from the coming together of individual sexual subjects, and a collective identity (not as 'cosy' a notion, he insists, as a 'community') is the prerequisite of social change. That collectivity is formed as much by exclusions as inclusions, however, and Sinfield assiduously delineates a number of ways in which established definitions of 'lesbian' and 'gay' leave out huge numbers of people, both in Western and non-Western cultures, who organize and conceptualize same-sex relations in different ways. His conclusion recalls, though is not identical to, that reached by Judith Roof: the political categories apposite for movements generated by the late 1960s may now be ending their useful life span; we may be entering the era of 'post-gay'. Vivien Ng's chapter 'Race Matters' endorses Sinfield's critique of Western tendencies to assume the universality of its categories, but she does not welcome any postmodern gesture towards the ending of identity. Ng points out that identity has many different meanings for lesbians and gays in ethnic 'minorities' – for them the shedding of identity may not have the allure it seems to exert over some white intellectuals. To amplify this argument, Ng provides a series of case studies that tellingly indict both Queer Theory and white lesbian and gay activism for their inability to address questions of race without falling into insensitivity, appropriation or tokenism. Ng is able to call on a growing body of work on race and sexuality, but class remains an almost entirely silenced factor in Lesbian and Gay Studies. Mary McIntosh's ground-breaking study of 'Class' is therefore forced to revisit a wide range of lesbian and gay texts and debates and bring to light the class discourses that were present in them but left unarticulated. She highlights the differences between the socialist underpinnings of early Gay Liberation and the widespread disregard for material questions in Queer Theory, looks (as Laura Gowing did in her chapter) at historical writing on same-sex love to foreground the class dynamics, and investigates the interconnections of class and gender identities in lesbian and gay subcultures. As she suggests, the rapid consumerization of gay and lesbian lifestyles is crying out for class analysis; that so little is forthcoming stems from the broader backlash against Marxism which has characterized recent intellectual life.

Jonathan Dollimore's chapter brings a sceptical eye to bear on recent developments in the theorizing and politicizing of bisexuality. He sees the new bi-theory, although not without insights and interest, as too eager to cast itself as the cutting edge of postmodern sexual theory, too quick to position lesbian and gay identities as clinging to outmoded notions of fixed certainty. Dollimore recognizes this as perhaps an understandable reaction to its opposite caricature, where lesbians and gays stigmatized bisexuals as indecisive and evading political commitment, but concludes provocatively by suggesting that any politically rationalized account of sexuality deludes itself by ignoring the destabilizing effect that intense sexual desire has on all forms of rationality. Bi-theory, he implies, may be falling into that trap just as fully as lesbian and gay theories did before it. Richard Dyer's chapter on 'Heterosexuality' has as its core claim the argument that any study of sexual identity needs to address the 'norm' as well as the 'margin'. Lesbians and gays have a head start in the analysis of heterosexuality, since they already recognize it as a concept and a construct, not the taken-for-granted 'naturalness' that even the most enlightened heterosexuals have trouble seeing beyond. The way to analyse, and hence demystify, heterosexuality is to 'make it strange', and Dyer's chapter offers some preliminary thoughts on how to go about this. He outlines the reliance of heterosexuality on concepts of difference and power, and indicates some cultural texts which contain particularly exemplary depictions of heterosexual relations.

My chapter on 'Camp' provides some frameworks for thinking about that troublesome discourse, indicates its relevance to many of the issues central to this book (the politics of identity; the history of sub-cultures; the tensions between experience and theory; the interconnections of gender, race, class and sexuality; the contours of Queer), and concludes with a polemical demand for a more gay-male-specific redefinition of camp, cleansing it of its associations with the spurious 'transgressiveness' of postmodern kitsch. Sarah Chinn's admirably accessible account of 'Gender

Performativity' will be especially welcomed by students held at bay by the barbed-wire prose of that theory's chief proponents. Chinn traces this key concept of Queer Theory back to its varied roots in linguistics, Marxism and deconstructionist criticism, and is careful not to neglect the more everyday sub-cultural manifestations of performative subversions. Her insights here might be productively cross-referenced with my arguments on camp, her call for queer thinkers to challenge 'heterocentrism' recalls the project of Dyer's chapter, and her recognition of the increasing importance of transgender theorists connects neatly to the following chapter by Jay Prosser. His rich and stimulating essay is, perhaps, more a future book in microcosm (*Transgender Studies: A Critical Introduction*) than a chapter which sits entirely at ease between these covers. That is not said in order to denigrate Prosser's contribution, simply to observe that transgender theory posits a fundamental threat to the categorizations of the sexual on which Lesbian and Gay Studies rests. For the moment, though, there are enough theoretical and activist links between transgender and lesbian/gay concerns to ensure that his chapter does belong here: it offers an illuminating guide to contested terminologies and identities (transgender, transsexual, cross-dresser, transvestite), to the inter-dependencies of transgender and Queer Theory, and to the burgeoning field of specific transgender theory.

Judith Halberstam concludes her chapter on 'Sex Debates' with an indication that she, like Prosser, expects transgender to be the most explosive and productive area of radical thinking about sex and identity in the near future. The bulk of her chapter is retrospective, however, looking back at the controversial role played in academic and subcultural discourses by sexual acts, as opposed to the more easily manageable and discussible topic of sexual identity. With a wide historical perspective and a welcome awareness of class and race dynamics (making this chapter one to read alongside those by Gowing, McIntosh and Ng), Halberstam declines the probably impossible stance of objectivity towards the subject of sex, advancing instead a wholehearted attack on 'sex-negative' cultural feminism and its 'asexual erotica'. While never suggesting that sexual acts are politically empty, she rejects reductive, prescriptive equations of sexual practice and ideological implication. Sex, after all, calls on the unconscious, the psychic and the theatrical, never simply on the logical and the literal. The sexual practice which has occasioned most disputes in gay and especially lesbian politics is sadomasochism, which is the focus of Lynda Hart and Joshua Dale's chapter. For them, SM is the key test case on which to explore the issues of pleasure and meaning, fantasy and identity, politics and interpretation which underpin all controversies over particular forms of sexual expression. Using both historical and theoretical perspectives, they survey the competing viewpoints surrounding SM with the overall aim of setting out to 'dispel some of the negativity' attached to it. Several essays in this collection refer to the 'pathologizing' of lesbian and gay sexualities; Cath Sharrock's chapter centres on that issue, looking at it in terms of the immediate context of the AIDS crisis and at some historical usages of pathologizing strategies, in particular at some eighteenth-century texts aimed at stigmatizing sexual diversity. Sharrock notes the prominence at both moments of a rhetoric of plague, contagion, infection and threat (similarly deployed at certain times to regulate independent female sexualities), extrapolating from this not that there is an unbroken ahistorical continuity across two centuries, but that the homophobic discourses unleashed by the onset of AIDS were able to draw on already existing ideological vocabularies which lent them a dangerous aura of legitimacy.

The final chapter of this Introduction to Lesbian and Gay Studies is a sizzling broadside against the perceived inadequacies of the field. Simon Watney's starting point concerns the specific issue of how AIDS figures so sparsely in the mushrooming enterprises of lesbian and gay academia, but he widens the attack until it becomes a mixture of fury and lament over the opportunities that will be wasted if Lesbian and Gay Studies becomes nothing more than another branch of institutionalized theorizing only interested in speaking to a tiny elite. He reserves particular scorn for the 'rigid orthodoxies' of Queer Theory, most of all the postmodern queers' rejection of stable, coherent lesbian and gay identities 'as if these were an embarrassing form of philosophical error rather than a most remarkable political and cultural achievement'. For Watney, what we need most right now is collective political endeavour, but this will be impossible to mobilize if we jettison any sense of collectivity in deference to the fashionable academic belief in multiple, shifting subjectivities. Politics means making a choice, postmodern abstraction defers choice in favour of an endless play of possibilities.

In its somewhat unguarded belligerence, Watney's essay no doubt sets itself up to be witheringly deconstructed by the brightest young things in university Lesbian and Gay Studies programmes (at present, after all, the smoothest route to professional success in lesbian and gay academia is to adhere to precisely the Queer agenda Watney so loathes), but his diagnosis does ring true to me. I sometimes teach students of Lesbian and Gay

Studies who airily dismiss what they see as the naïve unsophistication of 1970s identity politics, without stopping to realize that without the gains made via those ways of thinking neither they nor I would be able to study the course in front of us (or even have made certain personal decisions to get us into the room or the university). Making this point runs the risk, of course, of descending into a middle-aged rant about the ungratefulness of the young, but such lack of awareness of the political history of lesbian and gay thought can all too easily lead to the problems anatomized by Watney. This is not to say his intervention should be seen as the last word, even though it is the last essay. Then again, placing it there was an editorial decision we made to indicate how important we think his questions are. The other chapters in this book, and the debates and further writing we hope this book will generate, are some of the answers to those questions. Some, but not all: the arguments are just beginning. If Lesbian and Gay Studies is to flourish, it needs to proceed through passionate dialogue.

ANDY MEDHURST

Notes

1. Although, ironically, our decision not to title the volume as such falls prey to perpetuating hetero-sex as definitive. These choices, it seems, are always loaded.

2. The terms belong to Kath Weston; she made this point in the plenary session 'The State of Queer Studies' Sixth National Lesbian, Gay and Bisexual Studies Conference, Iowa City, 18–21 November 1994. The talk was published as 'Theory, Theory, Who's Got the Theory?', in *GLQ: A Journal of Lesbian and Gay Studies*, Vol. 2, No. 4, 1995, pp. 347–9.

3. See Shumway, David R. 'The Star System in Literary Studies', in *PMLA*, Vol. 112, No. 1, 1997, pp. 85–100.

4. It might be worth noting here that the co-editors of this book have rather different feelings on the use of the word 'queer'. I am usually much happier to use it, both about myself and generally, than Sally Munt. It thus occurs fairly frequently in my sketch of the book's chapters, primarily as a way of avoiding the plodding repetition of 'lesbian and gay', though I have tried to use the form 'Queer' when I want to signify a text, idea or writer that I consider to belong to a loosely identifiable school of Queer Theory.

References

Abelove, Henry, Barale, Michèle Aina, and Halperin, David (eds) *The Lesbian and Gay Studies Reader*. New York and London: Routledge, 1993.

Bristow, Joseph, (ed.) *Sexual Sameness: Textual Differences in Lesbian and Gay Writing*. London: Routledge, 1992.

Nussbaum, Martha, 'Why Gay Studies: A Classical Defense', *The New Republic*, 13 – 20 July, 1992, pp. 26–35.

Sinfield, Alan, *Cultural Politics – Queer Reading*. Philadelphia: University of Pennsylvania Press, 1994.

Acknowledgements

The editors would like to thank: Pat Baxendale, Sara Bragg, Sarah Chinn, Lynda Hart, Roz Hopkins, Alun Howkins, Kate Lacey, Kate O'Riordan, Alan Sinfield, and Phil Ulyatt for their friendship, collegiality, advice and support; all the contributors, particularly those who joined the project in its later stages; and each other, for staying friends despite the traumas and for proving a dyke and a queen can make a wonderful couple.

Part 1

Bodies of Knowledge

1

A Queer Geography

Affrica Taylor

RECENTLY, SEXUALITY has become a geographical affair. This is not because long-distance relationships are on the rise, but because of a new scholarly union between human geography, gay and lesbian studies, and queer and feminist theory. It is the productive relationship between space and sex, that intrigues writers with a geographical as well as a sexual bent. They are investigating the ways in which space is sexed and sex is spaced, or in other words, the ways in which the spatial and the sexual constitute each other.

I am attracted to these queer new geographies, and their spatial bent on sex, because of the different light they throw on gay and lesbian identities and communities. So, armed with some spatial theoretical tools, I have picked a couple of spaces which are of particular relevance to gays, lesbians and queers, to be my sites of study. These are the metaphorical space of the closet, and the real (as well as symbolic) space of the gay and lesbian urban ghetto community. I have chosen these spaces because they are full of interesting contradictions, and we can consider them, in Foucault's terms, as 'other spaces'.[1] As other spaces or spaces of difference, closets and communities function as counter-sites in hegemonic social space. One of my main concerns is to try and figure out just how counter-hegemonic or bent these 'other spaces' really are.

The route we will take is not a straightforward one. Before setting out for the urban ghetto community and the closet, I will make a couple of detours: first to recount a journey that I once made to Central Australia; and then to take in a couple of theoretical sites, each of which marks an important spatial intervention and challenges us to think differently about our position in the world.

My first deviation

It was an unusually hot November in 1983 when I made this particular trip from the east coast to the 'Red Centre', to take part in what is still known as the 'Pine Gap Women's Camp'. This was Australia's first Greenham Common affair, protesting the presence of a US spy base just outside Alice Springs. With what I can now refer to as a 'Priscilla-esque' spirit of the sexual frontier, we drove west in a cavalcade of cars, indelibly marking the entire 3,000-kilometre stretch of desert highways with our enamel spray-can insignia 'Lesbians are everywhere'. Several hundred city women, a large proportion of them lesbians, converged on the camp site outside the barbed-wire gates of the 'Pine Gap US and Australian Joint Defence Facility'. So did large contingencies of Pitjantjatjara, Luritja, and Arrernte women, who had travelled in from their various bush communities. When we arrived, the camp had already been set up and everybody was euphoric: there was a big mob of women (*arhele mape*).[2] Black and white, dykes and straights, we shared a common purpose: we were all there to do serious 'women's business' (*ara minymaku*).[3] Our business was to expel the foreign enemy ('the boys with their toys' we called them) from the (essentially female) heart of our country, or so we thought.

It was not long before it was painfully revealed that our glib appropriation of 'women's business' was highly problematic, and that this country of 'ours' was not singly conceived. A ruckus broke out when Aboriginal women insisted that the Aboriginal men who were also traditional owners of that country should take part in the inaugural march and address the rally. In their eyes this was clearly the 'proper way' of doing things, a mark of mutual respect and solidarity, and the appropriate formal gesture to hand temporary custodial responsibility over to the women who had come from elsewhere. To them it was a mark of honour. In response, many of the non-Aboriginal women were enraged. This simply confirmed their belief that all women are primarily the victims of patriarchy, and was evidence of the universal truth that 'as women we have no country'. This ' incursion', as it was widely interpreted, simply strengthened their resolve to close ranks around their Aboriginal sisters and help them to recognize and resist the domination of Aboriginal men.

The event became, for me, a hallmark of the ironies and contradictions that are inherent in identity-based politics, although this particular occasion had its own peculiar style and context. This was, after all, the era in which it was fashionable to espouse 'feminism the theory and lesbianism the practice'.

Desiring to be as close as possible to women, and as separate as possible from men, was the simple formula in popular currency at the time. But this particular experience compelled me to do some serious re-thinking about just who was 'my mob'. As we drove home, I read our flagrant markings on the road from a new angle. The brashness with which we assumed an omnipresence was no longer simply an unambiguous rebuff of heterosexism. Going back, 'Lesbians are everywhere' was a ghostly reminder of our own implication in colonialism. I had never been more acutely aware of the presumption and the territoriality inherent in the act of white Western women rendering generic the notion of 'women's business'.

Lesbian and gay spatial turns

The next year, across the world from me, but also disturbed by her white lesbian feminist position in it, Adrienne Rich wrote: 'It is that question of feeling at the centre that gnaws at me now. At the centre of what?' (1986, p. 212). She noted that in the preceding ten years the revealing writings by Black American feminists and radical women of colour, many of them lesbians, as well as the writings of non-Western women, had seemed to have made little impact on the myopic 'white eye' of Western feminist theory. The 'Eye of Feminism', as it saw itself, was not really engaging with these writings, and the complexities that they raised. For the contradictions of women's lives was the very stuff that these writers spoke of – contradictions, such as those that were so sharply highlighted for me at the Pine Gap Women's Camp, that are produced by the *differences* within and between us. It seemed that middle-class, white Western women had a lot vested in keeping things simple, on staying put in the centre of the feminist universe, and continuing, from this supreme position, to speak for *all* women.

This centrism was exactly what Rich sought to dislodge when she made her famous call for a move 'toward a politics of location'. In a re-angling of feminism's famed personal politics, she insisted on the importance of each of us knowing where we are speaking from, but at the same time understanding that we are not all speaking from the same place. She concluded: 'I need to move outward from the base and centre of my feelings, but with a corrective sense that my feelings are not *the* centre of feminism' (1986, p. 231). Pivoting around her question 'the centre of what?', Rich's 'politics of location' was an explicit strategy to de-centre identity politics, and to re-frame feminist inquiries around and about our multiple positionings. For letting go of the universal 'bird's eye view' that a central position assumes, involves giving up the privilege of seeing for all, deciding for all and speaking for all. It debunks the rhetoric of women as a whole (lesbians as a whole, gays as a whole . . .), and derails the reductive impulse to foreclose on the (one) 'truth' about 'us'. Assuming now that we are *not* all the same as we are situated in different places, the question of 'who we are' shifts across to 'where we are'. The shift is strategic, it is spatial, and it *spreads out*; tracing the very contradictions of our similarities and differences as political networks of proximity and distance. The geographical dimension of a 'politics of location' thus surfaces, as identity is transformed from a fixed state of being, into multiple contested and contesting positions, mapped across an expanding terrain of emerging differences.

Rich's call for a politics of location marked a spatial turn in the trajectory of feminist theories in the 1980s. Although her lesbianism was not a feature of this particular essay, as she was writing neither exclusively about lesbians nor to lesbians, it was still significant. Her sexuality, along with other important aspects of her multiple social positionings – such as being North American, white, middle class and Jewish – specifically situated her within feminist conversations about women's identities at that time. In other words, her lesbian sexuality partially twisted her angle on things. Rich's spatial twist also made a contribution to the development of feminist geography, which now, a decade later, in a kind of relay effect, is one academic route feeding spatial considerations back into the arena of lesbian and gay studies.

Within another line of contemporary critical inquiry loosely labelled 'poststructuralist' or 'postmodern', the work of the gay French philosopher/historian Michel Foucault has also precipitated a spatial turn. Like Rich, Foucault wrote to de-centre thinking, in his case within the field of the history of ideas. It was in *The Archaeology of Knowledge* that Foucault first made it clear that he was unimpressed by the 'total' history of Modernism, which he believed was always implicated in maintaining the centrality of existing regimes of 'truth', knowledge and power. Instead Foucault promoted 'local' critiques, where the 'subjugated knowledges' of those positioned in the social margins resist and contest the dominant social discourses. Foucault preferred these edges. As David Halperin points out in his book affectionately entitled *Saint Foucault*, 'as a madman . . . as a left-wing political extremist . . . as a sexual pervert', Foucault had good reason to want to expose the ways by which normalizing discourses both produce and silence 'social deviants' (1995, p. 130). This is what his major work on clinics, asylums and prisons was largely about. But despite producing three volumes of *The History of Sexuality*, Foucault's major work was never explicitly concerned with gay subjectivities, and his public commentary about gay concerns was restricted to a few interviews that he gave to the gay press in the later part of his life.[4] No matter how much Foucault's sexual 'deviance' underpinned the ways in which he provoked us to 'think differently', he was neither an outright gay theorist, nor a straightforward man. In fact, the brilliance of Foucault's work often lies concealed in its obscurity and its perversity, and the effects of his ironic twists can take some time to reveal themselves.

Nowhere is this more evident than in his closeted contributions to theorizing the spatial. As the postmodern geographer Edward Soja put it: 'The contributions of Foucault to the development of critical human geography must be drawn out archaeologically, for he buried his precursory spatial turn in brilliant whirls of historical insight' (1993, p. 16).

Other spaces

Although spatial terms such as 'positions', 'networks', 'thresholds', 'sites', 'territories', 'fields', 'strata', 'surfaces', 'gaps', 'dispersions' . . . , characterize the style of Foucault's writing, his major works were about history, not about geography. When prompted to reveal his ideas about the relationship between history and geography, in an interview entitled 'Questions on Geography', Foucault concurred that space had been devalued in (Modernist) social theory. 'Space was treated as the dead, the fixed, the undialectical, the immobile. Time, on the contrary, was richness, fecundity, life, dialectic' (1980, p. 70). With a sharp eye to the way that centrist thinking privileges itself, Foucault was noting that just as space had become the Other of time, so geography had become the Other of history. Consistently and brilliantly perverse, Foucault liberally deployed spatial metaphors, or the language of geography as Other, to subvert the centricity of history.

According to the geographer, Chris Philo, the subversive potential of geography is quite simple and obvious; it just took Foucault's (anti) historian bent to recognize it.

> Foucault recognizes the simple but telling 'fact' that the phenomena, events, processes, and structures of history . . . are always fragmented by geography, by the complicating reality of things always turning out more or less differently in different places. (1992, p. 140)

Foucault had actually written a lucid and forceful assertion of the importance and potential of space in contemporary life, back in 1967, but this collection of lecture notes remained unseen for nearly twenty years. Eventually they were published in the French journal *Architecture – Mouvement – Continuité*, and two years later in 1986, in the English journal *Diacritics*, as 'Of Other Spaces'.

Foucault named these 'other spaces' that so intrigued him, *heterotopias*. Taken from the Greek, 'hetero' means 'other' or 'different', and 'topia' means place. Thus heterotopia literally translates as 'places of difference'. But there is another layer of meaning, one that involves the effect of misplacement or displacement. In medicine, heterotopia is used in this way to describe an organ that is out of place or not in its right place.[5] I want to retain this double meaning, as I think that it is important to keep in mind that *difference or otherness is always about displacement*. Foucault himself described heterotopias as 'something like counter-sites, a kind of effectively enacted utopia, in which the real sites, all the other real sites that can be found within the culture, are simultaneously represented, contested and inverted' (1986a, p. 24). As other spaces, heterotopias are clearly disruptive sites which displace centres. What they reveal threatens to displace all that might be taken for granted as 'real'. It is no wonder that Foucault found them so appealing.

He referred to many and varied sites as heterotopias, including those sites of his famous studies: the asylum and the prison; and others of his expressed interest like brothels and bath-houses. He insisted that heterotopias, like a mirror, can be both real and unreal simultaneously. Always sites of contradiction, they can reflect an image of a perfect world, but at the same time they also reconfigure it. There are also heterotopias of imagination, movement and passage, such as the ship, which Foucault describes as a heterotopia 'par excellence', 'a place without a place, that exists by itself, that is closed in on itself, and at the same time given over to the infinity of the sea' . . . which has been for European cultures over the last few centuries 'the great instrument of our economic development' and 'simultaneously the greatest reserve of the imagination' (1986a, p. 27).

The function that Foucault attributed to heterotopias was one of disclosure. He believed that they not only reveal their own internal contradictions, but in their relations with each other, they render apparent the contradictions between all sites in the real world.

. . . heterotopias . . . have a function in relation to all the space that remains. This function unfolds between two extreme poles. Either their role is to create a space of illusion that exposes every real space . . . or else . . . their role is to create a space that is other, another real space, as perfect, as meticulous, as well arranged as ours is messy, ill constructed, and jumbled. This latter type would be the heterotopia, not of illusion, but of compensation, and I wonder if certain colonies have not functioned somewhat in this manner. (1986a)

In this way heterotopias, as sites of disclosure, reveal the illusions and the delusions of the so-called 'real' world and its centres. The postmodern geographer, Edward Soja, believes that in writing about heterotopias, Foucault was encouraging us '. . . to see the "other spaces" hidden in the more obvious and diverting multiplicity of real-world sights and situations . . .' and to use them to '. . . reveal the meaning of social being' (1995, p. 14). Very enthusiastic about the possibilities that heterotopias offer to us as critical tools, Soja poses them as a challenge worth taking up. As he points out: 'To get to these "other" spaces requires a different way of seeing, a different interpretive analytics' (1995, p. 15).

For the remainder of this chapter, I want to take up the 'different interpretive analytics' of Foucault's heterotopias in three ways. First, I will examine the mirror effects of the heterotopia as a site of compensation, a simultaneously real and unreal utopian site, which reflects back to us our imagination of a perfect place, and reconfigures it. Second, I will explore the potential of the idea of the heterotopia as a site of illusion, a site of simultaneous concealment and exposure, where things may be revealed to be not as they appear, and thereby disrupt the order of our thinking. Third, I will consider the passage between these two different heterotopias as their relations in movement, the to-ing and fro-ing which de-centres and transforms them.

Ghettos and communities

The alternative site of gay and/or lesbian lifestyles, the urban ghetto, the 'homeland' of gay and lesbian communities is a well-known place that we can now consider as a heterotopia. As I write, a particular site – Oxford Street – Sydney's gay precinct, comes to my mind. It is variously known as 'The Glitter Strip', the 'Golden Mile', or just 'The Ghetto';[6] or for those who know it less intimately but nevertheless recognize it by reputation, the site of the Sydney Gay and Lesbian Mardi Gras parade. It comes to my mind because it is obvious. Any Sydney-sider will tell you, Oxford Street *means* gay community. It is coded gay – pink triangles adhere to shop doors and windows, rainbow flags hang from its awnings. It is full of gay bodies on display, cruising, shopping, consuming gay-friendly products, spending pink dollars, occupying gay space, making out, marking gay territory. At a glance it appears unambiguously to be Sydney's gay heartland.

And yet, when we speak of gay or lesbian communities these days, the radical geographers who insist that we remember the political production of all spatial concepts, will remind us that our communities are in fact '*imagined*'. The term 'Imagined Communities' was first coined by Benedict Anderson in his book of the same name. He was using it to account for the origin and spread of nationalism, but his concept has since been widely taken up by those interested in smaller community formations. It is important to note here, that to speak of imagined communities is not simply to deny their existence, and I do not need to revisit Oxford Street to be convinced that Sydney's gay community has an undeniably physical form. But there is always more to a sense of community than just a spatial location: there is also a fictional aspect to the way that we imagine 'the community' to be our home. We dream up communities as utopias of belonging. We dream them up, because we are drawn to imagine a perfect place, a place that is everything that the 'real' world is not, a place without homophobia, without heterosexism, a place of tolerance and acceptance, a place where we can celebrate our sexual difference, where we can be ourselves.

As soon as we locate these utopic visions in real places: whether that be in Oxford Street, in the Castro, in Park Slope, Brooklyn, or wherever else; these community ghettos begin to function as heterotopias of *compensation,* as simultaneously real and unreal sites. From a distance, the actual scene is filtered through the utopian visions that we carry imprinted on our mind's eye. The closer we get to the 'real' centre of the ghetto, the more our imaginings of the ideal community are eclipsed by the scene that unveils before our eyes. Moving between our utopian imaginings and what we actually experience once we hit the streets, reconfigures the ways in which we (think we) know the ghetto community. The point of stressing the difference between the imagined and the real here, is not to make out that gay and lesbian ghettos are terrible places, but to come back to their terrible ordinariness. They are ordinary because they are not ideal places. Like all other social spaces, they are full of ambiguities and contradictions. This is exactly what the heterotopia of compensation reveals to those who come to occupy it. It mirrors its own contradictions of perfect imaginings and ordinary realities.

Within the actual ghetto then, we are confronted with the pervasiveness of difference in all sectors of the 'real' world. Despite distant imaginings of a place of comfortable sameness, it is the internal differences that confound many on entering the ghetto community. Herein lies the paradox of these alternative community places, these 'other' spaces: they are sites at which the lived experience of difference within difference, renders apparent the fiction of homogeneous gay and lesbian communities. It is only when we arrive in the ghetto with high hopes of belonging, expecting to feel an immediate affinity with all others there, that our experiences of the very real differences between us shatter the vision of 'we-ness' and render untenable the notion of a cohesive community, and its component unified lesbian or gay subjects.

Kath Weston describes this very process in her article entitled 'Get Thee to a Big City'. Drawing on the experiences of some of those who were part of the 'Great Gay Migration' to San Francisco in the 1970s, she points out that people coming from wide-ranging backgrounds, 'entered the urban space of the gay imaginary from very different trajectories', and that for some 'it culminated in sort of anti-identification' (1995, p. 289). The stories she relates of arrival in the 'gay capital' do not necessarily affirm a sense of homecoming and belonging, but emphasize the frequent and unanticipated sense of isolation and difference within it. Even though it is clear that gay or lesbian identities are configured differently by gender, race, age, class, place of residence, etc., somehow the logic of difference can be lost if we become caught up in the primacy of the gay imaginary. The question remains: why do we continue to hold on to a cohesive notion of the imagined community, and locate it centrally in the urban ghetto? Somehow the obviousness of our differences is obscured when we locate 'the community' in 'the ghetto', and we can see no reason why we should not all feel equally comfortable in the same place. Remembering Adrienne Rich's challenge to myopic vision, we might do well to interrogate the use of the ghetto as the central symbol of community, and to ask exactly whose world the ghetto represents.

Some geographers have already answered this question. In writing about urban spaces and sexuality, Lawrence Knopp was particularly blunt:

The largely urban-based, predominantly white, and male-dominated gay social and political movements . . . have taken their own alternative codings of space 'out of the closet' and into the public sphere, but usually within racist, sexist and pro-capitalist discourses. (1995, p. 158)

So perhaps in some ways gay and lesbian community ghettos are not that radically different from the straight world for which they wish to compensate. They have their own implicit centres which need to be challenged. Thinking back to my Central Australian deviation, they have a lot in common with the heterotopia of the Pine Gap Women's Camp. At that site, the revelation that 'women's business' did not mean the same thing to Aboriginal and non-Aboriginal women, ultimately exposed the hidden colonial relations that (white) 'sisterhood' sought to conceal. In gay and lesbian ghettos, the revelation that life in the urban heartlands is not equally cosy for all gays and lesbians, exposes the gender, racial, class and age differences that cohesive notions of 'the community' conceals. The final twist then, must be to de-centre the notion of the gay and lesbian community itself.

Queer spaces and closets

It has been the queer turn, traversing the fields of feminism, postmodernism and cultural geography, that has challenged the unitary idea of the gay or lesbian community and its concomitant territoriality. From a queer stance, the very idea of a gay or lesbian ghetto, set up in opposition to the straight world, simply reinforces the rigid heterosexual/homosexual binary, and thus limits the possibilities of both our sexualities and the spaces in which we can belong. Ghetto gay and lesbian politics often reinforce a strict sexual coding of social spaces, determining them to be either gay/lesbian or straight. By contrast, queer political actions, such as those 'performed' by Queer Nation in the US, Queer Nation Rose in Canada, Outrage in Britain, and ACT-UP all over the Western world, employ an 'everywhere in your face' strategy, to interrupt the dominant sexual codings of spaces by rendering visible the potential queerness of *all* space.

Exemplary of this attitude is Cindy Patton's proclamation:

Gay people have been the perpetual victim of liberal notions of public and private: come out and be beaten up, stay in the closet and the government refuses to deal with the HIV epidemic. To cope with the spatial paradox, queer nationalism invades the mall, kisses in on the Supreme Court steps, unstraightens the Classics to signal those territories have been co-occupied. . . . Social space is leveled and zero-sum: the existence of any queer body anywhere reduces the space for the kingdom of God. (Davis, 1995, p. 293)

Also embracing a queer spatial politics, Sue Golding rejects the oppositional and territorial politics of gay and lesbian identity and community. As an alternative to the restrictive, bounded and strictly coded territory of the ghetto community, Golding offers the model of the queer City as a site of open-ended difference. She suggests that hope lies in the postmodern, thoroughly decadent 'Urban' style of queer perverts who simply refuse to fit into the gay/straight, lesbian/gay binary categories of sexual identity, and their 'crushing . . . totalizing communities' (1993a, pp. 206–19).

dom, Master, bottom, whore-fem, butch, Daddy-boy, cruising, play, play-mate, and so on, have their place. Or, rather, they take a place and make a place. They make an impossible place take place. They describe, circumscribe, inscribe a spectacular space, a spectacle of space: an invented, made-up, unreal, larger-than-life-and-certainly-more-interesting space that people like myself sniff out and crave and live in and want to call 'Home'; a home I want to suggest that is entirely Urban; an urbanness I want to say that is entirely City and not at all – or at least not exactly – Community; a queer (kind of) city (or better yet, cities). (Golding, 1993b, p. 80)

In making a similar break with the conservative impulses of all idealized communities, Iris Marion Young pins her hopes for radical democracy on the model of the 'unoppressive city' of 'unassimilated otherness'. She sees in the life of the radically open city, public places that are simultaneously occupied by strangers, groups of people who can be together 'without suppressing or subsuming the differences' (1990, p. 320). She offers this vision as an alternative to the idealization of a close-knit ghetto-style community.

For both Golding and Young, a postmodern vision of the Urban symbolizes the cohabitation of unlimited differences, thus offering the very opportunities that 'the community' stifles. This immediately suggests that the Urban/unoppressive City would also be an interesting site to explore as a heterotopia of compensation, but not now. Touching base again with Rich's mantra 'my centre is not *the* centre', I am reminded that the 'larger-than-life-and-certainly-more-interesting space' that Golding calls 'Home', is not the place where we all hang out. It seems like a long way from the suburbs, the outer regions, and a million miles away from the closet.

If we take 'the gay and lesbian community' as the Modernist expression of a cohesive oppositional subculture, and the queer city to signify the open-ended possibilities of a postmodern existence, where does this leave the closet? I want to suggest that the metaphorical space of the closet is immutable and irresolute, that it vacillates between both Modernist and postmodern expressions of lesbian and gay life, with a range of counter-effects.

In the Modernist narrative, exemplified by 'coming out' stories, the standard trajectory of gay and lesbian identities *begins* in the closet. The closet is the repository in which we discover and then secrete the 'deviant' origins of our sexuality, where we hide our 'true selves' from a hostile society. In this sense it serves a dual function: acting as a refuge it protects us from persecution, but as a lonely cell it imprisons us within our own deception. Emerging from the closet, or coming out, is thus a move of mixed fortunes. The risk of self-disclosure entails making oneself vulnerable to hostility, but it also offers the promise of liberation in the assertion of one's 'true' lesbian or gay self. It is Modernism's 'truth imperative' which propels us to come out of the closet, and this is generally regarded as a progressive move, a move towards self-actualization. The passage between the closet and the lesbian and gay community is in fact the route by which most of us come into our lesbian or gay identities, even if it does not (as I have already suggested) always turn out quite as expected. In this narrative we tend to think of the closet negatively: as an invisible space of sad and lonely beginnings, or as a necessary hiding space from the dangers of persecution. And there is no doubt that it has functioned, and continues to function in these ways.

It might seem unthinkably retrogressive from a Modernist perspective, to reverse this movement, and return to the closet from *the* community, but from the confidently postmodern view, playful reversals can be strategically powerful. Considered as a paradoxical postmodern site, the closet becomes an 'other' space, a subversive site. Because the closet conceals something that can at any moment be revealed, it always has the potential to radically disturb what is taken for granted to be 'normal'. As a space of illusion, the closet functions as another kind of heterotopia, performing the role that Foucault described as exposing every 'real' space. This makes it very versatile, quite insidious, and definitely queer.

The queerness and the potency of closets has been well established by

Eve Kosofsky Sedgwick. In *Epistemology of the Closet*, she argues that the closet, representing a known secret, is a central trope structuring contemporary Western thinking (1990). Sedgwick makes it clear that sustaining heterosexual normativity requires some considerable effort. In other words, it is hard work to keep the known secret of homosexuality safely hidden away. In the light of such a struggle to maintain the illusion of normative heterosexuality, the closet is repositioned. Instead of always being a vulnerable site of shameful hiding, it can transform into a powerful site of deliberate ruse – the site of the wild-card, the mischievous joker.

When we wilfully play around with them, closets become our performance spaces. As sites of passing for straight, they allow us to be simultaneously (queer) inside and (straight) outside, a highly transgressive double position. The closet then becomes a stage for the (tricky) performance of sexuality. As long as anyone can successfully keep the (known) secret of homosexuality by carrying off the performance of heterosexuality, all heterosexuality can be seen as performance, all heterosexuality becomes open to question, and all spaces become sexually ambiguous. With an explicit interest in maintaining the sexual ambiguities of social spaces, the geographers David Bell and Gill Valentine place lesbian closet performance in the unremarkable realm of everyday occurrence, at the same time as they spell out its radical possibilities:

> by 'passing' as 'normal' in everyday life, lesbians who manage their identities also have the potential to shake the foundations of the 'stable' temple of heterosexuality if their 'deviance' is revealed. By destabilizing heterosexual identities they also have the power to destabilize the heterosexual space that those performing hegemonic heterosexual identities produce. (Bell and Valentine, 1995, p. 149)

Where to now?

If the spatial bent reveals anything new about gays and lesbians, it is that our 'other' spaces destabilize our own territories of meaning just as much as they destabilize the territories of heterosexuality. Lesbians and gays get shaken up while making the pilgrimage across the metaphorical closet, the symbolic community and the real ghetto. These are all unsettling grounds, where meanings can shift or double back at any moment. Within the closet we move between concealment and exposure, between protection and imprisonment, between vulnerability and subversion. Through imagining community we move between utopia and disillusionment, between solidarity and alienation, between cohesion and fragmentation. And in the downtown ghetto we move between the centre and the margins, between exclusion and inclusion, between regulation and resistance. In this way we are twisted and turned, pushed backwards and forwards, until we squeeze past our own limitations, to stretch the spaces of possible sexual meaning and the sexual possibilities of space.

Notes

1. First coined in a lecture Foucault wrote in 1967 entitled 'Des espaces autres', but not published until nearly twenty years later. My reference is taken from the translation by Jay Miskowiec, 'Of Other Spaces', in *Diacritics*, Vol. 16, 1986, pp. 22–7.
2. An Arrernte expression translating literally as 'women's mob'.
3. This is the Pitjantjatjara form of the well used expression 'women's business'. This form has a double meaning. Not only does it refer to those things that concern women, but it also suggests that women have a particular way of doing these things. There are numerous Aboriginal language expressions of this, but the English form is also common currency for Aboriginal women from all over Australia. Used in the English way, 'women's business' confirms the appropriateness of sex segregation in particular circumstances.
4. The most notable of these being an interview that he gave to *Le Gai Pied* which was re-published later as: 'Friendship as a Way of Life', in *Foucault Live* (*Interviews, 1966–84*), New York: Semiotext(e), 1989, pp. 203–9.
5. From *The Macquarie Dictionary*, 2nd edn, Sydney: The Macquarie Library, 1992, p. 828.
6. For a detailed history of Sydney's gay community see Gary Wotherspoon, *'City of the Plain': History of a Gay Sub-Culture*, Sydney: Hale and Iremonger, 1991; references to these names on page 191.

References

Anderson, Benedict, *Imagined Communities: Reflections on the Origin and Spread of Nationalism*. London and New York: Verso, 1991.

Bell, David, and Valentine, Gill, 'The Sexed Self: Strategies of Performance, Sites of Resistance', in Steve Pile and Nigel Thrift (eds), *Mapping the Subject: Geographies of Cultural Transformation*. London and New York: Routledge, 1995, p. 149.

Davis, Tim, 'The Diversity of Queer Politics and the Redefinition of Sexual Identity and Community in Urban Spaces', in David Bell and Gill Valentine (eds),

Mapping Desire: Geographies of Sexualities. London and New York: Routledge, 1995, pp. 284–303.

Foucault, Michel, *The Archaeology of Knowledge.* Andover: Tavistock Publications, 1972.

Foucault, Michel, 'Friendship as a Way of Life', in *Foucault Live (Interviews, 1966–84).* New York: Semiotext(e), 1989, pp. 203–9.

Foucault, Michel, *The History of Sexuality, Volume One: An Introduction* (trans. Robert Hurley). New York: Random House, 1978; *The History of Sexuality, Volume Two: The Use of Pleasure* (trans. Robert Hurley). New York: Random House, 1985; and *The History of Sexuality, Volume Three: Care of the Self* (trans. Robert Hurley). New York: Random House, 1986b.

Foucault, Michel, 'Of Other Spaces', in *Diacritics*, Vol. 16, 1986a, pp. 22–7.

Foucault, Michel, 'Questions on Geography', in C. Gordon (ed.), *Power/Knowledge: Selected Interviews and Other Writings 1972–77.* New York: Pantheon, 1980, pp. 63–77.

Golding, Sue, 'Quantum Philosophy, Impossible Geographies and a Few Small Points About Life, Liberty and the Pursuit of Sex (All in the Name of Democracy)', in Michael Keith and Steve Pile (eds), *Place and the Politics of Identity.* London and New York: Routledge, 1993a, pp. 206–19.

Golding, Sue, 'Sexual manners', in V. Harwood, D. Oswell, K. Parkinson and A. Ward (eds), *Pleasure Principles: Politics, Sexuality and Ethics.* London: Lawrence and Wishart, 1993b, p. 80, cited in the introduction to David Bell and Gill Valentine (eds), *Mapping Desire: Geographies of Sexualities.* London and New York: Routledge, 1995, pp. 16–17.

Halperin, David, *Saint Foucault: Towards a Gay Hagiography.* New York and London: Oxford University Press, 1995.

Knopp, Lawrence, 'Sexuality and Urban Space: A Framework for Analysis', in David Bell and Gill Valentine (eds), *Mapping Desire: Geographies of Sexualities.* London and New York: Routledge, 1995, pp. 149–61.

Patton, Cindy, 'Public Enemy: Fundamentalists in Your Face', *Voice Literary Supplement*, February 1993, p. 17, cited in Tim Davis, 'The Diversity of Queer Politics and the Redefinition of Sexual Identity and Community in Urban Spaces', in David Bell and Gill Valentine (eds), *Mapping Desire: Geographies of Sexualities.* London and New York: Routledge, 1995, p. 293.

Philo, C., 'Foucault's Geography', in *Environment and Planning D: Society and Space*, Vol. 10, 1992, pp. 137–61.

Rich, Adrienne, 'Notes toward a Politics of Location (1984)', in *Blood, Bread and Poetry: Selected Prose 1979–1985.* New York and London: W. W. Norton and Company, 1986, pp. 210–31.

Sedgwick, Eve Kosofsky, *Epistemology of the Closet.* Los Angeles: University of California Press, 1990.

Soja, Edward, 'Heterotopologies: A Remembrance of Other Spaces in the Citadel-LA', in Sophie Watson and Katherine Gibson (eds), *Postmodern Cities and Spaces.* Cambridge: Blackwell, 1995, pp. 13–34.

Soja, Edward, *Postmodern Geographies: The Reassertion of Space in Critical Social Theory.* London and New York: Verso, 1993, p. 16.

Weston, Kath, 'Get Thee to a Big City: Sexual Imaginary and the Great Gay Migration', in *GLQ*, Vol. 2, No. 3, 1995, pp. 253–77.

Wotherspoon, Gary, *'City of the Plain': History of a Gay Sub-Culture.* Sydney: Hale and Iremonger, 1991.

Young, Iris Marion, 'The Ideal of Community and the Politics of Difference', in Linda J. Nicholson (ed.), *Feminism/Postmodernism.* London and New York: Routledge, 1990, pp. 300–23.

Further reading

Angelides, Stephen, and Bird, Craig, 'Feeling Queer: It's Not Who You Are, It's Where You're At: Editors' Introduction', in *Critical inQueeries,* Vol. 1, No. 1, September 1995, pp. 1–6.

Berry, Chris, and Jagose, Annamarie, 'Australia Queer: Editor's Introduction' in C. Berry and A. Jagose, (eds), *Australia Queer: Meanjin,* Vol. 55, No. 1, 1996, pp. 5–11.

Bondi, Liz, 'Locating Identity Politics', in Michael Keith and Steve Pile (eds), *Place and the Politics of Identity.* London and New York: Routledge, 1993, pp. 84–101.

Edelman, Lee, 'Tearooms and Sympathy, or, The Epistemology of the Water Closet', in Andrew Parker, Mary Russo, Doris Sommer, and Patricia Yaeger (eds), *Nationalisms and Sexualities.* New York and London: Routledge, 1992, pp. 263–84.

Fuss, Diana, 'Inside/Out' in Diana Fuss (ed.), *Inside/Out.* London and New York: Routledge, 1991, pp. 1–10.

hooks, bell, 'Marginality as a Site of Resistance', in Russell Ferguson, Martha Gever, Trinh T. Minh-ha, Cornel West (eds), *Out There: Marginalisation and Contemporary Cultures.* New York: New Museum of Contemporary Art, 1992, pp. 341–3.

Jagose, Annamarie, *Lesbian Utopics.* London and New York: Routledge, 1994.

Johnson, Lynda, and Valentine, Gill, 'Wherever I Lay My Girlfriend, That's My Home: The Performance and Surveillance of Lesbian Identities in Domestic Environments', in David Bell and Gill Valentine (eds), *Mapping Desire: Geographies of Sexualities.* London and New York: Routledge, 1995, pp. 99–113.

Keith, Michael, and Pile, Steve (eds), *Place and the Politics of Identity.* London and New York: Routledge, 1993.

Lefebvre, Henri, *The Production of Space,* (trans. Donald Nicholson-Smith). Oxford and Cambridge: Blackwell, 1994.

Massey, Doreen, 'Politics and Space/Time', in Michael Keith and Steve Pile (eds), *Place and the Politics of Identity.* London and New York: Routledge, 1993, pp. 141–61.

Massey, Doreen, *Space, Place and Gender*. Minneapolis: University of Minnesota Press, 1994.

Munt, Sally R., 'The Lesbian Flâneur', in David Bell and Gill Valentine (eds), *Mapping Desire: Geographies of Sexualities*. London and New York: Routledge, 1995, pp.114–25.

Phelan, Shane, *Getting Specific: Postmodern Lesbian Politics*. Minneapolis: University of Minnesota Press, 1994.

Probyn, Elspeth, 'Lesbians in Space: Gender, Sex and the Structure of Missing', in *Gender, Place and Culture*, Vol. 2, No. 1, 1995, pp. 77–84.

Probyn, Elspeth, *Outside Belongings*. London and New York: Routledge, 1996.

Rose, Gillian, *Feminism and Geography: The Limits of Geographical Knowledge*. Cambridge: Polity Press, 1993.

Rothenberg, Tamar, '"And She Told Two Friends": Lesbians Creating Urban Social Space', in David Bell and Gill Valentine (eds), *Mapping Desire: Geographies of Sexualities*. London and New York: Routledge, 1995, pp. 165–81.

Smith, Neil, and Katz, Cindi, 'Grounding Metaphor: Towards a Spatialized Politics', in Michael Keith and Steve Pile (eds), *Place and the Politics of Identity*. London and New York: Routledge, 1993, pp. 67–83.

Soja, Edward, and Hooper, Barbara, 'The Spaces that Differences Make: Some Notes on the Geographical Margins of the New Cultural Politics', in Michael Keith and Steve Pile (eds), *Place and the Politics of Identity*. London and New York: Routledge, 1993, pp. 183–205.

Wiegman, Robyn, 'Introduction: Mapping the Lesbian Postmodern', in Laura Doan (ed.), *The Lesbian Postmodern*. New York: Columbia University Press, 1994, pp. 1–20.

2

Cyberqueer

Nina Wakeford

All the world, in feminist and Queer Theory, it would seem, is no longer a stage, but a screen.

Sue-Ellen Case, 'Performing Lesbian in the Space of Technology'

The queer Oz, cyberqueerdom, lesbigay digitopia – this new space invites everyone who steps on its shores to coin new names. Most of us just call it 'the net' and take the on-line world for granted after a few tours.

Jeff Dawson, *Gay and Lesbian On-Line*

WHY IS THE INTERNET of any relevance to the study of sexuality, and in particular the lives of lesbians, gay men, transgendered peoples and those living under the terminology of queer? Whatever the label – the Internet, net, cyberspace, on-line world – the recent development of resources and communication channels enabled by global networks of computers has generated intense excitement or panic for communities and governments, popular media and commentators within academia. In this chapter I will discuss how and why new information and communication technologies have been created, promoted and studied by those who subvert the norms of heterosexuality. It is through their actions that the term 'cyberqueer' makes sense.

Although the attention paid to the Internet in general, particularly in Europe and America, seems overwhelming, 'cyberqueer studies', as I will call them, are few. Therefore absent from this chapter is a summary of any central debate between protagonists advocating opposing theoretical or activist positions, as might be expected from a survey of a field of study. In years to come as studies in cyberqueer expand and insist on greater theoretical and methodological specificity, such an introduction will undoubtedly look very different. In the meantime this chapter will address the following questions: What do lesbian, gay, transgender and/or queer cyberspaces look like? What is their social, political and economic importance? What would be a critical reading of the themes in existing cyberqueer studies?

What do lesbian, gay, transgender and/or queer cyberspaces look like?

Just try it. This incitement permeates much of the writing which describes lesbian, gay, transgender and queer cyberspace. The message, from eulogizing testimonies of on-line experiences in popular print media such as *Gay Times, Diva, The Advocate, The Pink Paper, Girlfriends*, to anecdotal tales of love found or lost in electronic encounters, is that anyone who has not yet encountered the worlds of cyberspace cannot know the wonders which await them: the realization of global community! the remaking of queer identity! the discovery that whichever subculture of a subculture you inhabit, there will be a Web page, or discussion group, or real-time chat room just for your kind!

This view is exemplified by publications such as *Gay and Lesbian Online: The travel guide to digital queerdom on the Internet, the World Wide Web, America Online, Compuserve, plus BBSs coast to coast* (Dawson, 1996). Dawson begins his book by attempting to draw parallels between a 'real' lesbian and gay world and an on-line realm which awaits exposure:

> If you have ever stepped off the ferry on to Fire Island or pulled into Provincetown or any other gay and lesbian enclave, you know the feeling. It's as if a desert dweller had walked through a magical wall into lush tropics. The natives seem exotic and utterly normal. That's what this book is, a door opening into a world where gays and lesbians are the natural majority. (Dawson, 1996, p. 1)

While noting in passing the assumption of geographically and economically situated cultures of American gay and lesbian life which make this analogy work for Dawson (could Blackpool and Brighton really be substituted?), and the basis of native/exotic/other which functions as a foil to the normality which is revealed as we realize that 'they' are 'us', the key manoeuvre is his suggestion that entering cyberspace can be compared to arriving in an existing place where not only will we feel at home, but we are even the 'natural' majority.

The encouragement to experience cyberspaces at first hand and to assess for oneself their importance relative to other lesbian, gay, transgender and queer cultural representations, is a position with which many working in the field are broadly sympathetic, with one key proviso: access.

Just as Fire Island and Provincetown (Brighton and Blackpool) are only available to those with disposable income and sufficient cultural resonance with these locations, so too the door between on-line and off-line life is more magical for some than for others. Access to cyberspace requires the use, if not the ownership, of a computer, a modem, a telephone service and an Internet provider. These resources are surely not equally distributed amongst the diverse groups of lesbians, gay men, transgendered and queer folk, as far as we know from on-line demographics (Hall, 1996; Wincapaw, 1997). As well as celebrating a potentially new space in which to be queer, we must also pay attention to the kinds of queer which remain silent and unseen, blocked by Dawson's 'wall' of the new information technologies. How many individuals are not in a position to participate in screen- and textually-based information which is predominantly in English? Who bears the cost of strengthening our networks of activists via the computer rather than any other means? In reviewing the vast array of resources available, it is evident that the larger-scale socio-economic questions of the demographics of production and consumption of cyberqueer spaces remain largely unanswered.

Bearing in mind the probability that the computer-mediated worlds cannot be taken to be representative of the diverse population which they reference, what is queer cyberspace? It is probably more accurate to describe 'the on-line world' in the plural: overlapping cyberspaces (Fraiberg, 1995; Wakeford, 1995). Fraiberg indicates that much of the popular imagery of cyberspace presents it as 'a singular, dense and impenetrable space – a huge world populated by hackers and the like' (1995). Instead she insists that cyberspace is 'a multifaceted, multilayered, and very segmented place'. She implies that this is as true for queer spaces as for electronic on-line places which are not primarily defined as queer. Furthermore she suggests that the idea implied by theorists such as Mark Dery (1993) of a neatly separated diversity of cyberspace populations is unreliable. Cyberspaces, whether 'queered' or not, resist an orderly cartography. First, unlike geographically situated places, which have relative stability in terms of their locations on a map, many places in cyberspace tend to be mobile or transient. Second, each space may have different modes and costs of access, ease of use, graphical or textual forms, and levels of intervention from those who own and operate the system. Third, users of one space or system often participate in others; this adds to the impression that queer cyberspaces operate within distinctive cultural clusters, as well as within the global network of other computer-mediated spaces.

Nevertheless some delineation of these segments and layers helps to contextualize the kind of cyberspaces described in the studies of cyberqueer. Amy Goodloe, one of the pioneers in the creation of lesbian cyberspaces and also a researcher in the area, has traced the roots of the diverse lesbian computer networks and services (1997).[1] Her categorization structures my descriptions of the cyberqueer spaces more generally: [2]

Newsgroups
One of the oldest forums for computer-mediated communication, newsgroups allow users to post messages to an electronic message board which can be read by anyone else who accesses the system. The Queer Infoserver currently identifies thirty-five newsgroups of lesbian, gay, transgender and queer interest.[3] Some of those listed also have sub-groups associated with them, so this figure is probably an underestimate of the current number of active newsgroups. Goodloe identifies the first explicitly cyberqueer newsgroup as net.motss (later known as soc.motss) which was founded by Steve Dyer in 1983 (Goodloe, 1997). The acronym *motss* stands for Members Of The Same Sex. More recent newsgroups include soc.support.youth.gay-lesbian-bi, soc.support.transgendered, alt.journalism.gay-press and alt.politics.homosexuality, among many others. However, since newsgroups are public message boards, 'intruders' to soc.motss and other newsgroups can bombard the list with 'flames' (abusive messages) about the nature of the group or its positive stance towards lesbians and gay men (Hall, 1996, pp. 155–6). To prevent this tendency in many newsgroups messages are first received by a moderator who determines whether or not to forward them on to the newsgroup as a whole.

Bulletin Board Systems (BBSs) also exist on commercial services, and by way of small local systems which are not run for profit. These may offer both newsgroup functions, electronic mail and live chat, which I describe in the next section. For example in 1991 the Gay and Lesbian Community Forum (GLCF) was established with official support of one of the largest US service providers, America Online (Woodland, 1995). This space has both message boards and political and cultural resources: 'Daily AIDS reports from the Centers for Disease Control are available, as are pictures of members and PG-rated pinup photos, mostly of men' (Woodland, 1995). Woodland also points out that in addition to the official queer area on America Online there were over one hundred 'gay-related' message folders outside the GLCF. He attributes this proliferation beyond a recognizable cyberqueer zone to the official policies on America Online designed to combat verbal harassment.

Electronic mail discussion lists

In terms of lesbian spaces on the Internet, electronic mail discussion lists have enjoyed far more popularity than newsgroups, from the early Sappho list which itself generated regional sublists, to the flood of new lists generated since 1994 about more specific interests: kinky-girls, boychicks, politidykes and lesbian-studies, for example (Goodloe, 1997). This recent expansion of discussion lists is apparent throughout the range of potential interests of those who identify as lesbian, gay, transgender or queer. In early 1997 the Queer Resources Directory 'List of lists' catalogued more than 200 lists currently in operation, including lists for debate, activist announcements, support for specific sexual or ethnic communities, and special hobby or interest groups.[4]

The relative popularity of these lists may be due to the fact that communication is conducted via messages which are redistributed to a list of subscribers rather than being available to all on a public forum. This means of distribution creates a space which is more private than elsewhere in cyberspace. Women using lesbian and bisexual women's spaces confirm this impression of 'safer' space (Wincapaw, 1997), although it is as yet unclear whether the same motivation drives others who use electronic mailing lists rather than newsgroups for cyberqueer activities. Mailing list distribution restricts, although does not eliminate altogether, the amount of intrusion from those unsympathetic to the aims of the list. The varying success of an electronic mail discussion list in maintaining a group of users who are supposedly united around a topic is often a function of the way in which membership rights to the list are granted. Such gatekeeping of cyberqueer spaces has been one of the points of interest for researchers as it raises questions about who has the power to define or negotiate identity on-line (Case, 1995; Hall, 1996; Wincapaw, 1997).

Chat rooms

Both newsgroups and discussion lists are based on asynchronous communication. In contrast chat rooms and Internet Relay Chat (IRC) are based on 'live' real-time interactions on 'channels' with names such as *uk-poof or *leschat or within 'Lesbian and gay rooms' on services such as America

Online. The history of the queer chat room scene is much harder to trace than for many other cyberqueer spaces (Goodloe, 1997). Most channels exist only when there are participating users, and even for the channels which are persistent over a time period logs are not kept automatically of interactions which occur in these spaces. Nevertheless chat spaces have developed their own distinctive cyberqueer cultures.

Chat areas also exist as part of services offered by smaller private BBSs such as 'Modem Boy' in Los Angeles (Woodvale, 1995) and as part of large commercial services, for example the 'Lesbian Cafe' (Correll, 1995). One of the distinguishing features of such chat spaces in comparison to newsgroups and discussion lists is their explicit elaboration of spatial metaphors within which participation takes place:

> The system is Modem Boy High School; virtually every aspect of the system is made part of this metaphor, often humorously: users are *STUDents*, the Sysop [System Operator] is a crotchety old maid *principal* named Ms. Krump, areas devoted to different subjects are *classrooms*, each with a moderator called a *teacher* . . . email takes the form of *passing notes in class*. (Woodland, 1995)

Although these spaces are interactive chat environments, the images of cyberqueer space are creations of the moderators or owners of the forums. A variation on the chat space is the MUD or MOO space, in which users can create their own textual objects, including spaces, which are saved within the computer system itself. For example 'Weaveworld', inspired by the writings of Clive Barker, was for a time a cyberqueer space within one of the largest of these systems, LamdaMOO (Woodvale, 1995). On entering this space, the user is greeted by the following text:

> You are standing on the top of a hill covered with fragrant and unfamiliar flowers and grasses. From this vantage point you see a large part of Weaveworld, a riotous patchwork of geographies hastily rescued from some ancient peril.

Woodvale describes this space as one replete with markers of 'paganism and sensuality'. When a user 'eats' a 'giddy fruit' the subsequent visions give a clearer idea of the anticipated inhabitants:

You see Jorge Borges, saying 'Oh time, thy pyramids!'
Quentin talks with what appears to be a box containing Schroedinger's cat.
You see the two boys from the statue, wrestling.
You see Michel Foucault in white pants and a leather jacket.

Such scenarios tend to be textually much more complex than those on BBSs, as rooms can be entered revealing other rooms, objects and narratives. Users can add to the story, the spaces or the textual artefacts in a manner which is not possible in most other chat arrangements.

There also exist a small number of two-dimensional cyberqueer chat spaces which are based around images and text. For example Alison Bechdel, a lesbian cartoonist, was commissioned to design the space for a lesbian and gay area which opened in 1996 on the Microsoft Network (MSN). Instead of imagining a space using text which scrolls down the monitor, as in Weaveworld, entering graphical chat spaces is similar to seeing yourself in a cartoon strip. The scene on MSN's chat room is a cafe-bar where an expresso machine features prominently, and users are represented by avatars, or cartoon characters. Chatting in such spaces still appears as text on the computer screen, but the avatars also have a set of limited expressions or 'emote' features. The execudyke can flirt or open her jacket to reveal a Lesbian Avengers T-shirt, as the user selects different modes from a predetermined set of cartoon images. Although a similar virtual world called 'Pride! Universe' exists on the Fujitsu-Compuserve Worlds Away system, there are as yet no accounts of user experiences in these spaces, both developed as commercial ventures by large Internet service providers.

Web sites
As well as spaces within which to communicate, some segments of cyberspace have also become arenas in which text, graphics and sound are collected and stored. In recent years the World Wide Web has become the most prominent focus of many cyberqueer activities, and probably needs the least introduction here. The structure of the Web system, which links together files stored on computers in disparate locations, has enabled vast collections of lesbian, gay, transgendered and queer information to be indexed at central sites such as the Queer Resources Directory (QRD) which currently has 18,334 individual documents indexed by subject (see Note 4). The development of the Web itself is a very recent phenomenon,

aided by graphical browsers. Cyberqueer spaces have rapidly expanded in line with the development of the medium. For example Goodloe reports that between early 1995 and the summer of that same year, the number of Web sites of interest to lesbians had increased from a handful to over one hundred (Goodloe, 1997).

Although the general structure of hyperlinked information is common to all 'pages' on the World Wide Web, there is an extensive range of cyberqueer offerings. Some, such as the Queer Resources Directory or the Queer Infoserver, aim to index all the queer information which is available electronically. Others are both indexes of information and sites for communication, such as Planet Out (See Figure 1),[5] which is a commercial venture with spaces to buy products emblazoned with the Planet Out logo as well as newsgroups and chat room facilities. The Black Homie Pages[6] are hosted by the publishers of erotic literature for African-American lesbians and gay men. There are many unfunded activist pages, such as the FTM International Web site, which provides updates and resources for female to male transgender communities.[7] There are also pages detailing biographies and interests of individuals, with links to friends, institutions, or campaigns. Some of these individual pages are linked to a central list of 'People OUT on the Net'.[8]

What is the social, political and economic importance of cyberqueer spaces?

In the continuing struggles over cultural production and the politics of representation for lesbians, gay men, transgendered peoples and queers, intense interest has been paid in Queer Theory and lesbian/gay studies to conceptions of self, and identity politics. Often this preoccupation has taken place at the expense of an analysis that integrates the self into institutional and cultural practices (Seidman, 1993). Cyberqueer spaces are necessarily embedded within both institutional and cultural practices, and are a means by which the lesbian/gay/transgendered/queer self can be read into the politics of representation and activism confronting homophobia.

To show how struggles over cyberspace become struggles about the expression of sexuality we can return to the initial attempts to start net-motss, the first newsgroup. Dyer has described the battle with the homophobic hierarchies which had the authority to permit or deny the creation of a new forum on the newsgroup system (Dyer, 1988). He is scathing about the moral panic induced by his original suggestion which led to the mystified *motss* acroymn, and several months later was invited to rename the group with an explicitly 'out' signifier, although participants rejected this offer.

Prejudice is common in the day-to-day maintenance of cyberqueer space just as at the time of their creation. Amy Goodloe reports that she frequently receives electronic mails from men identifying themselves as her heterosexual saviours from lesbianism. The occurrence of such harassment was much reduced after she started to display these unsolicited messages on her Web pages. At one time her on-line resources were rendered inaccessible by her service provider after a heterosexual pornographic magazine on-line had linked the Lesbian.org site to its own, allegedly without realizing the content did not include the graphical images which users were expecting. Nevertheless there was enough volume from this link to close down her site on a daily basis until she protested and ensured the link was removed.

Cyberqueer spaces are constantly reconstituted as points of resistance against the dominant assumption of the normality of heterosexuality in ways which are familiar to activists engaged in other struggles against heterosexism. Artists such as Barbara Hammer are using the Web to create a 'lesbian community biography' (Willis and Halpin, 1996) and transgender activist Kate Bornstein used the metaphor of the virtual world to explore the difficulties of transgender transition in a recent stage production (Hall, 1996).

Although some cyberspaces are clearly signalled in their names as non-heterosexual, others are ambiguously labelled and open to a different form of queering (Dishman, 1995; Fraiberg, 1995). Fraiberg suggests that particular attention should be paid to queering of newsgroups which do not have overtly queer topics. In these places the 'potential for performance space' of queer can be tracked. 'In those realms, the queering of net space becomes not a given, but a site of contestation' (1995). With this focus in mind Fraiberg discusses the interactions on two discussion lists devoted to musicians who had recently come out at the time of her study: the Melissa Etheridge List and the Indigo Girls List. She finds that these lists function as a way to talk about sexuality as well as music. Such discussions unsettle fixed labels such as lesbian or queer for a fan population which cannot be assumed to be either, and who are often given only coded signals of sexuality from other participants. Fraiberg concludes 'That sense of discursive movement creates the dynamic that enables queer sexuality to constantly mark and yet always be up for grabs on these popular lists.'

On these music discussion lists queering of the electronic texts never becomes a threat to the existence of the electronic group itself, yet it is an example of the politics of representation in action. The portrayals of both the fans and the musicians are embedded in the cultural practices not only of gender and sexuality, but the logic of production and consumption within the music industry, the conventions of fandom, *and* the discursive norms of electronic discussions (cf. Baym, 1994). Although all cyberqueer spaces exhibit these overlapping practices, the fragility of such forums is evident when discussions of sexuality are conflated with pornography, and lesbian, gay, transgendered and queer spaces are subject to censorship. In the most drastic example, in December 1995, German government officials raided the Munich offices of Compuserve, at that time Europe's largest on-line service, and demanded that it block worldwide access to 200 discussion groups which allegedly contained pornographic materials or information harmful to children. Electronic forums which were targeted included lesbian and gay support groups, initially unavailable to any user since Compuserve could not block access on a country by country basis. One year later, all but four forums were restored to the system, after the company offered filtering software for individual users.

The cultural and political stakes of maintaining a cyberqueer presence are heightened still further given the extensive attention directed at new information and communication technology in terms of public policy and economic prosperity. Increasingly participation in on-line worlds is being signalled as a desirable component of citizenship on both a local and global scale. If citizenship is to be reconfigured in this way, then attention must be paid to the means by which cyberqueer will intervene in the redefinitions, whilst simultaneously facing the challenge of facilitating the equal participation of those who do not have access to computer mediated spaces.

Sexuality is embedded in both the spatial dynamics and the economics of late capitalism (Knopp, 1992), and the same can be argued for computer mediated forums. Sue-Ellen Case argues that cyberqueer intervention (in the form of 'screening' the lesbian) is crucial if the computer screen is to become *the* screen both to the world and for 'our own so-called private production' (Case, 1995). In this scenario the computer screen is the mechanism for the symbolic organization of both cultural *and* economic power. Case draws on the work of David Tomas who posits these new electronic spaces as 'the essence of a postindustrial society' which itself replicates via the exchange of global information and is driven by the dictates of a transnational computer-based economy (Tomas, 1991). If we accept this view, cyberqueer might be used strategically, both continuing to subvert the assumed superiority of heterosexuality within the politics of representation, and by making evident the silences and those silenced by the new computer-aided logic of global accumulation.

However, large-scale service providers have tried to generate profit-making cyberspaces to be consumed by the lesbian and gay population. It was recognized by America Online that the GLCF was one of the most frequently accessed of its services. There is profit to be made by hosting cyberspaces where the product sold is access to others of your kind. MSN and Com-puserve-Fujitsu have been developing their two- and three-dimensional virtual worlds not as a community service but as part of a business plan to cap-italize on the corporate construction of the lesbian and gay consumer. As Case points out, even the most anarchistically radical discourse of the cyber-punk movement can be reappropriated in the name of capital (1995, p. 334).

A critical reading of cyberqueer studies

Most of the commentary and research within the field which I have called cyberqueer studies is sympathetic to the alliances between lesbian, gay, transgender and queer experiences and computer-mediated worlds. How-ever, cyberqueer studies are in their infancy, and this is reflected by the high proportion of material which has been produced either outside the institutional mainstream, published on Web pages rather than in estab-lished print journals, or is innovative work-in-progress by graduate students. Up to this point, there has been significantly more analysis of les-bian cyberqueer practice than for other populations, and very little material on transgender experience despite the widespread participation of transgendered users in diverse cyberqueer forums. Almost exclusively the existing writing has focused on textual cyberspaces rather than those with graphical forms.[9]

The term 'cyberqueer' itself indicates an uneasy amalgam of two words – queer and cyber(space) – each of which has already been over-loaded with the definitions it has been required to contain.[10] If both words are reputed to have a lack of specificity, what is the purpose of creating a hybrid of the two? It is a calculated move which stresses the interdepen-dence of the two concepts, both in the daily practices of the creation and maintenance of a cyberspace which is lesbian, gay, transgendered or queer, and in the research of these arenas. There has been a persistent silence on matters of sexuality in critical cultural studies of technology, perhaps partially because technology was associated with the instrumental to the exclusion of the representational (Case, 1995). The creation of the term 'cyberqueer' is itself an act of resistance in the face of such suppression.

A common theme in the studies of cyberqueer is the relationship between sexuality and space, where space is taken to be the arena accessible by computer-mediated interactions. Cyberqueer spaces are framed as new places within which lesbian, gay, transgender or queer experiences can take place, with a particular focus on the advantages compared to 'real' physically-located space. Mainstream cyberspace has often been promoted as creating 'virtual communities' and cyberqueer spaces may compensate for the social or geographical isolation of sexual minorities by operating as a medium through which contacts can be more easily facilitiated (Case, 1995; Woodland, 1995). The research on cyberqueer discussion lists suggests that for many users the lists are places to socialize and meet new friends or lovers, but can also be an important 'space of refuge' from *other* lesbian, gay, transgender and queer worlds, some of which are themselves on-line (Hall, 1996; Wincapaw, 1997). Kira Hall names a strategy of 'radical cyberfeminism' which she locates within the women-only discussion list Sappho (Hall, 1996). Radical cyberfeminism – which includes screening of names and messages, a norm of support and an anti-flaming policy – is a response to the 'aggressive stylistics which characterize cybermasculinity' on other mixed gender discussion lists such as Gaynet and QSTUDY-L (Hall, 1996). This strategy is a way of imposing boundaries around the space, and is also often achieved by regulating as far as possible the gender, sexual orientation, and/or other criteria of those accessing the forum (Wincapaw, 1997).

Others have focused on how the detailed spatial imagery of each cyberspace itself contributes to the inclusion or exclusion of particular groups (Woodland, 1995). Whereas ModemBoy's cultural referents are 'horny, sexually compulsive adolescent boys' and a blatant ideal of 'hairless white boys', Weaveworld is drawn from a more subtle gay iconography of paganism, anarchy and sensuality. Woodland voices the claim, implicit in much of the other research, that the importance of such descriptions is that cyberqueer spacial imagery indicates the state of contemporary queer identities.

The construction of identity is the key thematic which unites almost all cyberqueer studies. The importance of a new space is viewed not as an end in itself, but rather as a contextual feature for the creation of new versions of the self. The possibility of anonymity on some services and the lack of face-to-face social cues lead authors to suggest that coming out may be easier on-line, thus transforming the notion of what it means to be gay (Dishman, 1995). Jodi O'Brien describes an advertisement in *The Advocate* which proclaims (over a naked male torso) 'There are no closets in Cyberspace'. This pronouncement plays both on the possibility of anonymity and reinforces a distinction between 'real' world (with closets) and cyberspace where we are led to believe that the closet/'being out' fix has no meaning (O'Brien, 1996). Additionally Dishman locates the origin for the desire for a sexual use of cyberspaces as connected to the impact of HIV and AIDS. He comments: 'Certainly, with respect to infectious disease, there can be no safer interactive sex than having it with someone with whom contact exists only through electronic pulses. Cybersex is safe sex' (Dishman, 1995).

Some authors have proposed that such a new kind of electronic sexuality would be particularly attractive to gay men (Dishman, 1995, 1997; Sheldon, 1996), although the terms 'cyberdyke' and 'cyberlesbian' have also been employed in the promotion of new lesbian identities (Case, 1995; Hall, 1996; Haskel 1996; Wakeford, 1995). Occasionally the kind of language used in such predictions mirrors the utopian rhetoric observable in mainstream predictions of cyberspace futures:

> Through the technology available on the Internet, gay men have become erotic hitchhikers in search of sexual stimulation beyond the physical body. The fact that we are able to use our imaginations for sexual pioneering is at once appalling and intimidating to straights. The Information Superhighway allows gays to realize the brain, and its creative transmissions, as our largest sexual organ. (Sheldon, 1996)

Although the precise way in which identity is invoked varies between accounts, certain theoretical assumptions underpin most cyberqueer studies.

First, it is usually taken for granted (if not explicitly stated) that the version of the concept of identity offered by recent prominent queer theorists, in particular Judith Butler and Eve K. Sedgwick, is unproblematically appropriate for cyberqueer (in particular see Fraiberg, 1995; Bromley, Hall, 1996; Woodland, 1995). Queer can be interpreted as a way to include all non-normative sexualities as identities, and at the same time allows a blurring of any necessary links between sexuality and gender (Walters, 1996) yet in cyberqueer it is also a way of describing identities which are mediated through electronic means. Dishman (1995) has claimed that cyberspace actually aids the production and expression of queer identity, yet that begs the question: What precisely does the *cyber* add to the *queer* identity which it lacked previously? Can queer identity reliably be theorized without also problematizing how it may be reconstituted or transformed by the nature of the individual cyberspace within which it is constructed? Several authors have attempted to discuss the ways in which evidence of the process of construction of queer can be spotted on-line. Yet there is still a resistance to suggest alternative modes of cyberqueer identity outside those proposed by dominant Queer Theory. As Biddy Martin has pointed out, in some versions of identity produced in the name of Queer Theory, sexuality becomes the primary figure of mobility and 'crossing', leaving race and gender as relatively stable (Martin, 1994). Such differential immobility in categories would be a weighty legacy for those trying to theorize cyberqueer, particularly given the fact that there are so few accounts which focus on race beyond the acknowledgement of white cultural dominance of cyberspace. Cyberspace has its own dominant history of how diverse sexual identities are expressed or silenced, yet this is rarely acknowledged. For the most part those producing and consuming cyberqueer spaces are obliged to work within what is technically possible within computer systems, and the representations which they have the skills to construct in each forum.

Second and as a consequence, the postmodernist heritage of this version of queer (accompanied by other postmodern influences) leads to versions of identity as fluid and/or performative (see Case, 1995; Dishman, 1995; Bromley, 1995; Hall, 1996; Broidy, 1996; Haskel, 1996; Woodland, 1995). The ideology of fluid identities is evident in the maxim that 'you can be whoever you want to be' in cyberspace, and this can change with varying presentations of self. Kira Hall cites lesbians who 'play' at being gay men (Hall, 1996). Hank Bromley talks of users who 'pretend' to be transgendered (Bromley, 1995). In fact the impression is that cyberspace is the postmodern space *par excellence*, whether or not the user is gay or straight, transgendered or not. Perhaps the closeness of fit is a bit too convincing? What is lost if cyberqueer research becomes merely a celebration of parody and performance, or the simplistic application of an author's reading of *Gender Trouble* or *The Epistemology of The Closet?*

One of the intersecting ways in which identity has been theorized by cyberqueer writers has drawn upon Donna Haraway's vision of the machine-human hybrid: the cyborg, itself iconic in some fields of technoscience studies (Haraway, 1985). Both Kira Hall and Hank Bromley frame their articles by highlighting Haraway's metaphor. Yet even though within Haraway's formulation there is a clear understanding of how multiple positioning of race and gender are integral to such a hybrid, it is a visionary metaphor, and proves problematic when applied to user experiences. From her study of the women of the Sappho discussion list, Hall concludes 'cyberspace is generating goddessses and ogres, not cyborgs' (1996, p. 167).

Third, as understood through cyberqueer research, identity appears to be attached primarily to signals of the body, whether they are codes for body parts or physical attributes in a Muff Diva Index of the lesbian body (Wakeford, 1995), the contention that a discussion list itself is an embodied lesbian form (Case, 1995), or in a forum where ideas about bodies become the central gatekeeping mechanism for access to the cyberqueer space (for example, the 'pre-op'/'post-op' transgender debate, Wakeford, forthcoming). Much is made of how users can change the descriptions of themselves which others may access while on a BBS (Tsang, 1994), or the fact that anonymity means that one starts with 'no body' and so is free to construct or reconstruct images of physicality at whim (Dishman, 1995). ModemBoy signals a specific kind of embodied power relationship, and

Figure 2.1: PlanetOut's Web site.

even PlanetOut's Web site (Figure 1) has a finite subset of body styles chosen from a wider cultural repertoire.

Despite the preponderance of such bodies, there has been much less attention to the body which is *not* screened, the one which is 'left' when the computer is turned off, or even what happens to the 'real' body when the computer is on. Lisa Haskel's account of cyberdyke life shows how both the machine and its connectivity provoke physical wants and desires when she is off-line as well as when she is connected (Haskel, 1996), but there is little research which attempts to examine the intersection and potential contradictions of bodies in the on-line and off-line worlds.[11]

The final assumption embedded within much of the discussion of identity recalls the issue of participation in cyberspace. Whilst cyberqueer research points to the economic costs of involvement (Woodland, 1995; Wakeford, forthcoming), there is a disturbing silence on the issue of ability to perform identities once users are in a cyberqueer space. Is this also economically related? Are users who can afford more time able to be more (convincingly) fluid? Is this ability culturally specific? If performance is the measure of identity, how does performance vary with cultural location? Most cyberqueer activities and research have their origins in the USA. There is a strong likelihood that this will influence the level and nature of participation, yet no cross-cultural work has yet been undertaken. Many of the cultures of cyberspace emphasize the 'newbie' phenomenon in contrast to the more experienced user, yet this dimension of time and performance is also lacking from the accounts of cyberqueer.[12] Drawing on Lisa Haskel's comments, the question might not be 'Are you lesbian?' but 'Are you lesbian *enough*?' to participate (Haskel, 1996, p. 52). Her comment is a reminder that the ability to enter many cyberqueer spaces involves conscious (re)construction of the self which may be learned over time.

There are multiple locations of cyberqueer activity in on-line worlds and resources. Nevertheless there remains a tendency for those who analyse these appearances to concentrate on the symbolic aspects of cultural production at the expense of the economic and structural features. Whereas the production and consumption of cyberqueer *activities* is flourishing, cyberqueer *studies* in general are at risk of lagging behind by ignoring economic and political conditions which are inevitably intertwined with the social and cultural features of their representations. There is also the danger that by reflecting present preoccupations in certain versions of contemporary Queer Theory, the focus on the performance of multiple fluid identities may be sustained at the cost of obscuring other potentially stimulating lines of enquiry, such as the institutional context of cyberqueer. This is a criticism which has been levelled at Queer Theory more widely (Seidman, 1993), yet it is particularly apt for research where the object of study is so intimately acquainted with economic conditions of production and consumption.

Notes

1. Amy Goodloe is also the creator and maintainer of the largest lesbian site on the World Wide Web (www.lesbian.org).
2. For a full list of spaces, the Yahoo directory at: http://www.yahoo.com/text/Society_and_Culture/Lesbians__Gays_and_Bise xuals/Computers_and_Internet/ is a good place to begin.
3. The Queer Infoserver is one of the large repositories of indexed information on the World Wide Web (www.infoqueer.org/queer/qis).
4. The Queer Resources Directory (www.qrd.org/qrd/) is the largest and one of the oldest collections of electronic information about the whole range of computer network spaces which are advertised as lesbian, gay, transgender and queer.
5. http://www.planetout.com
6. http://abacus.oxy.edu/BLK/blkhome.htm
7. http://www.ftm-int.org/intro.htm
8. This list can be accessed via an electronic link from the Queer Infoserver (see Note 3).
9. I have omitted from this discussion research on lesbians (Wood, 1997) and gay men (Nieto, 1996) which has used computer-mediated communication primarily as a means of data collection rather than as an integral concept for subsequent data analysis.
10. The earliest use which I have been able to trace of the term 'cyberqueer' is *Queer-e*'s call for papers exploring the term (see footnote 2, Hall, 1996).
11. But see Wakeford (1997) for an initial exploration of the connections between bodily practices in these two arenas.
12. An exception is Correll's study of the 'Lesbian Cafe' BBS, which is cited in the further reading for this chapter.

References

Baym, N., 'The Emergence of Community in Computer Mediated Communication', in S. G. Jones (ed.), *Cybersociety: Computer Mediated Communication and Community*. London: Sage, 1994, pp. 138–63.

Broidy, Ellen, 'Cyberdykes, or, Lesbian Studies in the Information Age', in Bonnie Zimmerman and Toni A. H. McNaron (eds), *The New Lesbian Studies*. New York: Feminist Press, 1996, pp. 203–7.

Bromley, Hank, 'Border Skirmishes: A Mediation on Gender, New Technologies, and the Persistence of Structure', paper presented at Subjects of Technology: Feminism, Constructivism and Identity, Brunel University, Uxbridge, June 1995.

Case, Sue-Ellen, 'Performing Lesbian in the Space of Technology: Part II', in *Theatre Journal*, Vol. 47, No. 3, 1995, pp. 329–44.

Dawson, Jeff, *Gay and Lesbian On-Line: The Travel Guide to Digital Queerdom on the Internet, the World Wide Web, America Online, Compuserve, plus BBSs Coast to Coast.* Berkeley, CA: Peachpit Press, 1996.

Dery, Mark, 'Flame Wars', in *South Atlantic Quarterly*, Autumn. Special Issue: Flame Wars: The Discourse of Cyberculture, 1993, pp. 559–68.

Dishman, Jesse Dallas, 'Digital Divas: Defining Queer Space on the Information Superhighway', paper given at Queer Frontiers: The Fifth Annual National Lesbian, Gay and Bisexual Graduate Student Conference, March 1995, pp. 23–6. Published online: http://www.usc.edu/Library/QF/queer/papers/dishman.html

Dishman, Jesse Dallas, 'Digital Dissidents: The Formation of Gay Communities On The Internet'. MA Thesis, University of Southern California, 1997.

Dyer, Steven, 'Re: Origins of soc.motss'. Message posted to soc.motss newsgroup, 27 May 1988, 20:31:15 GMT. Archived at: http://www.qrd.org/qrd/ electronic/usenet/soc.motss.beginnings

Fraiberg, Allison, 'Electronic Fans, Interpretive Flames: Peforming Queer Sexualities in Cyberspace', in *Works and Days*, 25/26, 1, 2, 1995. Published online: http://acorn.grove.iup/edu/en/workdays/Fraiberg.HTML

Goodloe, Amy T., 'Lesbian Computer Networks and Services', in Bonnie Zimmerman (ed.), *Encyclopedia of Homosexuality* (2nd ed.) *Volume I: Lesbian Histories and Cultures.* New York: Garland, 1997.

Hall, Kira, 'Cyberfeminism', in Susan Herring (ed.), *Computer-Mediated Communication: Linguistic, Social and Cross-Cultural Perspectives.* Amsterdam: John Benjamins, 1996, pp. 147–70.

Haraway, Donna, 'A Manifesto for Cyborgs: Science, Technology, and Socialist Feminism in the 1980s', in *Socialist Review*, Vol. 80, March–April, 1985.

Haskel, Lisa, 'Cyberdykes: Tales from the Internet', in Nicola Godwin *et al.*, *Assaults on Convention: Essays on Lesbian Transgressors.* London: Cassell, 1996, pp. 50–61.

Knopp, Lawrence, 'Sexuality and the Spatial Dynamics of Late Capitalism', in *Environment and Planning D: Society and Space*, Vol. 10, No. 6, 1992, pp. 651–69.

Martin, Biddy, 'Sexuality without Gender and Other Queer Utopias', in *Diacritics*, Vol. 24, No. 2/3, 1994, pp. 104–21.

Nieto, Daniel S., 'Who is the Male Homosexual? A Computer-Mediated Exploratory Study of Gay Male Bulletin Board System (BBS) Users in New York City', in *Journal of Homosexuality*, Vol. 30, No. 4, 1996, pp. 97–124.

O'Brien, Jodi, 'Changing the Subject', in *Women and Performance,* Vol. 17, 1996. Published online: http://www.echonyc.com/~women/Issue 17/

Seidman, Steven, 'Identity and Politics in "Postmodern" Gay Culture: Some Historical and Conceptual Notes', in Michael Warner (ed.), *Fear of a Queer Planet: Queer Politics and Social Theory.* Minneapolis: University of Minnesota Press, 1993, pp. 105–42.

Sheldon, Glenn, 'Cruising the Tearooms in Cyberspace', in *Gerbil,* Vol. 6, 1996. http://www.multicom.org/gerbil/cyb.htm

Tomas, David, 'Old Rituals for New Space: Rites de Passage and William Gibson's Cultural Model of Cyberspace', in Michael Benedikt (ed.), *Cyberspace: First Steps.* Cambridge, MA: MIT Press, 1991, p. 35.

Wakeford, Nina, 'Sexualised Bodies in Cyberspace', in Warren Chernaik and Marilyn Deegan (eds), *Beyond the Book: Theory, Text and the Politics of Cyberspace.* London: London University Press, 1995, pp. 93–104.

Wakeford, Nina, 'Theorising the Performance of "Identity" and "Community" in Lesbian (Cyber)spaces', in Sarah Oerton and Gill Plain (eds). *Coming Unstuck: Gendered Spaces, Places and Change.* London: Taylor & Francis, 1997.

Walters, Suzanna Danuta, 'From Here to Queer: Radical Feminism, Postmodernism, and the Lesbian Menace (or, Why Can't a Woman Be More Like a Fag?', in *Signs,* Vol. 21, No. 4, 1996, pp. 830–49.

Willis, Holly, and Halpin, Mikki, 'When the Personal Becomes Digital: Linda Dement and Barbara Hammer Move Towards a Lesbian Cyberspace', in *Women and Peformance,* Vol. 17, 1996. Published online: http://www.echonyc.com /~women/Issue 17/

Wincapaw, Celeste, 'Lesbian and Bisexual Women's Electronic Mailing Lists as Sexualised Spaces', in *Journal of Lesbian Studies.* Forthcoming, 1997.

Wood, Kathleen M., 'Narrative Iconicity in Electronic-Mail Lesbian Coming-Out Stories', in Anna Livia and Kira Hall (eds), *Queerly Phrased: Language, Gender, and Sexuality.* New York: Oxford University Press, 1997.

Woodland, Randall, J., 'Queer Spaces, Modem Boys, and Pagan Statues: Gay/Lesbian Identity and the Construction of Cyberspace', in *Works and Days* 25/26 13, 1&2, 1995. Published online: http://acorn.grove.iup/edu/en/workdays/ WOODLAND.HTML

Further reading

Case, Sue-Ellen, *The Domain Matrix: Performing Lesbian at the End of Print Culture.* Bloomington: Indiana University Press, 1997.

Correll, Shelly, 'The Ethnography of a Lesbian Bar: The Lesbian Cafe', in *Journal of Contemporary Ethnography,* Vol. 24, No. 3, 1995, pp. 270–98.

Duyves, Mattias, 'The Minitel: The Glittering Future of a New Invention' in *Journal of Homosexuality,* Vol. 25, No. 1/2, March-April, 1993, pp. 193–205.

Tsang, Daniel, 'Notes on Queer 'n' Asian Virtual Sex', in *Amerasia Journal,* Vol. 20, No. 1, Winter, 1994, pp. 117–28.

3

Literary Criticism

Vincent Quinn

LESBIAN- AND GAY-CENTRED literary criticism currently enjoys a
profile that would have been unthinkable fifteen years ago. Its stars
operate at the height of their profession. Their work has been widely
acclaimed, they attract many students to the programmes with which they
are associated, and they frequently occupy positions of institutional power.
Their recognition and visibility have contributed to the air of confidence
that now surrounds lesbian and gay criticism. An ever-increasing body of
work, originating from both established and aspiring scholars, continues to
expand the range of what can be said in this field. Indeed it is partly as a
result of such work on sexuality and textuality that terms such as 'English
Studies' and 'Literary Studies' now seem like potentially limited, and limiting, categories.

Visibility implies professional success, but establishment acceptance is
always a double-edged sword. This chapter will of course explore the successes of lesbian and gay criticism, but it begins by looking at an attack on
such work from within the university system. This opening section will
clarify the importance of lesbian and gay criticism by revealing what it is
about such research that makes the literary studies establishment feel
uncomfortable. After that I will look at some of the problems of definition
that surround lesbian and gay criticism, and then give a brief account of its
rise. The essay will close by considering some of the strategies that may be
necessary if we are to avoid the neutralizing effects of academic assimilation.

'Manfred' and the current state of literary studies

In the spring of 1996 a fake letter began to circulate on the Internet. Pur-
porting to be a job application from one 'Manfred Mickleson', the
document was actually a sustained attack on current developments within

English. The letter was an amusing, if crude, joke which allowed the unctuous Manfred – a supposed PhD student at Cornell – to boast of his inspirational seminars ('I have won several Most Exciting Teacher awards') and his considerable research potential (he claims to have books due out from Routledge, Verso, Methuen, and Cambridge University Press).

In the course of this hard sell, Manfred notes that his dissertation is 'informed by current thinking in feminist theory, Queer Theory, cultural materialism, eco-criticism, and post-colonial studies'. In particular, it focuses on 'masculine authority and feminine desire in eighteenth-century pirate literature'. His work argues that 'it is the absence of women in shipboard life that permits Defoe in his *History of the Pirates* to depict sea-going commerce in terms of a normative homosociality' and that here, 'piracy . . . embodies the eruption of a transgressive (and, implicitly, anti-imperialistic) sexuality'.[1]

Whatever the merits or demerits of this topic, the hand behind Manfred clearly believes that such research is absurd. The letter implies that piracy – a not uncommon subject in eighteenth-century studies – is an inappropriate and unduly faddish focus of attention because it is more concerned with cultural commentary than with literary history. Instead of sticking, for example, to Defoe's contribution to the rise of the novel, Manfred is using Defoe to illuminate questions of gender, sexuality and ethnicity. These categories – on which new generations of scholars have increasingly focused – are precisely the areas of interest that the author of the letter wants to expose as spurious. By emphasizing them, Manfred rejects the established paths of literary commentary, thus leaving himself open to unforgivable contextual errors:

> The manuscript will culminate in a detailed discussion of Mary Wollstonecraft's *Pirates of Penzance* as a feminist re-appropriation of the pirate motif, together with an account of the masculinist or patriarchal suppression that would for many years result in this work's being attributed to Gilbert and Sullivan, and [which] does not mention the use made [of it] in subsequent portions of work by Foucault, Althusser, Lacan, Deleuze, Bourdieu, Gayatri Spivak, Edward Said, Judith Butler, and others.

On one level, such comments are simply meant to be humorous, but there is a disturbing message implicit in the satire: queer studies, feminism, psychoanalysis, and post-colonial studies may be trendy, but they are not disciplines. Their misguided practitioners have replaced scholarly caution with name-dropping, jargon, and unverifiable assertions, and the solecisms committed by such academics are the inevitable by-products of their chosen methodologies. Candidates using such perspectives may be applying, in multiplying numbers, for jobs (in some cases, they may even get them), but as far as the author of the letter is concerned, they don't deserve to be successful.

Manfred, however, is only one aspect of the letter's attack on the state of English Studies. He may be pushy, but his pushiness is born of desperation and powerlessness. The letter's deeper targets are the academics that Manfred has chosen to emulate. Not all of the names he mentions are exponents of queer criticism, but the tone of his application suggests that it is this area, more than any other, that has led him astray. His title – 'Commerce, Homosociality, and the Engendering of the Body in Defoe and Wollstonecraft' – parodies Eve Kosofsky Sedgwick, as does the abstract that follows.[2] Even more pointedly, Manfred proudly announces that his topic is being supervised by Terry Castle, adding that she has written a letter in support of his application. Castle – whose work on sexuality has revolutionized eighteenth-century studies – is made to look ridiculous by association. How, we are encouraged to ask, could anyone have faith in a critic who is prepared to sponsor such an ignorant candidate?

This attempt to undermine Castle via her supposed graduate student suggests that the true concern of the Manfred letter is the question of academic control. The letter betrays its author's realization that English Studies is in a state of flux, and that established and aspiring professionals have a great deal invested in its future. That future, moreover, is far from clear. Should English concern itself with 'literature' or with 'culture'? May it employ methodologies that have been adapted from other disciplines? How valid are approaches that prioritize explorations of sexuality? Is it legitimate to politicize both texts and our responses to them? Or – alternatively – should notions of literary history and inherent literary value be the ultimate organizing principles of the subject?

In many ways such disputes are as old as English itself. The discipline began as a mistrusted alternative to Classics and has been keen to prove its significance ever since.[3] To be flippant, one long-established way of asserting the subject's importance (if only to other English professionals) has been to indulge in as much in-fighting as possible. In some ways, current debates over queer studies, psychoanalysis, feminism, deconstruction, cultural materialism, new historicism, and post-colonial studies are only the latest in a series of such arguments. What is new this time around is that changes across the general academic scene (including the rise of subjects such as Cultural Studies and Media Studies) threaten the existence of established, literature-based courses. It is against this background that the Manfred letter must be read, since its creator clearly believes that the methodologies that Manfred has adopted are foreign to English and that they will de-stabilize the subject, making literary scholarship (and literary scholars) redundant. If this trend continues, English, as it has usually been constituted, will cease to exist.

As far as Manfred is concerned, this melt-down has already been achieved: in his roll-call of mentors, philosophers rub shoulders with psychoanalytical and post-colonial theorists, as well as with literary critics. But to his creator, this shopping-list of critical perspectives is another aspect of Manfred's unworthiness – as far as Manfred is concerned, these methodologies are all the same and he will adopt any of them in order to get a job. Here the letter touches, almost accidentally, on a serious point, namely that lesbian and gay critics are not alone in proposing new ways of doing English. On the contrary, lesbian and gay criticism is one of several new strands in English, and it has partly evolved out of insights gained in other fields. I do not wish to deny the importance, originality or specificity of lesbian- and gay-centred work, but it is important to acknowledge that this work does not exist in a theoretical vacuum. On the contrary, it has come about via a process of disciplinary and theoretical cross-pollination. As such, the exaggerated methodological alliances of the Manfred letter are not wholly inappropriate because queer criticism *is* connected, historically and methodologically, to feminism, cultural materialism, psychoanalytical criticism, and post-colonial studies. Although such approaches are not interchangeable, they share a common scepticism about literary tradition, and they continue to evolve through a process of collective influence. Indeed, it is largely because of their rise that the very notion of unitary disciplines such as 'English', 'History', or 'Philosophy' has come into question.

That said, it is important to question the dichotomy that the Manfred letter implicitly draws between 'trendy' and 'traditional' approaches to English. Its creator clearly believes that if one has adopted a subject as allegedly modish as male–male relations on pirate ships then one will also, as a matter of course, be employing a jargon-filled vocabulary and a great deal of French theory. Conversely, a scholar writing about Jane Austen will have a suitably epigrammatic style. He or she will not be tempted to explore the erotic possibilities of same-sex friendship in the eighteenth-century novel let alone inquire – as Terry Castle has done – into the bedtime arrangements of Austen and her sister.[4]

It is this polarization between the 'trendy' and the 'traditional' that enables conservative critics to represent their perceived opponents as blindly anarchic and in need of suppression; it is a position that legitimates the contempt that the Manfred letter shows towards Castle, Sedgwick and others. As such it ought to be resisted; but a binary of 'trendy' versus 'traditional' is also dangerous for progressive critics because it denies the extent to which 'traditional' English is already a territory riven with disagreements and inconsistencies. The relationship between 'traditional' and 'trendy' versions of English is crucial because it illustrates the contested environment in which lesbian and gay literary criticism continues to develop. The charge of modishness has too often been used by establishment critics to stigmatize disruptive ways of reading. One might well argue that lesbian and gay critics should address their own community and not pay heed to accusations of faddishness from within the academy, but it is difficult to ignore such taunts when they originate from figures of institutional power. Indeed one of the most disturbing aspects of the Manfred letter is its provenance. It would be reassuring if one could read Manfred as the invention of a single embittered individual (the winner, perhaps, of several Least Innovative Teacher awards), but the framing narrative (circulated with the letter itself) asserts that:

> Manfred . . . is an imaginary candidate. He was created in a moment of sheer giddiness by several members of a search committee who had, collectively, just finished reading the dossiers of over one-hundred candidates for an actual eighteenth-century position. Manfred is, therefore, more than a product of the ironic or satirical imagination. He is a kind of 'composite candidate' representing the newest PhDs being produced by English graduate programs.
>
> The other thing that makes Manfred amazing is that a number of the departments to whom he applied did not realize that he was an imaginary candidate. He received over forty dossier requests, and six invitations to be interviewed at the MLA convention.

This commentary transforms the letter. It asserts that far from being one person's work, Manfred is in fact the collective invention of a group of senior academics. These are professionals whose position (as members of an interview board) means that they can deny jobs to junior colleagues if the latter produce certain kinds of ideologically-centred work. Moreover, the frame of the letter, whether it is 'true' or not, displays a contempt for those academics who supposedly called Manfred in for a full interview. Instead of merely being a joke at the expense of a single student, the letter becomes an acidic attack on an entire strain of literary studies. It depicts a system populated by academics who have been so misled by 'theory' that they are prepared to believe that Mary Wollstonecraft wrote *The Pirates of Penzance*. These people, it suggests, are willing to give Manfred a job because his work echoes their own, and because their critical standards are as slip-shod as his.[5]

I will return to these institutional questions later on because they impact on how lesbian and gay criticism should develop. However, I am now going to consider some of the implications of the term 'lesbian and gay criticism', as a prelude to sketching in a little of its history.

The growth of lesbian and gay criticism

In his job application, Manfred refers confidently to 'queer criticism' as if this were a single school adhering to a set of specific rules. It is not difficult to imagine the sort of critics who might fit into this category – Eve Sedgwick, Leo Bersani, and Alan Sinfield spring to mind as possibilities – but it would be impossible (and undesirable) to construct a unitary definition of what such a 'queer school' might represent. Bersani's work is largely concerned with psychoanalysis, while Sinfield's is driven by Marxism; Sedgwick's is broadly deconstructivist. Given these multiple and sometimes contradictory influences, it is limiting to conceptualize 'queer criticism' in a monolithic fashion since such a reification would suppress the multi-faceted nature of our work.

'Queer', of course, can be seen as a gesture towards multiplicity, but it is a word that carries problems of its own.[6] These might be avoided if we replace 'queer criticism' with 'lesbian and gay criticism', but even here there are uncertainties of definition. Obviously, 'lesbian and gay criticism' is a form of textual commentary that emphasizes questions of same-sex desire. But beneath this apparently uncontroversial formula are several difficulties. Jeffrey Meyers' *Homosexuality and Literature, 1890–1930* undoubtedly foregrounds sexual difference, but one would hesitate to describe the book as an example of lesbian and gay criticism. In his preface, Meyers announces that he does not 'imply a moral judgement when I use words like invert, pederast and perverse, which have negative connotations. I do hope, however, to maintain the sympathetic attitude that is necessary to understand any work of art' (1977, pp. 2, 3). In the readings that follow, homosexuals are 'they', not 'we', and as a result Meyers is able to sustain his pathologizing vocabulary. 'Sympathy', it is apparent, is not the same as identification. A crucial requirement of lesbian and gay criticism, then, is that the critic should find an allegiance among the marginal rather than the dominant. It is not enough to focus, as Meyers does, on 'deviant' material; one must also be willing to situate oneself within a dissident tradition. The issue, therefore, is the *way* one reads a text; it is not the sexual orientation of the critic, or of the writer whose work is being examined.

Another problem with the term 'lesbian and gay criticism' is that it implies that 'lesbian criticism' and 'gay criticism' are wholly congruent. The two have similar functions and a shared wish to interrogate heterosexist power structures, but they are not identical, either in terms of their histories or their professional visibility. For example, although many gay male critics have taken feminism as a model or exemplar of what gay criticism can achieve, there is undeniably a much closer link between feminism and lesbian-centred criticism than there is between feminism and gay-centred criticism. As a result, the two main branches of 'queer' criticism can be seen to have different trajectories and patterns of influence. The strength of 'lesbian and gay criticism' is that it acknowledges the valuable overlaps between lesbian and gay ways of reading. Its danger, however, is that it threatens to obliterate the specificity of each position, leading to a situation whereby each is subsumed in the other – and in institutional terms, this almost always results in the relative invisibility of lesbian-centred work.

That said, it is possible to make some general comments about the history of lesbian and gay criticism, and about the factors that have led to its current visibility. Although this prominence is a product of the last fifteen years, several ground-breaking texts pre-date this period. One such publication is the 1974 gay edition of *College English*, edited by Louie Crew and Rictor Norton. In his preface to *Displacing Homophobia* (1989), Ronald Butters pays tribute to Crew and Norton, and notes that the radical nature of such a project made it necessary for them to begin their text with a nineteen-page editorial on 'The Homophobic Imagination'. Butters' point is that lesbian and gay critics no longer have to be so defensive; for him, the essays in *Displacing Homophobia* 'evolve in a context in which their right to exist – indeed, the necessity of their existence – grows increasingly unquestionable' (Butters, 1989, p. 1). Such confidence is exhilarating, although it is worth noting that four years after *Displacing Homophobia* Mark Lilly begins *Gay Men's Literature in the Twentieth Century* (1993, p. 1) with a chapter entitled 'The Homophobic Academy' – a title reminiscent of Crew and Norton's 'Homophobic Imagination'. The substance of Lilly's argument suggests that institutional pressures continue to exert a malign influence on lesbian and gay criticism; it also implies that the freedom experienced by Butters may be more available in the United States than in Britain.

Leaving aside the question of editorial confidence, the factor that most separates the world of 1974 from the world of 1997 is the absence, in the Crew/Norton volume, of references to Michel Foucault. This is hardly surprising given that *La Volonté de Savoir* appeared in 1976 – two years after the gay issue of *College English* – and it was another two years before it was published in America as *The History of Sexuality: An Introduction*. But even then, it took some time before the implications of Foucault's work became clear. In his important contribution to gay criticism, *The Homosexual Tradition in American Poetry* (1979), Robert K. Martin makes only one mention of Foucault. This reference, in a footnote that alludes rather airily to 'critics like Michel Foucault and Guy Hocquenghem', implies that Martin has not fully digested the former's concept of the 'reverse discourse' (1979, p. 226, n.50). Indeed the reference is not backed up by any specific citations, and Foucault is absent from Martin's bibliography. This is not to criticize Martin, it is merely to indicate that there was a time lag before Foucault's work on sexuality assumed its current (though not unchallenged) pre-eminence.

In talking of Foucault's importance to the rise of lesbian and gay criticism, there are two factors to be considered. One is the specific contribution made by *The History of Sexuality*, and the other is the impetus that his work has given to inter-disciplinary studies. Foucault's notion of discourse as a means of enforcing power or expressing identity has proven to be congenial to professionals in a range of subjects including English, History, Classics, Anthropology and the Social Sciences; and this, combined with his particular interest in sexuality, has helped to create the climate of intellectual cross-pollination in which lesbian and gay criticism has flourished. Moreover, Foucault's emphasis on the construction of identity and culture through *discourse* has made it possible to radicalize the functions of traditional literary criticism. Thus, 'close reading' need no longer be an activity reserved for the study of canonical texts. Instead, it has become possible to 'close read' any number of 'literary' and 'non-literary' texts in order to probe the ways in which language, sexuality and power interact.

This implosion of difference between 'literary' and 'non-literary' texts is one of the tenets of new historicist practice, much of which has taken Foucault as its cue. I do not have the space to give a full account of new historicism, but I would like to note its enabling effect on lesbian and gay criticism. Besides its obvious interest in questions of power, and its refusal to dichotomize the 'literary' and the 'non-literary', new historicism – like feminism – has insisted that critics should situate themselves within their own discourses. This ideal of transparency has legitimated all sorts of apparently 'personal' gestures – including, of course, the disclosure of one's place on the continuum of sexual orientation.[7]

These quasi-confessional practices are in turn related to the larger issue of reader-response criticism. Again, this is a vast area, but it is undoubtedly the case that a variety of reader-response based techniques has contributed hugely to the rise of lesbian and gay criticism.[8] Because reader-response places a stress on the relationship between reader and text, the reader's sexual identity is an undeniable aspect of his or her reactions to the printed page. It therefore becomes acceptable to construct theories of what it means to read a text 'as' a gay man or 'as' a lesbian. This in turn frees critics from the need to focus exclusively on works produced by writers who are demonstrably homosexual. Much of the pre-history of queer criticism was taken up with the construction of alternative canons of neglected queer artists; this work – which took its cue from the feminist re-discovery of lost women writers – was valuable, but it inevitably involved a degree of historical anachronism and a rather simplistic approach to identity politics. There is the further problem that the creation of any canon, even a dissident one, involves an exercise of power through acts of exclusion. The value of reader-response criticism is that it adds range to such projects by making it possible to include a book like *David Copperfield* despite the (so far) unchallenged heterosexuality of its author. It also makes it possible for each reader to have his or her own list of significant texts without being dependent on academics drawing up a queer (and multi-cultural) version of Harold Bloom's *The Western Canon* (1994). Indeed different readers might uncover queerness in different parts of the same book: reading Dickens, I might respond to Copperfield's love for Steerforth while a lesbian friend would probably be more interested in the ambiguous Rosa Dartle.

As the Manfred letter shows, there are many other factors feeding into the rise of lesbian and gay criticism. Amongst these are psychoanalysis, post-colonial studies and deconstruction. The latter is particularly beguiling, perhaps because its terminology provides, at least rhetorically, a way of dismantling existing systems of control, and of re-figuring 'the marginal' as a site of empowerment. (Although it might be added that deconstruction's flight from the material world does little to address the problems of discrimination and governmental harassment that we continue to face.) The other decisive influence in our field is of course feminism, which has provided a model for many of the directions in which lesbian and gay criticism has moved. In particular, feminism radicalized literary and social commentary by replacing biological 'sex' with the culturally-constructed category of 'gender'. As David Halperin shows, this anti-essentialist stance anticipated queer work on the construction of sexuality and undermined traditional appeals to 'nature' as an unchanging and monolithic force (1990, pp. 6–8).

Feminism continues to inform queer studies although, as Sally Munt points out, academic structures necessarily create tensions between lesbian criticism and the areas with which it is institutionally associated, such as gay studies, Women's Studies and critical theory (1992, pp. xi–xviii). This is a point to which I will return in my conclusion, but at this point I want simply to say that, taken together, feminism and the other discourses I have mentioned have transformed literary studies, opening up spaces that were previously unthinkable. The volume of this work is astonishing, as is the speed with which it has appeared. In *Lesbian and Gay Writing* (1990), Mark Lilly complains of the 'staggering paucity of good books, from our own community, on lesbian/gay writing' (1990, p. 8).[9] This charge was already debatable when Lilly was writing; if someone made the same claim now it would be irrefutably inaccurate. In particular, post-Foucaldian critics such as Eve Sedgwick have inspired a great deal of theoretically sophisticated material that focuses not on an essentialist notion of homosexuality, but on what Thomas E. Yingling calls 'an investigation of the homosocial continuum (including how homophobia insistently informs that structure)' (1990, p. 2). The subtlety of this project is welcome, although there are undeniable tensions between Sedgwick's ahistorical tendencies and the more period-specific emphasis of lesbian and gay work drawing on new historicism and cultural materialism.

It is also true that although much has been said on the history of sexuality, there are still countless spaces on that map waiting to be filled. New historicism is particularly associated with Renaissance Studies, so it is hardly surprising that critics such as Stephen Orgel and Jonathan Goldberg have greatly enhanced our understanding of early modern configurations of desire. There is an equivalent wealth of research on nineteenth- and twentieth-century texts, but the eighteenth century and the medieval period have only recently come under scrutiny from lesbian and gay commentators. The coverage of genres within specific periods can also be spotty; for example, there is a huge amount of work on contemporary lesbian and gay fiction, but relatively little has been written about queer poetry. Such gaps are not disheartening: on the contrary, they provide a stimulus for further enquiry, while indicating how much has already been achieved. What *can* be disheartening, however, are the forces of institutional power that haunt this chapter, so I would like to close by returning briefly to that issue in order to suggest where lesbian and gay criticism might go if it is to evade establishment control.

Prospects and possibilities

One of the lessons of the Manfred letter is that is dangerous to place all of one's trust in an academy that is likely to satirize us and/or refuse us jobs. Indeed the greater our success, the more vulnerable we are to spiteful attacks: the *prominence* of lesbian and gay criticism is precisely the thing that makes it worth attacking. The authors of the Manfred letter would not have bothered focusing on this area if they did not think that 'queer' textual strategies constituted a threat to their own, established methodologies. The satire, ironically, is a measure of the success of lesbian and gay criticism.

It would be foolish, however, to invest too much in this ideal of professional visibility. The market forces implicit in the Manfred letter suggest that today's exciting vogue is tomorrow's tedious orthodoxy. Indeed the current prominence of lesbian and gay criticism has almost certainly been achieved at the expense of overlapping critical discourses, such as feminist theory. In America particularly, professional dominance can rarely be achieved without the displacement of potential allies. It is as if the academy will only accommodate one or two marginal positions at a time: the competing candidates have to fight it out for dominance, only to see the victor displaced, before too long, by the next hot topic. (Or, alternatively, lesbian critics and gay critics are put in a position which stresses competition and rivalry rather than collaboration and kinship.)

Exponents of lesbian and gay criticism can therefore be seen to tread a difficult path. On the one hand, there is the threat that we will be denied jobs; while on the other there is the threat that we will be assimilated into a system that views our work solely in terms of its marketability, and that refuses to engage with the realities of gay and lesbian experience. Thus it seems vital that we should define our success in terms that go beyond the literary studies establishment. It is not accidental that so many queer critics are also involved, on whatever level, with lesbian and gay activism. Besides keeping open these links between professional and political identities, it is also important to seek new ways of politicizing our presence within the academy.

One way of achieving this re-politicization of literary studies might be to re-emphasize the importance of *teaching* criticism, as well as *writing* it. The university system dictates that academics define their success in terms of publications but while it is indisputably important that lesbian and gay critics should continue to produce such texts, it is also vital that they should remember that there are other arenas in which to explore the relationship between sexuality and textuality. In particular, dissident critics should not just suggest new ways of approaching literary studies, they should also engage actively with existing university syllabuses in order to 'queer' traditional methodologies. In other words, the business of teaching mainstream courses can be disrupted by the choice of non-mainstream texts and by an insistence on politically sophisticated ways of reading.

The transmission of these textual strategies to students might in itself be seen as a form of modest activism, even more so when it moves on from the level of syllabus amendment to the establishment of entirely new programmes in cultural criticism centred specifically on questions of same-sex desire. A good example of this is the 'Sexual Dissidence and Cultural Change' MA at my own university, which arose directly out of the work of Jonathan Dollimore and Alan Sinfield.[10] Such a synthesis between writing and teaching seems a particularly productive way forward, not least because it can create a queer space within a given institution while simultaneously reaching beyond that institution to other parts of the lesbian and gay community. There are other possibilities – including a commitment to the sort of prose that is accessible to non-academics – but whatever gestures one makes, it is clear that lesbian and gay criticism should look primarily to communities of lesbian and gay readers for its validation, and *not* to the academic establishment.

Notes

1. This document came to me via an eighteenth-century discussion group; it is accompanied by a note indicating that the author is unknown and that the letter is unbound by copyright restrictions. Given its nature, the text is unpaginated.
2. It was Sedgwick who popularized the term 'homosocial' in *Between Men*, New York and Guildford: Columbia University Press, 1985 – a text that has had an almost incalculable influence on lesbian and gay criticism.
3. See chapter three of Chris Baldick's *The Social Mission of English Criticism, 1848–1932*, Oxford: Clarendon Press, 1983.
4. See Castle's 'Sister, Sister' in the August 1995 issue of *The London Review of Books*. The reception of this piece anticipates the tone of the Manfred letter. See Harvey Porlock's 'Critical List' in *The Sunday Times*, 13 August 1995, for a survey of reactions.
5. The discussion of the letter on the Internet was also illuminating. Many contributors objected to Manfred's caricatured version of theory, but when a couple of posters suggested that the text was homophobic, they were accused of being humourless and paranoid.
6. These are dealt with elsewhere in this book. Despite personal misgivings, I sometimes use 'queer' as a convenient umbrella term in the discussion below.
7. For a fuller discussion of this, and other aspects of new historicist practice, see H. Aram Veeser, 'The New Historicism', pp. 1–32 of *The New Historicism Reader*, ed. by H. Aram Veeser, New York and London: Routledge, 1994.
8. Reader-response covers many different critical practises; for a fuller account of the term, see *Reader-Response Criticism: From Formalism to Post-Structuralism*, ed. by Jane P. Tompkins, Baltimore and London: Johns Hopkins University Press, 1980.
9. Yingling is referring specifically to Sedgwick, but the point holds true of others of her academic generation.
10. For a reflective account of this MA programme, see Alan Sinfield, 'Playing The System: The Sussex MA and an Anxiety', *Radical Teacher*, Vol. 45, Winter 1994.

References

Bloom, Harold, *The Western Canon: The Books and School of the Ages*. New York: Harcourt Brace, 1994.

Butters, Ronald R., Clum, John M., and Moon, Michael, (eds), *Displacing Homophobia: Gay Male Perspectives in Literature and Culture*. Durham and London: Duke University Press, 1989.

Halperin, David, *One Hundred Years of Homosexuality and Other Essays on Greek Love*. New York and London: Routledge, 1990.

Lilly, Mark, *Gay Men's Literature in the Twentieth Century*. Basingstoke: Macmillan, 1993.

Lilly, Mark (ed.), *Lesbian and Gay Writing: An Anthology of Critical Essays*. Basingstoke: Macmillan, 1990.

Martin, Robert K., *The Homosexual Tradition in American Poetry*. Austin: University of Texas Press, 1979.

Meyers, Jeffrey, *Homosexuality and Literature, 1890–1930*. London: Athlone, 1977.

Munt, Sally R. (ed.), *New Lesbian Criticism: Literary and Cultural Readings*. Hemel Hempstead: Harvester Wheatsheaf, 1992.

Yingling, Thomas E., *Hart Crane and the Homosexual Text*. Chicago and London: University of Chicago Press, 1990.

Further reading

Baldick, Chris, *The Social Mission of English Criticism, 1848–1932*. Oxford: Clarendon Press, 1983.

Castle, Terry, 'Sister, Sister', *The London Review of Books*, August 1995.

College English. Gay issue (1974) edited by Louie Crew and Rictor Norton.

Dollimore, Jonathan, *Sexual Dissidence: Augustine to Wilde, Freud to Foucault*. Oxford: Clarendon Press, 1991.

Porlock, Harvey, 'Critical List', *The Sunday Times*, 13 August 1995.

Sedgwick, Eve Kosofsky, *Between Men: English Literature and Male Homosocial Desire*. New York: Columbia University Press, 1985.

Sinfield, Alan, *Cultural Politics – Queer Reading*. London and Philadelphia: Routledge and The University of Pennsylvania Press, 1994.

Tompkins, Jane P. (ed.), *Reader Response Criticism: From Formalism to Post-Structuralism*. Baltimore and London: Johns Hopkins University Press, 1980.

Veeser, H. Aram (ed.), *The New Historicism Reader*. New York and London: Routledge, 1994.

Acknowledgement

The author would like to thank Andy Medhurst, Sally Munt, Alan Sinfield and Annis May Timpson for their constructive comments on this chapter.

4

History

Laura Gowing

LESBIAN AND GAY HISTORY remains a unique kind of historical discipline. Its development over the last twenty years has been crucially shaped by broader shifts in historical paradigms: the development of a feminist historical practice, the growth of women's history, gender history, and black history, and the movement towards a new 'history from below' that restores historical agency to those whose voices have traditionally been suppressed.[1] It continues apart from these movements, a history that retains a core constituency outside the academy and a weight that is both personal and political. History for lesbians and gay men is both pleasure and necessity, referenced and reinvented in lesbian and gay historical fictions, political discourses, even computer quiz games. Lesbian and gay historians since the late nineteenth century have charged themselves with the tasks of countering homophobia, understanding contemporary politics, preserving popular memory, and creating a genealogy of the lesbian and gay past.

More than most areas of Lesbian and Gay Studies, history has developed as two separate disciplines. The experiences of lesbians and gay men in the past have been disparate and often entirely separate; source material is notoriously less available for lesbian history: only politics, it might seem, compels us to try and construct a joint history. The perspectives of gender history suggest, however, deeper possibilities of a lesbian *and* gay history.

Creating lesbian and gay history means reimagining the past, forcing the personal onto the public stage, asking questions of the sources that are often impertinent, sometimes anachronistic, and always difficult. Lesbian and gay history begins from an emphatically modern position, which might be summed up by the association of three key terms: sexuality, identity, and community. All need to be historicized and problematized. Here, I want to examine the ways in which historians have done so; the narratives that have emerged from the various historical needs and desires of lesbians and gays; and the possibilities of new historical horizons for histories of homosexuality, sexuality, and gender.

Defining the subject

Who are the subjects of lesbian and gay history? The lesbian and gay identities from which historians start is a recent construction, contingent on specific cultural, social, economic and political circumstances. The terms we use to define ourselves have no precise historical equivalents: every word used in relation to same-sex acts in the past has its own history. The terms 'homosexual' (coined in 1869) and, later, 'heterosexual' did not pass into usage until the 1890s, although the word lesbian was used to mean sexual relations between women from the early eighteenth century. While historians of sexuality have argued that earlier terms such as 'sodomite' and 'tribade' referred to acts rather than identities (and not necessarily to acts specific to same-sex couplings), a closer study of language use and textual meanings allows the complexity of sexual language and its power to emerge. 'Sodomy' has consistently defined sexual deviancy, though not necessarily homosexuality; 'tribade', by the sixteenth century, meant any woman who enjoyed sex with women; 'hermaphrodite' defined both sexual and gender roles.[2] Long before the nineteenth-century 'invention of homosexuality' and heterosexuality, then, there were terms that described acts *and* categories of same-sex sex. In this century lesbians and gays have transformed languages of sexual identification to suit their needs. 'Gay', originally used for anything pleasurable, came only gradually, between the 1940s and the 1960s, to define people rather than bars or outfits; up until the late 1960s it could be used as a code word rather than a public declaration. 'Coming out', the seminal political and personal term of the 1970s and 1980s, was used in 1930s America for the debut of black and white drag queens at drag balls (playing then on the aristocratic tradition of debutantes coming out); later it came to mean, for both women and men, the first same-sex encounter; only at the beginning of the Gay Liberation movement of the early 1970s did it become associated with the 'closet' and the public revelation of gay sexuality to the straight world (Chauncey, 1995). The languages of sexuality demand an historical understanding that reconstructs how men and women might use words 'tactically in diverse cultural settings to position themselves and negotiate their relations with other[s]' (Chauncey, 1995, p. 14).

The ambiguities of definition and the contingency of modern sexual identities have forced lesbian and gay historians to question what they are looking for in the past. Sexual acts between men or women? Affectionate relationships between persons of the same gender? Communities or identities based on sexual preferences? Historians have argued with force that we demand standards of proof for homosexuality that we would never require for heterosexuality. In effect, we assume heterosexuality.

An historical search based on such assumptions has limited results: it depends on precisely the kind of essentialist definition of homosexuality that historians have disclaimed. It is, as Eve Kosofsky Sedgwick has argued, a 'minoritizing' history (1991, pp. 40–44). It is also one that makes the construction of lesbian histories particularly hard. Gay male historians have tended to explain their largely male-centred histories with the convention that 'the sources are all written by men, for men and about men' (Spencer, 1995, p. 8). Certainly, the records of male and female same-sex acts can be very different: in Western Christian history female homosexuality has been much less often the target of repressive legislation and persecution than male (though for examples where women did suffer such consequences see Crompton, 1981; Eriksson, 1980; van der Meer, 1991). Sex and relationships between men have been culturally and legally more visible than those between women. But the relative invisibility of lesbianism in the historical records is not, as historians have sometimes argued, the necessary result of a phallocentric culture, in which lesbian sex could barely be imagined before the twentieth century, and in which consistent cultural and biological differences between male and female sexuality made women inherently less free and less likely than men to engage in genital same-sex acts. Early modern Western popular and medical culture, for example, held that women were *more* lustful than men, and in this culture sex between women was by no means inconceivable, featuring in texts ranging from midwifery manuals to erotica. Writing a lesbian past means making different efforts with the source material, and looking for changing conceptions of gender as well as sexuality. Doing so, a unified history of lesbians and gay men, as well as fuller separate histories, may become possible: one that traces shared cultures and categories, shared space, and linked identities (such as Esther Newton's pioneering study of Cherry Grove: Newton, 1993).

Partly through the perspectives of gender history, lesbian and gay history is coming to encompass heterosexuality as well as homosexuality. Passion, friendship, love and sex are part of a broad spectrum of relations between men and between women that demand a sensitive historical analysis. This is not to say that male and female homosocial bonds in the past are contiguous or continous with homosexual bonds. Rather it is the points of differentiation between homosociality and homosexuality that need attention as they vary and shift between cultures, religions, and communities: where, by whom, and why are the lines drawn and redrawn between bonds of homosociality and those of homosexuality? Such an approach, which moves in the direction Sedgwick has outlined for a 'universalizing' history, depends on an interest in the changing boundaries and overlaps between homosexual and heterosexual histories, and demands a consideration of the relationship between the history of sexuality and those of social, economic and political change; it requires thoughtful readings of the imagining, erasing, and transforming of same-sex relationships in a variety of historical sources.[3]

Nevertheless the urge to minoritize or essentialize history is in many ways what propels the gay historical project. Narratives of 'gay people' through history, such as the early work of John Boswell (1980), the most cogent defender of 'essentialist' approaches, both arouse lesbian and gay historians' misgivings and appeal to their historical desires. While the model of a socially constructed sexual identity fits in most usefully with our historical understanding of sexuality, the idea of a transhistorical gay sexuality actually represents the personal understanding of many lesbian and gay people of their sexual identity far better. David Halperin argues that this is bound to be so, that 'the constructionist thesis is not only counter-intuitive but is *necessarily* so' (1990, p. 44). The historian who stresses the historicity and contingency of homosexual identity is frequently forced, at the same time, to recognize the ahistoricity that continues to seem an essential component of desire.[4] Visions of the political utility of gay history compound these tensions; the story of the experiences of lesbians and gays in the past which seemed politically useful for the liberation movements of the late 1960s, 1970s and 1980s can also be turned to the service of homophobia.[5] In 1986 the US Supreme Court ruled in *Bowers v. Hardwick* against the right to consensual homosexual sodomy, appealing to precisely the transhistorical definition of sodomy that historians have found problematic. The decision traced a tradition of condemning sodomy through biblical texts, medieval sodomy trials and eighteenth-century legal texts, ignoring the historically variant meanings of 'sodomy' *and* the fact that the relevant state law technically applied to heterosexual as well as homosexual couples to interpret sodomy as any act performed by same-sex partners (Halley 1994).

Historicizing sexuality

The understanding of sexuality that underpins the lesbian/gay historical agenda is an extremely modern and a particularly Western one, in which sexuality constitutes an autonomous sphere and an aspect of identity. Historians of sexuality, inspired by the work of Michel Foucault, have demanded a complex historicizing of 'sexuality' as a cultural production. Simultaneously with the first volume of Foucault's *History of Sexuality* (1978), Jeffrey Weeks, in *Coming Out* (1990), was shaping an agenda for a history of homosexuality: 'There is no essence of homosexuality whose historical unfolding can be illuminated. There are only changing patterns in the organization of desire whose specific configurations can be decoded' (Weeks, 1985, p. 6).

Tellingly, it has been reinterpretations of that favourite homosexual past, ancient Greece, that have done most to reconceptualize the history of sexuality. Same-sex relations between men were manifestly intrinsic to the social, political and cultural functioning of the ancient world. But against John Boswell's interpretation of the category 'homosexual' as one rooted in ancient Greek culture, David Halperin (1990) has argued that sexuality itself is an alien concept in this period. Sex was understood not as a separate sphere but in relation to citizenship, age, and economic status, and sexual acts were defined not in terms of homosexuality and heterosexuality, but in terms of active and passive participation in penetration, an act with wider political and social meanings. For Halperin sexuality cannot be a stable category of historical analysis: historians must, instead, look for the historicity of the category of sexuality. This approach has wide implications outside ancient history. Sexuality and morality are cultural productions; making sense of them involves examining the discursive structures that determine the place of sex in different cultures. The history of homosexuality has led the way towards a history in which sex is not private, unchanging and natural, but key to the shifting patterns of society, politics and culture.

Constructing identity

If sexuality is modern, sexual identity is even more so. In many societies the term makes no sense at all. In Native American tribes, the institution of the 'berdache' involved women and men cross-dressing, taking on the labour roles of the opposite sex, and taking same-sex partners, but the defining identity was one of gender role – understood primarily in terms of occupation and dress – rather than of sexual object choice (Whitehead 1993). In the pre-industrial West before about 1700, the heterosexual family was primarily an economic unit, and marriage a stage in the life cycle: in this society, same-sex acts took place within the heterosexual matrix, and homosexuality was understood as a behaviour rather than a role. In this world, a history of homosexuality might encompass a whole range of erotic expressions: female transvestites; hermaphrodites; European fantasies of African and Egyptian sexualities; passionate friends; the men and women tried for sodomitical or lesbian acts; and the lesbian and homosexual visibilities and absences in Renaissance texts.

In this period the relationship between masculinity, male friendship and power has been a particularly fruitful one for gay historians. Alan Bray has illuminated the tensions at the heart of early modern masculinity, tensions which were intimately related to homosexual possibilities (1982, 1990). On one level sodomy was the monstrous sin, punishable in many places by execution; it might also be understood, in trials such as those of the Dutch Republic in the 1730s, as a national crime that mirrored economic and political degeneration and decline; and finding, imagining and combating male and female homosexuality in native cultures was part of the early modern colonial project in America (Katz, 1992, pp. 281–292). At another level, male homosexual relationships might go unnoticed or unremarked in local, particularly rural, communities. In between these two extremes, male friendship was in early modern Europe an increasingly important way of cementing and building political and social alliances. Sharing a bed had a public as well as an emotional significance: in England in 1625 Archbishop Laud recorded that he had dreamt that James I's favourite, the Duke of Buckingham, had come to him in bed, 'where he carried himself with much love towards me . . . and likewise many seemed to me to enter the chamber who did see this'. But the signs of friendship were underlaid by the threat of sodomy: the tension between the two was, Bray argues, at the heart of masculine power relations (Bray, 1990, p. 4). So intimate a relationship between power and same-sex bonding necessarily did not work for women, except at the highest levels: Queen Anne's relationship with Sarah, Duchess of Marlborough, and subsequently with Abigail Masham brought bonds, obligations, and conflicts between women to the centre of political power. Nevertheless, same-sex bonds between women seem to have aroused anxieties of their own in the seventeenth century. In some seventeenth-century texts, 'chaste' love between feminine women, previously treated as culturally insignificant, was coming to appear as transgressive as tribady and transvestism (Traub, 1996).

From this world where sex and identity were unrelated, the earliest movements towards the development of a modern gay identity have been traced by Randolph Trumbach. He has argued that, in European cities from around 1700, a major shift transformed the understanding of sexuality and identity. Sex with men and boys began to be understood no longer as part of other promiscuous, rakish sexual behaviour, but as characteristic of a deviant minority. In taverns and 'molly-houses', men held pretend marriages, used female aliases, and went to balls in women's clothes. This was 'the birth of the queen': mollies constituted a new gender group, between male and female, defined by effeminacy and sexual object-choice (Trumbach, 1991a). Women, Trumbach (1991b) argues, followed a similar pattern a hundred years later, with 'sapphists' (who might dress male to attract women) replacing 'hermaphrodites' (persons with both male and female attributes). This may be a simplification of lesbian identities, for lesbian sex was still often conceived as involving at least one feminine partner, the 'femme' whose history has been so little studied, and who might appear, at different times, transgressive or conforming (Traub, 1996; Donoghue, 1993).

These shifts in the meanings of friendship, sex and identity have been related to the various transformations of the early modern world: with industrialization, the development of an economy that did not depend on families, in which single men (and, although not until much later, single women) could participate; in the seventeenth century, the establishment of a Protestant-inspired ideal of companionate marriage, which the diversion of affections outside the heterosexual couple could be seen to undermine; in the eighteenth century, a growing separation of gender roles in which masculinity was coming to mean heterosexuality. This schema of change is necessarily partial; it leaves out any participants in homosexual acts who did not fit homosexual roles, such as the passionate male and female friends of the eighteenth and nineteenth century, and the 'masculine' men and 'feminine' women whose homosexual acts did not, apparently, threaten their gender identities. It tends to elide the heterosexual context that continued to define homosexuality, and to be defined by it: same-sex identities were still rarely conceived of as precluding heterosexual acts. Finally, stressing 'identity' may turn out to misrepresent the experiences of most early modern people: claiming a unique, self-fashioned identity was an elite male project from which most women, servants, and slaves were excluded (Hunt, 1994). The same-sex erotic and emotional world remained a broad and incoherent one: one whose framework was changing with capitalism, changing family life, and urbanization, but whose outlines remain essentially foreign to those of the modern sexual world.

For many historians the roots of modern lesbian and gay identities appear much later, marked by the new medical and sexological discourses of the late nineteenth century. The sexologists, many of whom identified themselves as homosexual and sought to establish a framework for toleration, explained homosexuality as the incurable characteristic of a fixed minority, predominantly manly women and effeminate men, congenitally predisposed to inversion, partnered generally by 'normal' women and men whose homosexuality could be transient, and with natural abilities, tastes and characteristics that reinforced their sexual preferences (Weeks, 1990). The discourses of sexology have been held responsible for a major shift in the world of same-sex intimacy and sexual relations in the 1880s and 1890s, with new anxieties about relationships between women and renewed legal sanctions against male homosexuality. Sexology, however, was not always a coherent movement; nor was it the only influence on the definition of sexual identity. Sexual definitions were negotiated and resisted in a complex dialectic.

Primarily the new definition of homosexuality described *gender* identity, and it did so using terms and concepts that were already familiar to men and to women. In the late nineteenth century, American street and bar culture defined 'fairies' as effeminate men with their own gender identity, and contrasted them with 'trade', men whose normal gender roles were not imperilled by sexual contacts with fairies (Chauncey, 1995). For lesbians, too, the masculine – 'inverted' - identity that sexologists identified struck a chord with many women, while for others it opened new possibilities. In the late nineteenth century the adoption of masculine roles, dress, and imagery was part of the development and aspirations of the New Woman; it made lesbians newly visible; and it gave some women a way of articulating the sexual desire supposed to be lacking in true femininity (Newton, 1984).

The twentieth century saw a shift, varying by class, race, and generation, from this idea of homosexuality as a gender role to homosexuality as a sexual identity. Butches of the 1950s defined themselves by their desire for women, while those of earlier decades saw themselves as masculine women with men's desires (Kennedy and Davis, 1993, p. 385); and the gender roles of 'trade' and 'fairies' were gradually replaced by the sexual identity 'gay' (Chaunce,y 1995). By the 1940s the lesbian butch-femme role system functioned as far more than a personal code: it was a collective social imperative that enabled participation in a community, and that enabled the manipulation and transformation of heterosexual gender norms in a lesbian context (Kennedy and Davis, 1993). But through the shifts in cultural constructions of identity, gender identity and sexual identity continued to be profoundly connected; and neither, it seems, develop continuously from the pre-modern to the modern.

Inventing communities

Increasingly, what lesbian and gay historians have searched for in the past has been the history of communities and subcultures which acknowledge and support sexual identity. Modern historians have seen the development of sexual identities as contingent on the growth of lesbian and gay communities. At the same time as homosexual *roles* were replacing homosexual *behaviour*, urban homosexual subcultures were appearing. In Amsterdam, London and Paris, men recognized each other through secret gestures, established cruising grounds, and code words (Gerard and Hekma, 1988). If they did not have communities, they did, at least, have temporary systems of contacts and networks.

Whatever their appeal as forerunners, early modern subcultures can be related only cautiously to the much more explicitly queer subcultures of the twentieth century, with their quite different understandings of sexuality, identity and community: the upper-class lesbian circles of 1900s Paris; the black artists, writers and musicians of 1930s Harlem, and the whole world of gay New York between 1890 and 1940; the lesbian and gay culture of pre-Nazi Berlin and the homosexual emancipation movement that emerged from it. In New York, gay men had their own map of the metropolis. They learned which bars, bath-houses, and streets were open to them, and which were not; how rules changed with the time of day or night; where drag and camp were celebrated and where they were to be hidden.

Women's relationship to public space, particularly before the 1940s, was fundamentally so different to men's that a women's history along these lines is hard to imagine. In New York between about 1890 and 1940, gay male culture was highly visible and integrated into the everyday life of the city in a way that lesbian culture was not. Much of lesbian subcultural life took place in spaces and spheres that have been largely invisible to historians. However, in America and Europe, large-scale migration to the cities, the effects, particularly in Europe, of the First World War, and the development of new leisure and labour patterns opened up new possibilities for women as well as men. Black and white women claimed space as dykes, bulldaggers and cross-dressers alongside 'horticultural lads' in, for example, Harlem and Greenwich Village in the 1920s and 1930s; elsewhere in America and in Europe lesbian subcultures, centred on bars or house parties, were developing. Elizabeth Lapovsky Kennedy and Madeline Davis's oral history of bar lesbians in Buffalo from the 1930s stresses the agency working-class lesbians had to shape their communities: they participated in an autonomous, powerful, if often hidden community with its own ethics, norms, and butch/femme roles, and its own ways of claiming a public space (1993, p. 14). For them, as for lesbians and gays throughout this century, 'community' has been established piecemeal; it has been divided or shared on the basis of race, gender, and class.

In many ways, the dominant approach to lesbian history has been premised on the absence of self-consciously *lesbian* communities. Instead, historians such as Lilian Faderman (1985) and Carroll Smith-Rosenberg (1975) have envisioned a nineteenth-century 'female world of love and ritual' in which relationships between women were romantic, primarily if not totally non-genital, and normative for middle-class family life. Such relationships between women and girls constituted the emotional world of boarding schools, underlaid marriages, and established autonomous networks between women. This narrative gives historical backing to Adrienne Rich's vision of a 'lesbian continuum' (Rich, 1980) on which all relationships between women have a place; but it performs its own work of erasure: of genital sex, of the experiences of black women and working women, and of the quite different understandings of friendship, sex, and bodily closeness that might obtain outside the world of white middle-class women. More recent archival work has begun to illuminate the place of sexual desire and sexual acts, both genital and non-genital, in such apparent 'romantic friendships'. The letters of Addie Brown, a black woman in 1860s Connecticut, reveal that close female friendship and sharing a bed was understood to also involve access to breasts (Hansen, 1995). Anne Lister, a property-owning gentlewoman of early nineteenth-century Halifax, established close friendships with other women which frequently involved 'grubbling' under their skirts and achieving 'kisses' (probably meaning orgasms), and which she envisaged leading to a 'marriage' of shared property and economic interests (Lister, 1988).

For Anne Lister and for many others, lesbian/gay identity was not, apparently, a collective affair. Narratives of community stress the establishment of visible cultures at their peril. For invisibility is also always part of the lesbian and gay experience, and the secrecy and individualism of sexual experiences is as crucial to the lesbian and gay past as publicity, visibility and community.

Reinventing the past

Changing discourses of sexual identity, inversion, and homosexuality have made their own contribution to lesbian and gay history. The concepts of sexual inversion and homosexuality were conceived as transhistorical, essential identities; the invention of homosexuality was itself premised on a seamless narrative of 'homosexuals in history'. Writers such as John Addington Symonds and Edward Carpenter established a list of great homosexual men and some women of the past. Very much the same list was transmitted between gay men and lesbians on a popular level: one gay prisoner told a New York doctor in the 1920s that 'most of the world's genius can be traced directly to the homosexual', citing 'Shakespeare, Coleridge, De Quincey, Rosa Bonheur, Joan of Arc, Beethoven, Wagner and Napoleon' as homosexuals. 'By constructing historical traditions of their own', writes George Chauncey, 'gay men defined themselves as a distinct community. By imagining they had collective roots in the past, they asserted a collective identity in the present' (1995, p. 286). It was an identity that, premised on the idea of the 'third sex', could include and involve both women and men. For the last century at least, an essentialist history has provided the oral tradition, the myths to live by, the genealogy of lesbian and gay life and love.

Such genealogies will always be necessary and potent. But the fragmentation of contemporary lesbian and gay identities and politics is generating new needs and desires. For lesbians and gays, identity is not homogenous or seamless; historical narratives cannot be seamless either. In both collective and personal terms, our modern identities, communities and politics are shaped by a past of contradictions, inconstancies and discontinuities, in which sexuality cannot be understood in isolation from gender, ethnicity and class.

Lesbian and gay historians, like black historians and feminist historians, are forced to read historical sources in their own ways. This methodological process of 'reading against the grain' has been even more of a necessity for lesbians and feminists than for historians of male homosexuality. But taking gender as well as sexuality as a category of historical analysis will demand that both lesbian and gay historians read more closely between the lines of the written and visual sources, looking for the possibilities of lesbian and gay readings; re-imagining the stories suppressed in historical texts; testing the tensions and stresses of the construction of heterosexuality as well as that of homosexuality. Between persecution and resistance, and behind the myth of invisibility, lesbian and gay history can establish a story of social, cultural and political resistances, collusions, manipulations and transformations.

Notes

1. See D'Emilio (1992). In contrast Patrick Higgins argues that the history of 'ordinary people' is misdirected and that 'homosexual history' should be studying 'the connection between homosexuality and genius' and the role homosexuality has played in the making of modern culture (1993, pp. 17–18).
2. On tribady, see Donoghue (1993, p. 4); but Martha Vicinus (1989) argues that only educated men used these terms: there was no *slang* language to denote lesbianism in this period as there was for male homosexuality. We do not know that any women were self-identified as tribades, which raises more questions about the meaning of 'identity'.
3. Recent examples of this approach include Simons (1994) and Chauncey (1995).
4. For an example of this tension, see Katz (1992), which recognizes on the one hand that 'gay' has a history, on the other that 'all homosexuality is situational'.
5. The recent history of lesbian and gay politics is examined in D'Emilio (1983).

References

Abelove, Henry, Barale, Michèle Aina, and Halperin, David, *The Lesbian and Gay Studies Reader.* New York and London: Routledge, 1993.

Boswell, John, *Christianity, Social Tolerance and Homosexuality.* Chicago: University of Chicago Press, 1980.

Bray, Alan, 'Homosexuality and the Signs of Male Friendship in Elizabethan England', *History Workshop Journal,* Vol. 29, 1990, pp. 1–19.

Bray, Alan, *Homosexuality in Renaissance England.* London: GMP, 1982.

Chauncey, George, *Gay New York: The Making of the Gay Male World, 1890–1940.* London: Flamingo, 1995.

Crompton, Louis, 'The Myth of Lesbian Impunity: Capital Laws from 1270 to 1791', *Journal of Homosexuality,* Vol. 6, 1980–81, pp. 11–25.

D'Emilio, John, *Making Trouble: Essays on Gay History, Politics, and the University*. New York and London: Routledge, 1992.

D'Emilio, John, *Sexual Politics, Sexual Communities: The Making of a Homosexual Minority in the United States*. Chicago: University of Chicago Press, 1983.

Donoghue, Emma, *Passions Between Women: British Lesbian Culture 1668–1801*. London: Scarlet Press, 1993.

Duberman, Martin, Vicinus, Martha, and Chauncey, George (eds), *Hidden from History*. Harmondsworth: Penguin, 1991.

Eriksson, Brigitte, 'A Lesbian Execution in Germany, 1721: The Trial Records', *Journal of Homosexuality*, Vol. 6, pp. 27–40

Faderman, Lillian, *Surpassing the Love of Men: Romantic Friendship and Love Between Women from the Renaissance to the Present*. London: Women's Press, 1985.

Gerard, Kent, and Hekma, Gert (eds), 'The Pursuit of Sodomy: Male Homosexuality in Renaissance and Enlightenment Europe', in double issue of *Journal of Homosexuality*, Vol. 16, No. 1/2, 1988.

Goldberg, Jonathan (ed.), *Queering the Renaissance*. Durham, NC: Duke University Press, 1994.

Halley, Janet E., '*Bowers v. Hardwick* in the Renaissance', in Goldberg (ed.), 1994.

Halperin, David, *One Hundred Years of Homosexuality and Other Essays on Greek Love*. New York and London: Routledge, 1990.

Hansen, Karen V., '"No *Kisses* is Like Youres": An Erotic Friendship between Two African-American Women during the Mid-Nineteenth Century', in *Gender and History*, Vol. 7, No. 2, 1995, pp. 153–82.

Higgins, Patrick, *A Queer Reader*. London: Fourth Estate, 1993.

Hunt, Margaret, 'Afterword', in Goldberg (ed.), 1994, pp. 359–78.

Katz, Jonathan Ned, *Gay American History: Lesbians and Gay Men in the U.S.A.* Rev. edn, New York: Meridian, 1992.

Kennedy, Elizabeth Lapovsky, and Davis, Madeline D., *Boots of Leather, Slippers of Gold*. New York: Penguin, 1993.

Lister, Anne, *I Know My Own Heart: The Diaries of Anne Lister (1791–1840)*. Helena Whitbread (ed.) London: Virago, 1988.

Newton, Esther, 'Just One of the Boys: Lesbians in Cherry Grove 1960–1988' in Abelove, Barale and Halperin (eds), 1993.

Newton, Esther, 'The Mythic Mannish Lesbian: Radclyffe Hall and the New Woman', in *Signs*, Vol. 9, No. 4, pp. 557–75, reprinted in Duberman, Vicinus and Chauncey (eds), 1984.

Rich, Adrienne, 'Compulsory Heterosexuality and Lesbian Existence', in *Signs*, Vol. 5, No. 4, 1980, pp. 631–60.

Sedgwick, Eve Kosofsky, *The Epistemology of the Closet*. Hemel Hempstead: Harvester Wheatsheaf, 1991.

Simons, Patricia, 'Lesbian (In)Visibility in Renaissance Culture: Diana and other Cases of Donna con Donna', in *Journal of Homosexuality*, Vol. 27, No. 1/2, 1994, pp. 81–122.

Smith-Rosenberg, Carroll, 'The Female World of Love and Ritual: Relations between Women in Nineteenth-Century America', in *Signs*, Vol. 1, No. 1, 1975, pp. 1–29.

Spencer, Colin, *Homosexuality: A History*. London: Fourth Estate, 1995.

Traub, Valerie, 'The Perversion of "Lesbian" Desire', in *History Workshop Journal*, Vol. 41, 1996, pp. 19–50.

Trumbach, Randolph, 'The Birth of the Queen: Sodomy and the Emergence of Gender Equality in Modern Culture, 1660–1750', in Duberman, Vicinus and Chauncey, 1991a.

Trumbach, Randolph, 'London's Sapphists: From Three Sexes to Four Genders in the Making of Modern Culture', in Julia Epstein and Kristina Straub (eds), *Body Guards: The Cultural Politics of Gender Ambiguity*. London: Routledge, 1991b.

van der Meer, Theo, 'Tribades on Trial: Female Same-Sex Offenders in Late Eighteenth-Century Amsterdam', in *Journal of the History of Sexuality*, Vol. 1, 1991, pp. 24–45.

Vicinus, Martha, '"They Wonder to Which Sex I Belong": The Historical Roots of the Modern Lesbian Identity', in Dennis Altman *et al.*, *Which Homosexuality?* London: GMP, 1989.

Weeks, Jeffrey, *Coming Out: Homosexual Politics in Britain from the Nineteenth Century to the Present*. London: Quartet, 1990.

Weeks, Jeffrey, *Sexuality and Its Discontents: Meanings, Myths and Modern Sexualities*. London: Quartet, 1985.

Whitehead, Harriet, 'The Bow and the Burden Strap: A New Look at Institutionalized Homosexuality in Native North America', in Abelove, Barale and Halperin (eds), 1993.

Further reading

Faderman, Lillian, *Odd Girls and Twilight Lovers: A History of Lesbian Life in Twentieth-Century America*. Harmondsworth: Penguin, 1992.

Foucault, Michel, *History of Sexuality*. London: Allen Lane, 1978.

Miller, Neil, *Out of the Past: Gay and Lesbian History from 1869 to the Present*. London: Vintage, 1995.

5

Film Studies

José Arroyo

THE COMPLEXITY OF MAPPING a history of lesbian and gay film
studies becomes evident when one begins to interrogate each term.
What 'lesbian' signifies is highly contested. The term 'gay' is also changeable and fluid with a history of signification varying from a strategic
cultural and political identity adopted by men and women attracted to
their own sex in order to combat oppression, to a sign which, while barely
describing the commodified culture and identity of white middle-class
men, actively occludes the culture and identities of members of racial and
ethnic minorities attracted to their own sex. Since the 1970s, 'Film Studies' has been an established academic discipline with a clear object of study,
thus the term seems initially transparent. Yet a comparative glance at the
field's introductory textbooks indicates substantial differences of opinion
as to what constitute appropriate movies and methods in the study of
cinema.

Lesbian and gay film studies, then, is a fiction in the process of construction, one which this article attempts to contribute to while hopefully
problematizing. To say that lesbian and gay film studies is a fiction is not to
say that it doesn't exist. In fact this article draws its references (with unfortunate if necessary selectivity) from over a quarter of a century of writings
that investigate the relations between various types of film and lesbian and
gay cultures. To say that the field is a fiction is merely to argue that the term
indicates a coherence and a unity that is at best an imaginary utopia, albeit
one not without descriptive and analytic potential. At a basic level, one
could delineate discrete if overlapping accounts of lesbian film studies and
gay male film studies, each with different foci, separate canons, and distinct literature. To bring the two together in their difference is a choice
based on historical, institutional and intellectual rationale: respectively, the
early monographs on gays and film took into account, although to different extents, both gay males and lesbians (Tyler, 1972; Dyer, 1977; Russo,

1981); the institutionalization of Lesbian and Gay Studies as a discipline requires particular constructions of objects of study; and the cross-fertilizing of lesbian with gay film scholarship, Lesbian and Gay Studies with film studies and all of the above with Queer Theory is potentially mutually informative and intellectually exciting.

Film studies became institutionalized in the 1970s upon the recognition that cinema was the twentieth century's premier art form and a powerful mass medium capable of influencing people's dreams, thoughts and actions. Lesbian and gay studies is an interdisciplinary field which encompasses any research that takes sex and sexuality as a central category of analysis. According to Abelove *et al*, 'Lesbian/gay studies, in short, cannot be defined exclusively by its subject, its practitioners, its methods, or its themes . . . Lesbian/gay studies does for *sex* and *sexuality* approximately what Women's Studies does for gender' (1993, p. 15). As I will demonstrate below, just as Joan Wallach Scott argues that taking on board the question of gender in history doesn't just entail adding on to history but rethinking the way history is done (1988, pp. 10–11), issues raised by lesbian and gay film studies can potentially change and at least inform our understanding of central concepts in film studies such as representation, narrative, stars, authorship, spectatorship and genre.

Questions of representation

Representation is a key issue in lesbian and gay studies of film. The logic behind the Gay Liberation movement's emphasis on 'coming out' was that it would make the invisible visible and that such visibility, an alternative form of grass roots cultural and political representation in itself, would help transform the ways gays and lesbians saw themselves, how they were seen and how they were treated. In accordance with this logic, how lesbians and gays are represented in film and other audio-visual media is crucial. As Richard Dyer writes, images matter because:

> how social groups are treated in cultural representation is part and parcel of how they are treated in life. How a group is represented, presented over again in cultural forms, how an image of a member of a group is taken as representative of that group, how that group is represented in the sense of spoken for and on behalf of (whether they represent, speak for themselves or not), these all have to do with how members of groups see themselves and others like themselves . . .

Equally re-presentation, representativeness, representing, have to do also with how others see members of a group. (Dyer, 1993, p. 1)

The most influential of the early monographs to deal with the representation of gays and lesbians in film was Vito Russo's *The Celluloid Closet*, a groundbreaking work because it combined what was, for its time, an exhaustive historical survey of the representation of lesbians and gays in the cinema with a cogent and damning political analysis of that history. Russo divided his chronicle into three parts: representation before the Hays Code of 1934 (the enforcement of which prevented the overt representation of 'perversion'), the period from 1934 to 1962 which he called 'the invisible years', and the period from 1962 to 1978 which saw first the relaxation of the code, its eventual replacement by a ratings system in 1968 and the liberalizing of sexual mores which accompanied the various civil rights movements in general and the women's liberation movement in particular. In the first part, Russo argued that homosexuality in cinema has always been depicted in relation to masculinity. Gay men were represented as being 'like women' while women were represented as being 'like men'. The apparent higher tolerance for 'mannish' women was deceptive because it rendered actual lesbianism all but invisible while homosexual men in this period were represented via negative visual and verbal codes: 'powerlessness, femininity in men, decadence and sometimes anarchy were consistently coloured with sexual references that became more explicit each year until the code clamped down in 1934' (1981, p. 36). In the second section on 'The Invisible Years' Russo argues that 'Gay characters and references to the existence of homosexuality were routinely laundered off the screen for the better part of half a century' (p. 63). However, this section of the book is also entitled 'The Way We Weren't' because as Russo argues, 'Technically, homosexuals were just as invisible onscreen as they were in real life. They continued to emerge, however, as subtextual phantoms representing the very fear of homosexuality' (p. 63). In the last section, 'Frightening the Horses', Russo would argue that 'the dirty secret of old emerged on the screen in those newly enlightened times as a dirty secret, still a subject to be whispered about but not to be explored in a meaningful way. Homosexuality had come out of the closet and into the shadows, where it would remain for the better part of two decades' (p. 122). Sissies would continue to be the butt of the joke while homosexuals of both sexes continued to drop like flies, 'In twenty-two of twenty-eight films dealing with gay subjects from 1962 to 1978, major gay characters onscreen ended in suicide or violent death' (p. 52).

Early scholarship on representations of lesbians in film highlighted the problems of invisibility and negative stereotyping. In her 1973 essay 'Lesbianism in the Movies', Joan Mellen argued that lesbians were largely invisible in feature films and those that were visible tended to be depicted as 'sick' (p. 71), while Caroline Sheldon went on to insist that this type of representation was not without social repercussions: 'Lesbianism is usually shown as an aberration, an individual psycho-social problem, which may not be the condition of every lesbian in the audience but may help to precipitate a few into believing that it is' (1977, p. 5). As late as 1992, Andrea Weiss in *Vampires and Violets* continued to decry the lack of lesbian images in the cinema while noting that 'Each lesbian image that has managed to surface – the lesbian vampire, the sadistic or neurotic repressed woman, the pre-Oedipal "mother/ daughter" lesbian relationship, the lesbian as sexual challenge or titillation to men – has helped to determine the boundaries of possible representation' (p. 1).

The conclusion that lesbians and gays were generally represented via negative stereotypes led lesbian and gay scholars to impressive and sustained theorization of the notion of stereotyping itself, its uses and effects, resulting in a body of work that constitutes a vital contribution to cultural scholarship in general. Richard Dyer argued that types are 'simple, vivid, memorable, easily-grasped and widely recognized characterization' (1977, p. 28). Dyer divides types into social types, stereotypes and member types before describing how stereotypes can operate in film through iconography and structure. Dyer argues that stereotypes help to establish a hegemony that results in ethnocentrism because, 'the dominant groups apply their norms to subordinated groups, find the latter wanting, hence inadequate, inferior, sick or grotesque and hence reinforce the dominant groups' own sense of the legitimacy of their domination' (p. 30).

T. E. Perkins' 'Rethinking Stereotypes' elaborates on Dyer's work, arguing that stereotypes are often valid, effective and structurally reinforced. They can condense and connote a wealth of meanings and are similar to ideology in that 'they are both (apparently) true and (really) false at the same time' (1979, p. 155). Perkins notes that gays differ from other social groups in their relation to stereotypes in that they may well encounter stereotypes before they come out to themselves, that there is no legitimate social role for negative stereotypes of gays and that gays, whether they accept stereotypes as accurate or not, will tend to be more conscious of stereotypes as stereotypes. Perkins claims that 'the non-visibility of gays combined with their illegitimacy' means that very often the only way they can communicate their gayness is by using stereotypes (p. 153). Dyer later extrapolated this point in relation to visual images, arguing that gayness doesn't 'show' but is communicated through a repertory of signs whose recognizability entails typicality. 'Typification is a near necessity' argues Dyer (1993, p. 20), before delineating four predominant gay types (in-betweenism, macho, the sad young man, and lesbian feminism) in order to demonstrate the importance of gender and of biology/nature in gay representation, and the pressure from both dominant and sub-cultural forces to produce gay types (p. 29).

The conclusion that lesbian and gay images in mainstream cinema were either invisible or negative stereotypes had several repercussions. Though Becker et al had argued that 'negative stereotypes about lesbians have a lot to teach us about the limitations of any "positive image" approach to the depiction of women in Hollywood film (because) positive images, like negative images, suppress contradiction and are thus static' (1995, p. 27), there was a widespread belief amongst those involved in the Gay Liberation movement of the 1970s that an appropriate response to invisibility and a history of negative images was the construction and circulation of positive ones. As a result there were several key films from this period that were both made by and addressed to gays and lesbians concretely involved in Gay Liberation politics or more broadly sympathetic to a liberationist agenda. Representative titles would include fiction films such as Nighthawks (GB, 1980) and Outrageous (Canada, 1977) but mostly, because they were cheaper to make and easier to distribute, documentaries such as Coming Out (USA, 1972), Greta's Girls (USA, 1978), Michael, A Gay Son (Canada, 1980), Some American Feminists (Canada, 1977) and Witches and Faggots, Dykes and Poofters (Australia, 1980).

Hidden from history

Another significant response to the perceived invisibility and negative imagery of the period was to comb through the past for lesbian and gay film-makers, images of gays and lesbians, or information about lesbian and gay spectatorship that had been 'hidden from history', and to reclaim them. This work was presented in a variety of spaces: periodicals that came from and for the movement (Gay Left, The Body Politic, The Advocate), specialized film journals (particularly Jump Cut) and books aimed at a popular audience (for example, Boze Hadleigh's Conversations with My Elders). Some of this work may be regarded as a form of 'queer-spotting', one which continues to play a valuable role in lesbian and gay cultures. Many lesbians and gays have found political affirmation in learning that important film-makers (Dorothy Arzner, perhaps, or Sergei Eisenstein) were 'like them', others just enjoy the gossip value; indeed, such interest indicates that for queer subcultures, gossip is not an opposite of political discourse but a vital part of it.

Whatever forum it appeared in, and whatever the form, this type of historical work asked important questions: What were the pioneering gay and lesbian films? Which directors or actors were homosexual and is this detectable in the films themselves? Which films from the past (with or without homosexual subject matter) or which stars (queer or not) had a special significance to past generations of lesbians and gays? This type of work brought new attention to directors such as Mitchell Leisen, 'rediscovered' the value of directors such as James Whale, while the works of directors already recognized by film studies such as Dorothy Arzner or George Cukor were re-viewed for evidence of a 'gay sensibility'. Furthermore stars who were thought to be gay or bisexual (Garbo, Dietrich, Montgomery Clift) or those who had special significance to lesbian and gay subcultures (Doris Day, Judy Garland, Marilyn Monroe) were profiled and analysed 'from a gay perspective'. Films which featured playful or sexually ambivalent representations of gender, especially when they included cross-dressing or a kiss between people of the same sex, elicited particular appreciation – *Morocco* (1930), *Queen Christina* (1933), *Sylvia Scarlett* (1935).

All this historical work of rediscovery and reclamation was activist in the sense that it was undertaken in the face of absence or exclusion in order to challenge dominant discourses of identity, sexuality and culture. As B. Ruby Rich stated, in her exemplary essay on the 1931 film *Mädchen in Uniform*, ' the first lesson of *Mädchen in Uniform* is that lesbianism has a much larger and finer history than we often suspect, that the film indicates as much, and that we need to do ever more work on reconstructing the image of lesbian culture that has so painfully been erased' (1981, p. 49). Attempts along such lines to reconstruct a history of gay male representation have included work on films as diverse as *Wings* (Sweden, 1916) and *Victim* (GB, 1961). The focus in this work was not just on whether these representations were 'positive' or 'negative' to a contemporary audience but on investigating the films' social context as a way of understanding their representations historically. Delineating such contexts involves researching not only into a film's production and initial reception, but also into what discourses of sexuality were prevalent at the time and how such discourses might have affected production, distribution, exhibition and reception (Finch, 1984; Medhurst, 1984).

Alternative sites

'Underground' (experimental or avant-garde) cinema and pornography are two modes of cinema that have received sustained scrutiny from lesbian and gay scholars. The 'underground', with its onus on innovation in form or subject matter, its insistence on personal expression, and its championing of the transgressive, provided a fertile context for lesbian and gay representations (although there are important differences in the structural position of lesbians and gay men within the 'underground' context). This type of film-making was relatively inexpensive and had its own parallel, albeit small-scale, cinematic apparatus which included production, distribution, exhibition and modes of reception. Moreover, producers and audiences could cloak their production and consumption of these images under the alibi of art. It is one of the few modes of cinema in which lesbian and gay audiences could not only see a varied range of representations but also feel directly addressed by them. In the case of women-only screenings of work by lesbian film-makers like Barbara Hammer, film exhibition could be as political as the texts themselves. Work by directors as diverse as Hammer, Kenneth Anger, Jean Genet, Jack Smith, Greg Markopolous, Jan Oxenberg and Sue Friedrich experimented with various forms to represent the previously unrepresentable, experiments which often, to the delight of their audiences, included multitudinous and delicious images of a desire and a love that still didn't quite dare speak it name outside the film theatre.

Pornography is a controversial mode of cinema that has in the past been largely ignored by conventional film studies (Williams, 1989 and the journal *Jump Cut* are important exceptions). It is also an historically divisive mode amongst lesbians and gay men. Many lesbian critics, in addition to supporting a general feminist critique of pornography as objectifying and exploitative, were particularly opposed to heterosexual porn's representation of lesbianism, wherein lesbians were shown to be objects of exchange amongst men, lesbian sexuality was depicted as a display for male consumption, and lesbianism was shown to be 'cured' when the right man came along. Gay male scholars were also critical of heterosexual porn, but claimed that pornography for gay men operated differently in terms of production, exhibition, consumption and representation, and deserved analysis as a cinematic genre (Dyer, 1985, 1993; Waugh, 1985). In an extensive body of work on the subject, Tom Waugh (1983, 1985, 1992, 1996) has analysed how various kinds of erotic imagery contributed to the construction of 'liberating' discourses on representation, identity (individual, subcultural and national) and community; what narratives, structures, codes and iconography were utilized in representing gay male desire; and how these works intersected with 'High Art' practices. Gay male work on pornography stresses the centrality of erotic imagery to contemporary gay cultures, a centrality that is acknowledged in critiques of pornography in relation to race (Marlon Riggs' *Tongues Untied* (1989) is especially moving and memorable in this respect).

Debates on the relations between pornography and lesbian and gay representations and cultures need to be historicized. Contemporary feminist work indicates that there has been a significant paradigm shift in discourses on pornography since the 1970s. Perhaps because of easy access to home video equipment, there has been a considerable proliferation in lesbian erotic self-representation which has substantially shifted the terms of the debate (Besigner, 1992). Recent scholarship has also investigated the relationship between gay male pornographic imagery and heterosexual women's desire. Perhaps because, as Kobena Mercer writes, 'The gendered hierarchy of seeing/ being seen is not so rigidly coded in homoerotic representations, since sexual sameness liquidates the associative opposition between active subject and passive object' (1991, p. 182), gay male pornography has been discovered to be pleasurable to heterosexual women to the extent that women are producing explicit images of gay male sex for their own consumption (Marks, 1996; Penley, 1992).

Stars and authorship

It is important to remember that lesbian and gay film scholars have not only challenged and redrafted film studies but also worked within its established concerns. Film studies as a field would be substantially poorer without the important contributions of Robin Wood, Andrew Britton, Teresa de Lauretis, B. Ruby Rich, Judith Mayne, Richard Dyer and others who, to paraphrase Wood (1978), placed equal emphasis throughout their work on the terms lesbian or gay, film and scholarship. Since a list of contributions in every area of film studies would probably be as exhausting to read as to compile, it might be useful to dwell on two characteristic examples: stars and authorship.

Contemporary scholarship on stars within film studies can in most cases be directly traced to Richard Dyer's pioneering *Stars* (1979), and other lesbian and gay scholars can claim credit for a disproportionate amount of key contributions in the area (Britton, 1984; Medhurst, 1986; Stacey, 1994). The point here is that it is significant that lesbians and gays were drawn to the subject. Knowledge of stars has traditionally constituted valuable cultural capital for lesbians and gay men. How much one knew about Bette Davis or Doris Day could code information about one's sexual orientation so that it would be evident to those who had access to the same discourses (other 'friends of Dorothy' for example) while not disclosing anything to society at large. Camp as a sub-cultural mode of communication also necessitated substantial expertise on stars and training in appropriate forms of 'reading' them. Knowledge of and about stars was an important component in the construction of subcultural identities. Just as Richard Dyer learned how to be gay by learning how to like Judy Garland, others did before in relation to Dietrich and Davis and after in relation to Sigourney Weaver and Madonna. Whereas conventional cultural hierarchies historically saw an interest in stars as intellectually disreputable and socially permissible perhaps only to lower-class women, lesbian and gay cultures have long understood the complexity of star signs and the sociological and semiological riches they could yield. Consequently lesbian and gay critics working on star analyses were able to draw on a rich heritage of subcultural insights in forging what has become not only a key area in film theory, but one which would be virtually unthinkable without gay and lesbian perspectives.

Authorship was a contentious issue in film studies long before the advent of gay and lesbian interventions. Under the guise of *auteurism* and its subsequent metamorphoses, the notion that Hollywood films could be said to have an author (and thus be considered in traditional art-historical terms as authentic works of personal expression rather than as factory products) enabled serious investigation of movies under the aegis of art. Various conceptualizations of authorship in film have also provided ready-made categories through which to analyse bodies of work and also supplied accompanying modes of evaluation. Roland Barthes' pronouncement on the death of the author was very influential in the wider field of film theory, but lesbian and gay scholars have insisted that it still matters who it is that makes films, resulting in a variety of historical and theoretical explorations of authorship by lesbian and gay scholars. Historical work worthy of note includes Judith Mayne's analysis of how discussions of Dorothy Arzner's work in terms of female authorship ignore the very visible image of the author as a lesbian, and Andy Medhurst's critique of how attribution of the authorship of *Brief Encounter* has changed historically from valorizing first the gay screenwriter (Noel Coward), then the heterosexual director (David Lean) and lately a shared 'structure of feeling' between film-makers and queer audiences (Mayne, 1991; Medhurst, 1991). Lesbian and gay scholarship tends to work with models that see authorship as multiple and hierarchical and produced within material and semiotic circumstances. In Richard Dyer's words, 'all authorship and all sexual identities are performances, done with greater or less facility, always problematic in relation to any self separable from the realization of self in the discursive modes available. The study of (gay/lesbian) authorship is the study of those modes and the particular ways in which they have been performed in given texts' (1991, p. 183). Lesbian and gay scholarship has been sensitive to the attention to the social implicit in Barthes' call to dethrone the author in favour of a focus on the reader and the moment of reading. Alexander Doty has remarked that lesbian and gay authorship can be attributed to directors, stars or other film-makers on the basis of their being queer, and even proposed that lesbian and gay authorship could be validly ascribed to heterosexual film-makers whose work has a meaningful place within lesbian and gay cultural histories (1993a).

Different modes of seeing: lesbian challenges to film studies

The map of lesbian and gay scholarship on film delineated so far could, with varying degrees of ease, be accommodated into traditional film studies paradigms. However, the challenges to film studies in general and feminist film studies in particular from lesbian theorists are less easy to assimilate, potentially and productively transformative. Teresa de Lauretis argues that the project of lesbian film is to devise 'strategies of representation which will in turn, alter the standard of vision, the frame of reference of visibility, of *what can be seen*' (1988, p. 171). In attempting to account for and explore the implications of that project, lesbian film scholarship has altered the entire frame of reference of feminist film theory. Early feminist film theorists raised crucial questions of representation, narrative, address, spectatorship, identification and desire in relation to women, but often took heterosexuality as an unquestioned given. They utilized notions of cross-dressing, transvestism and the masquerade while resolutely ignoring lesbianism, leading lesbian critics to conclude that 'Lesbianism is the hole in the heart of feminist criticism' (Becker *et al*, 1995, p. 43). The urgent task of lesbian film theory, then, was to 'dismantle some of the current feminist film theory and film history in order to build a more inclusive foundation' (p. 43). As Chris Strayeer points out, 'Feminist film theory based on sexual difference has much to gain from considering lesbian desire and sexuality. Women's desire for women deconstructs male/female sexual dichotomies, sex/gender conflation, and the universality of the Oedipal narrative' (1995, p. 43).

Film studies in general has much to gain by taking on board Strayeer's insights, as well as other issues introduced through lesbian scholarship. What, for example, does Mandy Merck's assertion that lesbians in art cinema 'suffer as the objects of a cinema which cannot come to terms with its own pleasures' teach us about Art Cinema (1986, p. 174)? How can we build on Judith Mayne's claim that 'lesbianism is simultaneously a limit and horizon of female narration and authorship' (1991a, p. 175)? How does Jackie Stacey's claim that 'lesbian romance is defeated by problems too great to deal with in narrative terms' contribute to a more complex understanding of the romance genre (1995, p. 98)? Rather than continuing to list these and other challenges it might be useful to simply dwell on the core question of film spectatorship.

In her broad-ranging *Cinema and Spectatorship*, Judith Mayne differentiates between 'the subject', the viewing position assigned to the film viewer by the text and the cinematic apparatus as a social technology, and the 'viewer', the real people who watch movies. 1970s film theory utilized a psychoanalytic paradigm based on a binary model of sexual difference to analyse spectatorship as a subject-position and bracketed away actual viewers altogether. Lesbian scholarship has demonstrated how 'sexual difference' is a heterosexist concept that ignores the possibility of same-sex desire and pointed to the need to 'separate gender identification from sexuality, too often conflated in the name of sexual difference' (Stacey, 1987, p. 53).

Although Tamsin Wilton argues that a sociological paradigm is more useful to thinking about relations between lesbians and the moving image than a psychoanalytic one based on sexual difference (1995, p. 16), recent scholarship has demonstrated that both paradigms offer useful forms of knowledge, that both spectators and viewers can be productively analysed from lesbian, gay and queer perspectives. Alexander Doty has indicated what sophisticated, agile and intertextual readers queers can be (Doty,

1993), and his theoretical arguments can be empirically corroborated by evidence ranging from the evocative autobiographical recollections of individual lesbian spectators (Whittaker, 1981) to the novelist James Baldwin's vivid account of what the image of Bette Davis meant to him as a black and gay teenager (Baldwin, 1976). The continuing value of psychoanalytic approaches is evident in the work of writers like Teresa de Lauretis and Jackie Stacey. For de Lauretis, the questions at stake in discussions of queers and film are 'to see or not to see, to be seen (and how) or not to be seen (at all?). Subjective vision and social visibility, being and passing, representation and spectatorship – the conditions of the visible, what can be *seen*, and eroticized, and on what *scene*' (1991, p. 223). De Lauretis' extraordinary work, along with much other recent lesbian scholarship, is an attempt to answer those questions, several of which traditional film theory has yet to ask, and which the discipline of film studies cannot begin to answer without to some extent changing itself.

The queer moment

Developments in lesbian and gay film scholarship are intimately interlinked with developments in lesbian and gay film-making. For example, one could map the key shifts in lesbian film theory by pursuing the debates over film-makers like Dorothy Arzner, Ulrike Ottinger and Monika Treut, or tracing changing responses to films like *Mädchen in Uniform* (Germany, 1931), *The Killing of Sister George* (USA, 1968), *Personal Best* (USA, 1982), *Lianna* (USA, 1982), *Entre Nous* (France, 1983), *Born in Flames* (USA, 1983) *Desert Hearts* (USA, 1985), *She Must Be Seeing Things* (USA, 1987), *Basic Instinct* (USA, 1991), *Thelma and Louise* (USA, 1991) and *Go Fish* (USA, 1994). The latest development in lesbian and gay film studies is especially closely connected to a specific body of films, those usually assigned the label of 'New Queer Cinema'.

That label demarcates a number of 1990s films, mostly directed by gay men, which includes *Looking for Langston* (UK, 1989), *Poison* (USA, 1990), *No Skin off My Ass* (Canada, 1990) and *Edward II* (UK, 1991). The term was coined to distinguish them from previous films like *Maurice* (UK, 1987), which used classical narrative to present 'positive' images of gay men and lesbians which in some sense pleaded for tolerance. According to Ruby Rich:

The new queer films and videos are not all the same, and do not share a single aesthetic vocabulary or strategy or concern. Yet, they are nonetheless united by a common style. Call it 'Homo Pomo': there are traces in all of them of appropriation and pastiche, irony, as well as a reworking of history with social constructionism very much in mind. Definitively breaking with older humanist approaches and the films that accompanied identity politics, these works are irreverent, energetic, alternatively minimalist and excessive. Above all they're full of pleasure. (1992, p. 32)

As Rich notes, queer films could be seen as a prime example of postmodern aesthetics. They utilize irony and pastiche, represent fragmented subjectivities, depict a compression and they are frequently dystopic – but what differentiates 'New Queer Cinema' from other types of postmodern movies is how their aesthetic relates to AIDS as a socio-political and discursive context.

'New Queer Cinema' was produced at a moment when AIDS had effected a profound epistemic shift in gay culture (changing our views on society, sexuality, bodies, relationship, time, history and culture) and spurred us into new mobilizations of community (one example of which is the proliferation of lesbian and gay film festivals). Queer films are purposely stylish because they are struggling to represent a new context against the legacies of both dominant cinema and, as we can see in *Looking for Langston* or *Tongues Untied*, a previous history of gay representation. Films like *Edward II* try to place gays in history because imagining gays in history is to a certain extent a way of legitimizing present existence and more importantly, a way of imagining a future. They represent a view of time and a view of sexuality which explicitly or subtextually conveys a changed sense of mortality (Arroyo, 1993). For film studies, New Queer Cinema raises challenging questions about representations of the liminal; about hybrid forms of textuality, address and reception; about notions of multiple spectatorship, social authorship; and about how intra-generic approaches to a particular thematic could themselves constitute a new genre.

This chapter has addressed the works and the issues that I think are significant in lesbian and gay film studies, yet I am conscious of many gaps. Many key film-makers are missing, and a whole series of explorations in short films and in video are unaccounted for here. An account of race in lesbian and gay film scholarship that would not just be added on but would fundamentally alter the map itself remains to be written: this is a glaring, and arguably structuring, absence in the field. Just as previous lesbian and gay scholars have had to work within and against the discipline of film studies, future ones will have to negotiate their own relationship to the emerging field that I have sketched here, which already has a history that privileges certain questions over others.

References

Abelove, Henry, Barale, Michèle Aina, and Halperin, David M. (eds), *The Lesbian and Gay Studies Reader*. New York and London: Routledge, 1993.

Arroyo, José, 'Death, Desire and Identity: The Political Unconscious of "New Queer Cinema"', in Joseph Bristow and Angela R. Wilson (eds), *Activating Theory: Lesbian, Gay, Bisexual Politics*. London: Lawrence and Wishart, 1993, pp. 72–98.

Baldwin, James, *The Devil Finds Work*. New York: Dell, 1976.

Becker, Edith, Citron, Michelle, Lesage, Julia, and Rich, B. Ruby, 'Lesbians and Film', in Corey J.Creekmur and Alexander Doty (eds), *Out in Culture:Lesbian, Gay and Queer Essays on Popular Culture*. London: Cassell, 1995, pp. 25–43.

Bensinger, Terralee, 'Lesbian Pornography: The Re/Making of (a) Community', in *Discourse*, Vol. 15, No. 1, Autumn 1992, pp. 69–93.

Britton, Andrew, *Katharine Hepburn: The Thirties and After*. Newcastle upon Tyne: Tyneside Cinema, 1984.

De Lauretis, Teresa, 'Film and the Visible', in Bad Object Choices (eds), *How Do I Look?*, 1991, pp. 223–76.

De Lauretis, Teresa, 'Lesbian Indifference and Lesbian Representation', *Theatre Studies*, Vol. 40, No. 2, May 1988, pp. 155–77.

Doty, Alexander, *Making Things Perfectly Queer: Interpreting Mass Culture*. Minneapolis: University of Minnesota Press, 1993.

Doty, Alexander, 'Whose Text is it Anyway: Queer Cultures, Queer Auteurs and Queer Authorship', in *Quarterly Review of Film and Video*, Vol. 15, No. 1, 1993a, pp. 41–54.

Dyer, Richard, 'Believing in Fairies: The Author and the Homosexual', in Diana Fuss (ed.), *Inside Out: Lesbian Theories, Gay Theories*. New York: Routledge, 1991, pp. 185–204.

Dyer, Richard, *Gays and Film*. London: BFI, 1977.

Dyer, Richard, *Heavenly Bodies: Film Stars and Society*. New York: St Martin's Press, 1986.

Dyer, Richard, 'Male Gay Porn: Coming to Terms', in *Jump Cut*, Vol. 30, 1985, pp. 27–9.

Dyer, Richard, *The Matter of Images: Essays on Representations*. London: Routledge, 1993.

Dyer, Richard, *Now You See It: Studies on Lesbian and Gay Film*. New York: Routledge, 1990.

Dyer, Richard, *Stars*. London: BFI, 1979.

Finch, Mark, 'Uncovering the Very First Gay Film', in *Body Politic*, October 1984, p. 107.

Hadleigh, Boze, *Conversations with My Elders*. New York: St Martin's Press, 1986.

Marks, Laura, 'Straight Women, Gay Porn, and the Scene of Erotic Looking', in *Jump Cut*, Vol. 40, 1996, pp. 127–37.

Mayne, Judith, 'Lesbian Looks: Dorothy Arzner and Female Authorship' in Bad Object Choices (eds), *How Do I Look?* Seattle: Bay Press, 1991, pp. 103–35.

Mayne, Judith, 'A Parallax View of Lesbian Authorship', in Diana Fuss (ed.), *Inside/Out: Lesbian Theories/Gay Theories*. New York: Routledge, 1991a, pp. 173–84,.

Medhurst, Andy, 'Dirk Bogarde', in Charles Barr (ed.), *All Our Yesterdays: Ninety Years of British Cinema*. London: BFI, 1986, pp. 346–54.

Medhurst, Andy, 'That Special Thrill: *Brief Encounter*, Homosexuality and Authorship', in *Screen*, Vol. 32, No. 2, Summer 1991, pp. 197–208.

Medhurst, Andy, 'Victim: Text as Context', in *Screen*, July–August 1984, pp. 22–35.

Mellen, Joan, *Women and their Sexuality in the New Film*. New York: Dell, 1973.

Mercer, Kobena, 'Skin Head Sex Thing: Racial Difference and Homoerotic Imaginary', in Bad Object Choices (ed.), *How do I Look?* Seattle: Bay Press, 1991, pp. 169–210.

Merck, Mandy, 'Lianna and the Lesbians of Art Cinema', in Charlotte Brunsdon (ed.), *Films for Women*. London: BFI, 1986, pp. 166–74.

Penley, Constance, 'Feminism, Psychoanalysis, and the Study of Popular Culture', in Lawrence Grossberg, Cary Nelson, Paula Treichler (eds), *Cultural Studies*. New York: Routledge, 1992, pp. 479–94.

Perkins, T. E., 'Rethinking Stereotypes', in Michelle Barrett, Philip Corrigan, Annette Kuhn and Janet Wolff (eds), *Ideology and Cultural Production*. London: Croom Helm, 1979, pp. 135–59.

Rich, B. Ruby, 'Maedchen in Uniform: From Repressive Tolerance to Erotic Liberation', in *Jump Cut*, Nos. 24/25, 1981, pp. 44–50.

Rich, B. Ruby, 'The New Queer Cinema', in *Sight and Sound*. September 1992, pp. 30–5.

Rich, B. Ruby, 'Women and Film: A Discussion of Feminist Aesthetics', in *New German Critique*, No. 13, Winter 1978.

Russo, Vito, *The Celluloid Closet: Homosexuality in the Movies*. New York: Harper and Row, 1981.

Sheldon, Caroline, 'Lesbians and Film: Some Thoughts', in Richard Dyer (ed.), *Gays and Film*. London: BFI, 1977, pp. 5–26.

Stacey, Jackie, 'Desperately Seeking Difference', in *Screen*, Vol. 28, No. 1, Winter 1987, pp. 48–61.

Stacey, Jackie, '"If You Don't Play, You Can't Win": Desert Hearts and the Lesbian Romance Film', in Tamsin Wilton (ed.), *Immortal Invisible*. London: Routledge, 1995, pp. 92–114.

Stacey, Jackie, *Star Gazing: Hollywood Cinema and Female Spectatorship*. London: Routledge, 1994.

Strayeer, Chris, 'The Hypothetical Lesbian Heroine in Narrative Feature Film', in C. Creekmur, and Alexander Doty (eds), *Out in Culture: Gay, Lesbian, and Queer Essays on Popular Culture*. London: Cassell, 1995.

Tyler, Parker, *Screening the Sexes: Homosexuality in the Movies*. New York: Da Capo Press, 1972, 1993.

Wallach Scott, Joan, *Gender and the Politics of History*. New York: Columbia University Press, 1988.

Waugh, Thomas, *Hard to Imagine: Gay Male Eroticism in Pornography and Film from their Beginnings to Stonewall*. New York: Columbia University Press, 1996.

Waugh, Thomas, 'A Heritage of Pornography: On the Gay Film Collection of the Kinsey Institute', in *Body Politic*, Vol. 90, January 1983, pp. 29–33.

Waugh, Thomas, 'Homoerotic Representation in the Stag Film, 1920–1940: Imagining an Audience', in *Wide Angle*, Vol. 14, No. 2, April 1992, pp. 4–19.

Waugh, Thomas, 'Men's Pornography: Gay Versus Straight', in *Jump Cut*, Vol. 30, 1985, pp. 30–5.

Weiss, Andrea, *Vampires and Violets: Lesbians in Film*. New York: Penguin, 1992.

Whittaker, Judy, 'Hollywood Transformed', in *Jump Cut*, No. 24/25, 1981, pp. 33–5.

Williams, Linda, *Hardcore: Power, Pleasure, and the 'Frenzy of the Visible'*. Berkeley: University of California Press, 1989.

Wilton, Tamsin (ed.), *Immortal Invisible: Lesbians and the Moving Image*. London: Routledge, 1995.

Wood, Robin, 'Responsibilities of a Gay Film Critic', in Bill Nichols (ed.), *Movies and Methods*. Berkeley: University of California Press, 1978, 1985, pp. 649–60.

Further reading

Bad Object Choices (eds), *How Do I Look? Queer Film and Video*. Seattle: Bay Press, 1991.

Brasell, R. Bruce, 'My Hustler: Gay Spectatorship as Cruising', in *Wide Angle*, Vol. 14, No. 2, April 1992, pp. 54–64.

Citron, Michelle, 'The Films of Jan Oxenberg: Comic Critique', in Charlotte Brunsdon (ed.), *Films for Women*. London: BFI, 1986.

Gever, Martha, Greyson, John, and Parmar, Pratibha (eds), *Queer Looks: Perspectives on Lesbian and Gay Film and Video*. London: Routledge, 1994.

Mayne, Judith, *Cinema and Spectatorship*. London: Routledge, 1993.

Suárez, Juan A., *Bike Boys, Drag Queens and Superstars: Avant Garde, Mass Culture and Gay Identities in the 1960s Underground Cinema*. Bloomington: Indiana University Press, 1996.

White, Patricia, 'Female Spectator, Lesbian Specter: The Haunting', in Diana Fuss (ed.), *Inside/Out: Lesbian Theories, Gay Theories*. New York and London: Routledge, 1991.

Acknowledgement

The author wishes to thank Sarah Goode, Adrian Heathfield, Jason Jacobs, Ros Jennings and Julianne Pidduck for their critical commentary on drafts of this essay.

6

Queer Representation in the Mass Media

Alexander Doty and Ben Gove

CONSIDERING LESBIAN, GAY AND QUEER representation in the mass media and in popular culture often requires moving beyond understanding the 'mass' or the 'popular' as necessarily meaning a mainstream media or culture that only addresses millions of heterosexuals.[1] Until the last decade or so, lesbians, gays and queers were generally represented in media contexts that most explicitly catered to a large heterosexual audience. Yet, especially since the 1970s, lesbians, gays and queers have themselves used the mass media in diverse ways to address audiences through popular forms. While they may often be reaching hundreds or thousands, rather than millions, these lesbians, gays and queers are part of mass media and popular cultural production. Even if we do focus on so-called mainstream mass media and popular culture, however, it is clear that heterosexuals haven't been the only ones doing the producing, performing or watching.

There are often political reasons – whether conservative, liberal or radical – for maintaining a division between 'mainstream' mass media and 'alternative'/'independent' (mass) media. One conservative view is that mainstream media express (or should express) the will and desires of the majority, and as such, should not be forced to represent positively anything that does not reinforce dominant ideology. On the other hand, some liberals, progressives and radicals want clearly demarcated 'alternative' media outlets that allow for a less censored (and censured) range of information and representation. In relation to lesbian, gay and queer representation, though, the lines between mainstream and alternative media have become significantly more blurred in recent years, with the advent of, for example, programmes produced by and for queers on television (*Gaytime TV, In the Life, Out on Tuesday/Out*) and radio (*Out This Week, This Way Out*); out lesbian and gay music performers in the charts (Melissa Etheridge, k. d. lang, David McAlmont, Jimmy Somerville); and national advertizing campaigns

(Ikea, Lee Jeans for Women) which include openly queer representations. However, while some out lesbian/gay/queer writers are published in heterosexually-oriented magazines and newspapers (usually by addressing an assumed straight readership), journalism and comic strips largely remain in their separate heterosexual 'mainstream' and lesbian/gay/queer 'alternative' mass media worlds.[2]

Although there is now a plethora of mainstream, alternative and 'in-between' sources of lesbian/gay/queer media representation, very little academic critical work has been published that discusses these representations, as opposed to the more developed field of lesbian/gay/ queer film studies. With regard to television, popular music, radio, comics, advertizing and other forms of mass media, the most vigilant and detailed media watch has been kept by lesbian, gay and queer newspapers and magazines (themselves forms of mass media) like *The Advocate*, *Attitude*, *Boyz*, *Christopher Street*, *Curve* (formerly *Deneuve*), *Diva*, *Gay Times*, *Genre*, *The Pink Paper*, *Out*, *Outweek*, *10 Percent* and many other national and regional publications. While our case studies below treat the two areas of mass media that academic criticism has focused upon most – television and popular music – many of the critical approaches to gay, lesbian and queer representation that we mention have been developed most consistently over the years in queer newspaper and magazine reviews and articles. Yet in turn, it is equally important to acknowledge that journalism and other popular discussion of mass culture is often 'compelled by necessity to draw key terms and assumptions from high theory, from the more systematic accounts of art, commerce, pleasure . . . [sexuality, gender, 'race', ethnicity] and class that are available' (Frith, 1990, p. 174).

Television

It could be argued that there has been some kind of queer representation on television from the late 1940s onwards. The most popular show of the early years of American television, *The Milton Berle Show*, often featured its star sashaying in front of the camera in drag. Forever after, 'Mr Television', as he was known, would don a dress for gag guest appearances on other shows. Fast-forward a little over four decades: 'Mr Television', sans dress, finds himself at the 1993 *MTV Music Video Awards* standing next to RuPaul, the premiere media drag queen of the 1990s. But all is not well. It appears Berle had been 'jokingly' goading RuPaul backstage. Once on camera, RuPaul, with great hauteur and barely-veiled hostility, gets in a few sly digs at the grand old man of television drag.

We can use this severely condensed history of Berle on television to begin discussing the issues that have structured critical approaches to lesbian and gay representation on television. To start with a very basic, very important question: What *are* the lesbian, gay and queer images on television?[3] Some would suggest that the only 'real' gay, lesbian and queer figures are those that the text overtly (denotatively) marks as such through dialogue or by showing affectional or sexual activity. Into this category we could place characters like Matt Fielding (*Melrose Place*); Ricky Vasquez (*My So-Called Life*); Barry and Colin, Binnie and Della, Simon and Tony (*EastEnders*); Beth Jordache (*Brookside*); and the RuPaul persona. Others feel that a text doesn't have to explicitly announce a character's sexuality in order for that character to be understood as gay, lesbian or queer on the basis of other signs. In this sense, Milton Berle's drag turns might be read as 'queer', if not exactly gay, while figures like Pee-Wee Herman, early Darlene and Jackie (*Roseanne*), Xena (*Xena: Warrior Princess*) and Mr Humphries (*Are You Being Served?*) are read as gay, lesbian or bisexual by many viewers.

Complicated and fraught with controversy though this naming process may be, determining who to include in a list of fictional lesbian and gay media representatives says little about the politics of representation, though it does reveal something about the political agendas of the critic doing the selecting. So once cultural critics decide how broadly or narrowly to cast their representational net, they are still faced with evaluating these images. In the immediate post-Stonewall rebellion period of the early 1970s, most gay and lesbian media commentators were concerned with the question of 'positive' and 'negative' images – a concern that continues in much journalistic and academic writing to this day (see, for example, Dyer,1993; Gross, 1991; Hemphill, 1995).[4] This approach considers how stereotyped (or not) representations of lesbian and gay lives are in the media, as well as the range of gay and lesbian representation the media offers.

Initially, most lesbian and gay critics noticed, with little surprise, how limited the representational range was, particularly on television. Not only were there few images of lesbians and gays (whether overt or suggested), but these images tended to represent gay men as hysterical prissy queens, and lesbians as violent predatory butches. Most of the media representations held up for praise by positive/negative image critics, and by America's media watchdog group GLAAD (Gay and Lesbian Alliance Against Defamation), have been those depicting lesbians and gays as being 'just like everyone else', or those which play down the character's sexuality (often in an attempt not to make it 'the issue' or 'the problem').

Critics of the positive/negative images approach have suggested that most definitions of what constitutes a 'positive' image would restrict the range of gay and lesbian representation as much as so-called 'negative', stereotypical images do, by encouraging only bland, saintly, desexualized mainstream figures who might as well be heterosexual (see, for example, Dyer and Medhurst, 'Queen'). By the late 1980s and 1990s, the recurring televisual image of gay men with AIDS sparked heated critical debates over exactly what kind of image it was: 'negative', because it depicted homosexuality as a victimhood that, yet again, ended in death; or 'positive', as it encouraged sympathy and even admiration for gay men through images of their courage in the face of death?

Closely related to positive/negative image critical approaches are sociological-anthropological studies that look at the effects of television images of gays and lesbians on test groups of queers and/or straights (see, for example, Hemphill, 1995; Simms, 1981). As with positive/negative image approaches, many of these studies are interested in the power of stereotyping.[5] Taken together, these studies suggest that there are many ways in which people (either straight or queer) decide an image is 'stereotypically' gay, lesbian or queer – and that what is pejoratively understood as a stereotype by many straight viewers will not necessarily be understood in the same way by queer viewers. For example, many queer viewers might not see a particular image as offensively stereotypical because they have a wider range of queer cultural representation within which to place the image, enabling them to conceptualize the image as a representation of only one (or some) of the many aspects of queerness. However, queers often have a 'double vision' when it comes to (stereo)typing: they recognize that a certain image might be understood pejoratively by other (mostly straight) viewers, but, for themselves, and considering a queer cultural context, that same image represents a type or a more complex queer character. On the other hand, there are situations in which queer viewers are responding positively or negatively (or a bit of both) to certain 'not-overtly-stated' images that they understand as gay, lesbian or queer, while other, mostly straight, viewers read these same images as straight ones. When presented with queer readings of these images, these latter viewers will often attempt to deny or otherwise dismiss these readings as 'wishful thinking', 'being overly sensitive' or simply as 'not there'. Most queer viewers (perhaps because of their 'double vision') are willing to entertain the possibility that the images could be read as both queer and straight because of the vague or contradictory cultural coding surrounding the characters.

One break from positive/negative image approaches was to consider the narrative position of the lesbian or gay character (no matter whether the queerness was overt or suggested, 'positive' or 'negative') in television programmes (Doty, 1993; Merck, 1993; Torres, 1993). Upon even a cursory examination, lesbian, gay and queer cultural critics found that no matter how 'positive' or complex the queer characters, they were almost always narratively positioned as secondary to, or on the margins of, some more centrally important heterosexual plot. Even when they appear to be the central character(s), as in the AIDS-and-coming-out telefilm *An Early Frost* (1985) or the 'lesbian kiss' episode of *Roseanne* (1994), heterocentric narrative construction will, finally, structure the plot to revolve around how straight characters and culture respond to lesbians, gays and queers. Programmes like these are only 'about' lesbians, gays and queers in a secondhand sense, as we see these characters primarily through straight gazes and narratives. One of the rare television programmes to construct its narrative largely from a queer position, in this case a lesbian one, is *Oranges Are Not the Only Fruit* (1990).

We could also use a programme like *Oranges Are Not the Only Fruit* to address four other factors that lesbian/gay/queer media commentators have become increasingly concerned with discussing in relation to media representation: production, promotion, distribution and exhibition (see Hinds, 1990; Florence, 1995). That is, who finances, creates, publicizes and exhibits the programme, and how might these factors affect the ways in which the programme represents queerness? One way of accounting for the type of representation found in *Oranges*, for example, might be to comment upon the fact that its source novel and script were written by a lesbian (Jeanette Winterson); that its director, Beeban Kidron, though straight, has also been interested in representing lesbians and gays in much of her subsequent work – *Hookers, Hustlers, Pimps and Their Johns* (1993), *To Wong Foo, Thanks For Everything, Julie Newmar* (1995), *Love At First Sight* (1996); and that BBC2, while not a particularly progressive channel to many British viewers, looks positively radical when compared to American networks, where something like *Oranges* would never have been shown, let alone funded.[6]

Although not much is widely known about the leading actresses in

Oranges, discovering something about their sexual orientation – or hearing rumours about them – could contribute to the production of context-based discussions of television representation. But information about the actual or rumoured sexual orientation of the people before and behind the camera is also an important issue in lesbian and gay approaches to mass media representation that centre on spectatorship/audience/reception studies (see Doty, 1993; Hallam and Marshment, 1995; Hemphill, 1995; Hinds, 1990; Schuyler, 1995). Considering how lesbian, gay and queer viewers understand what they see on television provides what is perhaps the broadest (although some would also say the least rigorous) response to the question, 'What are the lesbian/gay/queer images on television?' Because when we consider queer representation not only in terms of textual denotation, connotation and narrative construction, but also in relation to viewers' fantasies and any extra-textual information they might bring to their television viewing, we realize that almost every figure on television might be 'representing' queerness in some way, to some degree, for some viewer.

Take, for example, any television 'hunk' figure. Though he may be portrayed by a ravingly heterosexual actor in a thoroughly straight narrative, the desires and fantasies of many gay viewers might be said to 'homosexualize' or 'queer' the character in a certain way. Or consider the case of the out or closeted lesbian or gay performer whose sexual orientation is known by thousands of queer viewers – on some level, many of these viewers are investing the characters these actors play with an aura of queerness. Of course, this can also happen to performers who are rumoured to be lesbian or gay, but who are really straight, and to the characters they play.[7]

As with the other critical approaches mentioned above, describing the various ways in which viewers 'queer' television representation is often only the first step for lesbian/gay/queer reception criticism. Once noted, how might these spectatorial processes be understood politically? For example, some might contend that a lesbian viewer's enthusiasm and desire for a straight actress playing a straight character – such as Diana Rigg's Emma Peel in *The Avengers* – represents woefully misplaced energy (and even self-oppressive attitudes). Other critics would see this situation as a wonderful example of how a marginalized viewer can claim the products of dominant culture as her own, or, more radically, as an instance of how considering spectatorship can show us that queerness is always a part of the 'mainstream' in one way or another.

Popular music

On the first page of his autobiography, *Take It Like a Man*, Boy George recalls the supreme importance of pop in his childhood: 'Music was my only friend, a way of escaping the isolation. The World of Pop seemed the perfect place for a boy like me' (p. 1). Needless to say, the Boy grew up to embody an important part of that 'perfect' world for countless other marginalized listeners. But his words also exemplify the acute thrill and significance of pop for most boys – and girls – 'like him', and for adult lesbians and gay men as well.[8]

The particular intensity of this queer devotion to popular music can be explained to a large degree by the sexual preoccupations and connotations of the medium in all of its diverse forms: the term 'jazz', for instance, derives from ' 'jass' or 'jasz' (like the later 'rock 'n' roll', black slang for fucking)' (Gill, 1995, p. 49). Jon Savage writes that '[i]t is above all the body, enveloped in sound, in dance, that stands at the cross-roads of popular music and leisure time; here the word "Love" that is omnipresent in the pop lexicon reads not so much as a romantic cliche but as a coded entry into the world of the private, into the world of pleasure and self-discovery' (1990, p. 155). Given the suppression and stigmatization of same-sex desires by the heterocentric and homophobic elements of dominant culture, pop music's very public flaunting of the seemingly 'private' realm of sexuality provides an accessible, visceral space for lesbian and gay 'pleasure and self-discovery'.

This lesbian and gay exploration of sexuality through the relative safety of pop can be both covert – solitary longing and passion beside the bedroom stereo – and overt – hence the especially crucial role of club culture and dancing as a means of erotic expression and socializing for gays and lesbians. Pop therefore contributes in powerfully formative ways to a great many lesbians' and gay men's self-perception and communication with one another.

These individual and collective queer uses of pop often occur despite the specific sexual message of the music. Barbara Bradby's sociological research, for instance, shows how 'music that is clearly understood as mainstream and heterosexual can be enjoyed and used in a lesbian context' (1993, p. 170). However, another major reason that 'sharing a taste for music is one of the main glues of [lesbian and] gay culture' (Medhurst,1995, p. xvi) is that 'it is from the milieux and sensibilities of the sexually divergent that pop culture draws much of its sustenance' (Savage,

1990, p. 155). On the one hand, this means that mainstream and hetero-centric independent labels frequently appropriate musical styles that originated within gay and/or lesbian culture, while removing or minimiz-ing any queer signifiers: 'hugely successful commercial disco and house music, for example, had its origins in the Black gay dance floors of Chicago and New York' (Stein, 1994, p. 20).[9] But on the other hand, whether in the multiple 1920s–1930s recordings of the 'Sissy Man Blues' (Gill, 1995, pp. 43–4), or on Patti Smith's hugely influential rock album, *Horses* (1975), the critical and/or economic success of the music industry has often revolved around directly referencing or insinuating same-sex passions, in order to produce an enticing sense of 'transgression' – principally in youth-oriented music, as opposed to the normative heterosexuality of much 'adult' rock and pop.

Hypocritically enough, though, the music business (both in its main-stream and, in many cases, its independent forms) has historically also tended to be as heterosexist and homophobic as dominant culture in gen-eral. While the industry persistently makes use of the unorthodox inventiveness of gay men and lesbians, it rarely welcomes openly queer per-formers, never mind lesbian or gay representations that directly challenge the presumed 'supremacy' of heterosexuality; unless, like Bronski Beat briefly in the mid-1980s, they become commercially promising.

The same can be said of most music journalism and criticism outside the lesbian and gay press; when it is not blithely homophobic, it is still usu-ally loath to foreground the pervasive queerness of pop. Yet this widespread failure to sufficiently acknowledge lesbian and gay representation in pop is also due in part to the number of performers who flirt with queer mean-ings in their material and star image, while publicly denying or downplaying those connotations, and/or dodging the question of their own sexuality, in pursuit of mainstream acceptance: examples regularly cited include Joan Armatrading, Tracy Chapman, George Michael and Morris-sey. For many of those gay and lesbian fans who are convinced – by hints, evasions and rumours in the media – that their sexually ambiguous or androgynous idols are either queer, or at least indirectly addressing queer listeners, the delight in decoding such veiled references is also part of a long 'history . . . of being grateful . . . for whatever scraps the dominant culture might grant' them (Gill, 1995, p. 176), leaving them feeling, in Richard Smith's ingenious phrase, 'seduced and abandoned'. But queer critical opinion is, unsurprisingly, divided on the issue of ambiguity and androg-yny versus explicitness.

In one sense, the indirectness of sexual ambiguity and androgyny has been welcomed as an important part of the playful hybridity of so much pop music and imagery. After all, in its privileging of rhythm, melody and emotion over rational logic, all popular music necessarily deals in the more elusive subconscious and unconscious realms of fantasy, as well as responding to the specifics of material reality. For this reason, some critics have argued that pop is most gripping – if not necessarily most politically progressive – when it 'works . . . not by specifics and slogans, but by hints and inferences loose enough for the imagination to leap in and resonate' (Savage, 1996, p. 161). Moreover, in a number of cases, arguments against sexually 'ambiguous' representations can be seen to ignore the reality of bisexual desires, which cannot be fully conceptualized within the prevailing homo/hetero binary, and to ignore the resonance of such representations for bisexual audiences.

But in another sense, sexual ambiguity on the part of secretly lesbian and gay performers has been widely seen to reproduce the heterosexism of the music industry. To take an often-cited example, the Pet Shop Boys have frequently brought gay male vernacular, themes and attitude into the mainstream since the mid-1980s. Yet Neil Tennant only publicly admitted that he is gay in 1994, enabling heterocentric audiences to disavow the gay origins and connotations of the group's music (however unbelievable such ignorance may appear to knowing queer audiences).

Tennant has defended his long-term evasiveness by suggesting that being ambiguous 'works very strongly, because people imagine things about you . . . you are a creature of their imagination' (Newman, 1996, p. 37). But it can also be argued that gay, lesbian or bisexual musicians and singers who are, or have been, publicly evasive about their sexuality in pursuit of mainstream success help to perpetuate the mainstream myth that openly queer pop performers are, by virtue of their sexuality, necessarily only of interest to a 'specialist' audience, with no complexity, ambiguity or further resonances in their material: '[a] performer who makes her lesbianism known typically becomes categorized as a "lesbian artist", and is doomed to marginality' (Stein, 1994, p. 15). The other major assumption perpetuated by the heterosexist majority of the music industry, and by lesbian and gay performers who agree to 'engage in self-censorship' (Stein, 1994, p. 15), is that heterosexual audiences cannot, and should not, find such queer material engaging *on its own terms*, without it having to mirror and reiterate heterosexual concerns.

However, such heterosexist assumptions have been rejected by a range of proudly independent 1990s American and British bands like Pansy Division, Sister George and Vitapup, known collectively as 'homocore' or 'queercore', 'a media tag for fierce, loud, punk-inspired music that's queer [even though not all the musicians are lesbian, gay or bisexual]. The lyrics are unapologetic, in your face and openly gay, sometimes with a randy sense of humor' (Bent, 1996, p. 11). These performers, and their independent labels, indicate the current possibility of small-scale 'mass' success without stifling or marginalizing queer content. In doing so, they can be seen as indirect descendents of the 1970s American (lesbian *and* non-lesbian) women's music industry, which was 'based on the feminist rejection of the commercial music industry, and the belief that only through alternative cultural networks could affirmative images of women be produced and distributed' (Stein, 1993, p. 99). These 'homocore' performers and producers have reconfigured that earlier feminist resistance for their own queer, post-punk agendas (although a few of these bands have also sought mainstream success on their own terms).

Yet in the mid-1990s, a few lesbian performers – most notably Melissa Etheridge and k. d. lang – have found considerable mass market success, exemplifying the (rare) possibility of the 'crossover' artist, who 'embraces lesbian identifications while achieving mainstream success, simultaneously acknowledging both lesbian marginality and membership in the dominant culture' (Stein, 1994, p. 16). These artists' mass popularity is all the more significant if we consider the predominant sexism of the music industry, and of rock/pop criticism and journalism, which has frequently 'used traditional models of authorship to discredit female performers in the search for male authority figures such as "the producer"' (Bradby, 1993, p. 149).

Nevertheless, such queer 'crossover' stars are still precariously positioned in a capital-hungry mainstream overwhelmingly structured around heterosexual desires; as with Neil Tennant's career trajectory, '[w]hile these artists were able to (partially) incorporate their lesbianism into their music and images, they did so only after they had achieved considerable commercial success. It was much more difficult, and perhaps even impossible, to do the opposite, to "cross over" from margin to mainstream, and come out while one's career was still at the early stages of development' (Stein, 1994, p. 25). The mid-1990s chart success of an already-out fledgling artist like David McAlmont, though, suggests that an openly queer pop performer may occasionally achieve some degree of mass popularity – and, in this particular case, also challenge the white hegemony of most gay and lesbian pop.

But while McAlmont's chart hits (with straight ex-Suede member, Bernard Butler) are partly a sign of the considerable strength of independent music in the British charts, they also had sex/gender-neutral lyrics, raising once again the vexed question posed in the previous case study: What *is* a lesbian, gay or queer representation in pop music? There is, of course, no single answer – different audiences (and individual audience members) gather their information about stars and songs from different sources. The frequent disjunction between the messages of the pop record, video, magazine article and television or live performance complicates this issue all the more. Still, the many complexities and contradictions that characterize the supposedly 'perfect . . . World of Pop' can also be seen to create possibilities for change, despite the long-standing cultural constraints upon those music industry figures who are striving to 'queer' pop more thoroughly.

Taken together, these two case studies also suggest more generally useful critical questions for the study of lesbian/gay/queer representation in any mass media form:

- What are lesbian, gay and queer representations? What criteria are being used to determine this?
- What is meant by 'positive' and 'negative' representations? What is the ideological agenda behind these definitions?
- How are lesbian, gay and queer representations (including performers) positioned in relation to 'mainstream' (implicitly heterosexual) images and narratives?
- What are the production, promotion, distribution and exhibition contexts for the text and the representations contained therein?
- How might considering audience reception influence an understanding of texts and representation?
- How might differences of 'race', ethnicity, sex, gender, sexuality, class and other cultural factors influence the production, critical analysis and public understanding of lesbian, gay and queer mass media representation?

Notes

1. Throughout this chapter, the term 'queer' will be used in two ways: (1) in the phrase 'lesbian, gay and queer', to mark a position that is distinct from straightness, as well as from existing definitions of gayness and lesbianism; and

(2) as an umbrella term which pulls together gayness, lesbianism and other non-heterosexual (or non-normatively heterosexual) positions. When it is not used as an umbrella term, however, 'queer' is not meant to eradicate distinctly lesbian, gay, bisexual or other non-heterosexual positions.

2. Among the more notable by-and-for-lesbian/gay/queer comic artists and comic strips are Alison Bechdel (*Dykes to Watch Out For*), Kate Charlesworth (*Dyke's Delight*), Howard Cruse (*Wendel*), Diane DiMassa (*Hothead Paisan*), Grizelda Grizlingham (*The Grizzlers*) and Eric Orner (*The Mostly Unfabulous Social Life of Ethan Green*). At their best, lesbian/gay/queer comics can comment upon an unusually wide range of socio-political issues, queer history and popular cultural enthusiasms with great brevity and immediacy, using an entertaining and emotionally compelling blend of sitcom, soap opera and fantasy.

3. Because of space restrictions, this section will be limited to discussing critical approaches to fictional televisual texts. The representation of actual lesbians, gays, bisexuals and transgendered persons in nonfiction programmes (news, documentaries, chat/talk shows etc.) might be discussed in relation to some of the issues and questions raised in this section. But questions like 'What are the lesbian/gay/queer images on television?' become irrelevant, for the most part. For discussions of lesbian/gay/queer representation in nonfiction media contexts, see Alwood, Hamer and Ashbrook, Richardson, and Sanderson.

4. Most gay, lesbian and queer critical work in television that employs (or critiques) 'positive/ negative image' approaches has been conducted in popular newspapers and magazines such as those listed in the introduction to this chapter.

5. 'Stereotyping' means representing a certain group in a way that is perceived to be a pejorative caricature which presents a narrow and limited picture of group members. A 'type' is a representation of characteristic figures within a group. While types might be seen in positive or negative terms, they are not understood as representations that demean everyone in the group with which they are associated.

6. *Oranges Are Not the Only Fruit* was shown in the United States on the Arts and Entertainment cable channel.

7. Critical considerations of lesbian/gay/queer audience knowledge about the (homo)sexual orientation of performers, and of how such knowledge affects viewers' understandings of televisual representation, might also take into account the debates surrounding 'outing' public personalities, as well as the related topic of how gossip and rumour about the sexual orientation of certain celebrities work in lesbian and gay communities. See Larry Gross (1991).

8. The term 'pop' will be used in two overlapping ways in this section: as a shorthand for all types of popular music, and in reference to the more specific (but still extremely elastic) category of 'pop music.'

9. This is also a key example of the widespread white appropriation and reworking of black musical styles. For a detailed discussion of this phenomenon in relation to black gay dance music, see Anthony Thomas (1995).

References

Bent, Steve, 'Homocore: In-your-face Gay, Modern Rock Invades Philadelphia', in *Au Courant*, July 1996, pp. 16–22.

Bradby, Barbara, 'Lesbians and Popular Music: Does It Matter Who Is Singing?', in Gabriele Griffin (ed.), *Outwrite: Lesbianism and Popular Culture*. London and Boulder, CO: Pluto Press, 1993, pp. 148–71.

Doty, Alexander, *Making Things Perfectly Queer: Interpreting Mass Culture*. Minneapolis: University of Minnesota Press, 1993.

Dyer, Richard, 'Seen to be Believed: Some Problems in the Representation of Gay People as Typical', in *The Matter of Images: Essays on Representation*. London and New York: Routledge, 1993, pp. 19–37.

Florence, Penny, 'Portrait of a Production', in Tamsin Wilton (ed.), *Immortal Invisible: Lesbians and the Moving Image*, London and New York: Routledge, 1995, pp. 115–30.

Frith, Simon, 'Frankie Said: But What Did They Mean?', Alan Tomlinson (ed.), *Consumption, Identity and Style*. London and New York: Routledge, 1990, pp. 172–85.

Gill, John, *Queer Noises: Male and Female Homosexuality in Twentieth-Century Music*. London and Minneapolis: Cassell/University of Minnesota Press, 1995.

Gross, Larry, 'Out of the Mainstream: Sexual Minorities and the Mass Media', Michelle A. Wolf and Alfred P. Kielwassen (eds), *Gay People, Sex and the Media*, Binghamton, NY: Haworth Press, 1991, pp. 61–9.

Hallam, Julia, and Marshment, Margaret, 'Framing Experience: Case Studies in the Reception of *Oranges Are Not the Only Fruit*', in *Screen*, Vol. 36 , 1995, pp. 1–15.

Hemphill, Essex, 'In Living Color: Toms, Coons, Mammies, Faggots, and Bucks', in Corey K. Creekmur and Alexander Doty (eds), *Out in Culture: Gay, Lesbian and Queer Essays on Popular Culture*. Durham, NC and London: Duke University Press/Cassell, 1995, pp. 389–401.

Hinds, Hilary, '*Oranges Are Not the Only Fruit*: Reaching Audiences Other Lesbian Texts Cannot Reach', in Tamsin Wilton (ed.), *Immortal Invisible: Lesbians and the Moving Image*. London: Routledge, 1990, pp. 52–69.

Medhurst, Andy, 'Foreword', to Richard Smith, *Seduced and Abandoned*, 1995, pp. xv-xvii.

Medhurst, Andy, 'One Queen and His Screen: Lesbian and Gay Television', in Emma Healey and Angela Mason (eds), *Stonewall 25: The Making of the Lesbian and Gay Community in Britain*. London: Virago, 1994, pp. 238–50.

Merck, Mandy, 'Portrait of a Marriage?', in *Perversions: Deviant Readings*. London and New York: Virago/Routledge, 1993, pp. 101–17.

Newman, Jeffrey L, 'Opening up: Pet Shop Boys Confront Rumors About Their Sexuality', in *The Washington Blade*, 23 August 1996, pp. 37ff.

Savage, Jon, 'Androgyny: Confused Chromosomes and Camp Followers', in *Time Travel – From The Sex Pistols to Nirvana: Pop, Media and Sexuality 1976–96*. London: Chatto & Windus, 1996, pp. 156–62.

Savage, Jon, 'Tainted Love: The Influence of Male Homosexuality and Sexual Divergence on Pop Music and Culture since the War', in Alan Tomlinson (ed.), *Consumption, Identity and Style*. London and New York: Routledge, 1990, pp. 153–71.

Schuyler, Sarah, 'Confessions of a Sitcom Junkie', in Gail Dines and Jean M. Humez (eds), *Gender, Race and Class in Media: A Text-Reader*. Thousand Oaks, CA and London: Sage, 1995, pp. 476–8.

Simms, Steven A., 'Gay Images on Television', in James W. Chesebro (ed.), *Gayspeak: Gay Male and Lesbian Communication*. New York: Pilgrim, 1981, pp. 153–61.

Smith, Richard, *Seduced and Abandoned: Essays on Gay Men and Popular Music*. London and New York: Cassell, 1995.

Stein, Arlene, 'Androgyny Goes Pop: But Is It Lesbian Music?', in Arlene Stein (ed.), *Sisters, Sexperts, Queers: Beyond the Lesbian Nation*. New York: Penguin/ Plume, 1993, pp. 96–109.

Stein, Arlene, 'Crossover Dreams: Lesbianism and Popular Music Since the 1970s', in D. Hamer and B. Budge (eds), *The Good, the Bad and the Gorgeous*. London: Pandora, 1994, pp. 15–27.

Torres, Sasha, 'Television/Feminism: *HeartBeat* and Prime Time Lesbianism', in Henry Abelove, Michèle Aina Barale and David M. Halperin (eds), *The Lesbian and Gay Studies Reader*. New York and London: Routledge, 1993, pp. 176–85.

Further reading

Alwood, Edward, *Straight News: Gays, Lesbians and the Mass Media*. New York: Columbia University Press, 1996.

Boy George, with Spencer Bright, *Take It Like a Man: The Autobiography of Boy George*. London: Sidgwick & Jackson, 1995.

Cottingham, Laura, *Lesbians Are So Chic . . . That We Are Not Really Lesbians at All*. London and New York: Cassell, 1996.

Gross, Larry, *Contested Closets: The Politics and Ethics of Outing*. Minneapolis: University of Minnesota Press, 1993.

Hadleigh, Boze, *The Vinyl Closet: Gays in the Music World*. San Diego: Los Hombres Press, 1991.

Hamer, Diane and Ashbrook, Penny, 'Out: Reflections on British Television's First Lesbian and Gay Magazine Series', in Diane Hamer and Belinda Budge (eds), *The Good, the Bad and the Gorgeous: Popular Culture's Romance with Lesbianism*. London and San Francisco: Pandora, 1994, pp. 166–71.

Richardson, Colin, 'TVOD: The Never-Bending Story', in Paul Burston and Colin Richardson (eds), *A Queer Romance: Lesbians, Gay Men and Popular Culture*. London and New York: Routledge, 1995, pp. 216–48.

Sanderson, Terry, *Mediawatch: The Treatment of Male and Female Homosexuality in the British Media*. London and New York: Cassell, 1995.

Smith, Richard, *We Have Come For Your Children: The History of Homosexuality and Popular Music*. London and New York: Cassell, 1997.

Thomas, Anthony, 'The House the Kids Built: The Gay Black Imprint on American Dance Music', in C. Creekmur and A. Doty, *Out in Culture*. Durham: Duke University Press, 1995, pp. 437–45.

7

Visual Culture

Peter Horne and Reina Lewis

WE HAVE CHOSEN the term 'visual culture' where once we might have distinguished between art history, fine art, photography, fashion etc. There are several reasons for this, the most straightforward being that the category of fine art has often been challenged in the twentieth century by artists whose practice extends across boundaries that were previously seen as fixed (by using a range of materials, referencing or recycling images from popular culture).

Secondly, critics, theorists and historians are increasingly concerned to identify the political implications of visual codes and forms of representation that recur across a given culture and are not limited to fine art alone. In particular they often want to raise questions about fine art that other approaches would be unable to contemplate because of disciplinary boundaries. This includes the ways in which the idea of the autonomy of art and the definition of an aethestic realm has been used to exclude questions of politics and identity. Some critics have also used the term 'regime of representation' to draw attention to the contribution that representation makes to the workings of power and/or resistance. Often, the point is to stress that culture plays an active role in constructing identities, rather than simply reflecting existing categories or opinions. The implications of this for Lesbian and Gay Studies might be obvious but are not always drawn. One might, for example, want to study how the once invisible lesbian is now, in the era of lesbian chic, regularly occurring in magazines, advertisements, television and the media whilst patterns of prejudice continue. For Lesbian and Gay Studies, thinking about visual culture in broad terms also facilitates a recognition of the particular importance it has had in the formation and articulation of lesbian and gay sexualities and subcultures. This is obvious in the case of modern Western gay subcultures, where a sense of a recognizable identity may be variously signified by the wearing of certain clothes, and the consumption of certain magazines, films, posters and the visual packaging of music. But it has also been the case that queers have looked back to previous artists and art movements for exemplars of alternative identities.

The third reason for moving toward the term 'visual culture' is that, increasingly, practitioners and critics in the field wish to correct the Eurocentrism that was implicit in practices based on previous disciplinary definitions. By constituting visual culture as an object of study, practice and curatorship, one can include non-Western visual practices that were previously ignored and often devalued. If included, non-Western visual cultures tended to be violently wrested away from their original context and re-evaluated within a modernist fine art tradition. Within this aesthetic, the products of these cultures came to signify the 'primitive', as something untainted by the perceived constraints of Western modernity. This included an imagined freedom from the sexual conventions of modern society. The resultant denigration and exoticization of the racialized body is one of the things that has been explored and challenged by Asian and black lesbian and gay artists who have negotiated their relationship between metropolitan/gay cultures and cultures of origin (Karimjee, 1991; Mercer, 1994).

We have organized this chapter around the three terms of production, distribution and reception. Points in any section will cross-reference to other sections, but we want to demonstrate how sexuality is an important factor in all sections of the art world.

Production

Lesbians and gay men often find pleasure in discovering that present-day artists are gay, even when their work is not transparently affected by their sexuality. They also wish to discover artists from the past with whom to construct an alternative great tradition or sense of a homosexual sensibility. This was the case with the, mainly male, aesthetes of the late nineteenth century looking back to the Renaissance. Similarly, in the twentieth century lesbians have formed cults around figures like Gluck, whose work features on the front of the Virago reprint of 'The Well of Loneliness' (Cooper, 1994; Dellamora, 1990; Horne, 1996). But such terms as homosexual, lesbian, gay and queer arise at particular moments in history and there are difficulties in applying them outside the period in which they are current, and especially in implying that past artists' sexuality had a direct bearing upon their artistic production. The anachronistic use of sexual categories can often obscure the different organizations of sexuality and homosociality in the past, as well as obliterating the complex relations between artist, patron and model in the organization of fine art production.

The sexual identification of the artist remains problematic in the present. The alternatives for the contemporary artist are not just between 'coming out' and remaining in the closet. They may identify as lesbian and gay but prefer not to be thought of as a 'lesbian artist' or a 'gay artist', since these composite terms can ghettoize their work, limiting its viewership (Horne and Lewis, 1996, section 2). But, to come out still remains important in order to challenge the stereotype of the modern artist as a virile male, inspired by a succession of women, as in the popular mythologyzing of Picasso. The idea of the female model as muse to male genius still persists in spite of the fact that so many twentieth-century artists have been gay. It also makes the lesbian artist either invisible or especially transgressive, as indeed some contemporary queer work aims to be.

The visibility of gay artists is often ambiguous and the ways in which it is acknowledged and denied is a subject for Lesbian and Gay Studies. Many of the most popular artists of the late twentieth century, such as David Hockney and Keith Haring are, or were, gay. Yet the very fact of their success in the mainstream often means that their sexuality is 'overlooked' in favour of an appreciation of the universality of their art. Therefore, it often falls to less well-known artists to occupy the space of the gay-artist because the very famous by virtue of their stardom are considered to be non-partisan. The very success and acceptability of high-profile gay cultural producers can almost make them invisible again. The sexuality of many artists has been ignored or suppressed in the discussion of their work. For most of his life, critics never really talked about sexuality in relation to Francis Bacon, even though his paintings were so often homoerotic in content and he made no secret of his sexual orientation (Cooper, 1996). At its most obvious level this creates a problem for each generation of artists and viewers who have no role models or interpretative frameworks that can incorporate the significance of sexuality to meaning. This is not a new dilemma. Feminist art history had to re-discover/recover lost women artists before it could proceed onto more nuanced discussions of gender and creativity. Similarly, one of the early tasks of lesbian and gay visual studies has been to reclaim contemporary and past artists who are queer and simultaneously to insist on the relevance of sexuality to the discussion of art movements more broadly – thus moving beyond the individual.

Many of the bohemian cultures that have played an important part in the history of art cannot be understood without attention to the role within them of their countercultural sexual agenda. It is not coincidence that so many deviant sexualities were involved in groups such as the Aesthetic movement, Bloomsbury and the early Pop Art movement (Dellamora, 1990; Reed, 1994; Katz, 1993). Such movements were always based on an opposition to the dominant that was sexual as well as formal or aesthetic. Thus, it is not just the sexual practices of the individual that play a part in lesbian and gay revisions of art and visual histories, but also an attention to the role of deviant or transgressive groups and ideologies. Thus, the different periodization of lesbian and gay visual studies will also produce different 'movements' and significant moments, previously not on the art historical map (for example the grouping around Gertrude Stein and Natalie Barney in pre- and post-First World War Paris: Cooper, 1994).

Distribution

Art is not transcendent: it acquires audience and value through material processes such as exhibition, review, reproduction and commission. For lesbian or gay artists, this part of their work is inevitably complicated by the questions of identity and content that we have been discussing. In common with black and Asian artists, lesbian and gay artists have increasingly expanded their activities to include curatorial work in order to create spaces and sometimes gather funding for work which may otherwise be ignored by the mainstream art world. This is not just about exhibiting work, but about creating the conditions of possibility for its being made in the first place. Curatorship is not an add-on for artists; it does not simply distribute their work but also is part of the critical and creative process in that it may create new constituencies and subjects for art practice. For example, the exhibitions 'Ecstatic Antibodies' and 'Bodies of Experience: Stories about Living with HIV' did not just exhibit pre-existent work about AIDS: the very conceptualization of the exhibitions and processes of organizing tours, collecting work and editing books helped to create new ways of thinking about subjectivity and challenging previous protocols about the relationship between health, science and art (Boffin and Gupta, 1990; Boot and Harding, 1989).

AIDS activism has been very aware of the role of the visual. Where 'Ecstatic Antibodies' intervened in art spaces, other AIDS cultural activists have taken to the streets aiming to reach a wider audience. At the time of the Stonewall riots, the symbolic starting point for the Gay Libertion movement, a participant claimed that now gay people were street people (Weeks, 1990). In the context of AIDS, the street has now become a place where gay people can contest public meanings using visual propaganda. In North America in particular, groups such as Gran Fury have appropriated public spaces and popular forms to produce alternative adverts on buses and hoardings as well as placards for demonstrations that challenge prejudice and inactivity over AIDS and HIV. These images and words also circulate in the form of books, postcards, T-shirts and badges and therefore reach beyond their immediate street audience and play a crucial role in the construction of identities though the consumption of visual culture. The work often departs from the idea of the individual author since many groups work collectively and take shared responsibility for the final image, which generally has no signature. This frequently involves the appropriation of elements from other art works. Douglas Crimp sees this as an aspect of gay involvement in the postmodern project, as the visual work raises questions about production, meaning and distribution outside the context of the art gallery and its discourses (Crimp and Rolston 1990). For him, gay postmodernism retains the radical potential that in other forms of postmodernism have been very easily re-incorporated by existing structures of art. Postmoderism is not necessarily politically radical, but lesbian and gay street art/spectacle is.

Work on the streets is not just picture graphics; there is a variety of work that utilizes diverse forms and visual languages. Whereas some of the work in *AIDS Demographics* is overtly polemical, with a direct impact, there has also been work for the street which is more lyrical and elliptical in its references.

Felix Gonzales Torres has designed a street hoarding showing the imprint of two bodies in a previously occupied bed (Figure 7.1). Its acknowledgement of the viewer's familiarity with advertising imagery gives a poignancy to the emptiness of the intimate space, such as we are normally accustomed to see bursting with virile and healthy advertising bodies.

Lesbian and gay work also sometimes expands in unusual ways the representation of the street. Some recent revisionist art history has stressed the role of the gaze of the flâneur in the construction of modernist art representing the pleasures and anxieties of the modern city. As well as debates about the male privilege that some see as innate to the figure of the flâneur, it is also noted that these same modern metropolitan spaces have provided opportunities for lesbian and gay subculture (Wilson, 1991). Recent work has also discussed the lesbian flâneur (Munt, 1995). And, whereas many

Figure 7.1: Felix Gonzalez-Torres, 'Untitled' (Project for the Museum of Modern Art, New York), 1991. Billboard dimensions variable. Installation view in Glasgow as part of the 'Read My Lips' exhibition, Tramway Gallery, October–December 1992. Photograph: Tramway Gallery, Glasgow.

of the accounts of the male flâneur presume him to be heterosexual, artists such as Gilbert and George have made the homoerotic spectacle of the modern city their subject. Their interest is in the erotic potential of a masculine youth of the East End of London. There is a mixture of nostalgia and modernity in their gaze. They do not wish however, to limit their audience to male homosexuals, insisting that women also enjoy the spectacle of their work. Their appropriation of the discourse of the flâneur raises questions for the art-historical debate about the masculinist, objectifying and class-bound nature of the spectatorial gaze. Artists such as Gilbert and George are very successful, and illustrate the potential for art to be both homoerotic in its inspiration and yet mainstream in its audience. Gay art practice has a more central role in the continuing vitality of modern art than is often recognized.

In addition, gay subcultures are noted for their higher-than-average investment in the visual, much of which these days is consumed in the gay-coded, relatively safe space of the urban gay village. In this instance, it is not just the buying of postcards and other forms of material culture that registers a queer identity, but the very act of being part of the village as spectacle in itself. For many urban gays (or those who visit the city) the activity of seeing and being seen in a clearly gaycoded space (be it a bar, a Pride march, a cafe or a sex shop) is part of affirming and asserting an identity. Methodologically, this is compatible with the art historian's interest in material culture and the cultural geography of space (Bell, 1991; Healy, 1996; Mort, 1996). This allows Lesbian and Gay Studies to give attention to the cultural consumption of non-elite audiences.

One of areas that distinguishes the circulation and consumption of gay art and gay consumers from that of heterosexuals is censorship. Although censorship can affect all parts of the population, it does fall with especial heaviness and regularity on gay communities and their activities. This can affect all areas of cultural activity, from the withdrawal of state grants for gay art exhibitions, to the impounding of explicitly gay safe-sex material and erotica, to self-censorship on the part of artists and curators. For this reason alone, many gay artists and curators choose or are driven to operate outside of mainstream spaces. Although it must be noted that the effects are uneven; transgressions of societal norms that may be tolerated or even applauded in a private avant-garde Bond Street gallery may be impossible in a provincial municipal art space. One of the projects of lesbian and gay visual studies is, then, not just to examine art produced by lesbian or gay artists, but to examine the effects of homophobia on its production and distribution. This is particularly important when so much of the activity of the far right has concerned itself with the cultural sphere. Thus legislation like the British Section 28 and the Helms Amendment in the USA were overtly concerned with the suppression of references to 'alternative' families and/or sexual practices (in which sadomasochism is totemic) as they appeared in visual and literary culture. In the USA the immediate targets of the Helms Amendment controlling the use of public subsidy to the humanities were certain photographs by Robert Mapplethorpe and Andres Serrano, though the work of performance artist Ron Athea was also the subject of pressure form the 'new Right'. But, rather than restricting the distribution of specific disliked works, the impact of the initiatives has been to intervene in the construction of gay identities and to reassert dominant views of heterosexuality and gender (Stychin, 1996).

Reception

Although we have divided this essay into three sections, the arguments in each have implications for the other parts. Ideas about the production of art and culture have implications for the role of the reader or viewer. For some, gay or homosexual art is identified as that which is produced by a gay sensibility. In this case, the role of the viewer is that of discerning the signs of the sensibility of the artist with whom one can then feel an identification. Such senses of identification, especially with past artists, have often been important in the production of the sense of a homosexual identity for the viewer. But it can imply that such a sensibility is transhistorical and transcultural. In contrast, historians and theorists have pointed to the historical specificity of the categories and labels with which we think our identities. It can also imply that the work of art itself is a direct reflection or expression of the nature of the producer. But images are not unmediated in this way: they gather and change meanings as they are actively consumed by viewers whose readings are formed in relation to other images and texts. An alternative is to regard the artist not so much as the authentic source of perceptions to be discerned by the viewer, but as a producer using available codes to construct meanings for a community of interpretation. Such communities of interpretation can have great importance for lesbians and gays constructing senses of identity that are not transhistorical and transcultural. These interpretative communities sometimes operate reading practices based on special knowledges necessary to interpret secret codes whose meaning may be invisible or different for mainstream audiences (Morgan, 1996). They can also be communities of reading which are more 'out' and brazen in their appropriation of mainstream images.

Dominant accounts of modernism rely on a rigid distinction between authentic, high-value fine art and inauthentic, low-value popular culture. In contrast, postmodernism embraces the popular and breaks down previous distinctions and cultural heirarchies. Gay artists and consumers in the twentieth century have had a different investment in popular cultures, both mainstream and gay. Much that is now recognizable as gay cultural activity has been based on the appropriation of mainstream culture, in the form of kitsch, camp, etc. Many art historians and theorists fail to recognize the significance of this gay component in the contribution of many of the artists, such as Andy Warhol and Keith Haring, credited with the postmodern re-evalution of the popular. Another element of the modernist tradition questioned by postmodernism that gay artists have also had a particular investment in challenging, has been its denigration of the sentimental in favour of a macho insistence on form. This is often premised on the idea of a single meaning equated with the expression of an individual genius's vision. In contrast, postmodernism opens up the play of meaning and is marked by a delight in the activity of the reader – notably in parody and irony. This is particularly attractive for gay readers who have historically grown accustomed to reading in such ways, often through necessity.

With the revival of the notion of queer, there has arisen a suspicion of too complacent a notion of community that queer sees as lacking sufficient acknowledgement of multiplicity and diversity and the way difference is constructed in relation to a norm. This criticism would apply equally to notions of community of reading practices. Instead, Queer Theory would decipher homoerotic codes: not to claim works as the product of a gay sensibility; not to stress the construction of a common gay visual language; but to disturb the coherence of texts and paintings premised on the suppression or invisibility of same-sex desires. Some accounts stress the importance for patriarchal culture of the representation of homosociality. This incorporates all forms of male bonding whilst simultaneously denying the same-sex sexual desires that are prohibited by the structural homphobia on which these cultural and social formations are in fact reliant (Sedgwick, 1991). This locates homophobia as social or institutional rather than a matter of individual psychology. The consumption of visual culture has been seen as one of the key activities through which individuals are inscribed in these social formations (Hatt, 1993).

Another approach is to look for what is visible in the work, once you insert a queer, lesbian or gay viewer. This moves away from seeing meaning as being in the gift of the artist (gay or otherwise) and recognizes that gay readers may derive gay pleasures from images, regardless of the image's point of origin. This type of reading can read queer meanings into a painting without attributing a gay identity to the author. But it may confirm a gay or oppositionally queer identity for the contemporary reader who derives pleasure from this version of reading against the grain. Alternatively, it may be used to problematize the ascription of fixed, modern sexual identities to artists of the past (such as Caravaggio) but also to refuse a simple fixed socio-sexual identity for the contemporary audience.

The issue of visual pleasure has often been discussed in relation to what has come to be known as 'gaze theory'. This follows Laura Mulvey's influential analysis of the gaze in relation to classic Hollywood cinema. She argued that the putative gaze constructed by the mainstream film is inevitably masculine. Women on screen are objectified, positioned as the passive recipients of a male gaze and not as active operators of the gaze. This positions men in the audience as scopophilic, deriving pleasure from a fantasy of control via their identification with the male hero. Women viewers are situated as either passive and masochistic, in their narcissistic identification with the beautiful female object, or as transvestite if they adopt a male viewing position (Mulvey, 1975, 1981). In this initial formulation there is no possibility for an active gaze from a female position, although subsequent work has been concerned with precisely this (Gamman and Marshment, 1988). The psychoanalytically informed discussion of Mulvey's early work impacted heavily on fine art practices for a whole generation of women, for some of whom it became practically impossible to represent the female form without it being simply another example of the objectification of the female body that could be appropriated by men. Of course, for lesbians, to give up on an eroticized relationship to the female body had entirely other and more serious implications. In keeping with developments in lesbian fiction, many visual artists moved into a concern with erotica (at a time when many heterosexual women artists were still not happy with it) attempting to make images that spoke to lesbian desire. This necessarily complicates the monolithic notions of masculinity and femininity that characterize some gaze theories and insists on the specificity but nonetheless variable nature of the lesbian female gaze or male homosexual gaze. This has often been taken up in lesbian photographic practice concerned with the representation of an active lesbian desire in the visual. Some of the most prominent work in this field does not seek to construct a specifically lesbian gaze or a single image with which to identify. Rather, it uses masquerade to play with roles, depicting sexuality as fluid or in suspension rather than innate or 'deep'. The take-up for this photographic practice has been wide, with images circulating in books as well as exhibitions and in the gay press where photo spreads are often reproduced (Boffin and Fraser, 1991; Grace, 1991).

One of the other ways in which gay aesthetics differs from dominant trends within feminist and social history of art, is in its treatment of the body. Whilst many lesbians and gay men would share a feminist critique of the commodification of body fascism, some would argue that gay subcultural investments in the body beautiful have a different register and are necessarily less exploitative, as artists explore different ways of eroticizing the male body for the pleasure of male gay viewers. The body beautiful continues to be the subject of much gay art and popular culture. One could

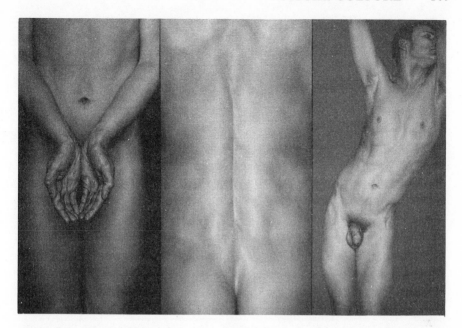

Figure 7.2: Matthew Stradling, 'Touch Me/Don't Touch Me', 1996. Oil on canvas, 192 x 122cm.

interpret this in several ways: that it offers possibilities of a narcissistic identification with the figure rather than an objectifying gaze towards it; that it plays ironically with the codes of representation often surrounding the body beautiful with feminizing and camp accessories; that it carries the conventions of masculinity to an excess that can be read as parodic (for example, as in the case of Tom of Finland). An artist who plays with all these different levels is Matthew Stradling who has been consistently concerned with exploring the male nude; representing bodies which although apparently open to the (homosexual) viewer's gaze are only ambiguously accessible (see Figure 7.2). Some of these issues have also been particularly focused on in debates about the eroticized, racialized black body in the work of Robert Mapplethorpe. Some black cultural critics and practitioners have wanted to recuperate these powerful and eroticized iconic images for black gay viewers without being reinscribed into a racially subordinate position (Mercer, 1994).

The other area where the body has featured prominently in lesbian and gay culture and critique is in debates about sadomasochism. Sadomasochism, and the forms of dress, adornment and body modification associated with it, has achieved a cultural capital far outweighing its actual demographic base. It has been much aired in the visual arena, not just in terms of art work but in terms of the forms of self-presentation fashionable in fine art venues. As such the spectacle of sadomasochistic visual codings – rather than acts of sadomasochistic practice – has come to function as the visual signifier for transgression and deviant sexuality par excellence (Lewis, 1994).

Conclusion

We have reviewed what happens to mainstream visual criticism when you insert a recognition of gay artists, lesbian and gay subcultures and lesbian and gay or queer viewers. Central to all these discussions is the need to recognize the pleasures that the visual offers to gay viewers, whether or not their gay coded pleasures are overtly recognized: by the image, the space that shows it or the artist that makes it. The debates also highlight the role of the visual in the construction of lesbian and gay identities. This critical practice challenges regimes of representation that privilege homophobia. The spaces of culture have had to be fought for and the increasing visibility of gay and lesbian cultural production and activities of cultural consumption has been achieved by our own efforts: lesbian and gay visual studies are part of the myriad ways in which we fight for recognition and the preservation of these spaces.

References

Bell, D. J., 'Insignificant Others: Lesbian and Gay Geographies', in *Area,* Vol. 23, 1991, pp. 323–9.

Boffin, T., and Fraser, J. (eds), *Stolen Glances: Lesbians Take Photographs.* London: Pandora, 1991.

Boffin, T., and Gupta, S. (eds), *Ecstatic Antibodies: Resisting the AIDS Mythology.* London: Rivers Oram Press, 1990.

Boot, C., and Harding, A. (eds), *Bodies of Experience: Stories about Living with AIDS.* London: Camerawork, 1989.

Cooper, E., 'Queer Spectacles', in P. Horne and R. Lewis, 1996.

Cooper, E., *The Sexual Perspective: Homosexuality and Art in the Last 100 Years in the West* (2nd edn). London: Routledge, 1994.

Crimp, D., and Rolston, A. (eds), *AIDS Demo Graphics.* Seattle: Bay Press, 1990.

Dellamora, R., *Masculine Desire: The Sexual Politics of Victorian Aestheticism.* Chapel Hill and London: University of North Carolina Press, 1990.

Gamman, L., and Marshment, M. (eds), *The Female Gaze: Women as Viewers of Popular Culture*. London: The Women's Press, 1988.

Grace, D., *Love Bites: Photographs by Della Grace*. London: GMP, 1991.

Hatt, M., 'Muscles, Moral, Mind: The Male Body in Thomas Eakins' *Salutat*', in K. Adler, and M. Pointon (eds), *The Body Imaged*. Cambridge: Cambridge University Press, 1993.

Healy, M., *Gay Skins: Class, Masculinity and Queer Appropriation*. London: Cassell, 1996.

Horne, P., 'Sodomy to Salome: Camp Revisions of Modernism, Modernity and Masquerade', in M. Nava, and A. O'Shea (eds), *Modern Times: The British Experience of Modernity*. London: Routledge, 1996.

Horne, P., and Lewis, R. (eds), *Outlooks: Lesbian and Gay Sexualities and Visual Culture*. London: Routledge, 1996.

Karimjee, M., 'In Search of an Image', in T. Boffin and J. Fraser, 1991.

Katz, J., 'The Art of Code: Jasper Johns and Robert Rauschenberg', in W. Chadwick, and I. de Courtivron (eds), *Significant Others: Creativity and Intimate Partnership*. London: Thames and Hudson, 1993.

Lewis, R., 'Dis-Graceful Images: Della Grace and Lesbian Sadomasochism', in *Feminist Review*, Vol. 46, Spring 1994, pp. 76–91.

Mercer, K., *Welcome to the Jungle: New Positions in Black Cultural Studies*. London: Routledge, 1994.

Morgan, T. E., 'Perverse Male Bodies: Simeon Solomon and Algernon Charles Swinburne', in Horne and Lewis, 1996.

Mort, F., *Cultures of Consumption: Masculinities and Social Space in Late Twentieth-Century Britain*. London: Routledge, 1996.

Mulvey, L., 'On *Duel in the Sun*: Afterthoughts on Visual Pleasure and Narrative Cinema', in *Framework*, Nos. 15–17, 1981.

Mulvey, L., 'Visual Pleasure and Narrative Cinema', in *Screen*, Vol. 16, No.3, Autumn 1975.

Munt, S., 'The Lesbian Flâneur', in D. Bell, and G. Valentine (eds), *Mapping Desire*. London: Routledge, 1995, pp. 114–25.

Reed, C., 'Making History: The Bloomsbury Group's Construction of Aesthetic and Sexual Identity', in W. Davis (ed.), *Gay and Lesbian Studies in Art History*. New York and London: Harrington Park Press, Haworth Press, 1994.

Sedgwick, Eve Kosofsky, *The Epistemology of the Closet*. Hemel Hempstead: Harvester Wheatsheaf, 1991.

Stychin, C., 'Promoting a Sexuality: Law and Lesbian and Gay Visual Culture in America', in P. Horne and R. Lewis, 1996.

Weeks, J., *Coming Out* (rev. edn). London: Quartet, 1990.

Wilson, E., *The Sphinx in the City*. London: Virago, 1991.

Further reading

Davis, W. (ed.), *Gay and Lesbian Studies in Art History*. New York and London: Harrington Park Press, Haworth Press, 1994.

8

Philosophy

Lisabeth During and Terri Fealy

Introduction: questions of definition

Ever since the news about sexuality and gender rudely interrupted philosophers' dogmatic slumbers, theorists have puzzled over the meaning of identity, desire, and difference. After a troubled relation with feminism, philosophy is finally developing a presence in Lesbian and Gay Studies. In North America, the tradition of philosophic liberalism, with its distinctive vocabulary of rights, representation, and equality, has enabled gay and lesbian critics to challenge a sexually oppressive social order, with some notable successes. Yet neither liberal reformism nor the more recent 'identity politics' have done much to check the virulent homophobia of the last twenty years. A demand for tolerance, insisting that private sexual practices of citizens must be left to individual choice, has brought us, paradoxically, less and less tolerance. Michael Warner writes:

> There are many people, gay and straight, who think that sexual orientation is a fairly clear and simple political matter, that discrimination should be eliminated but that gay people have no further political interest as a group. (Warner, 1993, p.xi)

Sexual orientation, we want to argue, is not a 'clear and simple' matter. Those who wish homosexuality obliterated will hardly be convinced by appeals to freedom and understanding. To disarm the paranoia which makes the homosexual socially invisible and psychologically abject, we must identify the *desire* which homophobia expresses, and speak for *another* desire. Any philosophical search for the specificity of lesbian and gay 'ways of being' will also reinterpret *human* eroticism. The oppression of dissident sexualities, the demonization of the queer body, are more than accidental interruptions on the road to universal recognition. As Diana Fuss remarks:

'Perhaps what we need most urgently in Lesbian and Gay theory right now is a theory of marginality, subversion, dissidence, and othering' (Fuss, 1991, p. 5).

Without underestimating the important work done in lesbian and gay philosophy by Claudia Card, Jeffner Allen, Sarah Lucia Hoagland, and Richard Mohr, our approach in this chapter is a different one. Responding to the urgency of Fuss's demand, we want to explore the resources of the European philosophic tradition, from Nietzsche to Foucault, Merleau-Ponty, Deleuze and Wittig. Philosophy's self-critique is pushed to radical conclusions here; the crises of reason and the self, which this tradition announces, resonate in the present conceptual struggles within Lesbian and Gay Studies. Postmodernists, inspired by Nietzsche, argue that philosophy has lost its 'good conscience', its conviction of universality and objectivity. The links between knowledge and power can no longer be denied; liberal humanism has had to admit the reality of conflicting desires and divergent schemes of value.

These changes, associated with postmodernism, have immediate relevance to the case of lesbian and gay philosophies. Philosophy has been called upon to justify its apparent indifference to sex, class, race and physicality. The games of power and seduction are far from alien to intellectuals who are as carnal as they are cerebral. Philosophers have continued to refuse such self-recognition, preferring the model of a community of scientific investigators, impassioned only by truth. Attempts by French feminists Luce Irigaray (1985, 1993) and Michèle LeDœuff (1989) to uncover the masculine sexual investment in knowledge have been met with polite disbelief. But the popular image of philosophy as a realm purged of domination and desire is already a caricature. If Michel Foucault is right that the aim of philosophy is to enable us to 'think otherwise than we are' (Foucault, 1985, p. 9), then it is philosophy which promises something of the resistance, something of the insubordination and potential for transformation which we desire.

In a Foucauldian spirit then, we want to use philosophy as a means to 'think otherwise' about the aesthetics of deviance, the ethics of homosexuality, and the lived experience of bodily identity. This project is conceptual as well as practical: the hegemony of a notion as problematic as 'normalcy' must be challenged. Feminists have shown us how the tools of philosophy can be used to identify the specific oppression which is based not exclusively on class but also on gender. For several generations, Marxist, Freudian, existential and deconstructionist analyses have attacked our culture's investments in patriarchy. Notions like freedom, identity, alienation helped to clarify the position of the 'second sex'. But at the moment, that vocabulary has reached exhaustion. While gays and lesbians also suffer from patriarchal oppression, homophobic antagonisms and erasures require a different kind of diagnosis than the one feminism has so powerfully developed.

Such a diagnosis is our aim in this chapter. We believe that a gay and lesbian point of view must change the way philosophy is done. The Nietzschean philosophy of difference and the twentieth-century movement called existential phenomenology offer powerful conceptual tools for reimagining sexual experience: its ethics, its politics, its subjectivity. But bringing sex to the foreground does not mean that everything characteristic of philosophy is to be abandoned: instead, the 'queering' of philosophy that we defend here, continues that 'art of making distinctions' which best describes the work of philosophy.

Eroticizing the philosopher

Nietzsche, the subject, the body, difference

It was probably the German philosopher Friedrich Nietzsche (1844–1900) who first asked what difference it makes to think with the body, with the passions. Yet early feminists found little to respond to in Nietzsche except his misogyny. Succeeding generations have modified that view, recognizing that Nietzsche and his followers (Gilles Deleuze, Michel Foucault, Jacques Derrida, Judith Butler) present the desiring lines of philosophy differently. Calling for a *re-evaluation of all values* (Nietzsche, 1969), Nietzsche distinguished between the 'ascetic' style of most traditional philosophic thought, and something new, a philosophy for free spirits, a philosophy of the future (Nietzsche 1989, 1968). The former was guilty of evading the constraints of the flesh, of disavowing the will to power and the stratagems of mastery which were the intellect's stock in trade. The latter – a 'gay science' – would bring the self and the body back into philosophy. It would not affirm or internalize the values of its culture, but create new ones.

Renouncing the ideal of detachment, a gay science promotes a way of life which is creative, affirmative, and agonistic: in Nietzsche's metaphor, 'Dionysian'. Nietzsche is ambivalent about his own sexual orientation. As Eve Sedgwick remarks, he is at once fascinated by phallicism and bewitched by feminine masquerade (Sedgwick, 1990, pp. 132–9; 148–70). For Nietzsche there is no single perspective from which all claims can be judged, no single sexual position that we can identify as 'affirmative'. Every desire hides within it its own prohibition, every sexual identity is also a pose, a strategy, a copy. Moral and epistemological positions are never neutral. They are always 'interpretations' of the world, expressing a certain force, a certain relationship to power. Thus the passions normally consigned to the 'inferior' domain of the body return, in Nietzsche's provocative genealogies, to the self of the philosopher. The knowing subject may aspire to a mastery of his or her own needs, revulsions, appetites. Yet all the while it is they, and their somatic representatives, who are in control.

Nevertheless, the Nietzchean recovery of the flesh and the passions is not a liberationist call for an end to sexual inhibition. 'Health', Nietzsche's favourite metaphor, suggests not the absence of sickness but the productive use of it. In his view, emancipation is of no use to a society unless it can also master its own decadence. Decadence is one of Nietzsche's most important concepts; in his time, as he was clearly aware, decadence was a code-word for homosexuality. Nietzsche's philosophy of the future, converting reactive forces into active forces, suggests a most intriguing possibility for the lesbian and gay influence on modern cultural life. Neither assimilation nor a self-identified and separatist 'ethnos', a Nietzschean 'queer culture' would exist within mainstream culture as its erotic alternative. The sexual body that insinuates its way back into the philosopher's thought is neither purely phallic nor effeminate; it is veiled, like the woman's, but also naked, struggling, restless. In place of a definite and proper body, Nietzsche imagines a mobile network of the senses, of appetites, repugnances, and incomplete corporealities.

Whatever Nietzsche's own evasions, his insistence on becoming rather than being allows us to imagine a sexuality for the future which is symbolically indeterminate. Its gender vacillates between male and female, and its sexual orientation wanders, not just between straight and gay, but between the hypervirility of the notorious 'philosophizing with a hammer', and the effete, melancholic, creativity of 'ressentiment'.[1]

Acknowledging the libidinal investments in every way of being and thinking, Nietzsche's philosophy of the future would be a way of becoming who one is, even of risking who one is. If he makes philosophy sexy again, he also challenges philosophy's identification with a comfortable normalcy, whether that be the matrimonial couple or the accepted discourse of reason. Philosophy, as Nietzsche asks us to practise it, does not shrink from the prospect of incomprehensibility, as it knows that the brave thoughts, the new thoughts, wear the masks of fools, madmen, deviants.

Foucault

Michel Foucault, widely considered the philosopher most significant to Queer Theory, saw that Nietzsche's critique of the normalizing culture of modernity had direct consequences in the realm of sexuality. Specifically, modernity is responsible for what Foucault calls 'the deployment of sexuality', a set of practices naming and regulating the expressions of desire. Rather than sexuality being a case of 'basic instinct' struggling against repressive moral law, there are multiple sexual politics and privileges (Foucault, 1979). If sexuality is not a natural drive, but a 'great surface network in which the stimulation of bodies, the intensification of pleasures, the incitement to discourse, the formation of special knowledges, the strengthening of controls and resistances, are linked to one another' (Foucault 1979, pp. 105–6), then why two sexes rather than four, or twenty? Out of an indefinite range of erotic possibilities, modern society determined on four species. Foucault identifies them: the hysterical female body; the masturbatory child; the procreative couple; the pervert. These are not natural kinds. They represent particular constructions of a homogenizing social order.

There is nothing metaphysically stable about the 'normal-deviant' opposition. The 'natural' is the result of complex discursive strategies, in which many confused social interests are invested. Against the tyranny of a normalcy which is a product of the combined energies of medicine, psychiatry, religion and the state, Foucault proposes that we explore 'bodies and pleasures'. Following him, many lesbian and gay writers have called for a refusal of identity and a cultivation of differences, with very few pleading the case for an 'essential' homosexual way of being.[2]

Deleuze and Guattari; Guy Hocquenghem

It is not enough just to be different. A theoretical position must give us the means to do something we could not otherwise do. If philosophy is to offer anything to lesbian and gay theory, it must show us a way to escape a system of sexuality which recognizes only the family unit and reproduction. Freudian analysis is of little help against the 'policing' of desire from which gays and lesbians (and not just 'hysterical women') suffer. As Gilles Deleuze and Felix Guattari argue in their famous critique of Freud, *Anti-Oedipus* (1972), psychoanalysis interprets sexual identity and sexual orientation as founded in the universal familial drama of the Oedipus. Although Freud described the raw material of desire as free-form, polymorphous, and indifferent to gender, once that libidinal energy has been channelled, object-choice becomes increasingly constrained. Psychoanalysis leaves us with a desire that, once 'matured', has nowhere to go if it does not follow the tracks of biology. If it deviates from the genital and reproductive norm, desire is classified as perverse.

It is for these reasons that Deleuze and Guattari attack 'Oedipal desire', imagining pleasure instead as a mobile plenitude, constantly searching out new regions of intensity, undeterred by respect for the law. The name they favour for desire is 'production'. Theirs is the most radical statement of a sexual postmodernism that decisively breaks with the ideals of humanism: sexuality is neither to be justified by reference to the species and the 'order of nature', nor by some code of respecting persons.

Sexuality does not need sentiment. Nor does it require the sanction of the state's disciplinary practices. Nor must it mean 'neuroticization', as if every eccentric desire introduced incest and guilt. Freud's psycho-sexual theory darkens any hope of erotic happiness; it offers a social 'norm' ill-suited to adult needs. For the 'Anti-Oedipeans', just as the pleasures of our bodies and organs are capable of different codings and rearrangements, so too the famous 'selves', fashioned by the state, the family, the law, are also dispensable. Deleuze and Guattari call for new forms of selfhood: don't copy the trees, they urge us; spread out from all sides, circulate, be like the rhizome which propagates itself as weeds do, make your own map. While others have made similar demands,[3] they are among the few since May 1968 to offer a philosophical programme in which new forms of subjectivity can be imagined.

Deleuze and Guattari's futurist vision of a world of 'a thousand tiny sexes' is not exclusively aimed at lesbians and gays (how could it favour any distinguishable genre?). But it clearly displaces the priority both of the genitals and of any sexuality based on a 'natural' order of genital reproduction.[4] Elizabeth Grosz attributes this to the fact that:

> (T)hey refuse to understand desire in negative terms, because they refuse to structure it with reference to a negative signifier, the phallus, and because they enable desire to be understood not just as feeling or affect, but also as doing and making . . . As production, desire does not provide blueprints, models, ideals, or goals. Rather, it experiments: it is fundamentally aleatory, inventive. (Grosz, 1995a, p. 180)

Not only does their model 'de-essentialize the body, sexuality, and sexed identities' (Boundas and Olkowski, 1994, p. 163); it endows bodily productivity with a host of differently styled metaphors. In *Anti-Oedipus* (1972) and *A Thousand Plateaus: Capitalism and Schizophrenia* (1980), bodily desire is 'mechanic'; it forms assemblages, effects linkages and performs temporary combinations of parts: some delirious and some almost imperceptible. Yet for all its energy – the pulsations of intensity it creates wherever there is a conjunction of two or more surfaces, bodily bits and mechanic bits, tongues and anuses, or skins and leather – the rhizomatic desire of Deleuze and Guattari is not working to order. It flourishes by spending itself, not by the conservation and re-investment which an economy of production requires.

This free and expansive wastefulness is what distinguishes rhizomatic desire from 'straight' desire and what recommends it to a queer sexual ethics. For straight sexuality, satisfaction must advance the aims of the species. But Deleuze and Guattari see the 'aims' of desire as effectuation, not satisfaction. Thus non-genital or same-sex couplings (like the couplings of the drinker to his bottle or the body-builder to her Nautilus) are not anomalous, even though they do create deviant passages, mixtures unauthorized by the logic of gender complementarity (see Grosz, 1995b, pp. 178–199).

The hybrid formations imagined by Deleuze and Guattari – not just the pre-oedipal mouth to the breast, but the pollen-seeking bee to the orchid – mean that sexual orientation has no script. There is, in a philosophy influenced by Deleuze and Guattari, no 'homosexual' as such. But there is 'homosexual production', which, as Guy Hocquenghem writes, 'takes place according to a mode of non-liminative horizontal relations' (Hocquenghem, 1978, p. 95). Reading male homosexuality 'against the Oedipus', as Deleuze and Guattari have taught him to do, the maverick French psychoanalyst Hocquenghem explains that the very idea of *homosexual* desire is meaningless:

> Properly speaking, desire is no more homosexual than heterosexual. Desire exists in a multiple form, whose components are only divisible a *posteriori*, according to how we manipulate it. Just like heterosexual desire, homosexual desire is an arbitrarily frozen frame in an unbroken and polyvocal flux. (Hocquenghem, 1978, p. 36)

Hocquenghem agrees with Foucault that the homosexual is an invention, or worse, a 'manufacture' of capitalism. There is no authenticity to this way of being: the homosexual only recognizes himself by his shame. As 'the phallus dispenses identity', and the homosexual is constituted by the anus, a body part whose existence society does not recognize, the homosexual has only a confused identity (1978, p. 87). But Hocquenghem does not end in pessimism: homosexual love can be neither shameful nor Oedipal. He draws our attention to a famous passage in Marcel Proust about the 'language of flowers'.

The 'strange' and 'beautiful' flirtation between Charlus and Jupien, which opens the section called 'Cities of the Plain' in *Remembrance of Things Past*, may be free of all allusion to the phallus, maybe even 'without sex'. The female flower coquettishly courts the male insect. The fat middle-aged Baron de Charlus opens expectantly to the flurrying little ex-tailor Jupien. It is a chance encounter in a sunny courtyard, the huge novel's only image of a happy passion among the 'accursed race' of Sodom to which the two secretly belong. For Hocquenghem, as for Deleuze and Guattari (who as we shall see in the final section, turn the insect-orchid seduction into the very trope of rhizomatic 'becoming'), the inter-species attraction is a moment of escape from phallocratic 'rule', a 'line of flight'.

Conclusion

From the reproductive couple to a world of shifting erotic incarnations: even if this is a possible image for gay and lesbian futures, it is neither universally shared nor philosophically unproblematic. A Nietzschean category of 'erotic becoming', in its eagerness to avoid fixation, risks turning ambiguity into a new universal, losing any specific focus on lesbian and gay desire. Homosexuality becomes lost within a continuum of 'queer' or anomolous evaluations. The 'politics of sexual ambiguity' championed by Judith Butler (1990, 1991) and Marjorie Garber (1992, 1995), and to a certain extent also Gilles Deleuze and Jacques Derrida, may indeed erase the very identity which homophobes would be all too pleased to see disappear. Of the French post-structuralist theorists it is only the radical Monique Wittig who insists on strengthening the lesbian category, not watching it blur into utopian waves of pleasure and mutation.[5]

The phenomenological tradition

It is not just Nietzsche who raises philosophic objections to the de-sexing of the one who knows. For Lesbian and Gay Studies, the very notion of universality presumes a male and heterosexual (as well as white and able-bodied) subjectivity. The phenomenological[6] philosophies which derive from Edmund Husserl and French existentalism also question the idea of a universal subject. But whereas Nietzsche is content to demolish the philosophical edifice in its unity and homogeneity, phenomenology imagines subjectivity from a different angle. It offers an alternative account of the causes of oppression and allows us to think of bodies and emotions in a more receptive relation to the world.

Rethinking oppression: the phenomenological alternative
Phenomenologists address the world as it is immediately lived, through the everyday ways life is experienced: 'The world is not what I think, but what I live through' (Merleau-Ponty, 1962, pp. xvi–xvii). To achieve this is harder than it looks. For phenomenology, the categories of scientific thought, which constructs dichotomies such as subject/object, must be 'suspended'. The subject experiencing its life-world is not a mind abstracted from and governing its body. Rather the world is presented 'pre-objectively', in what Merleau-Ponty calls a 'logic lived through' (1962, p. 49). Neither subject not object are consciously posited at this stage, only a fundamental indistinction between self and world, self and body. The objectifying categories suspended, experience becomes an ambiguous mixture.

Both physical and mental events inform the lived body. The lived body is phenomenology's field of analysis, '. . . an integrated structure of cognitive, sensorimotor and visceral processes' (Leder, 1990, p. 7). Immersed in the world and co-existing with it, rather than being set against it as is the Cartesian consciousness, the lived body is always situational. Therefore any consideration of the phenomenal subject must consider its facticity. The body, in acting upon the world, is also acted upon by it, constituting and constituted.

To claim phenomenology for lesbian and gay theory we need to begin with the everyday experience of homosexual subjects, to consider their situation in the world and their relations to others. In phenomenology there is no essential or innate norm that determines sexuality as heterosexual. The idea of a universal subject ceases to make sense if subjectivity is a result of embodied action in the world. Yet if phenomenology has no room for a universal subject, how can it account for the fact that lesbian and gay subjects are constituted as deviant? The reality of discrimination and oppression exists, and is verified in the abuses and discriminations that are a part of everyday life for those identified as lesbian, gay, queer or transgendered. How then does phenomenology explain this and does it offer any way out?

Existential phenomenology, which achieved a wide popularity through the work of Jean-Paul Sartre, insisted on the irreducibility of freedom, in particular the freedom of the active ethical agent. Some critics claim that this invalidates the politics of the existentialists. Their notion of radical freedom means that all subjects are equally free, that the slave is as free as the master, hence the lesbian or gay subject is as free as the male heterosexual subject. If determination by material conditions does not reach the core of what it is to be a self, then social oppression is in some sense irrelevant to existential politics, and such a politics in turn irrelevant to gays and lesbians. But Iris Marion Young and Jeffner Allen (1989) challenge this view of exisential phenomenology:

> Nothing could be further from the intentions of these philosophers, who saw action against oppression as imperative. . .. Far from counselling acceptance of one's slavery because deep down one is 'really' free, this philosophy counsels revolution: The fact that one is a slave today determines nothing about one's being tomorrow. (Allen and Young, 1989, p. 3)

Indeed phenomenology was applied to the problem of sexual oppression as early as 1954, by Simone de Beauvoir. *The Second Sex* looked beyond the mere correcting of social abuses into the disturbing psychic world of the sexist and his victim. Feminists since have found various ways to embrace the possibilities of phenomenology, asking how it may account for differently sexed bodies and the unequal distribution of freedom and power. Yet to put these analyses to work for our purposes would require significant changes. The stigmatizing of the homosexual as 'other' is quite different from the repressive tolerance of the woman within patriarchy. For de Beauvoir, woman is maintained in her place because she is useful, even necessary to man's self-understanding. But the homosexual is not useful. In patriarchal society, where the homosexual is often viewed as an impossible contradiction, s/he will rarely be imagined as the 'necessary' or concrete 'other' who fulfils the heterosexual's 'lack'. Yet if in some sense woman is, as de Beauvoir maintained, man's unconscious, the homosexual may be, as Eve Sedgwick argues, the unconscious fantasy or unacknowledged desire of the heterosexual: the gay 'other' is deeply buried within our culture. For Sedgwick (1985, 1990, 1993), the murkiness of homophobic fantasy means that the homosexual cannot be incorporated, even within a repressive structure. S/he can only be derided, abjected, pathologized. Woman is subordinate, but the lesbian or gay cannot even be acknowledged without risk.

Uncovering the fantasmatic operations of concealment and stigmatization does not automatically lead to a way out. But such an analysis may suggest more effective methods for gay and lesbian theory. If the phenomenologists are correct, radical alterity has a potential greater than either assimilation or separatism for imagining the relations between self and other, us and them, valuing and disvaluing, in different terms. One way in which this can be done is by increasing attention to the humanity and history of the body. For the body is also a site of oppression. Legal reforms, while important for homosexual freedom and security, only take account of the operation of *overt* oppressions. But oppression and domination devalue those perceived as 'other'. As Marion Young insists, it is not enough to develop theories of justice which 'assumes a point of view outside the social context where issues of justice arise' (Young, 1990, pp. 3–4). Oppression disfigures the relations between self and other, between self and self, between me and my body. It is the injustice within relations to bodies which we have not yet acknowledged.

Relying on Kristeva's notion of the ideal and the abject, Young argues that there is an implied universal body supporting the subject of knowledge. But whose body is that? When I am confronted by a body different from my own, I react with aversion or avoidance. Alien to my body, to the ideal body, are '. . . drab, ugly, loathsome or fearful bodies. Old people, gay men and lesbians, disabled people, fat people' (1990, pp. 123–4) occupy these positions. Prejudice exploits metaphors of bodies that are not recognizably ours: the Jew is subhuman, diseased; the Aborigine is from a different stock or at a different stage in evolution; the homosexual is sick because of the degeneration of his blood. While these attitudes may officially belong to past discourses, they survive in terms of unconscious reactions where we view those bodies as abject.

Phenomenology helps us to see the determining role of the body in the politics of aversion. It may also offer a different type of ethics, 'an ethos of habitation', modelled on the specific ways subjects live and act in the world, including, of course, sexuality. Normally, questions of morality do not take into account the lesbian and gay as moral positions: the 'ways of being and acting' are assumed to include only heterosexual choices. But lesbian and gay philosophy cannot go anywhere unless it attacks this invisibility of different sexual subjectivities. The project of thinking ethically about sexual relations and erotic practices must be refigured if the idea of a 'normal' sexuality is rejected as incoherent or irrelevant.

Rosalyn Diprose offers an interesting start to such a project in 'Generosity: Between Love and Desire' (1997). She argues for a model of sexuality and erotic subjectivity free from the individualism and sexual puritanism of much radical and liberal feminism. Drawing on de Beauvoir and Merleau-Ponty, Diprose defends diverse sexual encounters without ignoring the problem of sexual violence. She sketches the outline of 'a generosity of mind and body, love and desire . . . which, by assuming the ambiguity of existence, views the erotic encounter as one means of extending one's own existence through others without entrapment'.

Confronting the straight mind: Monique Wittig

In her collection *The Straight Mind and Other Essays* (1992), the French writer Monique Wittig undertakes what she calls a materialist analysis of the role of women in society, starting from a lesbian subject position. (By materialist she is referring to the ways specific social and political ideologies inscribe the body.) 'Woman', she states, is a social construction and not a natural category. The lesbian has been constituted as the one who is not a 'real' woman because she is not defined by her relationship to man. 'Thus a lesbian has to be something else, a not-woman, a not-man, a product of society, not a product of nature' (1992, p. 13).

According to Wittig, it is the co-implication of sex and gender which maintains heterosexual supremacy. Within this framework, man is constituted as the universal, while woman is known only in her relationship to this universal, and then only in terms of sex. Women are heterosexualized; imposed on them is the obligation to reproduce the species and heterosexual society. Feminists like Irigaray and Cixous who emphasize sexual difference play into this game when they celebrate the so-called positive aspects of woman. Far from destroying the tyranny of sameness, the exaltation of femininity maintains woman as a natural and essential category, thus continuing women's oppression. In the feminism of difference, women remain sexual objects, disallowed the position of subject.

However, the figure of the lesbian offers an alternative. If the lesbian exists, then the category of sex is not an essential category as heterosexual society would have us believe: '. . . to destroy 'woman' does not mean that we aim . . . to destroy lesbianism simultaneously with the categories of sex, because lesbianism provides for the moment the only social form in which we can live freely'. Outside the category of sex, resistant to heterosexual presumption, the lesbian reconceptualizes subjectivity in relation to sociality. Her subjectivity is not based on a relationship with man. For Wittig, this need not be only for lesbians, yet it is the lesbian who first actually achieves it. As Teresa de Lauretis describes her, 'Experientially autonomous from heterosexuality . . . [the lesbian] therefore exceeds the terms of its discursive-conceptual horizons' (1990, p. 143). It is in this sense that the lesbian can claim the universal subject/speaking position previously available only to men.

In the realm of desire, the radical lesbian also marks the threshold of change. In a curious formulation, Wittig insists that what lesbians desire is not 'women' but only 'lesbians'. This is the first intimation of an eros beyond 'the preliminary markings by sexes' (Wittig, 1979, p. 114). For lesbians (and gay men), sexuality cannot be reduced to a heterosexual model:

> Since sexuality has for us no finality apart from its own exercise, it must be above all an exercise of subjectivity that involves the search for pleasure and the creation of a unique being, self-sufficient, whom no heterosexual reduction would be able to account for. (1979, p. 119)

The force of Wittig's demand for a sexuality without 'finality' (reminscent of Deleuze and Guattari's rhizomatic desire) relies on her belief that the category of sex is mutable. She sees an escape from essentialized notions of what it means to be lesbian. Within the categorization of 'lesbian' there are differences which in turn can account for a diverse range of sexual practices. Because the lesbian's way of being is not based on gender opposition, it therefore 'opens onto another dimension of the human' (1979, p. 117).

Wittig's lesbian is not an individual with a specific sexual preference, nor a social subject with a particular political ideology. She is a subject who struggles to rewrite herself against the norm. Experimental in her expressions of desire, the lesbian still exists in a state of tension, both within and outside heterosexual society. It is she 'who historically must undertake the task of defining the individual subject in materialist terms' (1992, p. 19).

Homosexuality as style:
an anti-natural technology of the self

> The underground language of people who have no power to define and determine themselves in the world develops its own density and precision. It enables them to sniff the wind, sense the atmosphere, defend themselves in a hostile terrain. (Rowbotham, 1977)

By refiguring the category of lesbian, Wittig interrupts the discourse of gender more radically than most philosophers are willing to do: her 'lesbian ethos and aesthetics' does not invert heteronormativity but discards it. Recently within gay philosophy there have been voices speaking for another kind of 'surplus' that would exempt the homosexual from the 'category of sex'.

Two of the most original and influential gay writers, Roland Barthes and Michel Foucault, suggest a reinterpretation of gay eroticism as 'style'. Style has clear affinities with another image recently exercising a powerful attraction on theorists of gender/sexuality: the concept of 'performativity'.[7] Style, like performativity as Butler describes that in *Bodies That Matter* (1993), is at once individual *and* inflected with the history of our social and psychic relations. Barthes is the exemplary case of this phenomenon of 'stylization' as sexual personality. By developing an ethos of writerly self-creation he introduced his eroticism into his aesthetics. The personal carnal myth which the writer secretly breathes into his work, style springs 'from the body and the past of the writer', from his 'subnature of expression where the first coitus of words and things takes place.' It is explicitly phallic and masturbatory in *Writing Degree Zero* (1953), where it is described as:

> something crude . . . a form with no clear destination, the product of a thrust . . . a vertical and lonely dimension of thought . . . It is the writer's 'thing', his glory and his prison, his solitude, . . . a closed personal process, . . . the private portion of the ritual, . . . and the decorative voice of hidden secret flesh. (Barthes, 1987, pp. 31–34)

In Foucault's last writings on the history of sexuality, style becomes an idealized philosophic way of life, a way of 'fashioning the self'. He calls this an 'ascesis', or 'aesthetics of existence'. Greek sages cultivated such a life: disciplined, refined, but not without specialized sexual privileges. The aristocrat who made his life and thought into a work of art 'stylized' his existence to mark its difference from the vulgar unreflectiveness of the commonplace. Foucault identifies his 'technologies of the self' with experimentation of all sorts: mystic pursuits of self-dissolution, moral exercises like Jean Genet's cultivation of evil, individual attempts to relate differently in the over-familiar domains of sex. The challenge of this 'aestheticism' for contemporary gay and lesbian subjects is to create their own code of social deviance within a world whose appetite for experimentation has never been lower while the risks, as we know, have never been higher.[8]

For Barthes and Foucault, as for Proust, homosexuality is more a stylistic possibility than an identity. Like same-sex desire, style tends to be a problem for philosophy,[9] which likes its truth without adornment. For style is everything in writing which is not necessary to the content or message. Style is the surplus that confronts us with a decided personality, a particular way of looking and speaking, a peculiarity. Does not fetishism, for instance, 'stylize' sexual desire, give it a form and a discipline? Are not the perversions exercises of invention on some rather banal themes? As style is at once the most redundant and the most personal aspect of language, it is subject to the same suspicions which Jacques Derrida sees aimed at 'writing' (Derrida, 1976). Rousseau's work on language exposes an anxiety which is less metaphysical than sexual, condemning writing as a 'sterile' and 'monstrous supplement' to speech (1976, pp. 141–164). Writing is auto-erotic and unprocreative, shameful and secretive. Thus writing is on the side of decadence, impure and excessive.

It is tempting to pursue the parallels between a Derridean 'writing' and gay male sex, as Lee Edelman has done in *Homographesis*, a project which he describes as a 'putting into writing' of gayness (Edelman, 1994). Edelman, with writers like Harold Beaver (1981) and Eve Sedgwick (1990) recuperates 'the closet': the long enforced dissimulation of gay culture. While Gay Liberation believed that the compromising ambiguities of the closet must be denounced, this neglects the rich inventiveness and self-creation in the culture of an 'underground nation'. The euphemisms of those forced to hide are also a language: mimicry, innuendo and inversion, originally strategies of self-protection, have become part of the production of gayness, a distinctive aesthetic.

The gay world is not accidentally a culture of excess: in it the banal representations of the 'respectable' world are turned upside down, mined for their ironic and exorbitant potential. Queer culture, as Beaver writes, is a culture of signs or countercodes, 'transgressing against the contract of language' (Beaver, 1981, p. 100). 'In spite of the multiplicity of his signs,' Beaver claims, the homosexual 'is a double-dealer, moving incognito through a heterosexual world' (1981, p. 104). Homosexuality is an outrageous carnality next to the neutral murmur of straight behaviour. Just as philosophical discourse had to wipe out the distractions of style, so the sexual police must vilify homosexuality, whether male or female. Those exaggerated effects threaten to contaminate straight sexual norms, for what is monstrous about homosexuality is ultimately that it has no purpose except pleasure. In it, nature has gone awry.

Contra naturam: the theological insult meant to shame homosexual love into extinction is, as it happens, a description of a certain wilfulness essential to art. But even nature has perverse habits, not always reproducing through the sanctioned couple. Probably the most elegant of Deleuze and Guattari's rhizomatic 'becomings' is the formation made by the orchid and the insect, nature's playful response to the needs of Proust's sodomites, Charlus and Jupien. The orchid/insect is neither homosexual nor heterosexual, neither same-same nor same-different, and its reproductive intentions are almost entirely unreadable. Orchid and wasp come together in a chance, experimental construction. They do not revisit each other's childhood fantasies; they do not supply each other's lacks, they do not even exist in a register of mirroring parts or organs. We had better admit that attraction is unique, *sui generis*; given the futility of looking in it for any purpose, any rule, it would make more sense to ask of an attraction (as Deleuze and Guattari do): what does it make happen? What energies does it spread into the world? There is ultimately no guidebook in nature (and no consolation in custom) for the sexual lives of present and future humans. If we require a sexual morality free from violence and indifference, there is no escaping the fact: we must make it up for ourselves.

Notes

1. 'Ressentiment', French for 'resentment', is used extensively by Nietzsche to mean an impulse that wars against life and vitality, favouring negation, envy, decadence and, in general, all that is sick or mean-spirited in culture.
2. Bonnie Zimmerman writes: 'The primary strategies of the recent past, therefore, have involved the deconstruction of the lesbian as a unified, essentialist, ontological being and the reconstruction of the lesbian as metaphor and/or subject position' (Zimmerman, 1992, p. 3). For dissatisfactions of 'identity', see Fuss (1991), Butler (1990), Halperin (1990); and the objections of Leo Bersani (1995).

3. In the 1960s, the leaders of the rebellion against a repressive ego and the containment of desire included Norman O. Brown (1966), R. D. Laing (1960), and Wilhelm Reich, who all toyed with the idea that madness or schizophrenia could be preferable both to enforced sanity and social control.

4. See Boundas and Olkowski (1994), articles by Elizabeth Grosz (1995), and Rosi Braidotti (1994); Grosz, (1995a) pp. 173–85; and Probyn (1996) pp. 37–62.

5. On Wittig see Fealy (1997).

6. See Simone de Beauvoir (1972, 1994) and Maurice Merleau–Ponty (1962).

7. The essential text here is Butler (1990).

8. On this see especially Halperin (1995, pp. 81–119).

9. 'In its popular incarnations, the surfeit that marks off homosexuality from its normative other, heterosexuality, is 'gleaned' from the surface of the body: homosexuals are said to distinguish themselves by their extravagant dress, their exaggerated mannerisms, their hysterical intonations, their insatiable oral sex drives, and their absurd imitation of "feminine" and "masculine" behaviour.' (Fuss, 1993, p. 56)

References

Allen, Jeffner, and Young, Iris Marion (eds), *The Thinking Muse: Feminism and Modern French Philosophy*. Bloomington: Indiana University Press, 1989.

Barthes, Roland, *A Barthes Reader*, Susan Sontag (ed.). New York: Hill & Wang, 1987.

Beaver, Harold, 'Homosexual Signs (In Memory of Roland Barthes)', in *Critical Inquiry*, Vol. 8, No. 1, Autumn 1981, pp. 99–119.

Bersani, Leo, *Homos*. Cambridge, MA and London: Harvard University Press, 1995.

Boundas, Constantin V., and Olkowski, Dorothea (eds), *Gilles Deleuze and the Theater of Philosophy*. London: Routledge, 1994.

Braidotti, Rosi, 'Towards a New Nomadism', in Constantin V. Boundas and Dorothea Olkowski (eds), *Gilles Deleuze and the Theater of Philosophy*, London: Routledge, 1994.

Brown, Norman O., *Love's Body*. Berkeley, CA: University of California Press, 1966.

Butler, Judith, *Bodies That Matter: On the Discursive Limits of Sex*. London: Routledge, 1993.

Butler, Judith, *Gender Trouble: Feminism and the Subversion of Identity*. London: Routledge, 1990.

Butler, Judith, 'Imitation and Gender Insubordination', in Diana Fuss (ed.), *Inside/Out: Lesbian Theories, Gay Theories*. London: Routledge, 1991.

de Beauvoir, Simone, *The Ethics of Ambiguity* (trans. Bernard Frechtman). New York: Citadel Press, 1994.

de Beauvoir, Simone, *The Second Sex* (trans. H.M. Parshley). Harmondsworth, Middlesex: Penguin, 1972.

De Lauretis, Teresa, 'Eccentric Subjects: Feminist Theory and Historical Consciousness', in *Feminist Studies*, Vol. 16, No. 1, 1990.

Deleuze, Gilles, and Guattari, Felix, *Anti-Oedipus: Capitalism and Schizophrenia* (trans. Robert Hurley, Mark Seem and Helen R. Lane). Minneapolis: University of Minnesota Press, 1983, (first published 1972).

Deleuze, Gilles, and Guattari, Felix, *A Thousand Plateaus: Capitalism and Schizophrenia*, Vol. 2, (trans. Brian Massumi). Minneapolis: University of Minneapolis Press, 1987, (first published 1980).

Derrida, Jacques, *Of Grammatology* (trans. Gayatri Chakravorty Spivak). Baltimore and London: Johns Hopkins University Press, 1976.

Diprose, Rosalyn, 'Generosity: Between Love and Desire', in *Hypatia*, forthcoming, 1997.

Edelman, Lee, *Homographesis: Essays in Gay Literary and Cultural Theory*. London: Routledge, 1994.

Fealy, Terri, 'Wittig's Revolutionary Intent', in *Australian Feminist Studies*, forthcoming, 1997.

Foucault, Michel, *The History of Sexuality*, Vol. 1, (trans. Robert Hurley). London: Allen Lane, 1979.

Foucault, Michel, *The History of Sexuality*, Vol. 2, (trans. Robert Hurley). New York: Pantheon Books, 1985.

Fuss, Diana, 'Freud's Fallen Women: Identification, Desire, and "A Case of Homosexuality in a Woman"', in Michael Warner (ed.), *Fear of a Queer Planet*, Minneapolis: University of Minnesota Press, 1993.

Fuss, Diana (ed.), *Inside/Out: Lesbian Theories, Gay Theories*. London: Routledge, 1991.

Garber, Marjorie, *Vested Interests: Cross Dressing and Cultural Anxiety*. London: Routledge, 1992.

Garber, Marjorie, *Vice Versa: Bisexuality and the Eroticism of Everyday Life*. London: Hamish Hamilton, 1995.

Grosz, Elizabeth, 'Animal Sex', in Elizabeth Grosz and Elspeth Probyn (eds), *Sexy Bodies: The Strange Carnalities of Feminism*, London: Routledge, 1995b.

Grosz, Elizabeth, *Space, Time and Perversion: Essays on the Politics of Bodies*. New York and London: Routledge, 1995a.

Halperin, David, *One Hundred Years of Homosexuality*. London: Routledge, 1990.

Halperin, David, *Saint Foucault: Towards a Gay Hagiography*. New York: Oxford University Press, 1995.

Hocquenghem, Guy, *Homosexual Desire* (trans. Daniella Dangoor). London: Allison and Busby, 1978.

Irigaray, Luce, *An Ethics of Sexual Difference*. (trans. Carolyn Burke and Gillian Gill). Ithaca: Cornell University Press, 1993.

Irigaray, Luce, *This Sex Which is Not One* (trans. Catherine Porter with Carolyn Burke). New York: Cornell University Press, 1985.

Laing, R. D, *The Divided Self: A Study of Sanity and Madness*. London: Tavistock, 1960.

Leder, Drew, *The Absent Body*. Chicago: University of Chicago Press, 1990.

Le Dœuff, Michèle, *The Philosophical Imaginary* (trans. Colin Gordon). London: The Athlone Press, 1989.

Merleau-Ponty, Maurice, *The Phenomenology of Perception* (trans. Colin Smith). London: Kegan Paul, 1962.

Nietzsche, Friedrich, *On the Genealogy of Morals* (trans. Walter Kaufmann and R. J. Hollingdale). New York: Vintage Books, 1989.

Nietzsche, Friedrich, *Thus Spoke Zarathustra* (trans. Walter Kaufmann) in *The Portable Nietzsche*, New York: Viking Press, 1968.

Nietzsche, Friedrich, *The Will to Power* (trans. Walter Kaufman and R.J.Hollingdale). New York: Vintage Books, 1969.

Probyn, Elspeth, 'Becoming-Horse', in Elspeth Probyn, *Outside Belongings*. London: Routledge, 1996.

Rowbotham, Sheila, *Woman's Conciousness, Man's World*. Harmondsworth: Penguin, 1977. Cited in Sneja Gunew (ed.), *Feminist Knowledge: Critique and Construct*, London and New York: Routledge, 1990, p. 26.

Sedgwick, Eve Kosofsky, *Between Men: English Literature and Male Homosocial Desire*. New York: Columbia University Press, 1985.

Sedgwick, Eve Kosofsky, *Epistemology of the Closet*. Berkeley: University of California Press, 1990.

Sedgwick, Eve Kosofsky, *Tendencies*. Durham: Duke University Press, 1993.

Warner, Michael (ed.), *Fear of a Queer Planet: Queer Politics and Social Theory*. Minneapolis: University of Minnesota Press, 1993.

Wittig, Monique, 'Paradigm', in Elaine Marks and George Stambolian (eds), *Homosexualities and French Literature: Cultural Contexts/Critical Texts*. Ithaca and London: Cornell University Press, 1979.

Wittig, Monique, *The Straight Mind and Other Essays*. Boston: Beacon Press, 1992.

Young, Iris Marion, *Justice and the Politics of Difference*. Princeton: Princeton University Press, 1990.

Zimmerman, Bonnie, 'Lesbians Like This and That: Some Notes on Lesbian Criticism for the Nineties', in Sally R. Munt (ed.), *New Lesbian Criticism: Literary and Cultural Readings*, New York: Columbia University Press, 1992.

Further reading

Allen, Jeffner (ed.), *Lesbian Philosophies and Cultures*. Albany: State University of New York Press, 1990.

Butler, Judith P., *Subjects of Desire: Hegelian Reflections in Twentieth-Century France.* New York: Columbia University Press, 1987.

Card, Claudia (ed.), *Adventures in Lesbian Philosophy.* Bloomington: Indiana University Press, 1994.

Daumer, E., 'Queer Ethics, Or the Challenge of Bisexuality to Lesbian Ethics', in *Hypatia,* Vol. 7, No. 4, 1992, pp. 91–105.

Grosz, Elizabeth, *Sexual Subversions: Three French Feminists.* Sydney: Allen & Unwin, 1989.

Hoagland, Sarah Lucia, 'Lesbian Ethics and Female Agency', in E. B. Cole (ed.), *Explorations in Feminist Ethics,* Bloomington: Indiana University Press, 1992.

Moher, Richard D., *Gay Ideas: Outing and Other Controversies.* Boston: Beacon Press, 1992.

Moher, Richard D., 'Invisible Minorities, Civic Rights, Democracy: Three Arguments For Gay Rights', in *Philosphical Forum,* Vol.17, 1985, pp. 1–2.

Weed, Elizabeth. (ed.), *Coming to Terms: Feminism, Theory, Politics.* New York and London: Routledge, 1989.

9

Michel Foucault and the Uses of Sexuality

Elspeth Probyn

ONE OF THE MOST ENDURING QUESTIONS that confronts anyone interested in sexuality and gender is whether we are born with gender and sexual identities already intact or whether they are the result of various forms of socialization and conditioning. If for me it is clear that while I may have been born a female, the meanings attached – and that I attach – to being a woman are the result of where and how I live (the particular society and historical past and present into which I was born), the question of whether I was born a lesbian is a trickier one. And if for political reasons I do not subscribe to the idea that gays and lesbians are the result of a 'gay gene',[1] it is also unquestionable that for some gays and lesbians the idea that 'we were born that way' is reassuring. In an analogous fashion, feminists have deeply questioned the status of 'woman' as a universal term. Again, while at certain political moments it has been necessary to affirm 'women' as a collective group, it is increasingly evident that in so doing the differences amongst women have been erased to the detriment of non-white women.

On the surface, it may seem less threatening to heterosexual society to consider gays and lesbians as a fact of nature. However, this simple statement also begs the idea that we are an aberration of nature. Thus while at an individual level the idea of natural determination may seem quite innocent, the problem comes when one considers the range of debates and political arguments that support such a view. For, when we say that homosexuals are born that way, not only do we open the door to the regulation of foetuses in order to rid society of a 'parasitic gene' (one that does not encourage reproduction of the species), we also have to buy into the idea that gays and lesbians have always existed in much the same way as we do now, and that in all societies and cultures homosexuality has much the same meaning. Moreover, we also have to conclude that homosexuality is a category of person, and not a range of varying practices. In this chapter I will briefly engage with some of the problems associated with the debate over essentialism (the view that there is a meaning to gender and sexuality that is prior to social formations) and social constructionism (the view that biological attributes only come to have meaning within historical and social formations). The key point of my argument goes beyond this debate in order to consider the politics of sexuality – the use that sexuality is put to in our culture.

I have long had a stubborn conviction that things don't have to be the way they are now. This has been given intellectual comfort and support through my reading of the work of Michel Foucault who, across his numerous books and articles, consistently argued that what we take as natural is the result of particular historical forces and factors. This enduring political belief that human beings can rework ideas of destiny (be they historical or biological) and that we must always strive towards freedom, took many forms for Foucault, but was continually informed by an intellectual curiosity about all forms of social organization. Although the figure of Foucault is daunting, he inspires us to be supremely interested in life and politics. And he himself could be quite playful and displayed a wicked sense of humour in his writings. For instance, he once gave an anonymous interview to the leading French newspaper, *Le Monde*, under the title 'The Masked Philosopher'. Taking up the idea that curiosity is stigmatized as futility, he argued that 'To me it suggests something altogether different: it evokes "concern"; it evokes the care one takes for what exists and could exist; a readiness to find strange and singular what surrounds us . . . a fervour to grasp what is happening and what passes; a casualness in regard to the traditional hierarchies of the important and the essential' (1989, pp. 989–9). This 'casualness' led Foucault to study what were often seen as peripheral elements in the organization of society; of course, on reading his analyses it became obvious how central they are to modern conceptions of life and truth. Such was the case with sexuality, a subject that we now acknowledge as one of the major ways through which we know ourselves, and conceive of our individuality. Following Foucault countless studies have analysed sexuality as a key vector of power, and as the repository of truth – both individual and societal.

Indeed, it is hard to imagine writing about sexuality without the work of Foucault. And if Foucault is at the centre of the sex-theory industry, since his death of AIDS in 1984, there have been several biographies that try to get at the truth of Foucault through his own sexuality.[2] According to one of his more prurient biographers, it was the actuality of the leather culture that interested him more than writing about it. James Miller is fascinated by what he believes to be the essential link in Foucault's thought: that of death and s/m. Positioning himself as a wholesome straight, he can only manage to describe the s/m scene in the words of others (he borrows both from the Marquis de Sade and from another dead great French philosopher, Gilles Deleuze): 'Your hands will be strapped to the ceiling. Bands will be wrapped around each of your arms and tightened . . . to express passionately and actively an agonizing lust for blood and for death' (1994, p. 279). While this description and Miller's project have been the subject of much critique (the only analogy he can come up with to his own life experience is that of having a tooth filled), who could blame Foucault for seeking out this scene? I for one would have much preferred the bath houses of San Francisco to the trenches of hard lines about sexual positions and suitable partners.

Without overly generalizing, I recall the 1970s as a pre-Foucauldian time when the politics of sexuality were pretty straightforward, and deviation from certain lines of behaviour was not lightly tolerated. At the time, I was living some 1,500 kilometres up the road from San Francisco (where the bath house culture was in full swing) in the then very provincial town of Vancouver where (unbathed) hippy culture reigned. In the main, power was seen as unproblematic: the divisions of 'them' and 'us' staunchly in place. In terms of politics, being a tart on the dance floor and consorting with gay boys put me squarely in the camp of 'them' when it came to a certain strand of feminism, and in the terms of gay liberation, I would have been written off as a 'fag hag' – if, that is, the boys I hung out with had had a political thought in their bodies. Now, I suppose this type of behaviour might be regarded as queer *avant la lettre*; then it just got me into trouble.

Unbeknown to me, I was living through a moment of great debate within the loosely affiliated feminist, lesbian and gay movement(s) over the nature of sexuality. In order to think about the current possibilities of a Foucauldian politics of sexuality (and to atone for my youthful sins), I will sketch the outlines of the discussion over essentialism and social constructionism, and the role of some key concepts about power and sexuality as articulated by Foucault.

As Carole Vance argues, feminist and lesbian and gay theories have been instrumental in questioning the 'prevailing ideological frameworks for examining the "facts" abut sex and gender' (1989, p. 13). As she further states, the need to examine these concepts arose in great part because of the prevalence of essentialist views in the study of sexuality:

a belief that human behavior is 'natural', predetermined by genetic, biological, or physiological mechanisms and thus not subject to change; or the notion that human behaviors which show some similarity in form are the same, an expression of an underlying human drive or tendency. (p. 14)

In Diane Richardson's terms, this plays out in 'a continuing search for answers to two questions: "Who is a homosexual?" and "What makes a person homosexual?" . . . In such assumptions the term homosexual is used to refer to a core and enduring aspect of being of a group of individuals' (1983/84, p. 79). In the face of such questions, there has been a sustained effort on the part of many feminist and lesbian and gay theorists to assert that sexuality and gender must be conceived of as historically situated terms, in other words, the idea that 'individuals are sexually one essence or another is specific to history and culture' (Richardson, ibid.). Pursuing this line further, Diana Fuss defines the constructionist project as 'concerned above all with the production and organization of differences, and therefore reject[ing] the idea that any essential or natural givens precede the processes of human determination' (1989, pp. 2–3).

If the case against essentialism has been led by social and historical accounts of the changing specificities of homosexuality, we need to take into account the ways in which actual individuals live out their sexuality. Doing so reinforces the argument against essentialism when it is shown that a very large part of the population engages in homosexual activities. It is salutary to remember that even in the staid late 1940s the Kinsey Reports found that only half of the white male American population was exclusively heterosexual. This led Kinsey and his researchers to argue that individuals should not be 'characterized as heterosexual or homosexual, but as individuals who have had certain amounts of heterosexual experience and certain amounts of homosexual experience' (Kinsey, Pomeroy and Martin, 1948, p. 656). In turn, Jan Schippers takes Kinsey's findings as yet more proof that essentialism is 'a bed which is too small', given that it offers 'no satisfying answer to the question of why some people do change their sexual identity in the course of their lives' (1989, p. 143). In other words, if homosexuality or heterosexuality were indeed an essential attribute of a given individual, how or why would that person change her sexual orientation? If this would seem to challenge essentialist tenets, from his psychotherapeutic practice with gay men, Schippers also notes that many gay men have an essentialist approach to their own sexuality.

Even from this brief sketch, one can see that the debate between essentialism and constructionism has all the makings of an endless ping-pong game. If for some the jury is still out on whether sexuality is essential or constructed, along with many I would argue that the debate has passed its 'use-by date', or that, as Fuss puts it, the case of essentialism versus conructionism 'is a largely artificial (albeit powerful) antagonism' (1989, p. 119). And if much of the social constructionism side has used Foucault's first volume of *The History of Sexuality* to argue that homosexuality was only discovered as a category of person in the eighteenth century, I want to turn away from the debate about whether sexuality is either natural or social in order to follow through on what was more properly Foucault's concern. In his words,

> my main concern will be to locate the forms of power, the channels it takes, and the discourses it permeates in order to reach the most tenuous and individual modes of behavior, the paths that give it access to the rare or scarcely perceivable forms of desire, how it penetrates and controls everyday pleasure. (1980, p. 11)

Encapsulated in this quotation are many of the central themes to a Foucauldian understanding of the workings of sexuality, none of which have solely or properly to do with the debate over essentialism and constructionism. In fact, when asked a question about 'the distinction between an innate predisposition to homosexual behavior and social conditioning', Foucault replied 'No comment' (1989, p. 212). Rather, what interests Foucault, and in the order that I will explicate them, are the thematics of power, discourse, pleasure, desire, and more generally how all of these terms come to constitute us in our everyday individuality, modes of subjectification that are disciplinary as well as being manners of self-disciplining ourselves. In other words, these are key ways in which modern society exercises power over its subjects, but they also play important roles in fashioning how we come to perceive of ourselves as individuals. Indeed, one of Foucault's crucial points was that power does not solely bear down upon us; rather, it permeates our most intimate being. If it has become commonplace to say that for Foucault power is everywhere, this passage repeats what he argued over and over again through the analysis of many different sites: that power 'is not localized in anybody's hand, nor in classes but exercised and employed through a net-like organization' (1980b, p. 98). It seems to me that this statement (or any of a myriad of others) should lay to rest the oft-cited idea that Foucault's notion of power was nebulous. If it goes against the Marxist tenet that power is held by the ruling classes, it also shows up the fact that 'class' is also a sociological abstraction – albeit one that is certainly experienced at both individual and collective levels.

More immediate to the concerns of this chapter are the feminist critiques of Foucault about his lack of analysis of the gendered aspects of power.[3] As Meaghan Morris has famously argued, 'any feminists drawn in to sending love letters to Foucault would be in no danger of reciprocation. Foucault's work is not the work of a ladies' man' (1988, p. 355). However, as I have argued elsewhere, (Probyn, 1993, 1996) if Foucault does not overtly analyse the relations of gender he certainly gives us tools with which to consider how power is exercised across gendered and sexualized bodies. In Judith Butler's work (1990), this insight is extended in order to consider how categories of gender and sexuality are produced through our bodily performances of them. In this vein, gender and sexuality are nodal points of power where individual bodies are instrumental in reproducing dominant discourses. As François Éwald (1992) puts it, discipline and normalization are key techniques through which power is operated, specific techniques that focus on individuals as both the object and instrument of the exercise of power. And in modern societies, gender and sexuality along with race and ethnicity constitute the most evident nexus of normalization, discipline and power.

These techniques are more properly called 'discourse' in Foucault's work. While the definitions and implications of discourse are wide ranging, simply put one might say that what concerns Foucault are the limits and forms of what is, at any given time, sayable. The analysis of discourse thus aims at revealing the ground that allows for some things to be said, and renders others impossible: 'The question proper to such an analysis might be formulated in this way: what is the specific existence that emerges from what is said and nowhere else?' (in Hannah, 1993, p. 349). If the idea of 'discourse' may seem at first very ephemeral, it is quickly rendered immediate when we consider that networks of knowledge and power continually place us, fix and name us in our everyday lives. The term 'discourse' then refers us to statements, or sets of statements that map out reality. As Deleuze argues of this conception of discourse, 'Everything in them is real and all reality is manifestly present' (1988, p. 3). For example, if there are no words to describe anything other than heterosexuality, the acts that I perform with another woman are either rendered completely invisible or are named as the 'love that dare not speak its name'. This is a clear example of how the impossibility of certain statements then rules out particular forms of reality.

Even when statements are allowed, they are nonetheless always informed and constrained by other statements. If I can now say that 'I am a lesbian', this is nonetheless a statement that takes its weight from other statements and truths. It may be an individual statement but it also presupposes public knowledges. If I say it, it has certain implications that it may not have if others state it.

If, for example, a psychiatrist states that I am a lesbian, or an educational body states it, I may find myself excluded from employment, confined or subject to 'treatment'. Aligned with the way in which statements seek to portray truths is the concomitant need to analyse the ways in which that which is sayable regulates and constrains other statements. Thus, one has to look to what enables certain statements to be said. In order for me to say that I am a lesbian there have to be several other orders of statements in place. These range from the obvious such as a recognition that something called lesbian actually exists, to the publicly constructed truths about lesbians: that we are all man-haters, wear lumberjack shirts and have no sense of humour. And we can readily see that under certain circumstances, I may not want to utter such a statement because of the way it will interact with others. In this way, statements regulate what I can say – what is indeed sayable – and the type of effects that any statement will have .

For Foucault, power is always exercised through discourse, thus rendering the analysis of discourse central to understanding what he calls power-knowledge relations. And lest one thinks that discourse is only about words, it is helpful to remember that in French the terms that best capture Foucault's perspective are: *pouvoir, voir, savoir* (power, the visible, knowledge). Or in other words, it is to that which passes for self-evident that attracts a critical attention, remembering that 'evidence' comes from the Latin root of *evidere* – to see. In fact, one can say that the basis of systems of racism, sexism and homophobia is found in the sighting of difference, a difference which is taken to be self-evidently a perversion of the normal: the not-white, the not-heterosexual, the not-feminine that is expressed in such common refrains as 'Are you a girl or a boy?' (And after the nth time of getting called 'Sir', I sometimes think that the best reply might be 'Are you stupid or what?'). In the face of such statements and at a methodological level, Foucault draws our attention to three criteria which regulate the operations of discourse, and which are three principles to be kept in mind when analysing discourses: first, one looks to the formation of discourse, to the rules which underpin its operations; second, one examines the transformation of discourse, the conditions that must be brought together at any given time in order to allow for certain objects, concepts, and theories; and third, one studies the correlation between sets of discourses and the (institutional, social, economic and political) context in which they are deployed (Foucault, 1991).

While sexuality is not the only site where we can see this regulation and self-regulation of discourses in action, it is one of the most compelling. In *The History of Sexuality* Foucault convincingly argued that far from being regulated by repression, sexuality was controlled through a constant incitement to speak about it, and to speak about it as the very truth of our selves. This idea of Foucault's is now confirmed on a daily basis through television and other media accounts and confessions of all sorts of sexual practices. From the talk shows where you can experience at one hand removed the widest range of sexual activities, to important gains in civil rights, to the contested area of same-sex marriage (which probably does more to enhance straight marriage than anything else), to the mainstream portrayals of gay and lesbian 'lifestyles' (as if one merely bought into being a lesbian), to really awful depictions of supposed lesbian eroticism touted in films like *As Night is Falling* or *Claire of the Moon* – the examples of publicly aired (self-) representations of sexuality are seemingly endless.

In such accounts we can clearly see the types of linkages that Foucault argued were set in motion by sexuality: 'the correlation between a domain of knowledge (a field of knowledge – concepts, theories, disciplines), a type of normativity (a set of rules – what is allowed or not allowed, the natural or the monstrous, the normal and the pathological . . .), and a way of relating to the self (the relation of an individual to him/herself – by which he/she comes to know him/herself as a sexual subject in relation to others)' (1994, p. 578). Thus, when Ricki Lake or Oprah Winfrey tackle the 'problem' of lesbian s/m we will see these correlations in action (and it is interesting to note that even in the explosion of representations of sexuality, some will still be marked as acceptable and others as abnormal). In the talk show format, and closely following Foucault's framework, concepts and theories will be brought forward by an 'expert' (more likely than not a sexologist or a psychologist); from their statements definitions of what is normal and not, pathological or regular, will be defined or assumed to be self-evident; and those foolhardy enough to be interviewed will no doubt say that this is how they are, that it makes them feel good about themselves and that they feel secure in having a network of friends who are into the same thing. That this may be perfectly true does not stop the fact that the entire operation has sought to correlate what is normal sexual activity and what is abnormal through the discourse and testimony of certain bodies. If the lesbian into s/m constructs her identity around a set of practices in which she may get pleasure, she has also served as a body across which public representations and knowledges are confirmed.

While we might say that this example shows that lesbians are now free to speak about their different sexual practices, we also need to pay attention to how confessions and testimony play within the machinery of discipline and power. Indeed, the encouragement to 'confess' on television or anywhere else is a fundamental part of modern systems and regimes that govern sexuality. The more visible the body, the finer nuanced are the degrees of what is acceptable or not.

This example (or any number of others) shows how discourses contract sexuality as a major site in the definition of what is normal or pathological in our society. It also raises the ways in which sexuality operates to define the truth of certain bodies and how bodies are the site where we can see in action the effects of the power to name and define. This is what Foucault argued in regard to the exteriority of discourse, and the public workings of power. From the church confessional to the talk show, ours is a society wherein power is exercised through talk: we are a thoroughly confessing bunch. Sex is thus the prime site to study the production of truth and the construction of the norm. As Leo Bersani has argued of *The History of Sexuality*, Foucault shows 'that power in our societies functions primarily not by repressing spontaneous sexual drives but by producing multiple sexualities, and that through the classification, distribution, and moral rating of those sexualities the individuals practising them can be approved, treated, marginalized, sequestered, disciplined, or normalized' (in Halperin, 1995, pp. 19–20). While Bersani is quite right that this is central to *The History of Sexuality*, it was not the final point of Foucault's interventions into the domain of sexuality in general and homosexuality in particular.

As the final part of this chapter, I want to turn now to a more pointed discussion of how we may use our bodies, sexual practices and pleasures in order to formulate a sexual politics that goes beyond merely drawing attention to our marginality. If in much commentary on Foucault, it is bemoaned that he depicted powerless bodies at the mercy of discursive systems of naming and classification, it may be that theorists too often consider one or another of Foucault's books in isolation. Read by itself *The History of Sexuality,* Vol. 1, 1980 may yield a picture of what has been famously called Foucault's 'docile bodies'. But this image is harder to maintain if one considers that Foucault also argued 'that we have to understand that with our desires, through our desires, go new forms of relationships, new forms of love, new forms of creation. Sex is not a fatality; it's a possibility for creative life' (1984, p. 27). Here and elsewhere Foucault explicitly articulated sexual choices and practices with 'the technologies of the self', a concept he elaborated in the 2nd and 3rd volumes of *The History of Sexuality* (1986, 1988). Freely admitting that he had perhaps paid too much attention to technologies of domination, Foucault then elaborated on the ways in which forms of societal discipline interact with other operations that individuals perform on themselves. He describes the latter as 'techniques which permit individuals to affect, by their own means, a certain number of operations on their own bodies, their own souls, their own thought, their own conduct, and this in a manner so as to transform themselves, modify themselves' (1988, p. 367). While the object of Foucault's study in *The Care of the Self* was historical (ancient Greece and its citizens – in other words, neither women nor slaves), we can take from his argument in order to think about how contemporary sexual practices might play within an ethical project that, as Foucault argued, 'always refers to an active political and erotic state' (1988b, p. 24).

The type of gay and lesbian sexual politics that I see emerging from these key tenets of Foucault's thought are fundamentally to do with the relationality that homosexuality in our society encourages. As Foucault argued, 'Homosexuality is an historic occasion to re-open affective and relational qualities, not so much through the intrinsic qualities of the homosexual, but due to the biases against the position he occupies; in a certain sense diagonal lines that he can have in the social fabric permit him to make these virtualities visible' (1989b, p. 207). This is then to seek new forms of relationships 'through homosexuality [that] can be established, multiplied and modulated . . . to use sexuality to arrive at a multiplicity of relationships' (ibid., p. 204).

From this perspective, we have moved considerably from the debate between essentialism and social constructionism that I outlined at the beginning of this chapter. Rather than worrying about whether or not we are born gay or lesbian, or whether society has formed us as such, it is now a question of what we can do with our bodies and desires in order to make the social relations we live within better, more equitable and more pleasurable. As AIDS activists such as Simon Watney have clearly and urgently argued,

> identities and alliances are not natural or inevitable, but have to be forged in collective experience and in shared aims and objectives . . . through the many different aspects and arenas of the social formation, whether through gender, nationalism, religion, health issues, regionalism, race and so on. (Watney, 1989, p. 183)

Moving beyond an essentialist conception of sexuality, and considering homosexuality as relational means that we now are confronted with the need to conjugate our differences. Homosexuality then becomes a challenge to ourselves and not just to heterosexual society. Following Foucault's injunction, this means that we cannot be content with increased visibility, we cannot rest on the fact that some aspects of gay and lesbian lifestyles are now acceptable (and can be seen in *Newsweek* or on television). While these representations are important, they are not enough. Indeed, they may herald that the effects of power are merely shifting in intensity from one site (affluent gays and lesbians) to another (the poor, or minoritarian homosexuals, or to those who have sex with the same gender but who cannot or will not take up the identity of gay or lesbian). While it is for me important to be able to lay claim to being a lesbian, to be able to state it in contexts that have been rendered safer because of the long battles led by gays, lesbians and feminists, it is nonetheless an identity that is only of use if put to work in the service of creating more equitable relationships. Or as Foucault puts it, 'if identity is only a game, if it is only a procedure to have relations, social and sexual-pleasure relationships that create new friendships, it is useful' (1984, p. 28). If, as he hoped, it would be homosexuality as friendship that finally most threatened the normal order of heterosexual society, then it is the relationships we forge by way of our sexual practices that are important – not whether or not we were born gay and lesbian, nor even, in the final count, that we are socially constructed. Moving beyond the general level of such arguments, the politics of sexuality can only be enacted through the tangible and material study of these lines, the minute following of the lines of gender, class, ethnicity, and age that produce bodies that yearn, open and close on others.

Notes

1. The recent work of Simon LeVay and others has brought this question to the pages of mainstream publications. See LeVay, *The Sexual Brain*, (Cambridge, MA: MIT Press, 1994). In essence, LeVay argues on the basis of his research on the hypothalamus, that this region of the brain is central to the regulation of 'male-typical sexual behavior', and that gay men have differently formed brain structures than straight men.
2. Notably, Didier Eribon, *Michel Foucault*. Trans. Betsy Wing. (Cambridge, MA: Harvard University Press, 1991); Eribon, *Michel Foucault et ses contemporains*. (Paris: Fayard, 1994); David Macey, *The Lives of Michel Foucault*. (London: Hutchinson, 1994); David Halperin, *Saint Foucault: Towards a Gay Hagiography*. (New York and Oxford: Oxford University Press, 1995); James Miller, *The Passion of Michel Foucault*. (New York: Doubleday, 1994).
3. To my mind, the most cogent of these is Teresa de Lauretis' argument that analysing the technologies of gender surpasses Foucault analysis of sex. See her *Technologies of Gender*. (Bloomington: Indiana University Press, 1988).

References and Further Reading

Altman, Dennis, Vance, Carole, Vicinus, Martha, and Weeks, Jeffrey (eds), *Homosexuality, Which Homosexuality? Essays for the International Scientific Conference on Lesbian and Gay Studies*. London: GMP Publishers, 1989.

Butler, Judith, *Gender Trouble: Feminism and the Subversion of Identity*. New York and London: Routledge, 1990.

Deleuze, Gilles, *Foucault* (trans. Sean Hand). Minneapolis: University of Minnesota Press, 1988.

Eribon, Didier, *Michel Foucault* (trans. Betsy Wing). Cambridge, MA: Harvard University Press, 1991.

Eribon, Didier, *Michel Foucault et ses contemporains*. Paris: Fayard, 1994.

Evans, David T., *Sexual Citizenship: The Material Constructions of Sexuality*. New York and London: Routledge, 1993.

Éwald, François, 'A Power without Exterior', in *Michel Foucault Philosopher* (trans. T. J. Armstrong), New York and London: Routledge, 1992.

Foucault, Michel, *The Care of the Self* (trans. Robert Hurley). New York: Vintage Books, 1988.

Foucault, Michel, 'Friendship as a Way of Life', in S. Lotringer (ed.), *Foucault Live*, (trans. J. Johnston), New York: Semiotext(e), 1989c.

Foucault, Michel, *The History of Sexuality*. Vol 1. (trans. Robert Hurley). New York: Vintage Books, 1980.

Foucault, Michel, 'An Interview: Sex, Power and the Politics of Identity', with Bob Gallagher and Alexander Wilson, in *The Advocate 400*, 7 August 1984.

Foucault, Michel, 'The Masked Philosopher', in S. Lotringer (ed.), *Foucault Live* (trans. J. Johnston), New York: Semiotext(e). (*Le Monde*, 6 April 1980), 1989.

Foucault, Michel, 'Préface à l'Histoire de la sexualité', in Daniel Defert and François Éwald (eds), *Dits et écrits*, 4 vols, Paris: Gallimard, 1994.

Foucault, Michel, 'Questions of Method', in Graham Burchell, Colin Gordon and Peter Miller (eds), *The Foucault Effect: Studies in Governmentality*, Chicago: University of Chicago Press, 1991.

Foucault, Michel, 'Sexual Choice, Sexual Act', in Sylvère Lotringer (ed.), *Foucault Live* (Interviews, 1966–84) (trans. John Johnston), New York: Semiotext(e), 1989b.

Foucault, Michel, 'Truth, Power, Self: An Interview with Michel Foucault', (by Rux Martin), in Luther H. Martin, Huck Gutman and Patrick H. Hutton (eds), *Technologies of the Self*, Amherst: University of Massachusetts Press, 1988b.

Foucault, Michel, 'Two Lectures', in Colin Gordon (ed.), *Power/Knowledge: Selected Interviews and other Writings. 1972–1977.* New York: Pantheon Books, 1980b.

Foucault, Michel, *The Use of Pleasure* (trans. Robert Hurley). New York: Vintage Books, 1986.

Fuss, Diana, 'The "Risk" of Essence', in her *Essentially Speaking Feminism: Nature & Difference*, London and New York: Routledge, 1989.

Guibert, Hervé, *To the Friend Who Did Not Save my Life.* New York and London: Serpent's Tail/High Risk Books, 1991.

Halperin, David, *Saint Foucault: Towards a Gay Hagiography.* New York and Oxford: Oxford University Press, 1995.

Hannah, M., 'Foucault on theorizing specificity', in *Environment and Planning D: Society and Space*, 11, 1993.

Kinsey, A. C., Pomeroy, W. B., and Martin, C. E., *Sexual Behavior in the Human Male.* Philadelphia: W. B. Saunders Company, 1948.

Macey, David, *The Lives of Michel Foucault.* London: Hutchinson, 1994.

Miller, James, *The Passion of Michel Foucault.* New York: Doubleday, 1994.

Morris, Meaghan, *The Pirate's Fianceé: Feminism Reading Postmodernism.* London: Verso, 1988.

New Formations. Special Issue: 'Michel Foucault: J'Accuse', No. 25, 1995.

Probyn, Elspeth, *Outside Belongings.* New York and London: Routledge, 1996.

Probyn, Elspeth, *Sexing the Self: Gendered Positions in Cultural Studies.* New York and London: Routledge, 1993.

Richardson, Diane, 'The Dilemma of Essentiality in Homosexual Theory', in *Journal of Homosexuality*, Vol. 9, 1983/84, pp. 2–3.

Schippers, Jan, 'Homosexual Identity, Essentialism and Constructionism', in Dennis Altman, Carole Vance, Martha Vicinus and Jeffrey Weeks (eds), *Homosexuality, Which Homosexuality? Essays for the International*

Scientific Conference on Lesbian and Gay Studies. London: GMP Publishers, 1989.

Vance, Carole S., 'Social Construction Theory: Problems in the History of Sexuality', in Dennis Altman, Carole Vance, Martha Vicinus and Jeffrey Weeks (eds), *Homosexuality, Which Homosexuality? Essays for the International Scientific Conference on Lesbian and Gay Studies*, London: GMP Publishers, 1989.

Watney, Simon. 'Practices of Freedom: "Citizenship", and the Politics of Identity in the Age of AIDS', in Enca Carter and S. Watney (eds), *Taking Liberties: AIDS and Cultural Politics*, London: Serpent's Tail, 1989.

10

Feminism

Bonnie Zimmerman

Introduction

Feminism is a term so ubiquitous that few of its users bother any more to define it. Nevertheless, in this essay I will attempt to explain its history, its multiple meanings, its role in the development of, first, Women's Studies and then Lesbian and Gay Studies, and its current status among scholars and activists. Feminism, in its most transparent definition, is the belief in the full potential of women and the equality of the sexes. But the matter is much more complex than that. Feminism may signify a political position, a theoretical methodology, a personal lifestyle, or a mode of interpretation. It may be all of these (and more) to one individual; it may be only one to others. An individual's understanding of what constitutes 'potential' and 'equality' may be radically different from another's. These factors, in part, account for acrimony among those who would call themselves feminists – including disagreements over who else may so name herself (or himself).

In all its forms, feminism has been a motivating force in the initiation and growth of the lesbian and gay movement, and even more influential in the development of gay and lesbian studies. Lesbians, not surprisingly, have embraced feminism more adamantly than have gay men, but the latter have found it to be a source of powerful arguments and theories as well. But in the 1990s, the influence, indeed dominance, of feminism over lesbian and gay theory has diminished considerably. This chapter will discuss how feminism came to be so influential, and how that influence waxed and waned. Perhaps of more value – for the uneasy relationship between lesbianism and feminism has been thoroughly analysed and polemicized – this chapter will attempt to distinguish between various strands within feminism and demonstrate which have come to be understood within Lesbian and Gay Studies as useful and influential ('good') and which pernicious and retrograde ('bad').

History

'Feminism', in the contemporary political climate, is a term of both approval and opprobrium. A product of the so-called second wave of feminism, beginning around 1968, the term was actually avoided by early proponents of the movement in favour of the more radical 'women's liberation'. In the 1990s, however, 'feminism' has come to signify all efforts to remove material and psychological barriers in women's path, and is simultaneously embraced by its adherents and rejected or questioned by its critics who include members of the political right as well as, ironically, the ideological left.

There is no consensus over the origin of the word 'feminism', although the best guess is that it entered the English language from France in the late nineteenth century, during what is now called the first wave of feminism. Historians can identify feminist individuals (such as Christine de Pisan or Mary Wollstonecraft) or discrete historical moments, but the great mass movement that resulted in profound social and ideological changes in the United States and Western Europe arose in the mid-nineteenth century, declined after the First World War, and then re-emerged in the late 1960s as one contingent in the social movements of the dispossessed that swept across much of the globe.

Feminism re-emerged, first, as the political agenda of the women's movement, which included a liberal or reformist wing devoted to changes in social policy (including equal pay for equal work, legalization of abortion, improved child care facilities, and so on) and a radical wing, which proposed a thoroughgoing revolution – the exact nature of which tended to be vague or utopian – as the only solution to women's oppression. As a politics, feminism is concerned with the material conditions of actual women's lives, and the relations of power that constrain or free them.

But feminism also developed as a mode of consciousness or understanding, a principle of self-development for individual women. A woman became a feminist, not necessarily by joining an organization, but by changing the way she viewed herself and the world through the process of 'consciousness-raising' (CR). CR, based roughly on the Chinese Communist process called 'speaking bitterness', was a kind of exorcism of traditional thoughts and beliefs through shared story-telling. In the 1970s, the feminist magazine *Ms.* popularized CR as 'the click! experience': one suddenly realized that everything one had been told about, for example, housework or vaginal orgasm was wrong, false, and oppressive, and replaced that false consciousness with a more honest and accurate knowledge developed through an analysis of one's own experience and that of other women. Early feminists took for granted that true and correct knowledge could be constructed out of shared experience, vastly underestimating the influence of social ideologies (including feminism itself) upon experiential knowing. Nevertheless, the centrality of CR underscores yet one more meaning for feminism: as a principle of knowledge-building and ultimately the theory and methodology of the discipline of Women's Studies.

Women's studies emerged concomitantly with the women's movement and powerfully solidified its influence in society. The first courses and programs in the US began in the late 1960s, and by the end of the 1970s a network of degree-granting programmes, scholarly journals and academic presses, and regional and national organizations had spread across that country and throughout the world. There is no doubt that feminist political agitation has had a tremendous impact in the West, leading to the legalization of abortion, the opening of numerous professions, the lessening of the wage gap, to name just a few concrete examples. Nevertheless, the most enduring success of feminism may well be in the academy. Millions of women and men have been introduced to feminism through a Women's Studies class in colleges and universities, and increasingly, secondary schools. And integral to the institutionalized discipline of Women's Studies in the 1970s and 1980s was lesbian studies.

Feminism, which feminism?

Before moving to a discussion of the influence of feminism on lesbian (and gay) studies, it may be helpful to distinguish some of the main variations of feminist theory and politics. General introductions to feminism often break it down into a number of fairly rigid typologies: liberal feminism, radical feminism, socialist feminism, and so forth. Such typologizing is often unhelpful in that it presents fluid, unstable, and interconnected variations as rigid and exclusive categories. Nonetheless, there were definite distinctions among various types of feminism, distinctions that often led to schisms within feminist groups and produced profoundly different agendas. The current status of feminism within contemporary Lesbian and Gay Studies depends largely upon which variety of feminism is being referenced.

Women's liberation activists in the late 1960s tended to position themselves in relation to one of three different approaches to the oppression and liberation of women. *Liberal* feminists in the USA joined structured organizations like the National Organization for Women or the National Women's Political Caucus, articulated a politics of equal access to jobs and reproductive freedom, emphasized individual choice, and worked for changes within the mainstream, usually legislative, arena. Liberal feminism was (and is) a politics of incremental social change and personal transformation.[1] *Marxist* or *socialist* feminism grew out of the student and anti-war movements known as the New Left (to distinguish it from the Old Left of the Communist party). Socialist feminists worked in either left-wing organizations or in autonomous women's groups, based their politics on Marxist class theory, emphasized women's role as workers within the family as well as the paid workforce, and worked for revolutionary changes in the modes of production.[2] *Radical* feminism developed in part as a reaction to both liberal and socialist feminism. Radical feminists argued, counter to socialist theory, that sex, not economic class, was the primary contradiction in women's lives; further, women *as women* constituted a class in struggle against men as a class. Radical feminists tended to create small, short-lived organizations, placed sexual issues like rape, objectification, and reproductive freedom at the heart of their political programme, and, like social feminists, believed in total revolution – although how that revolution was to proceed was less clear than in socialist feminism (which had the long Marxist tradition to provide a model).[3]

This division was never as sharp as a retrospective narrative makes it out to be. Most feminists might agree wholeheartedly with the revolutionary goals of radical or socialist feminism, while still supporting the evolutionary aims of liberal feminism. Many feminists aligned themselves with different approaches at different points in their lives. The history of feminist thought in the 1970s illustrates the ongoing attempt to modulate the central concerns of all approaches into an inclusive feminism that balanced the claims of class and sex, of production and reproduction, of revolution and reform.

At some point during the 1970s, a new variation on the feminist theme began to emerge, one that would have considerable repercussions for feminism as a whole. Named *cultural* feminism primarily by its critics, this variation tended to accept traditional 'essentialist' constructions of femininity or the female, yet invert the value that had been placed upon it. In other words, women or the female are *essentially* peaceful, nurturing, relational, sensitive, closer to nature – and these are the qualities necessary for

the survival of humanity. In place of political activity – which was conceptualized as male – cultural feminists offered creative forms, counter-
institutions, and lifestyle choices as an agenda for change.[4]

Historians of the period differ in their assessment of how influential
cultural feminism was. Some, like Alice Echols, argue that cultural feminism became virtually synonymous with the women's movement by the
end of the 1970s. In my opinion that is a gross over-estimation, but I certainly agree that cultural feminism became very influential and seeped into
all kinds of feminist statements and politics through the decade. This was
particularly momentous for lesbian feminism.

Like generic feminism, lesbian feminism is a politics, a theory, an ideology, a point of view, and a way of life. As such it is equally difficult to
define. Lesbian feminism postulates that lesbianism is more than a sexual
behaviour or lifestyle; it has, rather, political implications and ramifications. Because the oppression of women is based fundamentally upon their
position within the patriarchal family, and because the heterosexual relationship is structurally unequal, women who opt out of that system –
lesbians – are *de facto* revolutionaries. Moreover, because patriarchy is also
rooted in misogyny – the hatred of women by both men and women –
women who choose to give their love to women are undermining the fundamental assumptions of society. As Charlotte Bunch wrote, when
lesbians become feminists and feminists become lesbians, patriarchy tot-
ters on its last legs.

Lesbian feminism in the early 1970s was theoretically similar to radical feminism, sharing its emphasis on women as an oppressed group, sex
as the primary determinant of women's oppression, and total change, both
societal and individual, as its goal. But socialist feminism also left its mark,
especially in the importance of class differences and a material analysis of
lesbian lives. By the end of the decade, however, the tenets of cultural feminism had decidedly taken hold among women who identified as lesbian
feminists. This made lesbian feminism vulnerable to the sharp attacks on
cultural feminism that developed in the 1980s, primarily from postmodern
feminism and women of color feminism, both of which I will discuss
below.[5]

The transformation of feminism(s)

Whether liberal, radical, socialist or cultural, feminism describes lesbianism primarily as a gender identity. In this sense, lesbians are first and

foremost women who love women – emphasis on the 'women'. But that description was to change dramatically by the end of the 1980s – and in a number of different ways. First, the primacy of 'gender' over 'sexuality' as the cornerstone of lesbian identity was questioned by a number of prominent theorists (in conjunction with significant changes in society). And second, the assumption that gender (or any other discourse) in and of itself is sufficient to define the existence or identity of any individual woman was profoundly undermined by the theoretical positions articulated by women (mostly lesbians) of colour.

The first aspect of this 'deconstruction' of feminism can be found in the writings of a number of theorists associated with 'Queer Theory'. Gayle Rubin's 1975 article, 'The Traffic in Women', first coined the term 'sex-gender system', which gave to early feminist theory a powerful tool for analysing women's oppression across cultures. Her equally influential 1984 article, 'Thinking Sex', on the other hand, argued for the separation of sex and gender as categories of analysis. Sex, in the sense of sexual behaviours, structures, and meanings, needs to be theorized independent of its location in (male, female, or otherwise) gendered bodies. This controversial proposition is quite antithetical to classic feminism, which is rooted in the notion that all institutions, structures, and concepts have different impacts and meanings for women and for men. Hence, in *The Epistemology of the Closet*, Eve Kosofsky Sedgwick (1990) illustrates the distinctions between a politics and theory rooted in gender (feminism) and one rooted in sexuality (a precondition of Queer Theory). Clearly, the distinction is most crucial for lesbians, who may be conceptualized primarily as women in a gender-analysis (feminism) or as homosexuals in a sexuality-analysis (Queer Theory).

The relationship between gender and sex has been argued most influentially by Judith Butler, whose work can be said to have revolutionized feminism, in both its lesbian and heterosexual varieties. Unlike Rubin and Sedgwick (both of whose work has been more fruitful for gay male scholars than for lesbians), Butler does not separate sex and gender. But she also does not conceptualize it in the same way as 'classic' 1970s and 1980s feminism. For classic feminism, sex refers to the biological sub-stratum (nature, the real) upon which gender roles (society or culture, the representational) are built. Sex (male and female chromosomes, hormones, bodies) is the origin or base upon which a particular culture constructs an edifice of roles, behaviours, images and expectations which are transmitted through education, socialization, media, and so forth. Sexual difference cannot be changed, but gender can and must. Some feminists championed elimination of gender difference entirely, in favour of androgyny; others promoted the valorization of traditional feminine virtues (like pacifism and nurturance) for the betterment of society at large. But few questioned the equation 'sex is to nature as gender is to culture' until Butler.

For Butler, gender is a system of representation that makes sex possible. In other words, gender is the origin of sex (insofar as it is meaningful to even talk about origins) rather than the other way around. Gender is mandated by a compulsory heterosexuality (the term is borrowed from the feminist poet and theorist Adrienne Rich) that needs to construct human beings as two different and opposite sexes. Gender cannot be done away with as long as heterosexuality remains one of the regulatory regimes (the language is from Michel Foucault, a major influence upon Butler and all queer theorists) of society. But to accept gender constructions as they are is to remain locked into that very regulatory regime. One solution, insofar as there are any, may be to undermine naturalistic assumptions about sex and gender – that a particular gender 'belongs' to a particular sex, that any particular constructions of gender are natural and necessary – through inversion, parody, and play. Interestingly enough, this idea has led to the elevation of the drag queen and the transgendered individual into the political heroes of Queer Theory.

The writings of Rubin, Sedgwick, and Butler are part of the onslaught of postmodern theories that have profoundly influenced all academic work, including academic feminism. In addition to critiquing assumptions about the relationship between sex and gender, postmodern feminism questions a number of other widely-accepted propositions. For example, classic feminism is rooted in liberal humanist assumptions about unified identities, about experience as the grounding of knowledge and truth, about a pre-discursive reality that is represented in language and imagery. Postmodern feminism discards all these notions. Postmodern feminism instead argues that 'identity' is a fiction, a misrepresentation, the effect of discourse. Subjectivity is produced across multiple discourses of gender, sexuality, race, class, of which no single discourse can be isolated from the others. There is no access to 'reality', 'truth', or 'essences' except through their representations; in fact, reality and truth are nothing more than effects of representation. Identity categories such as 'woman', 'lesbian', or 'gay' are themselves sites of exclusion and limitation, because every identity (every sign) produces an excess that deconstructs it. For example, to define 'lesbian' as 'woman-identified woman' excludes butch lesbians, who then represent the excess that proves the insufficiency and instability of the definition (the sign). It is the very instability of these signs that produces radical resignifications and radical politics.

Postmodern feminism has been extremely influential within academic Women's Studies and generally productive of the new disciplines of gay and lesbian studies and Queer Theory. But it has not succeeded without controversy, protest, and resistance. Scholars who adhere to classic feminism and lesbian feminism dispute the idea that identities and labels are fictions and misrepresentations, arguing instead that an effective politics must be built upon unified and coherent social identities. Similarly, there is much resistance to the idea that everything is constructed in discourse, that there is no reality prior to discourse. Not only is this notion counter-intuitional (but then, so is much of feminism!), it seems to undermine feminism's political project of changing the material conditions of real women's lives. Postmodern feminism has difficulty articulating materiality and reality except as effects of representation, and that does not sit well with all feminists.

What have been unambiguously influential over all varieties of feminism and all academic feminists are the theoretical articulations of women of colour, both lesbian and heterosexual. Although many individuals might be named, including Cherríe Moraga, Paula Gunn Allen, Patricia Hill Collins, and Barbara Smith, arguably the most influential have been the African-American poet and essayist Audre Lorde and the Chicana multi-genre writer Gloria Anzaldúa. Not only are these writers foundational in the development of woman-of-colour feminism, they are also claimed (whether legitimately or not) for white feminism and Queer Theory.

Lorde and Anzaldúa, among many other theorists, identify the key limitation of classic (white) feminism: its tendency to construct monolithic representations of women and their needs. One problem with deriving politics from personal experience is that personal experience is always limited by the specific conditions and locations of race and class. If a white, middle-class feminist generalizes from her experience within a racist and classist society, then she will create a feminist politics and theory that speaks to and for only other white, middle-class women. And that is what happened, in both the first and second waves of Western feminism.

Hence, Lorde, Anzaldúa, and others anticipated postmodern feminism by critiquing the notion of a unitary feminist subject and politics. Instead, as the title of one of Audre Lorde's essays suggests, that subject and politics must be derived from the totality of women's experiences within related systems of 'age, race, class, and sex' (as well, of course, as nationality, religion, physical ability, and other systems). Anzaldúa created the figure of the 'mestiza' – a figure who stands 'in the borderlands' – to represent that multiplicity of identity markers; this figure has been adopted and metaphorized by numerous (non-Chicana) theorists and writers. On the other hand, women of colour, with some exceptions, have not typically theorized in the terms and concepts of postmodernism. While they dismiss the unified subject constructed by white middle-class feminism, their ideal is not the fragmented subject of postmodernism, but a 'whole' subject that integrates all the disparate parts that have been separated by racism and classism. Members of the Combahee River Collective (who included Barbara Smith), popularized the term 'identity politics' – and most theorists who are women of colour still argue that politics is necessarily rooted in an understanding of and commitment to *identity*: a social location that is external to the self, yet becomes part of the self. Far from dismissing the values of truth and reality, they tend to argue that there is a core of true knowledge and a real world that can be accessed through poetry and myth. Virtually all theorists of colour locate themselves within a materialist feminism in which real relations of production and reproduction precede representation and discourse.

I (like many others) would argue that lesbians of colour such as Anzaldúa, Lorde, and Smith, developed a third way within generic feminism – neither the monolithic feminism of white middle-class women in the 1970s nor the discursive feminism of postmodernists in the 1990s. For that reason they are claimed by both camps, yet retain insistently their own independent and vastly influential voice. That is certainly not to say that either lesbian feminism or postmodern feminism has thoroughly integrated these insights nor exorcized the pernicious effects of racism and classism. Too often, the works of Anzaldúa or Lorde are set in a course outline like a precious gem in a piece of jewellery – and then admired and praised without in any way becoming essential to the design of the whole. And yet, these writers and their ideas may well represent the future of feminist theory.

Feminism, Women's Studies, and lesbian studies

When academics began to address lesbian and gay issues in the 1970s, they faced a generally hostile environment. Homosexuality, when it was taught at all, was explained away as a deviant social behaviour or an abnormal psychological condition. The history and literature of lesbians and gay men was ignored, as was the wide range of sexual behaviours to be found across cultures. Lesbian and gay studies was not merely marginal – it was invisible.

Lesbian and gay academics began to express themselves in two locations. One was in caucuses of a few professional associations, most notably the Modern Language Association at whose meetings notable scholars and writers presented the opening salvos of an emergent field of inquiry. The second location was outside academic institutions, including community organizations such as the male-dominated Gay Academic Union (in the US) and local lesbian centres, and publications like *Sinister Wisdom* and *Conditions*. Not until the late 1980s did a united gay and lesbian studies find its place within mainstream academia.

However, lesbians did find in the newly emergent if marginalized Women's Studies courses and programmes a crack in the door through which it was possible to enter the universities and often thrive. Lesbian studies initially developed as one part of feminist education, within both independent Women's Studies programmes and organizations and the feminist sub-fields of specific disciplines such as literature and history. For this reason, there is a quite separate history of an independent lesbian studies in addition to the co-educational gay and lesbian studies that would emerge over a decade later. Despite the quite public and well-documented homophobia of many feminists, virtually all institutionally-based lesbian scholarship through the 1980s was accomplished within the context of Women's Studies. Gay male studies did not have such a 'home', and lagged behind lesbian studies to some degree. Exceptional works of individual scholarship are evident – for example, the work of John Boswell, Claude Summers, and Martin Duberman might be noted – but no substantial academic movement can be identified until the late 1980s.

Women's studies was a relatively hospitable place for lesbian scholarship because of its ideological base in feminism. Two different tendencies within feminism account for this. The first might be called its liberal idealism, specifically the emphasis upon the diversity and variety of women (which was, in fact, a long and hard-fought battle within feminism). Most Women's Studies courses and programmes paid at least lip service to 'women of all ages, races, classes, ethnicities, sexual preferences' – even if that litany did not make its way into the heart and soul of feminist knowledge-production. Hence, lesbians might be made welcome as one of those variations on womanhood to which all feminists were supposed to be sensitive. The second tendency within feminism was its radical critique of patriarchy or male dominance, including the institution of heterosexuality. It was within this critique that lesbian feminism and lesbian studies grew. The explicit theory and methodology of lesbian studies as it developed through the 1970s and 1980s, was feminism.

Feminism and the future of Lesbian and Gay Studies

As we approach the end of the twentieth century, the status of feminism as the privileged discourse of lesbian studies, the role of feminism in Queer Theory, and the relation of lesbian studies to gay male and queer studies are all heartily and healthily debated. As gay and lesbian studies has been institutionalized within universities and other sites of academic production, many argue (myself among them) that lesbian feminism and the particular history of an independent lesbian studies is increasingly being marginalized. Those of us who share this view worry that lesbians may become a subset of the universal gay male – thus returning us to the condition of silence and invisibility that helped to produce feminism in the first place. I will close, then, with these questions:

- Is feminism still relevant to the theoretical discourse of gay and lesbian studies?
- If so, what kind of feminism is it?
- If not, can gay and lesbian studies be meaningful to lesbians in particular, inside and outside the academy?

Since the early 1990s, it has been fashionable to question the relevance of feminism for Lesbian and Gay Studies. Feminism in general has been portrayed as impossibly homophobic and insufficiently multicultural, and lesbian feminism in particular as old-fashioned, 'essentialist', and anti-sexual. Whatever the truth of these allegations (and most are based upon mythmaking and ahistorical assumptions), the question must be posed: If not feminism, then what? To what alternate theory can Lesbian and Gay Studies turn? The answer seems to be Queer Theory, a rather loose and undefined (indeterminate) set of ideas and texts that derive largely from Foucault, but that would also claim feminism for itself. Many gay male scholars have found in feminism a powerful theoretical statement about the interconnection between sexism and homophobia. That is, much of the overt and covert hatred directed against gay men and lesbians can be traced to the challenge they pose to traditional gender roles: the sissy boy and diesel dyke. Progressive gay men have come to understand that their fight is closely aligned to the feminist movement. However, the version of feminism typically cited in Queer Theory is strictly postmodern and emphasizes gender play rather than gender oppression, sexual expression rather than sexual objectification, the realm of discourse and representation rather than that of material reality. For many lesbians in and out of the academy, this feminism is insufficient to fight against and transform patriarchy (or the sex/gender system).

Many (although not all) lesbian academics are also concerned that the type of feminism that is cited within Queer Theory (and thereby Lesbian and Gay Studies) is one that does not sufficiently analyse the actual differences of power and privilege between women and men – any more than it does differences of race and class. It is a feminism (and a race/class analysis) that is palatable to members of the privileged classes. This may result in lesbian studies being marginalized, or in (white) gay male interests and perspectives being falsely universalized. If lesbian interests have not been met within Women's Studies because of the difference of sexuality, then they will not be met any better within gay studies because of the difference of gender. Somehow the specificity of lesbian feminism and lesbian studies must be retained – even as individual lesbian scholars and students work within existing institutional locations, which rarely means lesbian studies programmes. How to do that, while reaffirming the critical role of feminism as the key theory of Lesbian and Gay Studies and thoroughly incorporating a race and class analysis: that is one of the clear challenges facing Lesbian and Gay Studies in the future.

Notes

1. On liberal feminism, see Gloria Steinem, *Outrageous Acts and Everyday Rebellions*. New York: Holt, Rinehart, and Winston, 1983.
2. On socialist feminism, see Nancy C.M. Hartsock, *Money, Sex, and Power: Toward a Feminist Historical Materialism*. Boston: Northeastern University Press, 1983.
3. On radical feminism, see Alice Echols, *Daring to be Bad: Radical Feminism in America 1967–1975*. Minneapolis: University of Minnesota Press, 1989.
4. On cultural feminism, see Echols.
5. No single text has yet been written defining and outlining lesbian feminism. For a general introduction, see Bonnie Zimmerman and Toni A.H. McNaron, *The New Lesbian Studies: Toward the 21st Century*. New York: The Feminist Press, 1996.

References

Anzaldúa, Gloria, *Borderlands/La Frontera: The New Mestiza*. San Francisco: Spinsters/Aunt Lute, 1987.

Bunch, Charlotte, *Passionate Politics: Essays 1968–1986*. New York: St. Martin's, 1987.

Butler, Judith, *Gender Trouble: Feminism and the Subversion of Identity*. New York: Routledge, 1990.

Echols, Alice, *Daring to Be Bad: Radical Feminism in America 1967–1975*. Minneapolis: Minnesota, 1989.

Lorde, Audre, *Sister Outsider*. Trumansburg: Crossing, 1984.

Rich, Adrienne, *Blood, Bread, and Poetry*. New York: Norton, 1986.

Rubin, Gayle, 'Thinking Sex: Notes for a Radical Theory of the Politics of Sexuality', in *Pleasure and Danger: Exploring Female Sexuality*, Boston: Routledge & Kegan Paul, 1984.

Rubin, Gayle, 'The Traffic in Women', in Rayna R. Reiter (ed.), *Toward an Anthropology of Women*, New York: Monthly Review Press, 1975.

Sedgwick, Eve Kosofsky, *Epistemology of the Closet*. Berkeley: California, 1990.

Further reading

Evans, Sara, *Personal Politics: The Roots of the Women's Liberation*. New York: Vintage, 1980.

Garber, Linda, *Tilting the Tower: Lesbians Teaching Queer Subjects*. New York: Routledge, 1994.

Hartsock, Nancy C. M., *Money, Sex, and Power: Toward a Feminist Historical Materialism*. Boston: Northeastern University Press, 1983.

Moraga, Cherríe, and Anzaldúa, Gloria (eds), *This Bridge Called My Back: Writings by Radical Women of Color*. New York: Kitchen Table: Women of Color Press, 1983.

Spender, Dale, *Feminist Theorists*. New York: Pantheon, 1983.

Stein, Arlene (ed.), *Sisters, Sexperts, Queers: Beyond the Lesbian Nation*. New York: Plume, 1993.

Steinem, Gloria, *Outrageous Acts and Everyday Rebellions*. New York: Holt, Rinehart and Winston, 1983.

Zimmerman, Bonnie and McNaron, Toni A.H., *The New Lesbian Studies: Toward the 21st Century*. New York: The Feminist Press, 1996.

11

Psychoanalysis and Sexual Identity

Christopher Lane

Does PSYCHOANALYSIS PRESCRIBE or demythologize gender and sexuality? Lesbian and Gay Studies seems unable to answer this question without doubt or occasional rancour. While feminism addressed a similar question in the 1970s and 1980s, using psychoanalysis to clarify an interminable debate between essentialism and constructivism, lesbian and gay scholars generally have ignored or rejected psychoanalytic arguments about sexual identity. Since medicine and psychiatry have defined homosexuality as a perversion and pathology for much of the twentieth century, psychoanalysis, to many lesbians and gay men, represents another coercive attempt to 'cure' them.

We need only recall the role of electroshock therapy and other brutal 'treatments' to understand that psychiatry and conservative psychology are generally hostile to homosexuality, and why lesbians and gay men are averse to 'scientific' definitions of same-sex desire. But since psychoanalysis and psychiatry view sexuality quite differently, given their respective definitions of the unconscious, it is not historically accurate to merge psychoanalysis with psychiatry in order to dismiss both. Nor would it be wise to do so, as psychoanalysis has advanced invaluable points about fantasy, desire, identification, and phobia.

As feminism needed to identify the complex history of psychoanalysis to clarify its diverse lineages and sometimes contradictory perspectives on femininity, so Lesbian and Gay Studies has begun recently to erode a set of assumptions about psychic accounts of homosexuality. Among others, Leo Bersani, Arnold I. Davidson, Tim Dean, Teresa de Lauretis, John Fletcher, Diana Fuss, Lynda Hart, Noreen O'Connor and Joanna Ryan, Judith Roof, and Kaja Silverman have stressed the immense value of identifying the stakes of public and psychic fantasy, not least to grasp the complex history of homosexuality in the West.[1] Many of these critics have also begun to clarify the remarkable implications of Freud's undertaking, using psychoanalysis to interpret the role of fantasy and desire in all sexual arrangements.

Henry Abelove has also documented that key psychoanalytic figures waited impatiently for Freud's death to reverse his arguments about homosexuality and his growing critique of heterosexuality (1985–86, pp. 59–69). Abelove notes the subsequent emergence of ego-psychology in North America, showing how psychology and psychiatry revised Freud's arguments about male and female homosexuality. Such revisions endorsed a normative account of sexual identity and an intolerance of homosexuality. In *The Repression of Psychoanalysis: Otto Fenichel and the Political Freudians* (1973, pp. 5–8, 12–15, 77, 112–13, 115) Russell Jacoby further demonstrates that conservative clinicians and psychiatrists in the 1930s found psychoanalytic inquiry too threatening; they transformed Freud's arguments about sexuality's inherent tension with society into a demand that their patients adapt their desires to fit social norms. Ironically, Freud's *Civilization and Its Discontents* (1930) emphasizes the *price* we endure for subjectivity in such cultural and social conditions.

Given his historical period, Freud's disbelief concerning most of these contemporaneous arguments about sexual normativity and perversion is remarkable. His frustration with sexology and ego-based psychology led him to identify the unconscious, which then generated his interest in the 'perverse' dimension of all human desire. By 'perverse', Freud meant that sexuality is fundamentally at odds with social identity. In this respect, psychoanalysis *cannot* make adaptive arguments – or suggestions about treatment and cures – without going against the grain of Freud's thought. Indeed, in defeating claims that sexuality is entirely self-evident and subjectivity thoroughly coherent, the unconscious *assists* Lesbian and Gay Studies' claims about sexuality's 'queer' properties. By downplaying the unconscious, however, and suggesting that desire is conscious, performative, and malleable (i.e., a matter of political choice), Lesbian and Gay Studies not only ignores the 'queerest' dimension of psychoanalysis but also fosters normative (and sometimes antisexual) arguments about lesbian and gay egos. As Tim Dean contends, Freud represents the ego as 'hostil[e] to both difference and desire' (1995, p. 122). In this respect, claims of sexual coherence, of the sort routinely advanced by lesbian and gay critics, ultimately defeat suggestions that lesbian or gay desire is inherently radical. By analysing the unconscious, Freud shattered many of the ruling assumptions of his time, compelling people to recognize that they could not attribute all of their thoughts, words and actions to conscious behaviour.

Many feminists have argued that Freud was simply looking for additional methods to suppress women, as though he and psychoanalysis were another cog in a vast patriarchal machine.[2] As before, however, we must distinguish between Freud's intentions for psychoanalysis and the ways in which turn-of-the-century European culture (and many later psychologists and psychiatrists) tried to use Freud's work for repressive effects. By addressing developments in Freud's work and the history of psychoanalysis, Jacqueline Rose and Juliet Mitchell clarify that psychoanalysis reframes the idea of femininity and female sexuality as respectively social and biological entities. Refusing to see gender and sexuality as innate or self-evident, psychoanalysis adds a crucial political dimension to cultural demands that we reduce female sexuality to femininity, and vice versa. As Rose argues,

> [The unconscious's] challenge to the concept of psychic identity is important for feminism in that it allows into the political arena problems of subjectivity (subjectivity *as* a problem) which tend to be suppressed from other forms of political debate. [The unconscious] may also help us to open up the space between different notions of political identity – between the idea of a political identity for feminism (what women require) and that of a feminine identity for women (what women are or should be). (Rose, 1986, p. 103; Mitchell, 1974)

Psychoanalysis therefore allows a form of 'protest' to surface that is rarely heard or allowed in conventional political debates; it also refutes the idea that language, sexuality and reality are simple, commonsense terms. As Rose explains, 'psychoanalysis, through its attention to symptoms, slips of the tongue and dreams (that is, what *insists* on being spoken against what is *allowed* to be said) appears above all as a challenge to the self-evidence and banality of everyday life and language, which have also, importantly, constituted the specific targets of feminism' (1986, p. 86).

Rose and Mitchell argue that Freud established psychoanalysis precisely to *alleviate* the misery and suffering of his patients, many of them women, who went to him voluntarily; such claims are entirely consistent with Freud's arguments about hysteria. Yet these points disappear in the feminist argument that 'consent' as such could not exist in this scenario (a claim depriving women entirely of agency). Overall, the psychoanalytic argument that the unconscious resists meaning and bedevils identity gets lost amid related feminist claims that women refusing psychological treatment by advancing hysteria were somehow championing their freedom. Similar points about female and childhood sexuality also get absorbed by the 'Foucauldian' claim that psychoanalysis was a site of 'power/knowledge', anxious to make its patients confess their desires and errors. Foucault did attribute power to late-nineteenth-century fields of knowledge but, as we shall see, his relation to psychoanalysis was much more complicated than this summary implies.

Freud rejected conventional accounts of hysteria because he grasped that hysteria is not emancipatory or enjoyable, but in fact the reverse. Many women undoubtedly were reacting against the material and psychic strictures they endured in Victorian culture, but to see psychoanalysis as complicit in – or even, improbably, as the cause of – their illness overlooks all of the arguments Freud formulated at the time in their defence. Unlike many of his contemporaries, who responded to their patients' complaints by depriving them of stimulation or compelling them to endure the notorious 'rest cure', Freud insisted on taking these women seriously. As Rose argues, correcting Jeffrey Masson, 'To argue that Freud dismissed the traumas of his patients as "the fantasies of hysterical women who invented stories and told lies" is a total misconstrual of the status psychoanalysis accords to fantasy, which was never assigned by Freud to the category of wilful untruth' (1986, p. 13). Rose notes that Masson, much later in his book, eventually concedes that Freud did not say that the hysterical fantasy was a lie (1986, p. 13n).

To engage the Foucauldian argument that psychoanalysis compounded medical and psychiatric sites of power/knowledge, we must note that Foucault's relationship to psychoanalysis was inconsistent and ambivalent, and that only certain elements of this ambivalence surface in his published work. Foucault's recent biographer, David Macey, attests that prior to Foucault's early formulations of psychoanalysis, he had asked the Parisian analyst Daniel Lagache about the prerequisites for a career in psychology (1993, p. 37). Didier Eribon, another of Foucault's biographers, claims that Foucault simultaneously considered beginning analysis with Lagache (1989, pp. 61–62). Rejecting Louis Althusser's advice that he receive hospital treatment for depression, Foucault eventually began a brief period of analysis in 1948, and he attended Jacques Lacan's seminars in the 1950s while following his work with interest (Macey, pp. 36, 69; p. 513, n.26). Macey further notes that Foucault wrote a brief tribute to Lacan, after his death in 1981, calling him 'the liberator of psychoanalysis' (quoted in Macey, p. 422). For these reasons, it may not surprise us that Foucault concluded *The Order of Things* (1966) by supporting Freud's account of the unconscious:

> It must not be supposed that the Freudian approach is the combination of an interpretation of meaning and a dynamics of resistance and defence. By following the same path as the human sciences, but with its gaze turned the other way, psychoanalysis moves towards the moment – by definition inaccessible to any theoretical knowledge of man, to any continuous apprehension in terms of signification, conflict, or function – at which the contents of consciousness articulate themselves, or rather stand gaping, upon man's finitude. (1970, p. 374)

Foucauldians often invoke *The History of Sexuality, Volume One* as indicative of Foucault's later frustration with psychoanalysis, but Foucault deliberately (and correctly) did *not* include Freud in his critique of 'the repressive hypothesis' (1978, pp. 81, 119); to suggest he did misrepresents both thinkers.[3] Foucault attributed this hypothesis to Wilhelm Reich and, implicitly, to Herbert Marcuse, each claiming that because society represses human sexuality, 'liberating' this sexuality must somehow revolutionize contemporary society (Foucault, 1978, p. 5). From 1908 on, Freud did critique what he disdainfully called '"civilized" sexual morality', but he did not (and with good reason) advance claims about sexuality's revolutionary potential; he grasped that the unconscious is not a simple herald of political change (1908, pp. 181–204). Noting Freud's divergence from Reich and Marcuse in a way that Foucault's Anglo-American readers surprisingly have not, Foucault represents psychoanalysis as an ally for lesbians and gay men precisely against narrow contemporaneous emphases on sexual normativity:

> It is very well to look back from our vantage point and remark upon the normalizing impulse in Freud; one can go on to denounce the role played for many years by the psychoanalytic institution; but the fact remains that in the great family of technologies of sex, which goes so far back into the history of the Christian West, of all those institutions that set out in the nineteenth century to medicalize sex, [psychoanalysis] was the one that, up to the decade of the forties, *rigorously opposed* the political and institutional effects of the perversion-hereditary-degenerescence system. (1978, p. 119, my emphasis)

Those who insist otherwise, Foucault implies, have simply not read Freud. Later in this volume, Foucault draws heavily on Freudian-Lacanian arguments to conceptualize his own claims about power-without-repression. Unfortunately, Foucault declares no sooner than at the start of the fourth section of *Volume One*:

> In point of fact, the assertion that sex is not 'repressed' is not altogether new. Psychoanalysts have been saying the same thing for some time. They have challenged the simple little machinery that comes to mind when one speaks of repression; the idea of a rebellious energy that must be throttled has appeared to them inadequate for deciphering the manner in which power and desire are joined to one another; they consider them to be linked in a more complex and primary way than through the interplay of a primitive, natural, and living energy welling up from below, and a higher order seeking to stand in its way. (1978, p. 81)

Had this argument surfaced in the first few pages of Foucault's study, where it clearly belongs, the resulting confusion about psychoanalysis and the 'repressive hypothesis' probably would not have occurred. Foucault is heavily indebted to Jacques Lacan in this passage (and does not say so), but he does argue correctly that Freud rejected a 'hydraulic' notion of repression, in which external pressure manifests itself as internal symptoms. Freud advanced a more complex and interesting argument about the subject's asymmetrical relation to the external world – an argument Reich, Marcuse, and many others misunderstood in their endeavour to translate Freudian psychoanalysis into a radical, emancipatory tool for social transformation.

Drawing then on Foucault's insistence that pre-1940s psychoanalysis was not a site of power/knowledge, we can clarify that Freud advanced a more sophisticated understanding of sexual desire than most of his contemporaries seemed able to tolerate. In the 1910 and 1915 revisions of his *Three Essays on the Theory of Sexuality*, first published in 1905, Freud made the following astonishing claim: 'Psycho-analytic research . . . has found that all human beings are capable of making a homosexual object-choice and have in fact made one in their unconscious' (1905, p. 145n). And he elaborates: 'From the point of view of psycho-analysis, the exclusive sexual interest felt by men for women is also a problem that needs elucidating and is not a self-evident fact based upon an attraction that is ultimately of a chemical nature' (1905, p. 145n). As Dean shows, such arguments reveal that Freud's theory of sexuality is not only antidevelopmental but also profoundly antiheterosexist (1995, pp. 129–30).

Many lesbian and gay scholars acknowledge some, even most, of these points, seeing Freud as a helpful precursor to Queer Theory; nonetheless they reintroduce social and cultural context as the fly in the ointment. In her influential study *Epistemology of the Closet* (1990), Eve Kosofsky Sedgwick summarizes her thoughts on psychoanalysis in the following hurried and abstruse way:

> It was in the period of the so-called 'invention of the homosexual' that Freud gave psychological texture and credibility to the countervalent, universalizing mapping of this territory, based on the supposed protean mobility of sexual desire and on the potential bisexuality of every human creature; a mapping that implies no presumption that one's sexual penchant will always incline toward persons of a single gender, and that offers, additionally, a richly denaturalizing description of the psychological motives and mechanisms of male paranoid, projective homophobic definition and enforcement. Freud's antiminoritizing account only gained, moreover, in influence by being articulated through a developmental narrative in which heterosexist and masculinist ethical sanctions found ready camouflage. (p. 84)

Freud's claims are much more sophisticated than Sedgwick acknowledges, for psychoanalysis deliberately does *not* propose that homosexuality affects only a sexual minority, Freud is refuting the conservative (and ultimately coercive) notion that there is an innate or 'congenital' predisposition to same-sex attraction (Sedgwick calls this argument 'minoritizing'). Freud underscored the limitations of *both* 'minoritizing' and 'universalizing' perspectives on homosexuality when insisting in 1905, 'libidinal attachments to persons of the same sex play no less a part as factors in normal mental life . . . than do similar attachments to the opposite sex' (p. 145n). Recognizing both the social relevance and psychic particularity of homosexual and heterosexual attachments, Freud strove to clarify the meaning of sexuality for each register without dissolving homosexuality into heterosexuality. Indeed, his thoughts on the efficacy of interpreting dreams, fantasies and psychic conflicts in his patients could not have proceeded without attending to the particularity of sexuality in individual subjects.

Alert to the dangers of proposing only a 'minoritizing' perspective,

Freud declared that 'psychoanalytic research is most decidedly opposed to any attempt at separating off homosexuals from the rest of mankind as a group of a special character' (1905, p. 145n). Why? Because the role of unconscious fantasies and identifications in every subject challenge the 'minoritizing' perspective, regardless of the subject's sexual preference. Freud also grasped that contrary claims – that is, support for 'innate' definitions of sexuality – would foster spurious debates about congenital predispositions, in which lesbians and gay men represent a 'third sex', as advocated by such sexologists as Magnus Hirschfeld and Karl Heinrich Ulrichs.

Freud's twofold critique of 'minoritizing' and 'universalizing' accounts of lesbian and gay desire mystified Hirschfeld, who strove to retain a model of congenital predisposition while ridding it of assumptions about pathology and sickness: 'I have sincerely tried to fathom the views put forward in recent years by Freud and his school, designed to show the influence of non-congenital factors. But the more I have done so, the more clearly I have found that what Freud's doctrine maintains as to the effect of external childhood events on human sexual development is fundamentally incorrect' (1926, pp. 39–40). Using contemporary terms, we could say that Hirschfeld critiqued Freud for 'de-gaying' the minoritizing argument Hirschfeld wanted to shore up.

In the citation above, Hirschfeld refers to Freud's seduction theory, which Freud revised in the late 1890s by defining sexuality as the complex result of external events and internal fantasies (this recalls Rose's argument with Masson). Where then does this leave Sedgwick, who, despite rejecting the congenital model, nonetheless reproduces most of Hirschfeld's complaints about psychoanalysis? Freud's case studies of 'Dora' (1905, 1901), 'Little Hans' (1909), 'the Rat Man' (1909), President Schreber (1911, produced only from an interpretation of Schreber's writing), 'the Wolf Man' (1914, 1918), and 'the Young Woman' (1920)[4] in themselves refute the idea that psychoanalysis is simply 'universalizing'. Since Sedgwick insists otherwise, she contradicts the Foucauldian claim that psychoanalysis is oppressive when analysing patients *in their particularity*. Let us draw out the implications of these different claims; they clarify a persistent mischaracterization of psychoanalysis: as the above quotations from Freud's *Three Essays* attest, psychoanalysis is neither 'minoritizing' nor 'universalizing'. Sedgwick nonetheless wants to *retain* a specific focus on lesbians and gay men in order to prevent a more expansive reading of homosexual desire. In doing so, she ends up supporting the 'reverse discourse' that Foucault critiques as a nineteenth-century tendency to consider 'the homosexual . . . [as] a species' (1978, pp.101, 43). Like Freud, Foucault rejected the idea that homosexuals constitute a 'species'; like Freud, too, Foucault rejected the idea that sexuality is revolutionary and an obvious precursor to social change.

Unconcerned by these contradictions, Sedgwick tries to critique psychoanalysis in every conceivable way. When psychoanalysis addresses individuals in their particularity (as Sedgwick presumably would want), she rejects it as oppressive, intrusive, and definitional – a claim immediately forgetting that analysis was voluntary and formed to alleviate suffering (1990, pp. 23–24); Foucauldians also might heed this point. And when psychoanalysis *critiques* late-nineteenth-century culture for defining individuals in terms of their sexuality – a critique, Foucault notes, that lasted until Freud's death in 1939 (recall: psychoanalysis 'up to the decade of the forties, *rigorously opposed* the political and institutional effects of the perversion-hereditary-degenerescence system' [1978, p. 119]) – Sedgwick accuses it of despecifying issues particular to lesbians and gay men (1990, p. 90).

We can deduce that Anglo-American Foucauldians are confused (in a way Foucault generally was not) about the repercussions of defining homosexuality by 'types' of people rather than sexual acts. In promoting what Foucault calls sexuality's 'veritable discursive explosion' (1978, p. 17), 'the bourgeois order' (p. 5) becomes a factor Sedgwick and others need almost to thank for promoting the homosexual visibility they are intent on retaining. John D'Emilio (1983) has at least acknowledged that late-nineteenth-century capitalism and culture profoundly enabled this century's civil rights and liberation movements by promoting economic and familial independence, and by forging the sexual identities that lesbians and gay men have since wrested from medicine and science (1983, pp. 104–6). Yet Foucault was less conflicted than his readers in responding to this sexual visibility, preferring to represent sexuality as a set of acts rather than a form of identity or speech. Such indeed is the logical effect of his wish to dismantle assumptions about 'the uniform truth of sex' (1978, p. 69). Paradoxically, Freud's arguments about psychic drives fully endorse Foucault's suspicions here, an irony critics who characterize psychoanalysis in simplistic ways fail to note.

Contemporary Queer Theory is ambivalent about Foucault's preference for 'acts' rather than 'identities', however, since it wants to celebrate 'perverse' visibility without the constraints of identity politics. All the same, Queer Theory at crucial points rebels against its push for sexual diffusion, seeing the side effects of its arguments as coercive bids to repress or absorb homosexuality's radicalism. Queer theorists such as Sedgwick, Judith Butler, Ed Cohen, and Elizabeth Grosz accept that sexuality marshalled in the name of identity is bound to reproduce a 'discursive regime' very similar to the one Foucault critiqued when remarking of sexology and psychology, 'The nineteenth-century homosexual became a personage, a past, a case history, and a childhood, in addition to being a type of life. . . . The sodomite had been a temporary aberration; the homosexual was now a species' (1978, p. 104).[5] Countering these constraints, these and other theorists aim to produce a fluid politics that tries to displace binary logic (heterosexuality versus homosexuality) by promoting a form of polymorphous perversity. In her Introduction to *Tendencies*, for instance, Sedgwick provides several long lists characterizing the types of sexuality she calls 'queer' (1991, pp. 105–6). Yet since this fluidity is also despecifying (i.e., 'antiminoritizing') and therefore 'de-gaying', many proponents of Queer Theory try to define the 'perverse' *against* the apparent coherence of a sexual 'norm', thus setting up their own binary and in the process forgetting Freud's argument that the unconscious undermines such binary oppositions. As Dean astutely observes, many queer theorists are forced disingenuously 'to *reinvent* fundamental psychoanalytic concepts, such as the unconscious and sexuality – that is, to eschew Freud while nonetheless insisting on all the ways in which sexuality is unnatural, difficult, perverse' (1995, p. 122). The result is a good deal of substantive and conceptual confusion, in which psychoanalysis seems to be both the perpetrator of a monstrous crime – heightened sexual scrutiny, increased social surveillance – and an interrogative force challenging our society's insistence on sexual conformity.[6] What does it mean to adopt a discourse suffused with such terms as 'fetishism', 'disavowal', 'projection', and 'displacement', only to contend that one hundred years ago these terms were tantamount to political and sexual oppression? Is there not something opportunistic – even critically dishonest – in adopting these terms for a 'queer' critique without acknowledging their debt to Freudian psychoanalysis? By dismissing the conceptual work informing 'the repressive hypothesis' (and thus most of the sexual arguments formulated by the Frankfurt School), Queer Theory produces quite impoverished notions of sexual desire and identification. Emphasizing 'performativity' as a strategy to avoid psychoanalysis and the unconscious not only eclipses crucial chapters in the history of Western homosexuality, but also can produce facile and voluntaristic – that is, ego-based – notions of sexual desire (Dean, 1995, p. 122).

By insisting that men and women are subject to the unconscious, psychoanalysis is 'anti-identitarian', in the sense that it pits sexuality against coherent and normative definitions of identity. Indeed, that psychoanalysis comes closest to offering the type of sexual fluidity Queer Theory wants to promote attests to the way the latter has advanced confused and contradictory notions of the unconscious, fantasy, and identification (Dean, 1995, pp. 126–27, 132–3).

Since psychoanalysis is not the enemy of homosexual desire, but just the reverse, we can begin to see how useful it is for Lesbian and Gay Studies. When formulating arguments that are critical of both society and ego-based definitions of desire, Freud did not excuse psychoanalysis from cultural prejudice, intolerance, and homophobia, as many Foucauldians and queer theorists claim (Sedgwick, 1990, pp. 23–24). On the contrary, to invoke only three examples, in '"Civilised" Sexual Morality and Modern Nervous Illness' (1908), 'Thoughts for the Times on War and Death' (1915), and in his 1930 book, *Civilization and Its Discontents*, Freud consistently criticized modern Western societies for compelling their subjects to live 'beyond their psychic means'.[7] In such circumstances, Freud argued, neurosis is the subject's only reprieve from society's relentless and intolerable demands. 'Experience teaches us', Freud wrote in 1908, correcting Christian von Ehrenfels, W. Erb, and Ludwig Binswanger, 'that for most people there is a limit beyond which their constitution cannot comply with the demands of civilization. All who wish to be more noble-minded than their constitution allows fall victim to neurosis; they would have been more healthy if it could have been possible for them to be less good' (1908, p. 191). For contemporary identity politics, this insistence on internal obstacles to full sexual expression appears to restrict our capacity for self- and group invention. Yet since it is erotophilic in a way that society is not, psychoanalysis offers us a vital reprieve from the demand to be 'good'. For this reason, I want to conclude by highlighting the ramifications of arguments ignoring Freud's interest in psychic and sexual resistance to consciousness and 'civilization'.

Freud's arguments about resistance are complex, in part because they supplement perspectives that address only the history of prejudice and limited public representation of same-sex desire. The way society represents stable roles for lesbians and gay men powerfully affects how we and others internally represent our desire, but to consider this difficulty merely a reproduction of cultural forms does not help us; it limits our grasp on the astonishing discrepancy between laws and their internal enactment or denial. Nor is it valuable simply to dismiss what is psychically difficult about sexual identity in order to forgo an encounter with psychoanalysis. Psychoanalysis neither 'robs' people of sexual security nor forgets how difficult it is to reach sexual self-acceptance. On the contrary, psychoanalysis emphasizes the value of striving for this acceptance, given its precise understanding of the difficulties besetting such a task. Claiming that psychoanalysis undermines 'sexual identity' misjudges the very field that formulates what an identity based on sexuality might be.

This point compels us to rethink popular accounts of subjectivity that extend only to the 'construction' of desire, personality, and identity. Such accounts assume that the subject acts according to its 'choice' or, conversely, is acted on by forces that take this choice away. More sophisticated arguments about the compromise of identity and the performance of desire do not fundamentally alter the precepts of this theory; despite claiming otherwise, they return us to the idea that desire is moulded or shaped by 'choice' or its absence. Every long and heated debate in the 1970s and 1980s over the 'construction' and 'essential nature' of same-sex desire reproduced this binary by suggesting that sexual-identity choices are fully conscious (i.e., determined by the ego) or non-existent (i.e., predetermined by the body's 'biology'). For the reasons I have elucidated, as well as a mistaken conflation of psychoanalysis with psychiatry's appalling institutional record, neither side has properly understood or advanced psychoanalytic accounts of identification. Psychoanalysis contends that internal constraints, psychic history, and an ineluctable resistance to speech and self-knowledge radically affect our object choice, regardless of our performative aims.

Reframing the idea of choice without fixing desire in nature (hormones, chromosomes, and so on), psychoanalysis falls between constructivism and essentialism. To suggest that one decides to be gay or lesbian is psychically distinct from maintaining that one elects to produce homosexual desire. This distinction raises a crucial but often ignored point about heterosexual anxiety regarding the presence of lesbians and gay men in the military and classroom: although we have a certain (albeit limited) choice about symbolizing sexual identity, we cannot master or consciously regulate sexuality's unconscious meanings. That is why constructivist accounts of desire – and phobic appropriations of them in the service of homosexual 'cures' – misunderstand the crucial dynamism of sexuality in its unconscious forms.

This paradox of identity illustrates the stakes informing modern theories of gay and lesbian identity. Sometimes engendering discomfort and anxiety, and always engendering uncertainty, this paradox prevents us from representing homosexuality and heterosexuality as stable and separate phenomena. Such emphasis denies that external impositions of discourse and power alone create homosexuality's structure. Beyond the crucial point that sexuality does not simply correlate with politics and history, we cannot understand past or present forms of identification without accepting the unbridgeable gap between public symbolizations of sexuality and internal – often unconscious – patterns of fantasy and self-definition. Another factor – the unconscious – insists on being *heard* in all these discussions, though it is notoriously difficult to talk about because it disturbs consciousness and reminds us that sexuality is not always self-evident and commonsensical.

We cannot override this gap by fantasizing that interpretation or politics will eventually master sexual enigmas. If psychoanalysis has taught us anything, it is to recognize that identities 'lean' on absence and doubt. This gap between the subject and its symbolic register is a space allowing identity to function and turn awry; without this gap, we would indeed be robbed of psychic and political transformation, since we would be locked in determinism. To consider the performative a path to freedom and emancipation is thus to misunderstand a crucial point: this gap returns 'sexual communities' to their uncertain and fragile consistency; there is unfortunately no psychic guarantee of their permanence or stability. This is the flip side of what can otherwise appear so liberating: a loss of guarantees.

For an example of this gap, consider the confusion arising from within lesbian and gay politics when 'protective' legislation fails to safeguard against social homophobia. Acts of legislation cannot mandate levels of tolerance, public fantasy, or urban hatred, but they can influence climates of official discrimination. Protective legislation is therefore a worthwhile and justifiable goal, but we must also recognize that the impossibility of safe and coherent communities obtains precisely from 'a resistance to identity at the heart of psychic life' (Rose, 1986, p. 91). Acknowledging that this resistance partly determines the shape and vigour of lesbian and gay identities, studies, and communities would give us more leeway in interpreting these phenomena. Indeed, by accepting this fluidity in its diverse psychic and communal forms, we might achieve more purchase on the ambivalence surrounding our desires' remarkable persistence.

Notes

1. See Leo Bersani, *The Freudian Body: Psychoanalysis and Art*. New York: Columbia University Press, 1986; Arnold I. Davidson, 'How to Do the History of Psychoanalysis: A Reading of Freud's *Three Essays on the Theory of Sexuality*', in Françoise Meltzer (ed.), *The Trial(s) of Psychoanalysis*. Chicago: University of Chicago Press, 1988, pp. 39–64; Tim Dean, 'On the Eve of a Queer Future', in *Raritan*, Vol. 15, No. 1, 1995, pp. 116–34; Teresa de Lauretis, *The Practice of Love: Lesbian Sexuality and Perverse Desire*. Bloomington: Indiana University Press, 1994; John Fletcher, 'Freud and His Uses: Psychoanalysis and Gay Theory', in Simon Shepherd and Mick Wallis (eds.), *Coming On Strong: Gay Politics and Culture*. London: Unwin Hyman, 1989, pp. 90–118; Diana Fuss, *Identification Papers*. New York: Routledge, 1995; Lynda Hart, *Fatal Women: Lesbian Sexuality and the Mark of Aggression*. Princeton: Princeton University Press, 1994; Noreen O'Connor and Joanna Ryan, *Wild Desires and Mistaken Identities: Lesbianism and Psychoanalysis*. New York: Columbia University Press, 1993; Judith Roof, 'Freud Reads Lesbians', *A Lure of Knowledge: Lesbian Sexuality and Theory*. New York: Columbia University Press, 1991, pp. 174–215; Kaja Silverman, 'A Woman's Soul Enclosed in a Man's Body: Femininity in Male Homosexuality', *Male Subjectivity at the Margins*. New York: Routledge, 1992, pp. 356–73.
2. For instance Elizabeth Wilson, 'Psychoanalysis: Psychic Law and Order', in *Feminist Review*, Vol. 8, 1981, pp. 63–78.
3. For instance Nancy Armstrong, *Desire and Domestic Fiction: A Political History of the Novel*. New York: Oxford University Press, 1987.
4. Freud, 'Fragment of an Analysis of a Case of Hysteria' (1905 [1901]), *Standard Edition*, VII; 'Analysis of a Phobia in a Five-Year-Old Boy' (1909), *Standard Edition*, X; 'Notes upon a Case of Obsessional Neurosis' (1909), *Standard Edition*, X; 'Psychoanalytic Notes on an Autobiographical Account of a Case of Paranoia (Dementia Paranoides) (1911 [1910]), *Standard Edition*, XII; 'From the History of an Infantile Neurosis' (1918 [1914]), *Standard Edition*, XVII; and 'The Psychogenesis of a Case of Female Homosexuality' (1920), *Standard Edition*, XVIII.
5. See Sedgwick, 'Queer and Now', *Tendencies*. Durham: Duke University Press, 1993, pp. 7–8; Judith Butler, *Gender Trouble: Feminism and the Subversion of Identity*. New York: Routledge, 1990, pp. 35–78; Ed Cohen, 'Foucauldian Necrologies: "Gay" "Politics"? Politically Gay?', in *Textual Practice*, Vol. 2, No. 1, 1988, pp. 87–101; and Elizabeth Grosz, *Volatile Bodies: Toward a Corporeal Feminism*. Bloomington: Indiana University Press, 1994.

6. For examples see Sedgwick, *Epistemology of the Closet*, 1990, p. 84; Dollimore, *Sexual Dissidence*, Oxford: Clarendon Press, 1991, pp. 191–204; Butler, *Gender Trouble*, New York: Routledge, 1990, pp. 35–78.
7. Although this argument appears in all these texts, the quotation is from Freud's 'Thoughts for the Times on War and Death', *Standard Edition XIV*, 1915, p. 284.

References

Abelove, Henry, 'Freud, Male Homosexuality and the Americans', in *Dissent*, Vol. 33, No. 1, 1985–86.

Dean, Tim, 'On the Eve of a Queer Future', in *Raritan*, Vol. 15, No. 1, 1995, pp. 116–34.

D'Emilio, John, 'Capitalism and Gay Identity', in Ann Snitow, Christine Stansell and Sharon Thompson (eds), *Powers of Desire: The Politics of Sexuality*. New York: Monthly Review Press, 1983.

Eribon, Didier, *Michel Foucault*. Paris: Flammarion, 1989.

Foucault, Michel, *The History of Sexuality, Vol. 1: An Introduction* (trans. Robert Hurley). New York: Pantheon, 1978.

Foucault, Michel, *The Order of Things: An Archaeology of the Human Sciences*. New York: Pantheon, 1970.

Freud, Sigmund, '"Civilised" Sexual Morality and Modern Nervous Illness' (1908), in *The Standard Edition of the Complete Psychological Works of Sigmund Freud, VIII*, (ed. and trans. James Strachey). London: Hogarth, 1953-74.

Freud, Sigmund, *Three Essays on the Theory of Sexuality. Standard Edition, VII*, 1905.

Hirschfeld, Magnus, *Geschlechtskunde*. Vol. 1. Stuttgart, 1926, p. 194, quoted in Martin Dannecker, *Theories of Homosexuality* (trans. David Fernbach), London: Gay Men's Press, 1981.

Jacoby, Russell, *The Repression of Psychoanalysis: Otto Fenichel and the Political Freudians*. New York: Basic, 1973.

Macey, David, *The Lives of Michel Foucault*. New York: Pantheon, 1993.

Mitchell, Juliet, *Psychoanalysis and Feminism*. London: Allen Lane, 1974.

Rose, Jacqueline, 'Femininity and Its Discontents', in *Sexuality in the Field of Vision*. London: Verso, 1986.

Sedgwick, Eve Kosofsky, *Epistemology of the Closet*. Berkeley: University of California Press, 1990.

Sedgwick, Eve Kosofsky, 'Queer and Now', in *Tendencies*, Durham: Duke University Press, 1993, pp. 7–8. See also Jonathan Dollimore, *Sexual Dissidence: Augustine to Wilde, Freud to Foucault*. New York: Oxford University Press, 1991.

Further reading

Bersani, Leo, *Homos.* Cambridge, MA: Harvard University Press, 1995.

Bersani, Leo, 'Is the Rectum a Grave?', in Douglas Crimp (ed.), *AIDS: Cultural Analysis/Cultural Activism*, Cambridge, MA: MIT Press, 1988, 1993, pp. 197–223.

Brenkman, John, *Straight Male Modern: A Cultural Critique of Psychoanalysis.* New York: Routledge, 1993.

Butler, Judith, *Bodies That Matter: On the Discursive Limits of 'Sex'.* New York: Routledge, 1993.

Dean, Tim, 'Sex and Syncope', in *Raritan*, Vol. 15, No. 3, 1996, pp. 64–86.

Domenici, Thomas, and Lesser, Ronnie C. (eds), *Disorienting Sexuality: Psychoanalytic Reappraisals of Sexual Identities.* Foreword by Adrienne Harris. New York: Routledge, 1995.

Fuss, Diana (ed.), 'Pink Freud', in a special issue of *GLQ*, Vol. 2, No. 1/2, 1995.

12

Postmodernism

Judith Roof

As AN HISTORICAL DESIGNATION, an indication of a particular set of styles, and a socio-political condition created by the disappearance of legitimating metanarratives or the precedence of commodity culture, 'the vaporous buzzword' postmodern (or so Barbara Kruger calls it) connotes a loss of the unified subject, the impotence of positivist narratives, and the self-reflective pastiche of a commodified art. The postmodern's relation to gay and lesbian studies is both coincidental and constitutive. Arising at the same historical moment (mid-1950s) that American gays and lesbians began overt activism, postmodernism's opening of categories and dissolution of meta-narratives both enables the political emergence of categories defined as sexually variant and delimits their reliance upon the unifying possibilities of identity politics. Thus, Lesbian and Gay Studies' relation to postmodernism is always both consonant and contradictory, felicitous and dangerous. The contradictions and dangers reside not only in threats to the political agency of identity politics or the commodification and appropriation of lesbian and gay lives and styles, but also in the too easy alignment of gay/lesbian to the postmodern as itself an inherent feature of lesbian or gay identity.

Since the designation 'postmodern' is itself a kind of pastiche, it is useful to consider briefly how its various conceptualizations might enable the increased visibility or production of the sexual identities and positions that deviate from normative heterosexuality as well as a sustained corpus of gay and lesbian theory and criticism that circulates around them. If, for example, we rely upon Ihab Hassan's dialectical comparison of literary modernism and postmodernism, the terms he associates with modernism – 'form', 'purpose', 'master code', 'metaphor', 'God the Father', and 'genital/phallic' to name a few – easily appertain to a traditional, familial, heterosexual order, while the opposite terms 'antiform (disjunctive, open)', 'play', 'idiolect', 'metonymy', 'The Holy Ghost', and 'polymorphous/androgynous' – are all culturally associated in one way or another with perversity, deviance, and homosexualities (1985, pp. 124-5). In the sense that these associations already emerge from cultural stereotypes, they prove to be little other than a kind of stylistic opening for a gay/lesbian presence, but insofar as the organized advent of a postmodern defined against a modernist tradition legitimates styles not previously recognized, acknowledging this series of postmodern traits takes stylistic and organizational account of homosexualities, providing a place for them. In this context, postmodernism provides a systematic locus for homosexualities, even though that position is in relatively the same relation to heterosexuality (the perverse in relation to the normative, the incomplete in relation to the full, etc.) as before a modern/postmodern dichotomy was devised.[1]

If we understand the postmodern as a shift in our relation to knowledge, then Jean-François Lyotard's characterization of the postmodern as signalling the loss of 'legitimating metanarratives' of knowledge would seem to permit the emergence of homosexualities as subject positions. If we understand legitimating metanarratives to be a part not only of scientific inquiry in the broad sense, but the ideological alibi for reproduction/production systems such as the family and capitalism, then the loss of such narratives removes the systemic barrier to the emergence of positions that seem somehow outside of or counter to such metanarratives. If the loss of legitimating metanarratives undoes not only the science of science, but also its necessary narrative of cause and effect – if postmodernity imposes a 'severe reexamination on the thought of the Enlightenment, on the idea of a unitary end of history and of a subject' – then the 'anything goes' of postmodern eclecticism would seem to include subjects freed from the 'unitary end' of history – from the heterosexualized notions of production/reproduction which have excluded homosexualities as 'degenerescence' (according to Foucault) in the first place.[2] It would also enable a critical method freed from the necessity of knowing or accounting for all.

This version of the postmodern might be employed to explain the emergence of gay and lesbian as subject categories as an effect of the loss of particular narratives that have defined the production of, have ordered, and in a sense have restricted knowledges to components of a larger metanarrative of reproduction and patriarchal family. The loss of such metanarratives would enable the emergence of homosexualities that presumably have already been present. Lesbian and gay are enfranchised as a part of postmodern's multiplication and dispersal of categories. Any new metanarratives that account for diversified subject position include gay and lesbian as two of many possibilities, as part of a variety that had become *status quo* even if nostalgia for the metanarratives of old continually tries to limit imagined gay/lesbian interference with familial order.

This shift from an Enlightenment belief in an orderable knowledge to the apparent variety of postmodern commodity cultural pastiche may also be 'characterized by a shift from an "epistemological" to an "ontological" dominant' (Harvey, 1990, p. 41). David Harvey's interpretation of Brian McHale's reading of the postmodern novel suggests a shift from knowledge to being, 'from the kind of perspectivism that allowed the modernist to get a better bearing on the meaning of a complex but nevertheless singular reality, to the foregrounding of questions as to how radically different realities may coexist, collide, and interpenetrate' (p. 41). This is really more than a trajectory from knowledge to being; it represents a shift from singular to plural, from controllable meaning to multiple, entangled, diverse, but perhaps inseparable possibilities, from the possibility of truth to the emergence of truths. While this shift seems to suggest that the acquisition of a truth is no longer possible, what it also suggests is a change in the idea of truth. The truth of truth is that truth is not singular and if truth is not singular, then the moral imperatives attached to religion, ethics, and familial ideologies are no longer absolute. What McHale sees as a shift to ontology is also a shift to a markedly different economy of value which permits homosexualities as several truths among many.

All of the previous understandings of postmodernism imply a space for gay/lesbian as categories produced either by stylistic analogy or metanarrative collapse, emerging through the agency of a postmodern re-envisioning of totality and truth. Lesbian and gay, along with other 'minorities', become the markers – the symptoms – of the emergent 'other' that Andreas Huyssen suggests can 'subvert, through the perspective of marginalization, both the high/low cultural split articulated in the dominant realm and that realm's representational (political as well as artistic) homogeneity' (Wiegman, 1994, p. 8). Huyssen's suggestion of a linear, reactionary relation between an ensconced modernism and an ensuing anti-modernist artistic practice certainly correlates with the historical co-emergence of gay/lesbian and postmodernism. But which causes which? Does the emergence of a postmodern anti-aesthetic enable the visibility of lesbian/gay, does it produce gay/lesbian in the forms that begin to dominate in the 1980s, or is the pressuring presence of gay/lesbian part of the impetus toward postmodernism? Or do all of these work together in a constellation of cultural change that is difficult to order? Is Andy Warhol's 1950s challenge to high/low cultural practice, for example, a gay practice or a burgeoning postmodern one, or both?

What if we challenge Huyssen's fairly traditional historical account with the more crafty implications of Lyotard? What if the postmodern does not succeed the modern in an oedipalized development within the logic of avant-gardes in general? What if instead, as Robyn Wiegman suggests, 'the postmodern doesn't transcend the modern; it rereads the modern, not from beyond, but from within' (1994, p. 14). The absence of a clear historical cause/effect narrative of modern/postmodern renders their relation a tension, an interdependent dynamic where each defines the other. While we might be tempted to align lesbian/gay with postmodernism in this dynamic, the tension between modern and postmodern actually replicates the tension within gay/lesbian studies between the political value of modernist identity strategies and the enfranchising liberation of postmodernism's opening of identity categories. This tension between modern and postmodern plays through Judith Butler's observation that 'to install myself within the terms of an identity category would be to turn against the sexuality that the category purports to describe; and this might be true for any identity category which seeks to control the very eroticism that it claims to describe and authorize, much less "liberate"' (1991, p. 14).

Butler's identification of the paradox inherent to the modernist/post-modernist trade of identity and free play locates the attributes of gay/lesbian categories on the side of a stereotypical postmodern whose value lies precisely in its lack of as well as its challenge to limit. 'I'm permanently troubled by identity categories', Butler says, 'consider them to be invariable stumbling-blocks, and understand them, even promote them, as sites of necessary trouble' (p. 14). At the same time, the category is instrumental precisely because it is unstable and challengeable. Butler continues, 'in fact, if the category were to offer no trouble, it would cease to be interesting to me; it is precisely the *pleasure* produced by the instability of those categories which sustains the various erotic practices that make me a candidate for the category to begin with' (p. 14). This suggests that at least a lesbian erotic is produced from the interplay of modernist and postmodernist terms, that the connection between gay/lesbian and post-modern is really a connection among lesbian/gay, postmodern, and modern.

This more complex formulation of the necessary inter-relation of modern/postmodern underwrites what seem to be fairly straightforward postmodernist conceptions (if such a thing is possible) of 'postidentity' sexualities, which is not the 'limitless and boundless shifting of positions and forms', as Judith Halberstam notes, but rather as a condition that 'indicates the futility of stretching terms like *lesbian* or *gay* or *straight* or *male* or *female* across vast fields of experience, behavior, and self-understanding' (1994, p. 210). Relocating sexual and gender identities as 'styles rather than lifestyles, as fictions rather than facts of life, and as potentialities rather than as fixed identities' Halberstam shifts modernist categories or identities into the realm of fiction, the consciously produced, performance, and perhaps even performativity. As in Butler's formulation, the putatively postmodern depends upon the modernist even as it rejects it. While seeming to portend a politics of dislocation and potential, Halberstam's discussion of 'new sexual vocabularies' also points out the all-too-omnipresent modernist subject who wields these fictions and who often reverts to type. The point is not that Halberstam's call for new sexualities is not an interesting or even necessary move in a postmodern view of the world, but rather to suggest how such a move is still appended to modernism, to the very categories it might like to eschew.

The category 'queer' also attempts to stretch or even dislocate discrete sexual categories with a more fluid, less locatable nomenclature which in itself suggests and sometimes tries to enact a disruption of categorization itself. While the designation 'queer' tends to prevent any easy location of subjects within sex/gender boundaries, and while the verb 'queering' suggests that such boundaries have never been stable, exclusive, or centred, the appeal to queer still makes sense only in relation to the modernist positions it eschews. In the sense that queer tries to occupy an identifiably postmodern position in relation to modernist identity categories, queering might be seen as a postmodernist move. To the extent that queering itself finally comes to stand in for gay/lesbian/transgender/transsexual (i.e., anything not purely heterosexual or aligned with traditional gender categories), it is retamed by a modernist impetus that locates queer as a substitute for homosexual. Queer may well permit thinking beyond modernist categories, but because it is appended to those categories as their performative dislocation, it sometimes has a tendency to come full circle, not in enabling a wholesale rejection of sex/gender categories, but in finally enfranchising even heterosexuality as queer. While this might be in some ways a desirable result, it also represents a levelling of queerness and its return to a *status quo*.

What might make arguments such as Halberstam's, or tactics such as

queering useful as ways to a gay/lesbian (queer) postmodern critical practice is the need to break down the dichotomy between modern and
postmodern, between before and after, between singular order and multiple possibilities as the way to a praxis paralyzed by the identity conundrum
Butler so clearly defines. To feminists critical of the postmodern's seeming
erasure of identity categories, postmodernism seems an arrivist bane, a
way of cancelling the fresh gains of several decades of struggle. But if we
understand some modernist notion of identity necessarily continuing at
the same time it is challenged, evacuated, stretched, and mutated, then the
identity categories that seem to constitute lesbian/gay studies also become
the premier points of its interrogation. In a way this has already long been
the case; as Lesbian and Gay Studies of the 1970s and 1980s struggled to
reclaim work by lesbian and gay authors or to reread texts in lesbian/gay-
inflected ways, what seemed so clearly to constitute the categories also
become less clear. The process of defining and refinding was simultaneously a process of discovering categorical uncertainty, wide diversity, and
multiple differences. One conclusion that might be made by such recovery
methods is that there is indeed a gay/lesbian literary tradition; another is
that we no longer have such a clear idea of what it might mean to be a
gay/lesbian author.

At the same time, however, the modernist impetus toward identity categories becomes a postmodern commodity. In the academy and in the
larger market, lesbian, gay, and even queer, simulacratized versions of an
alter-heterosexual ethos, become the chic trademarks of a broadening gen-
der/sex market. While gay and lesbian people become the objects both of a
consumer curiosity and their own critical and fetishizing eye, the potential
gender dysphoria associated with gay and lesbian positions opens vast
markets to unisex, ambi-sex, and the marketed visibility of any other-than-
heterosex possibility. Commodity culture itself both secures and evacuates
any modernist meaning still attached to these positions which become
wearable tradable styles within a larger logic of global capital. Commodity
identity is as much a paradox as Butler's observation about the tensions
adhering to lesbian identity.

Even so, like the postmodern, commodity culture and its appurte-
nances – style, simulacra, mutability, dislocation – seems almost too like
stereotypes associated with homosexualities, particularly with gay men.
Style, as a commodified entity itself, is associated with the kind of useless
(but totally desirable) decorativeness, a Wildean triviality important for its
very shift of focus and comment on the nature of bourgeois emphases. See-

ing style studies as themselves postmodern especially if the study is of post-modernism itself as the organizing aegis of style, carries with it the same paradox as that of identity. While studying the postmodern may seem to be postmodern, the study often is more modernist, inquiring for system and the truth of a commodity logic.

The problem, then, with associations between postmodernism and gay and lesbian studies is that while lesbian and gay might be easily associated with the postmodern, neither gay and lesbian studies of the postmodern nor postmodern studies of gays and lesbians tend to be postmodern, but instead share in the same tension between identity and dislocation, mod-ernism and postmodernism discussed above. This may well be because the postmodern, finally, does not cause or even abet the emergence and recog-nition of lesbian and gay as categories. For if the postmodern is neither an organized movement nor a unified and definable historical moment, then the coincidental relation between postmodernisms and emergent homo-sexualities may be the product of a structural parallel. In other words, the set of categories dubbed 'postmodern' and homosexualities are different manifestations of the same complex cultural impetus. If this is the case, the association of postmodern and gay/lesbian is finally perhaps opportunistic, providing a potential loosening of the strictures and ideologies that have circumscribed lesbian/gay presence and practice.

What kinds of specific critical practice do these various understandings of postmodernism bring to gay and lesbian studies? Postmodernism as an aesthetic category easily spawns studies of gay and lesbian 'postmodern' authors. While much of this criticism is very like traditional new critical, identity-based readings of gay/lesbian authors, occasionally such practice tries to correlate lesbian or gay with postmodern style itself as in Laura Doan's 'Jeanette Winterson's Sexing the Postmodern' or Sally Munt's '"*Somewhere over the rainbow* . . . " Postmodernism and the Fiction of Sarah Schulman.' Linking postmodern literary styles to postmodern texts, of course, derives not so much from any new lesbian/gay epistemology, but rather from the identification of postmodern literary style in works by gay or lesbian authors or works about lesbian or gay characters. In the end this is still a modernist criticism that tends to understand postmodern as a styl-istic category that leads to knowledge of how literary works challenge, redefine, stretch and fabricate gender and sexual categories.

More postmodern lesbian/gay work locates itself in the critique of cul-ture itself, particularly in studies of postmodern understandings of power, cultures, and sexual subjectivities informed by poststructuralist thought.

Often challenging a modernist notion of the subject, such work ranges from Judith Butler's analysis of gender, power, and subjectivity to work by Thomas Yingling, Lee Edelman, Sue-Ellen Case, Robyn Wiegman, Cindy Patton, Leo Bersani, Elizabeth Grosz, D. A. Miller, E. L. McCallum, and Camilla Griggers[3] (to name a few) that begins to challenge the foundations of gender/sex categories, modernist methodologies, and identity-centred epistemologies through appeals to post-structuralist theory, performativity, and rereadings of psychoanalysis.

While postmodernism and poststructuralism are not synonymous, the poststructuralist thought associated with postmodern worldviews enables the sophisticated analyses of sexuality, culture, and history produced in Lesbian and Gay Studies. Foucault's work on power and Barthes' understandings of representation and narrative join with the more structuralist psychoanalytic analyses of language and subjectivity provided by Lacan and Freud. This conceptual arsenal empowers trenchant gay and lesbian critiques of commodity culture (Doty, Koestenbaum), simplistic identity categories (Sedgwick, Phelan), gender (Butler, Halberstam), narrative (de Lauretis, Miller), the politics of representation and sexuality (Sedgwick, Goldberg, Bersani, Watney, Halberstam), and the basic precepts of sex/gender systems such as desire (de Lauretis), the phallus (Butler, Grosz), and the fetish (Grosz, McCallum).

Poststructuralist thought offers more possibility to an intellectual project that might effectively challenge sex/gender systems, perhaps enabling both the dissolution of categories and an effective queer politics. Any political practice that does not fall back into modernist identity categories must be theoretically informed, especially since our notions of politics tend to be highly modernist in their reliance upon identity categories. Breaking down the dichotomy between modernist and postmodernist means also breaking down the false opposition between theory and practice. Postmodernism holds the promise of a different order, poststructuralism might get us there, but only if we recognize that we might have to relinquish our modernist comfort in identity categories. It may well be that what has begun as lesbian/gay studies can become an inquiry that extends its understandings beyond identity.

Notes

1. See Teresa de Lauretis' reading of Freud's notion of the perverse in *The Practice of Love*. See also my *Come As You Are: Sexuality and Narrative* for a further analysis of the inter-relation of the perverse and the normative.

2. See Michel Foucault, *The History of Sexuality: An Introduction*. Lyotard's continued commentary is from 'What is Postmodernism?', p. 76.
3. The essay was published under the name Catherine Griggers. She has since changed her name to Camilla.

References

Barthes, Roland, *The Pleasure of the Text* (trans. Richard Miller). New York: Hill and Wang, 1975.

Bersani, Leo, 'Is the Rectum a Grave?', in Douglas Crimp (ed.), *AIDS: Cultural Analysis Cultural Activism*, Cambridge, MA: MIT Press, 1988, pp. 197–222.

Butler, Judith, 'Imitation and Gender Subordination', in Diana Fuss (ed.), *Inside/Out*, New York: Routledge, 1991, pp. 13–31.

Case, Sue-Ellen, 'Towards a Butch Femme Aesthetic', in *Discourse* 11, 1, Fall-Winter, 1988–89, pp. 55–73.

de Lauretis, Teresa, *The Practice of Love: Lesbian Sexuality and Perverse Desire*. Bloomington: Indiana University Press, 1994.

Doan, Laura, 'Jeanette Winterson's Sexing the Postmodern', in her *The Lesbian Postmodern*, pp. 137–155.

Doan, Laura (ed.), *The Lesbian Postmodern*. New York: Columbia University Press, 1994.

Doty, Alexander, *Making Things Perfectly Queer: Interpreting Mass Culture*. Minneapolis: University of Minnesota Press, 1993.

Edelman, Lee, *Homographesis: Essays in Gay Literary and Cultural Theory*. New York: Routledge, 1994.

Foucault, Michel, *The History of Sexuality*. Vol I (trans. Robert Hurley). New York: Vintage Books, 1990.

Fuss, Diana (ed.), *Inside/Out: Lesbian Theories, Gay Theories*. New York: Routledge, 1991.

Griggers, Catherine, 'Lesbian Bodies in the Age of (Post)Mechanical Reproduction', in L. Doan (ed.), *The Lesbian Postmodern*, New York: Columbia University Press, 1994, pp. 118–33.

Grosz, Elizabeth, 'Fetishism, Identity, Politics', in Judith Roof and Robyn Wiegman (eds), *Who Can Speak? Authority and Critical Identity*, Champagne: University of Illinois Press, 1995, pp. 155–64.

Halberstam, Judith, 'F2M: The Making of Female Masculinity', in Laura Doan (ed.), *The Lesbian Postmodern*. New York: Columbia University Press, 1994, pp. 210–28.

Harvey, David, *The Condition of Postmodernity*. Cambridge, MA: Blackwell, 1990.

Hassan, Ihab, 'The Culture of Postmodernism', in *Theory, Culture, and Society*, Vol. 2, No. 3, 1985, pp. 124–5.

Huyssen, Andreas, 'Mapping the Postmodern', in Joseph Natoli and Linda Hutcheon (eds), *A Postmodern Reader*. Albany: SUNY Press, 1993.

Koestenbaum, Wayne, 'The Queen's Throat: (Homo)sexuality and the Art of Singing', in Diana Fuss (ed.), *Inside/Out*, New York: Routledge, 1991, pp. 205–34.

Lyotard, Jean-François, *The Postmodern Condition: A Report on Knowledge* (trans. Geoff Bennington and Brian Massumi). Minneapolis: University of Minnesota Press, 1984.

Lyotard, Jean-François, 'What is Postmodernism?', in Julian Pefanis and Morgan Thomas (eds), *The Postmodern Explained* (trans. Don Barry, Bernadette Maher, Julian Pefanis, Virginia Spate, and Morgan Thomas). Minneapolis: University of Minnesota Press, 1993.

McCallum, E. L., 'How to Do Things with Fetishism', in *differences*, Vol. 7, No. 3, 1995, pp. 24–46.

Miller, D. A., 'Anal Rope', in Diana Fuss (ed.), *Inside/Out*, New York: Routledge, 1991, pp. 119–41.

Munt, Sally, '"*Somewhere over the rainbow*" . . . Postmodernism and the Fiction of Sarah Schulman', in *New Lesbian Criticism*, New York: Columbia University Press, 1992, pp. 33–50.

Patton, Cindy, 'Hegemony and Orgasm, or, The Instability of Heterosexual Pornography', in *Screen*, Vol. 30, No. 3, Autumn 1989, pp. 72–7.

Roof, Judith, *Come As You Are: Sexuality and Narrative*. New York: Columbia University Press, 1996.

Sedgwick, Eve Kosofsky, *Epistemology of the Closet*. Berkeley: University of California Press, 1990.

Watney, Simon, *Policing Desire: Pornography, AIDS and the Media*. Minneapolis: University of Minnesota Press, 1989.

Wiegman, Robyn, 'Introduction: Mapping the Lesbian Postmodern', in Laura Doan (ed.), *The Lesbian Postmodern*, New York: Columbia University Press, 1994, pp. 1–20.

Yingling, Thomas, 'AIDS in America: Postmodern Governance, Identity, and Experience', in Diana Fuss (ed.), *Inside/Out*, New York: Routledge, 1991, pp. 291–310.

Further reading

Bad Object-Choices, *How Do I Look: Queer Film and Video*. San Francisco: Bay Press, 1991.

Butler, Judith, *Gender Trouble*. New York: Routledge, 1990.

Jagose, Annamarie, *Lesbian Utopics*. New York: Routledge, 1994.

Jameson, Fredric, *Postmodernism, or, The Cultural Logic of Late Capitalism*. Durham: Duke University Press, 1991.

Roof, Judith, 'Lesbians and Lyotard: Sexuality and the Naming of the Postmodern', in L. Doan (ed.), *The Lesbian Postmodern*, New York: Columbia University Press, 1994, pp. 47–66.

Warner, Michael (ed.), *Fear of a Queer Planet: Queer Politics and Social Theory*. Minneapolis, University of Minnesota Press, 1993.

13

The Personal, Experience, and the Self

Sally R. Munt

THE COMMONSENSE READING of Lesbian and Gay Studies is that it emerged out of an identity politics in the 1970s where its motor was the anger of exclusion, to be reclassed twenty years later as a professionalized, diminished and rarefied intellectual practice. But it is lesbian, gay, bisexual and transgendered bodies that fashion this intellectual labour; bodies which live, move and feel their queer sensibilities as they put them onto paper. The personal is intrinsic to, performed in, and produced by Lesbian and Gay Studies, it is the reason we do what we do. My thoughts are inscribed upon my butch dyke body, and my writing emerges from a commitment to that self; it comes out of the belief that this particular kind of speaking matters. Theodore Roszak, writing in 1979, argued that 'we live in a time when the very private experience of having a personal identity to discover, a personal destiny to fulfil, has become a subversive political force of major proportions' (Roszak, 1979, p. xxviii) encapsulating the liberation movements of the previous decade which had grasped the experience of personal oppression and structured it into forms of social resistance. Such movements appropriated the ideology of liberal pluralism, that accorded the private and personal realm value (although this value remained secondary to the public), and conjoined it with emancipatory aims.

Feminism was one of the key instigators of a shift from these emancipatory politics (ascendant in the early years), to what are now called 'life politics', characterizing the social movements of the 1980s and 1990s which were concerned with the desire for new identities and new selves. Michel Foucault (1976) historicized the self as a reflexive project which has become closely related to sexual development and satisfaction. He saw sexuality as a central focus for 'experience', and critically outlined the mechanisms by which 'sex' apparently produces the truth of a person. For lesbians and gays this temptation, to see our sexuality as the truth of our identity because it is perceived as the most oppressed part of us, belies an enduring fiction. To 'come out' as lesbian or gay is to speak the truth of that oppression. We formulate this identity as a way of reversing the pain of homophobia, claiming in doing so a common experience, in Raymond Williams' term a 'structure of feeling' which functions as a subjective witness to the transformation of emotion into an identity. Michel Foucault saw the link between the confessional and the Christian religious ritual as endemic to Western practices of sexuality, and the confession is also structurally associated with testimony and witness, processes which evangelize experience as transcendentally meaningful. What is clear from this conjunction is the way feelings become performative: they materialize and metamorphose into states of being and legitimation.

This chapter explores the thorny conjunction between notions of the personal, the private experience and the self, categories which contain tangled intellectual histories, which in turn have informed, and are critically informed by, Lesbian and Gay Studies. No intellectual work is commenced without the prick of emotion, that particular personal investment in a subject which moves somebody to write; however, attempts to cover the self, to slough off this emotion, persevere. My own work is still periodically rejected for being 'too personal', an accusation levelled at me around the very first piece I published, which was to link lesbian detective novels to my mother's death (Munt 1988). As a synonym for critical naïveté, the action remains a/shaming, it separates me from my fantasy of belonging to an academic community, a prospective family who can favour me with a cognitive self. Aspiration for something called a 'family' is contentious, given its heterosexist connotations, but I do want to think about how we can foreground the connections, rather than the disjunctions, between lesbian, gay, and queer academics, to try and reinvigorate that Old Left concept of 'solidarity'. The accusation of inappropriate affect is so predetermined anyway, given that anyone working in Lesbian and Gay Studies is assumed to be a protagonist, and that the collapsing of the personal into the political and the theoretical has already occurred, and resulted in marginalization. This conflation is endemic to any discipline which has emerged from an identity politics, as anyone also working in women's studies, or black studies, can attest. Whilst the moral weight of history witnesses the necessity of these endeavours, the academy insists on an interminable rearticulation of proof of our existence: we work within this vice – that our presence always testifies to our absence. I recall one of many instances, when being interviewed for a university post I was asked by the panel if I allowed men in my classrooms. The Equal Opportunities Officer monitoring the interview didn't even notice.

It has been argued by Slavoj Zizek (1989) and Judith Butler (1993), and others that identities function phantasmatically as rallying points within political discourse, something we saw in Britain during the late 1980s when lesbians and gays mobilized in their tens of thousands to fight the infamously homophobic new law, Section 28. For many, this was their first public articulation of a homosexual *identity*. These critics have underscored how important it is to understand how Lesbian and Gay Liberation movements have successfully mobilized a romantic promise of fulfilment. But identities are alternately compelling *and* disappointing; they always work by exclusion and repudiation. It may be argued that the modernist dream of fixing lesbian and gay identity returned as the postmodernist nightmare dissolution of identity when Queer arose from those dispossessed, displaced by a seemingly assimilationist agenda. The dysphoric, those who cannot be included in the prevailing categories of identity, remain not just materially, but also epistemologically excluded, they are placed beyond the parameters of knowledge. There always appears to be someone who exceeds the phantasm of identity, someone who cannot be known, who is 'beyond reason'.

'Experience' was first privileged by and then problematized by feminists. Consciousness raising had implied that there was a pre-existing consciousness of woman to be unearthed. There occurred a conflation between being/becoming a woman and a feminist, as though one naturally slid into the other – to express 'woman-ness' was to embody feminism. But black and feminists of colour began to question the preconception of woman during the 1970s, challenging the ethnocentric image being evoked (Moraga *et al*, 1983). Implicitly, woman meant white woman. The totalizing notion of women's experience revealed an ahistorical and transcultural assumption of the sameness of oppression, which was itself anchored in the European construction of the individual self. (White) women's experience became *the* evidence and legitimation of a feminism which was selective in its aims, a feminism which saw gender as the primary – or even the only – structure of oppression. This tendency can be detected in lesbian and gay politics too, when sexual identity is allowed to subsume all other categories of experience. In Lesbian and Gay Studies, institutionalization effects the same elision, where learning about one social category is separated from, or hierarchically organized over, another.

Experience is contested, it is a product of oppressive discourse *and* it also produces that discourse. As Joan Scott puts it: 'experience is at once always already an interpretation and is in need of interpretation' (1992, p. 37). In this model, whose experience becomes representative, and whose becomes appropriated to resemble the norm? It is difficult to evade the twentieth-century creed 'I feel, therefore I am', or 'I feel, therefore it is true', which can degenerate into a complacent and narcissistic avoidance of accountability to others. Later feminism of the 1980s tended towards a politics of location, which too often became reduced to seeing identity as a mere effect of race, class, or gender. A further defensive simplification then occurred, as Nancy K. Miller has parodied: 'If I like it, it's personal, it caresses me; otherwise, it's just positional, it aggresses me' (1991, p. 19). Thus feelings, once again, became the arbiters of knowledge. The allure of personal testimony is that it does endow an argument with moral inspiration. The rhetoric of emotion – a trick of assumed identification – can manipulate the reader's subtle agreement when other methods fail. Is this merely disguising persistent individualism, the idea that because it's me, it's right? This accusation is a simplification, although it succeeds in silencing both the tentative and the gratuitous use of the personal in the text, as we are induced to abjure the personal in favour of, not a political community, but an academic one. Karl Kroeber, writing in the October 1996 PMLA on the 'dangers of the New Personalism' twists the argument again by posing individualism as a free, expressive humanism inhibited, even effaced, by identity politics in a rhetorical and implicitly homophobic and racist caricature:

> What seems an autobiographical impulse is in truth a contorted masquerade of its opposite, the loss of meaningful individuality. Our critics speak personally not for a real self but for a self conceived as representative of an approved ideology, race, or sexual preference – self-stereotyped as a subaltern postdeconstructionist, a black male lesbian, and so on. (p. 1163)

The catch is that both the conservative and the radical positions are imbued with nostalgia for (albeit different forms of) individualism.

Central to the deployment of experience as knowledge is the call to synthesize, in order to organize. Experience is irreducible to discrete political programmes, the myriad of particularities which make people unique seems to resist attempts to homogenize, and unify identity. But if we can deploy identity temporarily and strategically in order to resist, as a somewhat arbitrary fiction, by approximating coherence this closure can produce a space of resistance – the 'I am' of homosexuality (Fuss, 1989). The catch is, of course, that identities deploy us too, unconsciously as much as consciously. If psychoanalytic theory is right, that identity is a process always doomed to fail, because the desire for wholeness and integrity is disrupted by the unconscious, then perhaps here we have another explanation for the disillusionment with lesbian and gay liberation and the rise of Queer. Identities keep slipping away from us, and yet we keep calling them back – why? Reinventing identities is bound up with the continued validation of our experience; we keep trying to recover the self. As Bonnie Zimmerman has stated, 'Experience seems to resist our every attempt to dethrone it':

> If lesbians cannot or choose not to belong to the category woman, can we claim 'lesbian' as a more meaningful category or identity? How can we develop a politics and theory that draws upon lesbian experience, or lesbian existence? . . . without some kind of general acceptance of lesbian as a category, there can be no lesbian identity, no lesbian community, lesbian culture, lesbian literature, lesbian theory, or lesbian criticism. And yet, I feel sure that all these do exist. (1993, p. 113)

What I find interesting in this quote is Zimmerman's appeal to emotion; I know not all lesbians feel that they belong to a community. I know I do. Is this simply due to the privileging of my sexuality over all those other social mechanisms? Call me peculiar, but I still go to Lesbian and Gay Studies conferences in order to feel part of things – and I do. I still thrill at the experience of several hundred queers together *thinking* (yes, and invariably fucking). I also want to know why, whenever I read a theory and I *feel* it's wrong, in spite of it making intellectual sense, I tend to trust my gut. Now, I know I am in danger of being accused of presenting the heart as being somehow separate from the mind, or at least posing that one realm is at least less negatively constructed than the other. This can be understood as a reversal and perhaps a reinscription of the (gendered) binary opposition rationality = good/emotion = bad, and therefore a capitulation. It can also be interpreted as an indulgent exhibitionism, an essentialist solipsism, or a leap of faith, a risk taken to push against the territory of representation.

'Theory' is the bogey here: theory is still seen as antithetical to emotion, in that hoary polarity. Theory is the oedipal father whom we love, hate, and desire. But theory seems unmoved by our desires, unseduced by our approaches. There are scholars who are trying to theorize the 'I am' out of the experience of queer sexual spaces, who manage the delicate synthesis of analysis with affect, paradigmatically Eve Kosofsky Sedgwick in her essays, for example 'A Poem is Being Written', or 'White Glasses' (1993). In Britain we are lucky to have the work of 'first wave' cultural critics such as Richard Dyer and Elizabeth Wilson, who came out of the Leftist activisms of the post-1968 gay liberation front and womens' liberation. Such approaches encapsulate what Nancy K. Miller (1991) has identified as authored spectacles, which move beyond self-display into an engaging personal materialism, which simultaneously binds the reader and opens up an enquiry into those effects. This aesthetic of writing is connectivity, not bourgeois individualism. Certain pieces, like these of Sedgwick's, elicit affection from, and create, communities of reader/scholars, not least because they inscribe and invite spaces of identification through feeling. Similarly structured, but in a different field, is the historical writing of researchers such as Jonathan Ned Katz (1976), Joan Nestle (1988), Elizabeth Lapovsky Kennedy and Madeline D. Davis (1993), whose publications are clearly labours of love, attempt to reveal and reproduce the hidden selves of lesbian and gay history through time. Although the authorial self is not always consciously foregrounded in these narratives, the representation of their subjects is replete with affection. The sensitivities of the author similarly frame the reader's response, of affective identification. Lesbian and gay studies is ghosted by selves, by the under-represented and the un-representable, by the selves we desire and the selves we desire to be. Because its primary ambition is to materialize those desires, to make them possible, it cannot be driven just by intellect. Perhaps we can take Kath Weston's (1995) distinction between 'straight theory' and 'street theory' to heart, and think of theory (with a small 't'), as that which is critically engaged with experience, and, implicitly, emotion.

Listening to emotion bespeaks the Foucauldian shift from the Enlightenment epistemology of knowing the self to the ethical integrity of caring for the self. In his later work Foucault introduced 'technologies of the self': 'a certain number of practices and techniques through which individuals *actively* fashion their own identities' (McNay, 1992, p. 3). The technologies of the self enable the individual to come to an understanding of her self as a thinking/feeling subject, avoiding victim-hood (the traditional passive and dominated blank slate), and a recognition of her relational identity as a form of resistance. Latterly, Foucault tried to put the affect back into theories of regulation. How can we develop a theorizing self? Elspeth Probyn comments wryly on how theorists don't know what to do with the self, becoming paralyzed due to the crisis of representation which aborts any deployment of experience as instructive. She sees the self as a doubled entity: '. . . it is involved in the ways in which we go about our everyday lives, and it puts into motion a mode of theory that problematizes the material conditions of those practices' (1993, p. 1).

In enunciating our self, we are continuously reworking it, ideally in the direction of another, not in order to interpellate, but in an attempt to connect (as E. M. Forster would have put it, 'only connect'). Thus, our experience becomes conspicuous and undefended, a matter to work with, rather than inviolably reify. Probyn argues that there is a mode of reworking the self which exists between the epistemological (knowing) and the ontological (being), and that knowing and being the self is implicitly relational. She asks us to fold and bend the experiential in upon itself, in a warp and weave of critical self-knowing which results in a kind of multi-textured entity, a material self whose edges are connecting threads:

> The self is not an end in itself, it is the opening of a perspective, one which allows us to conceive of transforming our selves with the aid of others. Far from being a self-centred or self-centring action, this is to radically de-centre our selves, to work at the extremity where my self can be made to touch hers. (1993, p. 167)

This description is not unlike Nancy K. Miller's (1991) notion of the 'relay' of personal criticism, which travels between identity positions to create critical fluency. The questions 'Who am I?' and 'Who is she?' cease to have a separate logic in this intersubjective space, so that the focus shifts towards desire and becoming, and in a sense, becoming-Other. This desire to become is also a desire to belong. Be-longing is a familiar desire to all those inhabiting the notional outside, denuded, as we are, of the security of a fixed, ontological identity. So, perhaps, we can see a doubled movement: be-longing (towards the centre), and be-coming (towards the edge). Within Lesbian and Gay Studies, the most influential theorists have proselytized the latter over the former, adjunctive to the general deconstructive project of contemporary critical thought. Lesbian and gay studies itself vacillates between these desires: it wants to belong, but it also wants to become. To return to Probyn's work, she points out that the desire to belong always puts us on the outside, that the centre for us can only be a place of nostalgic erewhon, that 'belonging hinges on not belonging' (1996, p. 14). We need to turn our gaze toward those that live on the outside with us, and develop this outside-belonging as a form of political and intellectual practice; significantly, Probyn observes how Foucault maintained that 'one writes in order to become other' (1996, p. 52). Writing thus becomes less of the expressive author/master, and more of the inscribing subject, as the rise in autobiographical theory would suggest. Representing oneself, then, entails figuring identity as a movement, not a possession. This is not, however a simple romanticism of the outside as a guarantor of radicality, seeing it as a kind of mirror which miraculously discloses 'real' selves, and not the vampiric oppressor who will conveniently disappear. Writing a self invokes the introjected nastinesses as well as utopian desires. Writing a self can hone the self-reflexivity which provides the recognition that we cannot afford to wax lyrical with importunity, for at the edges we are touched by the implications of our words.

How can we avoid that split wherein we theorize nicely in class and then over coffee make bitchy remarks about the radical feminist, or the spotty boy in the corner? We enlist all sorts of theories to prove our liberal qualities which are often contrapuntal to (and never entirely separate from) our emotions. Our feelings are problematic for lots of reasons (there goes that binary again), and one function that theory can have is precisely to show us the disjunction between the two. As Linda S. Kaufmann has said, 'We are always beside ourselves in multiple senses' (1993, p. 138). She calls struggling for integration 'quixotic' though, and abandons the expressive project as misled. But I disagree, and would argue that this attempt is fundamentally dissociative in its effort to disengage the emotions. The split between theory and emotion is founded on the intractable dichotomy of Western thought between the mind and the body, where emotions discursively reside in the (female) body. Of course, emotions are actually in the body *and* the mind, and cannot be extricated by the self-conscious application of reason; the attempt is oxymoronic. I began this chapter with the observation that it is lesbian, gay, bisexual and transgendered bodies which perform the intellectual labour of queer theorizing, and it is this thought to which I want to return, by looking at the work of Elizabeth Grosz. In her book *Volatile Bodies* (1994), she takes issue with mainstream and feminist theorists who have executed the mind/body dualism in their writing. Grosz provides a way of:

... problematizing and rethinking the relations between the inside and the outside of the subject, its psychical interior and its corporeal exterior, by showing not their fundamental identity or reducibility but the torsion of the one into the other, the passage, vector, or uncontrollable drift of the inside into the outside and the outside into the inside. (p. xii)

Grosz is a leading figure in the recent shift in queer and feminist theory against the perceived perilous and complicit deployment of dichotomous modes of thought. She highlights the profound somatophobia (body-hatred) which has characterized philosophy since the ancient Greeks, and her book exhorts us to reintegrate our bodies into the production of knowledge. The body is not a trolley for getting the brain around, but constitutive of the subjectivities which consolidate Lesbian and Gay Studies. Thus, understandings of embodied subjectivities, and psychical corporealities, need to be evolved. Recalling my previous points, Grosz argues:

If, as feminists have claimed, 'our politics start with our feelings' and if the very category of experience or feeling is itself problematized through a recognition of its ideological production – if, that is, experience is not a raw mode of access to some truth – then the body provides a point of mediation between what is perceived as purely internal and accessible only to the subject and what is external and publicly observable, a point from which to rethink the opposition between the inside and the outside, the private and the public, the self and other, and all the other binary pairs associated with the mind/body opposition. (p. 21)

To recap: the private, the personal, experience and the self in Lesbian and Gay Studies must not – cannot – be conceptualized apart from the body, which is itself the mediator in the theory/emotion split. My 'gut' appears not to be such a simplistic response after all. However, this is not to hide behind the body as a manifestation of a natural truth, the body is a product of culture too, and its contours reflect the rhythms of discursive patterning. The ground of inquiry for Lesbian and Gay Studies must therefore consist of the zones of interactivity between the mind and the body, and hence theory and emotion. We do not study or indeed live in these separate spheres, we move around, betwixt and between them, our bodies are material reminders of the co-implication of our thoughts and feelings. When we examine the specificities of lesbian and gay bodies, we can begin to understand the impulses of Lesbian and Gay Studies.

Strikingly, Grosz turns to Deleuze and Guattari's idea of 'becoming-woman' as a way out of binary thinking. Noting that this concept is not without its problems for feminists (pp. 179–83), she takes up their proposal that becoming-woman can take us beyond the projected woman of patriarchal fantasy, and that this aim can make (feminist) sense for both men and women, and presumably gays and lesbians:

> Becoming-woman involves a series of processes and movements beyond the fixity of subjectivity and the structure of stable unities. It is an escape from the systems of binary polarization of unities that privilege men at the expense of women. It gradually becomes clear that what becoming-woman means or entails for men is different than for women. For men it implies a de- and restructuring of male sexuality, of the forms of genital domination, bringing into play the microfemininities of behaviors, the particles of another sexuality, or many sexualities, n sexes, or as Deleuze and Guattari elsewhere describe it, 'a thousand tiny sexes'. (p. 177)

In terms of wanting to explore what Lesbian and Gay Studies, with its historical debt to feminism, could be becoming, there are worse aspirations. The trajectory of becoming-woman, in the specific sense articulated by Deleuze and Guattari, could relieve us of the intractable hierarchies of reason and emotion, and enable us, as Queer Theory has espoused, to get beyond identity and yet manage to retain a sense of political movement. This kind of radical antihumanism is antipathetic to a preconceived goal, it is exploratory, motivated by the unpredictable productivities of desire. It is also beyond the material boundary of the body, rather, they prefer the concept of the 'desiring machine', which is no more than the intensities and flows of desire interfacing and connecting with all aspects of our living environment. It is this emphasis on connectivity, combined with Foucault's idea of the 'sexual mosaic', in common with the spirit of empathetic diversification in recent writing by feminist and lesbian women of colour (e.g. Gloria Anzaldúa's 'mestiza consciousness', 1987), which can caution Lesbian and Gay Studies against the tendency to typify or stagnate into reductionist remoteness. Theorizing emerges from the intricacy of our lived experience, bodies and all. The trick is to resist the self-righteous fragmentation which can result from identities being set against desires, when identification is used as a sledgehammer to crack a nut, wielded as the proof of belonging to an ever-diminishing group. Thus, we can make our desires work for us, rather than against us, not as a vortex which pulls people in (to be like us), but as – to use an analogy from my Yorkshire roots – a spinning jenny: 'a machine by which a number of threads can be spun at once',[1] in that warp and weave of critical *self*-knowing.

Notes

1. 'Spinning Jenny', *Chambers Twentieth Century Dictionary*, W. & R. Chambers Ltd, Edinburgh, 1972.

References

Butler, Judith, *Bodies that Matter*. New York: Routledge, 1993.

Dyer, Richard, *Heavenly Bodies: Film Stars and Society*. (See chapter 3 'Judy Garland and Gay Men'.) London: Macmillan, 1987.

Foucault, Michel, *The History of Sexuality: An Introduction*, Vol. 1 (trans. Robert Hurley). Harmondsworth: Penguin Books, 1976.

Katz, Jonathan Ned, *Gay American History*. New York: Thomas Y. Crowell Company, 1976.

Kauffman, Linda S., 'The Long Good-bye: Against Personal Testimony, or, An Infant Grifter Grows Up', in Gayle Greene and Coppélia Kahn (eds), *Changing Subjects: The Making of Feminist Literary Criticism*, London: Routledge, 1993, pp. 129–46.

Kennedy, Elizabeth Lapovsky, and Davis, Madeline D., *Boots of Leather, Slippers of Gold: The History of A Lesbian Community*. London and New York: Routledge, 1993.

Kroeber, Karl, 'Problems With Personal Criticism', in *PMLA*, Vol. 111, No. 5, 1996, pp. 1163–4.

McNay, Lois, *Foucault and Feminism*. Cambridge: Polity Press, 1992.

Miller, Nancy K., *Getting Personal*. New York: Routledge, 1991.

Moraga, Cherríe, and Anzaldúa, Gloria (eds), *This Bridge Called My Back*. New York: Kitchen Table: Women of Color Press, 1983.

Munt, Sally R., 'The Investigators: Lesbian Crime Fiction', in Susannah Radstone (ed.), *Sweet Dreams: Sexuality, Gender and Popular Fiction*. London: Lawrence & Wishart, 1988.

Rich, Adrienne, 'Notes Toward a Politics of Location', in her *Blood, Bread, and Poetry*. New York: W. W. Norton, 1986.

Roszak, Theodore, *Person-Planet: The Creative Destruction of Industrial Society*. London: Gollancz, 1979.

Scott, Joan W., 'Experience', in Judith Butler and Joan W. Scott (eds), *Feminists Theorise the Political*, New York: Routledge, 1992, pp. 22–40.

Weston, Kath, 'Theory, Theory, Who's Got The Theory', in *GLQ*, Vol. 2, 1995, pp. 347–9.

Williams, Raymond, *The Long Revolution*. New York: Columbia University Press, 1961.

Wilson, Elizabeth, *Hallucinations: Life in the Postmodern City*. London: Radius/Century Hutchinson, 1988.

Zizek, Slavoj, *The Sublime Object of Ideology*. London: Verso, 1989. Discussed in Judith Butler, *Bodies that Matter*, New York: Routledge, 1993.

Further reading

Anzaldúa, Gloria, *Borderlands: La Frontera: The New Mestiza*. San Francisco: Aunt Lute Books, 1987.

Fuss, Diana, *Essentially Speaking: Feminism, Nature and Difference*. New York: Routledge, 1989.

Game, Ann, 'Sociology's Emotions', in *Canadian Review of Sociology and Anthropology*, forthcoming 1997.

Grosz, Elizabeth, *Volatile Bodies: Toward a Corporeal Feminism*. Bloomington and Indianapolis: Indiana University Press, 1994.

Nestle, Joan, *A Restricted Country*. London: Sheba Press, 1988; new edition London: Pandora Press, 1996.

Probyn, Elspeth, *Outside Belongings*. New York: Routledge, 1996.

Probyn, Elspeth, *Sexing the Self: Gendered Positions in Cultural Studies*. London: Routledge, 1993.

Sedgwick, Eve Kosofsky, 'A Poem is Being Written' and 'White Glasses', in her *Tendencies*, Durham: Duke University Press, 1993.

Zimmerman, Bonnie, 'In Academia, and Out', in Gayle Greene and Coppélia Kahn (eds), *Changing Subjects: The Making of Feminist Literary Criticism*, London: Routledge, 1993, pp. 112–20.

Part 2

Debates and Dilemmas

14

Identity and Subculture

Alan Sinfield

ARE OUR SEXUAL IDENTITIES – gay or straight – essentially ours, or are they social constructs? Most men who identify as gay, and many lesbians, believe they were born that way and are pleased to hear that they may have a 'gay gene'. For these people, Lesbian and Gay Studies have been profoundly counterintuitive, for they have tended to assert that our sexualities are socially constructed.[1]

In the social sciences generally, constructionism has been a leading assumption since Peter Berger and Thomas Luckmann published *The Social Construction of Reality* in 1966. They took as a brief instance how, in a society that has institutionalized military homosexuality, the heterosexual would be regarded as deviant and a subject for therapy (Penguin edn 1971, pp. 131–3). In literary, philosophical, media and cultural studies, constructionism has correlated with the prominence of postmodernism as a notion of where we are in history, and of deconstruction as a mode of textual analysis. In many academic books and articles, showing that a text manifests identity as fluid, unstable, elusive, self-parodying (as opposed to fixed, natural, essential) is taken as sufficient demonstration that the text is both valuable and progressive. After all, heterosexuality appears to be profoundly *there* – normal, natural, human, god-given, essential – so demonstrating the instability of sexualities/textualities promises to undermine all that. If heterosexuality is constructed, it can be deconstructed. Queer Theory, in the early 1990s, depended largely upon this move.[2]

Despite the difficulties, which I hope will prove eventually productive, I mean to argue that modern Western les-bi-gay identities are products of our place and time. (In this essay I am trying out the term 'les-bi-gay' to see how it feels. I like its casual tone, and its economy; I am aware that it risks the problems we have had before: some people are not explicitly included, and some of those who are may feel at risk of incorporation by hegemonic male gayness.) My title is 'Identity and Subculture' because I believe that our identities derive from social process, in our subcultures and in interaction with the mainstream. I will be looking not at sexuality as deeply implanted in the individual, like some secular version of the soul, but at the place of same-sex passion in the sex-gender system. For we are not going to understand our local situations without addressing the wider ensemble of sexual practices in its historical specificity.

It seems sensible to suppose that this book will be read for the most part by people whose expectations fall largely within the modern Western sex-gender system (I use 'Western' in the conventional sense of mainly North American and North-west European). Therefore, in order to unsettle and refocus such expectations, I begin with other places. The question I will be asking of other cultures is not how far they seem to approve of gayness as we understand it, but what part same-sex passion plays in their lives.

Different differences

Anthropologist Susan Seizer describes how she and her partner, both US citizens, spent time in South India. 'For most Tamil women there are only two desirable identities, and they both revolve around her position within a male lineage: one is that of girl-child, living with her father's family, and the other is that of woman-wife, living with her husband's family.'[3] When Seizer was by herself in the field, she slept with the other women of the house – like sardines, as was the custom. Intimacy was common – 'having a woman lay her head in my lap, so her hair could be stroked' – but none of that signified lesbianism (p. 78). 'In Tamilnadu, lesbianism doesn't exist. It has not been marked. It has not been named' (p. 87). When a rare incident of female same-sex activity is reported, it is probably called 'homosex' – 'as though this problem, too, were strictly a Western one; yet another modern, imported evil' (p. 88). Seizer was perceived as the kind of woman who is moved primarily toward affectionate attachment. When her partner visited the village, she disliked the lack of recognition for their relationship: it was assumed that all the women were loving in an affectionate way.

The gender separation in Tamil culture does allow for a woman to have a dear friend, a confidante, a co-worker, a chaperone – accompanying her out of the house where it would be disreputable to go alone. In Madras, Seizer and her partner were generally assimilated to this model – which was a good deal more prestigious and unremarkable than being a lesbian couple in the United States: 'The signs of same-sex intimacy that mark us as dykes in the US – a visibility which we have only relatively recently begun to trade on to our advantage as a dyke movement – were the same signs that allowed us to blend seamlessly, invisibly into the norms of a female gender world' (p. 89). However, their serving woman was highly suspicious of the wish to shut themselves away behind closed doors (for the privacy which Westerners associate with sex). Eventually it was discovered that she suspected them of coining money! Whether this was a subliminal, metaphorical awareness of same-sex passion can be only a matter for conjecture.

What is plain from this account is that there is plenty of same-sex passion among Tamil women. However, the mismatch between their framework of expectations and that which prevails among Western activists did not assist mutual comprehension. Even when Seizer did eventually encounter a few women whom she considered lesbian, in Madras, their priorities were not those of lesbians in the West. First, they want to establish their right to operate in the world as independent women – not contained by the kinship network – and therefore they are in no hurry to overthrow the screen of womanly affection. They 'were struggling, not to be validated as women *together*, but as women alone' (p. 98).

I have begun with the experiences of Susan Seizer and her partner because they point up the difficulty that besets any cross-cultural work. Obviously we want to know about and learn from other cultures but, equally obviously, that involves abstracting from other people's lives. Such appropriation is particularly risky where it follows the lines of global imbalances of wealth and power. That said, because I have been able to find some helpful texts and because it throws up notable comparisons with the west, I want to instance the scope of same-sex male relations in Islamic countries. The accounts I have been reading are written from within Islam, by people from Turkey, Pakistan and Tunisia; they describe the dominant sex-gender system, the range of ways of negotiating it that have traditionally been deployed, and the struggles of sexual dissidents today.[4] Plainly I cannot, myself, write in that vein. This will be a self-confessed exercise in Western self-referentiality, with the aim of unsettling assumptions about identity and pointing to the cultural specificity of same-sex practices and identities everywhere.

Of course, Islam, like Christianity, is diverse, but a basic pattern of sex-gender relations may be observed. In Islamic countries, it is not usual for men and women to associate freely. Any kind of sex outside marriage is a crime in Islamic religion; divorce is very rare. Men normally live at home until they marry; if a man has sex with an unmarried woman then they are expected to marry. The family is the necessary base for any decent life, and the only resort in times of difficulty. Badruddin Khan writes: 'This is not just one model of life in Pakistan; it is not a choice; it is the only way of life. Individual love is recognized only in the context of this environment, and it is supported only if it furthers its development' (Khan, pp. 94–5). In such a context, a Western gay or lesbian identity is difficult to conceive.

At the same time, male dominance and the seclusion of women correlate with strong male friendships and allow men to be physical together. 'In the Arab world, every man is more or less open to an experience with a man – at different degrees of involvement', Muhammed says (Rose *et al.*, 1996, p. 59). In Turkey, adult male friends hold hands, embrace and kiss; mutual masturbation is regarded not as homosexual behaviour, but as something (heterosexual) men do together. In fact, provided a husband takes care of his family and is discreet, his personal sex life doesn't much matter. 'From the standpoint of "family", it is less risky for men to have affairs with other men than with women', Badruddin Khan observes.[5]

In brief, males in Islamic countries are expected to exercise phallic power, and they do this by asserting themselves over women and other subordinates, and as men together. To be sure, not everyone lives in this way, but this is the normative framework of expectations.

What a man in Turkey must not be is an *ibne* – an 'effeminate' male. Such a person does not marry; he may be a transvestite, earning his living by dancing, singing or prostitution; sexually, he is thought to be impotent, to play only the 'passive' role. This is the crucial distinction: between the 'active', 'masculine' inserter and the 'passive', 'feminine' insertee. Whether the insertee is a male or a female is relatively unimportant. Being attracted to boys is not regarded as unnatural or abnormal; just rather second-rate. Mehmet Ümit Necef explains:

> Any married man 'too full of lust' or separated too long from his wife looks for prostitutes, mistresses, animals (dogs and donkeys) or *lbneler*. Nobody would consider himself as 'abnormal', 'perverse', 'sinful', let alone 'homosexual' for fucking an *ibne*. He would not identify himself with a (minority) group of 'men-fuckers' or 'animal-fuckers'. To bugger an *ibne* is an enjoyment open to all; any man may be seduced by one of those. (Necef, pp. 73–4)

The reason why bisexuality is 'such a mass phenomenon in the Arab world', Muhammed says, is that 'the active bisexual sees the passive gay whom he has sex with as an extension of the/a woman. It is not badly considered at all to fuck, but to be fucked is a catastrophe' (Rose *et al.*, p. 59). (From this point, I cease putting quote marks round 'masculine', 'feminine' and 'effeminate'. However, it must be remembered that these are ideological constructs, not natural attributes.)

The sex-gender system in Islamic countries is far less preoccupied with same-sex passion, then, than is the case in Western societies. The gender of one's partner is not so important. The crucial point is that a man should maintain the dominant, masculine role, and hence a conventional gender hierarchy. There are feminine men, but they are regarded as freakish. In this framework, it is hard to conceive the gay man as we have constituted him in the West.

Becoming a man

I have been stressing the differences between Western and some Third World sex-gender systems. Indeed, if mutual masturbation had been regarded in twentieth-century Britain as heterosexual behaviour, as Huseyin Tapinc says it is in Turkey, many men who went to prison would have walked free. Nevertheless, gender hierarchy and the notion that dissident sexuality should be interpreted in terms of freakish gender abnormality are not foreign to the West. The notion of the female soul in the male body and the male soul in the female body was propounded by the sexologists at the turn of the century and only partly qualified by Freud. It fed into the older idea that leisure-class men were effeminate – idle and dissolute – anyway; Oscar Wilde conveniently supplied the confirmation that they were likely to be homosexual, to the point where he became the defining instance. When Quentin Crisp, who was born in 1908, writes in the 1960s that male homosexuals 'must, with every breath they draw, with every step they take, demonstrate that they are feminine', he almost describes the Turkish *ibne*. The partner of the queer gent, according to the dominant model, was lower-class and therefore masculine, and probably married. He did not need to regard himself as other than normal.[6]

The central project in the self-assertion of gay men, since the riot at the Stonewall Inn in New York in 1969, has been the attempt to rehandle gender assignment and gender hierarchy, and hence to repel the stigma of effeminacy. This has involved claiming masculinity for gay men, declaring that gay femininity is all right, and various combinations of these. The story is further complicated by the fact that we have been pursuing divergent modes of validation. Some of us want to say that our gender attributes (whatever they are) don't make us very different from other people and homophobia is just a misunderstanding; others want to say that les-bi-gay versions of gender attributes are fundamentally dissident and subversive of hetero-patriarchy, and hence are indeed, and properly, disconcerting to other people.[7]

Overall, among all this urgent defensive work, I locate six tendencies among gay-identified men in North America and North-western Europe today:

1. Any gay man may wear masculine jeans and T-shirts (and perhaps boots and a moustache), regardless of his preferred role in bed;
2. Any gay man may wear feminine or androgynous clothes, regardless of his preferred role in bed;
3. A gay man may do almost anything in bed, without regard to conventional gendered roles;
4. Even if two men maintain gendered roles in appearance and/or in bed, this does not thereby constitute a hierarchy (it does not bear a particular relation to who does the housework or drives the car);
5. Any gay cultivation of gendered roles may be either parodic or in earnest, and sometimes both at once;
6. Above all, there are few distinct terms for gendered roles: *all these men are gay.*

Mapping the influences upon this Western gay identity – in its diverse manifestations – would be a substantial task. We would have to consider the initial radical influence of the Gay Liberation Front, the countervailing pressure to conform, and the persistence of both into the present time; the (partial) decline in class and familial deference; how the women's movement has interacted with changing patterns of employment and family to redefine femininity, and to some extent masculinity; the development of the notion that citizenship is mainly a matter of consuming; and the hegemony of the United States (for 'pioneer' notions of maleness are deeply inscribed in US ideology and the Western male gay image is very 'American').

These influences have affected lesbians also. However, because women are likely to be perceived as aspiring to masculine prestige, rather than declining into feminine indignity, their situation is not symmetrical with that of men. They are coping with the subordination of women, as well as the stigma of 'wrong' gender assignment, but still the rehandling of gender hierarchy has been important. Sue-Ellen Case describes how the butch/femme pattern was suppressed during the hey-day of radical feminism, but is now reasserted both as a notable historical formation (for instance by Joan Nestle), and as productive in the current situation – 'playfully inhabiting the camp space of irony and wit, free from biological determinism, elitist essentialism, and the heterosexist cleavage of sexual difference'.[8]

The extent to which Western les-bi-gays have succeeded in repelling gender hierarchy may be registered partly in the extent to which Turkey, Pakistan and Tunisia seem strange to Westerners. However, the dominant sex-gender ideology is hardly to be overthrown, nor even notably reoriented, by some gay men, or for that matter some lesbians, growing moustaches. In practice, we all know, the stigma of effeminacy is fully available today to the press, in the playground, and in male-bonding contexts of all kinds. And, enveloped in this hostile ideology, many gay men themselves still believe, though perhaps residually, that the insertee is feminine and hence inferior.

Inclusions and exclusions

A problem with the work on Islamic societies upon which I have been drawing is that it is written mainly by people who have found themselves more comfortable with the Western concepts. Thus Badruddin Khan, who is living in Toronto, concludes: 'There is some reason to hope that, in the coming decades as the world draws closer, gay life in Karachi may yet develop in the inhospitable soil there' (Khan, p. 104). The temptation, as Stephen O. Murray observes, is to suppose a 'developmental' model: third world countries should 'catch up' by producing homosexuals like those in the West – even as at one time the economies of third world countries were envisaged as 'underdeveloped', then as 'developing', in the direction marked out by the West. In some aspects that is happening: there are gay men in the Western mode now in big cities in Turkey and throughout the third world, and often their Western orientation is marked by the adoption of the word 'gay'.

But it would be arrogant to suppose that Western ideas of sexuality will simply sweep aside indigenous modes. For, as Arjun Appadurai observes, 'the new global economy has to be understood as a complex, overlapping, disjunctive order, which cannot any longer be understood in terms of the existing center-periphery models' (Appadurai, 1990, pp. 295–310). We know only too well that gay, lesbian and bisexual identities are not coherent in the west; they are conflicted in themselves and in their interfaces with other aspects of the sex-gender system. So how could they be simply planted, like a flag on a pole, in other countries? 'At least as rapidly as forces from various metropolises are brought into new societies they tend to become indigenized in one or other way', Appadurai says (p. 295).

Nor should we suppose that the Western sex-gender system offers the optimum scope for same-sex expression among humankind. Muhammed says he feels less free as a bisexual in London than in Tunisia, where same-sex passion is little spoken of, scarcely acknowledged as a preference, and hardly stigmatized: 'For me, liberation of any kind is not a matter of a group of intellectuals starting off a movement. It means liberation at the level of the people (the man in the street), of society in its entirety'.[9] In other words, although a small number of committed gays may be fulfilled in the West, very many men are able to enjoy same-sex relations unselfconsciously in Tunisia.

For every identity is an exclusion as well as an inclusion. In North America and North-Western Europe, the years since 1969 have afforded good opportunity to those who want to be gay or lesbian. But for those who have felt themselves to be interested in same-sex passion but somewhat to one side of those models, gay identity has been a constraint. Lately, people living in the West have been saying this; I will discuss, briefly, racial minorities, the Queer movement, bisexuals, and men who have sex with men.

Generally in the West, gay identity has coincided with and depended on a weakening of family ties. Partly as a consequence of education, many younger people do not share, or expect to share, the outlook of their parents. Capitalism requires us to learn work skills that our elders do not comprehend, and to move around the country and the globe. In such a context, to disaffiliate from family and acquire an alternative identity – a class identity, for instance – is customary. So if our parents don't understand our sexualities, it is not too surprising and we can probably cope with it. We hope that, when we come upon hard times, friendship networks, pension schemes and social services will sustain us. But this disaffiliation from family does not suit members of racial minorities. Cherríe Moraga writes of the situation of American Chicana lesbians:

It seems my life has always been a kind of Catch 22. For any way you look at it, Chicanas are denied one another's fidelity. If women betray one another through heterosexism, then lesbianism is a kind of visible statement of our faithfulness to one another. But if lesbianism is white, then the women I am faithful to can never be my own. And we are forced to move away from our people.[10]

The writing of people such as Moraga will gradually reorient ideas of what Chicana women may do; they will help Chicana lesbians to take same-sex passion back to their families and communities. Thus they may produce new modes of relating that will be valuable for many in those communities, and instructive for the rest of us.

The Queer movement was a call to resist continuing harassment by government, the media and queerbashers, to denounce the feeble establishment response to AIDS, and to reassert the revolutionary potential of kinky sexuality. It condemned the complacency of many lesbians and gay men, especially those who have found convenient niches for themselves and who believe that keeping quiet may lead to social acceptance. The anonymous leaflet 'Queer Power Now' (London, 1991) demanded:

Queers, start speaking for yourself! Queers, Dykes, Fags, Fairies, Arse Bandits, Drag Queens, Trannies, Clubbers, Sluts . . . Call yourself what you want. Reject all labels. Be all labels. Liberate yourself from the lie that we're all lesbians and gay men. Free yourself from the lie that we're all the same . . . Liberate your minds. Queer is not about gay or lesbian – it's about sex![11]

The use here of the terms of our stigma is designed as much to confront conventional gays as to seize a language from the straight system. In fact, a problem for Queer as a movement was that its programme entailed rejecting most of its potential constituency – many of whom were still struggling in difficult circumstances to make out as lesbians and gay men, and didn't want to be told off because they weren't ready to adapt to Queer. Hence the movement was composed almost entirely of vanguard, and the exhaustion that afflicts activists set in quite rapidly.

Bisexuals became more assertive at about the same time as, and partly through, the Queer movement. Lesbians and gay men have been inclined to regard self-proclaimed bisexuals as lacking the courage to abandon a protective stake in heterosexuality. In the 1970s and 1980s, to declare yourself gay or lesbian was such a strenuous project that to blur the effect by adding that sometimes you were a bit straight after all seemed just too complicated, and scarcely plausible. Now, in the mid-1990s, some young people are not daunted by that kind of pressure. And some established lesbian and gay activists, who can hardly be accused of running scared, have been venturing beyond customary identities.

People from racial minorities, queers and people who term themselves 'bisexual' are still, for the most part, declaring a relation to existing lesbian and gay constructs and institutions. A group that does not, by definition, offer itself for federation is men who have sex with men while living generally as heterosexuals and regarding themselves as basically 'normal'. Until recently these people have hardly been considered – they have come to attention because they are difficult to reach with guidance about safer sex. They don't read the gay press or pick up condoms as they leave the pub; they may not have private space in which such matters may be negotiated; they may even think that HIV is what gays get, and therefore not relevant to them. I don't know of work that indicates how far these points apply to women.

Once, we supposed that the opportunity to be openly gay would attract many husbands away from their marriages and save younger men from making such a mistake; so married homosexuals would die out as a breed. But this is not happening. Some gay men of my acquaintance are meeting married men on a casual basis, others are having substantial affairs with them. Sometimes these husbands declare that they enjoy family life, love their spouses, and see no inevitable contradiction between occasional or secondary gay experience and a heterosexual lifestyle.

What has happened, I think, is that while the majority of men who are now leading an openly gay life would once have been married and covert, a further cohort that would once have scarcely allowed themselves gay fantasies is now having covert sex with men. And, beyond that, almost certainly, there are men who are thinking, but as yet hardly doing anything, about it. The relative legitimation that the gay movement has achieved has allowed everyone to move one space across. If this is the case, the proportion of males likely to engage in same-sex experience is larger than we have supposed – far larger than the proportion of males who will ever (as we can conceive it) identify as gay.

With these four disturbances of lesbian and gay orthodoxy in view (racial minorities, the Queer movement, bisexuals, and men who have sex with men), I conclude that we may now be entering the period of the *post-*

gay – a period when it will not seem so necessary to define, and hence to limit, our sexualities. To be sure, proclaiming that whatever most of us thought we were doing is passée because it's 'post-' is an easy way for the trendsetter to make a mark. And many people in Britain are still working at becoming lesbian and gay. Nevertheless, we may need to recognize that, despite our anti-essentialist theory, we have imagined sexuality to be less diverse and less mobile than, for many people, it is. Even as the sex-gender systems of some non-Western countries do not correspond to the scope of same-sex relations in the west, so the current Western lesbian and gay identities will never account for more than a proportion of same-sex passion in our society.

Subculture and politics

As feminists and commentators from racial and ethnic groups have remarked, it is ironic that just at the moment when subordinated peoples begin to centre ourselves as agents in our own lives, anti-essentialist criticism tells us that the centred subject is a delusion. Straight WASP men have abandoned the game and taken their ball away. And how are we to found an effective political movement on dispersed subjectivities? Many les-bi-gays believe that asserting that we can't help being gay will help defend us against homophobia. However, essentialist assumptions have not protected Jews, or Blacks, or innumerable native peoples from oppression and exploitation. They have not protected women. Conversely, religious faith is not generally reckoned to be innate, and that has not discouraged believers from asserting rights.

Does this mean, then, that we can or should abandon gay and lesbian?[12] And if our identities are contingent, multiple and provisional, how are we to build a community, let alone a political movement? Three points.

First, there cannot be a culture without categories, and I doubt that there can be one without hierarchies. A culture is a pattern of preferences for some modes of relating over others. All we can do is try to avoid making those categories and hierarchies where we have some influence more oppressive than they need be.

Second, the question of a les-bi-gay community is often bizarrely posed, as if it should mean total harmony – endless choruses of Tom Robinson's 'Glad to be Gay'. I prefer the term 'subculture' because it doesn't connote cosiness. Of course, we manifest the divisions of class, gender, race, age and education that occur in the wider society. Some of us are conservative by instinct, some are radical; some are sceptical, some religious. It would be absurd to expect otherwise. Nor is such complexity a weakness; what would be enfeebling is if our subcultures were no more than 'the scene' – clubs and bars. The diversity of our potential constituency is a source of strength.

For, third, we live in a dangerous world, and cannot risk trying to manage without subculture and politics. We have to build on from existing lesbian and gay identities; they offer the best chance of a political constituency. In the last analysis, our identities are situated at the most sensitive friction points of sexuality, love, power, gender, intimacy, stigma, nakedness, risk, and vulnerability. They have been acquired in the face of extreme hostility, not just from strangers, but from people whom we believed we could trust. They have the complexity and strength, and perhaps brittleness, that derive from resistance including, in most cases, our own resistance to our selves. In other words, they could hardly have a stronger basis in social interaction and in our subjectivities. Sarah Schulman summarizes this in *People in Trouble*, her novel about fighting AIDS in New York:

> 'The gay community', James said, 'is a unique community because our family is bonded on love. Each one of us has defined our lives by love and sexuality – the two greatest human possibilities. We have all recognized these truths in the face of great denial'. (1990, p. 118)

If such identities are indeed compelling, there is no reason to expect them to be simple.

Notes

1. Women who identify as lesbian are more likely to believe that they have made a choice: see Vera Whisman, *Queer by Choice*. New York: Routledge, 1996.
2. See Michael Warner (ed.), *Fear of a Queer Planet*. Minneapolis: Minnesota University Press, 1993.
3. Susan Seizer, 'Paradoxes of Visibility in the Field: Rites of Queer Passage in Anthropology', *Public Culture*, Vol. 8, 1995, 73-100, p. 98. I am grateful to Wei-cheng Raymond Chu for drawing my attention to this article. There are several first-person accounts by South Asian lesbians in Rakesh Ratti (ed.) *A Lotus of Another Color*. Boston: Alyson, 1993.
4. I draw principally upon Mehmet Umit Necef, 'Turkey on the Brink of Modernity: a Guide for Scandinavian Gays', and Badruddin Khan, 'Not-So-Gay Life

in Karachi: A View of a Pakistani Living in Toronto', both in Arno Schmitt and Jehoeda Sofer (eds), *Sexuality and Eroticism among Males in Moslem Societies*. New York: Haworth Press, 1992; Huseyin Tapinc, 'Masculinity, Femininity and Turkish Male Homosexuality', in Ken Plummer (ed.), *Modern Homosexualities*. London: Routledge, 1992; 'Bisexuality in the Arab World: Interview with Muhammed by Francoise Gollain', in Sharon Rose, Cris Stevens *et al.*, eds., *Bisexual Horizons*. London: Lawrence and Wishart, 1996. Also I have been reading through issues of *Trikone Magazine*, San Jose, California, and *Dost,* Bombay. I am very grateful for the help and advice of Pratap Rughani.

5. Badruddin Khan, 'Not-So-Gay Life in Karachi', in Schmitt and Jehoeda Sofer (eds.), *Sexuality and Eroticism*, p. 95. In my view, this is probably how it was in Shakespearean England: see Alan Sinfield, 'How to Read The Merchant of Venice without being Heterosexist', in Terence Hawkes, (ed.), *Alternative Shakespeares 2*. London: Routledge, 1996.

6. Quentin Crisp, *The Naked Civil Servant*. New York: Plume, 1977, p. 21. See John Marshall, 'Pansies, Perverts and Macho Men: Changing Conceptions of Male Homosexuality', in Kenneth Plummer (ed.), *The Making of the Modern Homosexual*. London: Hutchinson, 1981, pp. 146–7; Marjorie Garber, *Vested Interests*. New York: Routledge, 1992, pp. 137–41; Sinfield, *The Wilde Century*. London: Cassell, 1994, chs. 6–8.

7. For a recent analysis, see Murray Healy, *Gay Skins*. London, Cassell, 1996, ch. 6.

8. See Sue-Ellen Case, 'Towards a Butch-Femme Aesthetic', in Henry Abelove *et al.* (eds.), *The Lesbian and Gay Studies Reader*. New York: Routledge, 1993, pp. 297, 305.

9. 'Bisexuality in the Arab World', in Rose, Stevens *et al.*, (eds), *Bisexual Horizons*. p. 61. These points are strongly made by Martin F. Manalansan IV, 'In the Shadows of Stonewall: Examining Gay Transnational Politics and the Diasporic Dilemma', *GLQ* (*Gay and Lesbian Quarterly*), 2 (1995), 425–38.

10. Cherríe Moraga, *Loving in the War Years*. Boston: South End Press, 1983, p. 116. See also Sunil Gupta, 'Black, Brown and White', in Simon Shepherd and Mick Wallis (eds), *Coming on Strong*. London: Unwin Hyman, 1989, p. 176.

11. See also Warner (ed.), *Fear of a Queer Planet*; Cherry Smyth (ed.), *Lesbians Talk Queer Notions*. London: Scarlet, 1992; Healy, *Gay Skins*. pp. 172–86.

12. See Leo Bersani, *Homos*. Cambridge, Mass.: Harvard University Press, 1995, prologue and chs. 1 and 2; Mark Simpson (ed.), *Anti-Gay*. London: Cassell, 1996.

References

Appadurai, Arjun, 'Disjuncture and Difference in the Global Cultural Economy', in *Theory, Culture, Society*, Vol. 7, 1990, pp. 295–310.

Berger, Peter L., and Luckmann, Thomas, *The Social Construction of Reality*. Harmondsworth: Penguin, 1971.

Khan, Badruddin, 'Not-So-Gay Life in Karachi', in Arno Schmitt and Jehoeda Sofen (eds), *Sexuality and Eroticism among Males in Moslem Societies*. New York: Haworth Press, 1992.

Murray, Stephen O., 'The "Underdevelopment" of Modern/Gay Homosexuality in MesoAmerica', in K. Plummer (ed.), *Modern Homosexualities*. London: Routledge, 1992, pp. 29–38.

Necef, Mehmet Ümit, 'Turkey on the Brink of Modernity', in Arno Schmitt and Jehoeda Sofen (eds), *Sexuality and Eroticism among Males in Moslem Societies*. New York: Haworth Press, 1992.

Rose, Sharon, Stevens, Cris *et al.* (eds), *Bisexual Horizons*. London: Lawrence and Wishart, 1996.

Schulman, Sarah, *People in Trouble*. London: Sheba Feminist Publishers, 1990.

Seizer, Susan, 'Paradoxes of Visibility in the Field: Rites of Queer Passage in Anthropology', in *Public Culture*, Vol. 8, 1995, pp. 73–100.

15

Race Matters

Vivien Ng

> Disfigured faces, denied identities – such is the plight that afflicts us Asian gay men, and to a larger degree, our lesbian sisters. In the 'liberal' white media, be it gay or straight, our race is marginalized; it is handy for identification purposes only. In our own Asian communities, our sexualities are invisible. If mentioned sometimes, it is only done so to be knocked down, dismissed, and sent back to the hell of silence and nonentity.
>
> Eric C. Wat, *Preserving the Paradox*

> In short, legally speaking, there is no race to homosexuality.
>
> Mary Eaton, *Homosexual Unmodified*

THE BROADWAY MUSICAL *Miss Saigon*[1] opened in New York City in April 1991 amidst a chorus of protests. Coverage of the controversy in mainstream press focused almost entirely on the casting of the show. Mary Suh reports in *Ms.* on Actor's Equity's initial decision to bar Jonathan Pryce, a Caucasian, from the Broadway production because Asian actors had not been given the chance to audition the role. Equity subsequently strategically retreated when Cameron Mackintosh, the producer, threatened to kill the show altogether (1990, p. 63). In the same vein, Jessica Hagedorn writes in *New York Newsday* (1991) about the double bind Asian American actors faced: 'Do we protest and attempt to block the hiring of a fellow Asian like Ms Salonga, just so the job could go to an Asian-*American* actress? Do we protest the furthering of stereotypes by this musical, on the one hand, while clamoring for the right to play these well-paid roles on the other?' What readers of these mainstream publications did not know, however, was that there was another layer to the controversy surrounding *Miss Saigon* – the decision by Lambda Legal Defense and Education Fund and the Lesbian and Gay Community Services Center, both based in New York City, to use the musical as their major fundraiser in April and October, 1991, respectively. I relate the controversy here because it illustrates the entrenched racism (both conscious and unconscious) that plagues the white gay and lesbian community, as well as the shortcomings of single-identity-based politics.

When members of Asian Lesbians of the East Coast (ALOEC) and Gay Asian and Pacific Islander Men of New York (GAPIMNY) found out about Lambda's and the Center's fundraising plans, they met for the first time as a coalition in December 1990 to devise ways to make the two organizations abandon *Miss Saigon*. Deciding to target Lambda first because their fundraiser was earlier, the coalition sent a letter, dated 21 December, 1990, to Tom Stoddard, executive director of Lambda, demanding that Lambda develop an alternative plan for its benefit. They made it plain that they understood Lambda's need to raise money, but *Miss Saigon* was unacceptable because of the racist and misogynist nature of its plot and lyrics.[2] In his reply of 15 January 1991, Stoddard expressed sensitivity to issues raised by ALOEC and GAPIMNY; at the same time, he hinted that Lambda's decision was irreversible, citing the need for raising funds.[2] After meeting with representatives of ALOEC and GAPIMNY on 19 February 1991, the Lambda board decided to go ahead with *Miss Saigon* (Yoshikawa, 1994, p. 286).

Theorizing identity politics

Since the late 1980s, constructs such as 'identity', 'identity politics', and even 'community' have been subject to critical examination by postmodernist and queer theorists. Fuelling their rhetorical fire is the simplistic and globalizing construction of 'women' that typified white feminist theory of the 1970s. Judith Butler is on the mark when she writes,

> That form of theorizing has come under criticism for its efforts to colonize and appropriate non-Western cultures to support highly Western notions of oppression, but because they tend as well to construct a 'Third World' or even 'Orient' in which gender oppression is subtly explained as symptomatic of an essential, non-Western barbarism. (1990, p. 3)

Extending her investigation to the categories of 'sex' and 'gender', Butler asks, 'Is there "a" gender which persons are said to *have*, or is it an essential attribute that a person is said to *be*, as implied in the question, "What gender are you?"' (p. 7) Her skepticism is such that when she was asked to participate in a conference on lesbian and gay theories, she pondered,

> At first I considered writing a different sort of essay, one with a philo-sophical tone: the 'being' of being homosexual. The prospect of *being* anything, even for pay, has always produced in me a certain anxiety, for 'to be' gay, 'to be' lesbian seems to be more than a simple injunction to become who or what I already am. . . . To write or speak *as a lesbian* appears a paradoxical appearance of this 'I', one which feels neither true nor false. For it is a production, usually in response to a request, to come out or write in the name of an identity which, once produced, sometimes functions as a politically efficacious phantasm. I am not at ease with 'lesbian theories, gay theories', for as I have argued else-where, identity categories tend to be instruments of regulatory regimes, whether as the normalizing categories of oppressive structures or as the rallying points for a liberatory contestation of that very oppression. This is not to say that I will not appear at political occasions under the sign of lesbian, but that I would like to have it permanently unclear what precisely that sign signifies. (1991, pp. 13–14)

In a similar vein, Diana Fuss (1989) opens her chapter, 'Lesbian and Gay Theory: The Question of Identity Politics' with the query: is 'gay identity' real or fictive? She then explains the significance of such interrogation:

> Central to the controversy over the invention of homosexuality is the related issue of 'identity politics', a phrase with notably wide currency in gay and lesbian communities. In common usage, the term identity politics refers to the tendency to base one's politics on a sense of per-sonal identity – as gay, as Jewish, as Black, as female. . . . It has been endorsed by both gay men and lesbians as a working theoretical base upon which to build a cohesive and visible political community. . . .
>
> It should be clarified at the outset that although identity politics has been embraced by both lesbian and gay theorists, this is not to say that gay and lesbian subjects, as I have linked them here, inevitably share the same concerns or necessarily represent a unified political coalition. (1989, p. 97)

The *trouble* with Butler and Fuss (and other postmodernist/queer theorists) is the absence of the voice(s) of lesbian feminists of colour in their studies, and in the few instances where they are mentioned, (notably, Cherríe Moraga and Barbara Smith), they have been either misrepresented or marginalized. In her provocative essay, 'Postmodernism, "Realism", and the Politics of Identity: Cherríe Moraga and Chicana Feminism', Paula M. L. Moya discloses the 'misappropriation of women of color' by postmodernist theorists (1997, p. 128). Regarding *Gender Trouble*, Moya criticizes Butler for taking Moraga out of context, thus commiting the same offence that Butler herself has earlier faulted white feminist theorists for:

> Butler extracts one sentence from Moraga, buries it in a footnote, and then misreads it in order to justify her own inability to account for the complex interrelations that structure various forms of human identity. . . . She reads Moraga's statement that 'the danger lies in ranking the oppressions' to mean that we have no way of adjudicating among different kinds of oppressions. . . . This misreading of Moraga follows on the heels of Butler's dismissal of Irigaray's notion of phallogocentrism (as globalizing and exclusionary) and clears the way for her to do away with the category of 'women' altogether. Thus, although Butler at first appears to have understood the critiques of women (primarily of color) who have been historically precluded from occupying the position of the 'subject' of feminism, it becomes clear that their voices have been merely instrumental to her. (p. 133)

Not only has Butler misread Moraga in the section of her book that raises doubts about the efficacy of coalitional politics, but she has also ignored the intellectual contributions of other women of colour who have written extensively about the theory and practice of such politics. Is it possible that Audre Lorde and Barbara Smith, among others, have been dismissed as too 'essentialist' because of their persistent (and consistent) self-identification as Black lesbian feminists?

Harriet Malinowitz correctly names Audre Lorde as 'the theorist perhaps most often cited for galvanizing the lesbian feminist community to think about the nature and politics of difference' (1996, p. 265). In her essay, 'Age, Race, Class, and Sex: Women Redefining Difference', Lorde criticizes the women's movement for its 'pretense to a homogeneity of experience covered by the word *sisterhood* that does not in fact exist'

(1984a, p. 116). At the same time, she acknowledges that within the Black community, the 'need for unity is often misnamed as a need for homogeneity, and a Black feminist vision mistaken for betrayal of our common interests as a people' (p. 119). However, rather than becoming paralysed by 'difference' into accepting the impossibility of community or coalition building, as Butler and other postmodernist theorists appear to be, Lorde is mobilized to 'take our differences and make them strengths' (1984b, p. 112). She opens 'The Master's Tools Will Never Dismantle the Master's House' with the statement that, 'It is a particular academic arrogance to assume any discussion of feminist theory without examining our many differences, and without a significant input from poor women, Black and Third World women, and lesbians' (p. 110). Later in the essay, she makes the critical point:

> As women, we have been taught either to ignore our differences, or to view them as causes for separation and suspicion rather than as forces for change. Without community there is no liberation, only the most vulnerable and temporary armistice between an individual and her oppression. But community must not mean a shedding of our differences, nor the pathetic pretense that these differences do not exist . . .
> *I urge each one of us here to reach down into that deep place of knowledge inside herself and touch the terror and loathing of any difference that lives there. See whose face it wears.* Then the personal as the political can begin to illuminate all our choices. (pp. 112, 113; emphasis in original)

In her critique of identity politics, Diana Fuss endorses the analysis of Jenny Bourne, who regards identity politics as reactionary. Bourne faults the blind faith in 'the personal is political' for much that is wrong with identity politics (1989, p. 100–1). Fuss gives passing reference to 'A Black Feminist Statement' by the Combahee River Collective, identifying it correctly as an early manifesto for identity politics (ca. 1977), and expresses her philosophical reservations over Barbara Smith's insistence that her politics and her identity as a Black woman are causally related. The Combahee River Collective and Barbara Smith are thus discussed in the context of her criticism of 'the politics of identity politics'; yet, when she moves on to 'theorize' identity and 're-politicize' identity politics, Smith and other women of colour disappear from her scope. What Fuss fails to consider (or take seriously) is that unlike other single-identity groups that organized around only gender or race or sexual orientation, the Combahee

River Collective, of which Barbara Smith was a founding member, recognized from the start multiple forms of oppression (and the embodiment of multiple identities in individuals) and rejected pointedly the essentialist (and separatist) politics of white lesbian feminists:

> Although we are feminists and lesbians, we feel solidarity with progressive Black men and do not advocate the fractionalization that white women who are separatists demand. Our situation as Black people necessitates that we have solidarity around the fact of race, which white women of course do not need to have with white men, unless it is their negative solidarity as racial oppressors. We struggle together with Black men against racism, while we also struggle with Black men about sexism. . . .
>
> *A political contribution which we feel we have already made is the expansion of the feminist principle that the personal is political.* In our consciousness-raising sessions, for example, we have in many ways gone beyond white women's revelations because we are dealing with the implications of race and class as well as sex. (1983, p. 213; my emphasis)

In other words, 'A Black Feminist Statement' anticipates many of the questions raised about 'identity politics' by 1990s theorists, and yet this fact has been subsequently ignored. The dismissal of the intellectual and political contributions of lesbian feminists of colour, whilst not fatal, calls into question the efficacy of Butler's and Fuss's theoretical (and political) positions. Nonetheless, it should be acknowledged that their viewpoints are not without application, as the lessons from the *Miss Saigon* controversy can show. Certainly, their effort to problematize concepts such as 'sexual identity' and 'identity politics' helps to answer the question posed by Urvashi Vaid in her criticism of mainstream gay and lesbian politics, 'How did a movement about sexual politics – a politics centred on the idea that sexuality is the intersection at which so many of our identities meet – become limited to a movement divided by sexual and racial and gender-based identities?' (1996, p. 281).

The protest against *Miss Saigon* instigated not only the first-ever collaboration between Asian Lesbians on the East Coast and Gay Asian and Pacific Islander Men of New York, but perhaps more importantly, it also brought together gay and straight Asian American political and community activists. Thus, even though their intervention with Lambda failed and the show still goes on today on Broadway, the struggle marked a high point in the history of Asian American political activism. At the same time, this Asian American 'success' has an ironic twist which illustrates once more the complexities of identity formation that both Butler and Fuss have addressed in their writings. Nina Reyes, in her article on Asian lesbians and gays in the magazine *Outweek*, reported that not all Filipinos agreed with the protests because the star of the musical, Lea Salonga, was a Filipina, a fact that was a source of pride to many Filipinos (Manalansan, 1996, p. 56). And, at the anniversary celebration of Gay Asian and Pacific Islander Men in New York in the summer of 1992, one of the drag performers, a Filipino gay man, refused to be talked out of doing a lipsynch performance of Lea Salonga's songs in *Miss Saigon*, thus upsetting many revellers who found his choice appalling, given the protest a year earlier against the show (p. 56). As Martin Manalansan points out, 'It is important to note not only the effects of the *Miss Saigon* controversy on Asian American gay politics, but also how the representations and characters of this Broadway show have become icons of Filipino gay men.' (p. 57) Perhaps one factor that must be taken into account in constructing and/or understanding gay/ lesbian Asian American identities is the degree of 'Asian-ness' or 'Ameri-can-ness' in these identities. In the case of Filipino gay men, for example, Manalansan discovers that for many of the first-generation immigrants, the issues of race and racism are not significant to them and are definitely secondary to their goal of realizing the American dream (pp. 57–58). The acculturation divide is manifested in the issue of crossdressing and effem-inacy. The more self-consciously Americanized Filipino gay men (many of them go to gyms and act 'masculine') view the crossdressing habits of other Filipinos to be anachronistic and low-class. On the other hand, the cross-dressers 'accuse these "masculine" men of mimicking white Americans and of having illusions of being "real" men' (pp. 54–55). Perhaps in terms of performative 'subversiveness', the Filipino drag queens have a point there (Butler, 1990, p. 128). In any case, Dana Takagi's point is well taken: '[A]ttempts to define categories like "Asian American" or "gay" are necessarily incomplete. . . . Moreover, our search for authenticity of voice – whether in gay/lesbian Asian American writing or in some other identity string – will be tempered by the realization that in spite of our impulse to clearly (de)limit them, there is perpetual uncertainty and flux governing the construction and expression of identities.' (1996, pp. 32, 33)

Denied identities

On 10 January 1993, around 1:30 a.m., Truong Loc Minh, a Vietnamese immigrant, was viciously beaten by a gang of young white men in Laguna Beach, California, in an area of town where three gay bars were located. Police who were called to the scene suggested that it was a hate crime. But what kind of hate crime was it? The *Los Angeles Times* covered it as a gay-bashing incident and Truong's ethnicity was mentioned only once in the story. The Chinese-language *International Daily*, on the other hand, reported it as a case of Asian-bashing and went out of its way to assure its readers that Truong was not gay. There was no mention of the fact that Truong had pleaded guilty several years earlier to a charge of 'lewd conduct with another man' (Wat, 1996, p. 78). How can one explain the two radically different accounts? Did the two newspapers lie? In Eric C. Wat's opinion, neither lied, but their 'truth' had been mediated by racial and cultural assumptions about gay men and Asian men. He sees a parallel between newspaper accounts of the Truong attack and the lived reality of many gay Asian men:

> Like Truong, many gay Asian men are run over at the intersection of racism and homophobia. When each part of ourselves is not acknowledged at one time or another, it becomes difficult to define who we are. We are forever left in the middle of the road, unacceptable to those at either side of the street. . . .
>
> Somehow, sometime, somewhere, gay Asian men must find that third side of the street where we can grow, find our voices, learn about ourselves, and educate others about who we are, so that eventually we can join both sides of the street. (1996, pp. 79–80)

Wat's article appears in *Asian American Sexualities: Dimensions of the Gay & Lesbian Experience* (Routledge, 1996), a collection of essays whose publication represents a breakthrough in Asian American studies as well as Lesbian and Gay Studies – the third side of the street, so to speak. The influence of postmodernist and queer theorists such as Diana Fuss, Judith Butler, Eve Sedgwick, and Monique Wittig on this emergent field is obvious, as the footnotes of a number of articles show. However, regardless of their theoretical orientation, almost all the essays in this volume address different ways in which racism, ethnicity, sexuality and desire intersect. David L. Eng's deconstruction of the Tony Award-winning play *M. But-*

terfly, for example, reveals how the straight mind of Asian America, functioning in the milieu of racist America, has produced a literature that is compulsorily heterosexual, to the detriment of any anti-racist and anti-homophobic project. Eng is troubled by this development, because '[t]he erasure of homosexuality from the arena of Asian American literature is finally limiting, denying both a rich artistic heteroglossia and a fecund political opportunity for Asian Americans to once again vex majority expectations of well-worn stereotypes' (1996, p. 146).

Eric C. Wat's rendering, 'All the Asians are straight, all the queers are white, but it was a while before we found out that some of us are brave' (1996, p. 79) – borrowed from the title of Barbara Smith's book, *All the Men are Black, All the Women are White, But Some of Us are Brave* (1982) – encapsulates the experience of many lesbians and gay men of colour. Mary Eaton, in her article, 'Homosexual Unmodified: Speculations on Law's Discourse, Race, and the Construction of Sexual Identity', analyzes *Williamson v. A. G. Edwards & Son Inc.* and *Watkins v. United States Army* – the only two cases in the vast body of legal opinions on lesbian and gay rights where the race of the litigants is mentioned – and concludes from studying the legal reasoning in these two cases that 'legally speaking, there is no race to homosexuality' (1995, p. 51).

In *Williamson v. A. G. Edwards & Son Inc.*, Williamson, an African American man, accused his employer of discriminating against him because of his race and sued for reinstatement. A. G. Edwards, however, insisted that Williamson was dismissed solely because of his homosexuality – specifically, that he wore makeup at work and talked openly about his 'lifestyle'. Williamson did not dispute that he flaunted his homosexuality at work but countered that heterosexual employees talked about their sex life with impunity; moreover, although his white gay co-workers were censured for wearing ear-rings to work, they were nonetheless not dismissed. Therefore, since he was the only one fired, his race must have been a factor in his termination. The judge, however, ruled against Williamson. Eaton concludes: 'What distinguishes makeup and earrings is . . . a question of degree, not of kind. . . . Williamson's race disappears as a concern of any legal consequence because he was much too queer to be black or, to put matters somewhat differently, because the rouge was thick enough to conceal the *noir*' (p. 56).

In *Watkins v. US Army*, Sgt Perry Watkins, an African American, appealed successfully to the Ninth Circuit after his discharge from the army in 1981 because of his homosexuality. This case has been widely touted as a victory for lesbian and gay rights because the Ninth Circuit found the army's policy unconstitutional because it singled out homosexuals on the basis of who they were – i.e., their sexual identity. Eaton's research reveals that Watkins' race has been practically ignored; indeed, except for the occasional reference to his race in the original discharge papers, the fact that he is Black would not have surfaced at all. These references suggest to Eaton that the effort to remove Watkins from the army might have been racially motivated but this possibility was not raised by Watkins in his suit, nor did the court consider it. She notes, 'Watkins' race never rose to prominence because the method by which the court conceptualized his sexual orientation claim presupposed that race and sexual identity were mutually exclusive' (p. 59). The erasure of Watkins' race is even more remarkable in light of the fact that Judge Norris, who wrote the majority opinion, used race as an analogy to sexual orientation throughout his reasoning without once alluding to (let alone discuss) the fact that Watkins is Black.

Eaton reads the erasure of race in both suits to mean that 'homosexuality has been legally coded as white, or to put matters conversely, that race has been legally coded as heterosexual' (p. 59). Applying what she characterizes as modified Foucauldian analysis, she suggests that 'this whitewashing of sexual identity is . . . required to sustain the dichotomized system of straight and queer sexualities' (p. 59). She argues that if it is the intent of Queer Theory to disrupt boundaries between say, queer and straight, then the centrality of racial erasure cannot be ignored:

> Insofar as these strategic disruptions take as their point of departure racially unmodified notions of homosexuality and heterosexuality, they isolate only one of the infrastructural elements in the architecture of dichotomy, continue to operate within the dyad mode, and risk reinstallment of its imperative. Re-racializing the homosexual is thus not only a matter of feel-good politics of inclusivity, it is crucial to the deconstruction of the category 'homosexual'. (p. 68)

The invisibility of lesbians and gay men of colour is a reality that has been socially scripted. This is illustrated by the experiences of Truong, Watkins and Williamson. How to make visible what has been rendered invisible is a challenge that activists and scholars (especially those of colour) have had to wrestle with. Eaton's call for re-racializing the homosexual must be handled with care, because coexisting with the erasure of race in certain discourses about homosexuality are stereotypes of people of colour that have resulted in some instances in their sexual appropriation or, worse, exploitation.

Race, sex and desire

Frantz Fanon, in *Black Skin, White Masks,* writes, 'the Negro is eclipsed. He is turned into a penis. He *is* a penis' (1970, p. 120). This incisive analysis resonated at the first OUT WRITE conference in 1990 when poet and essayist Essex Hemphill used part of his paper for a panel on 'AIDS and the Responsibility of the Writer' to criticize Robert Mapplethorpe for perpetuating racial stereotypes of Black men in his photographs. His tearful delivery received generally favourable response from the audience and he was praised for bringing to the fore the concerns of lesbians and gay men of colour. John Champagne, author of *The Ethics of Marginality: A New Approach to Gay Studies,* is less positive about both the form and substance of Hemphill's talk. He faults Hemphill for using tears to 'shame the audience into refusing to interrogate the terms of his address' (1995, p. 58). He agrees that gay culture often eroticizes racial difference but does not accept Hemphill's reading of Mapplethorpe's work. He suggests that Hemphill is hypocritical in his contention that Mapplethorpe's photographs reduce the Black man to the image of a big, black penis because Hemphill's own poetry 'in fact contains numerous references to dicks – presumably black ones, and some of them big' (p. 84). Champagne juxtaposes Hemphill's criticism of Mapplethorpe with the rhetoric of foes of pornography such as Dworkin and Stoltenberg and finds almost word-for-word similarity. In particular, he tries to unveil a middle-class bias in both Hemphill's and 'contemporary feminist disgust with pornography'. And he discerns a 'hybrid quality of Hemphill's (discursive) position, a position that exceeds the nominations "Black" and "gay"' (pp. 59–60).

Champagne is equally disenchanted with Marlon Riggs, in particular his film *Tongues Untied* (1989). He criticizes the film for privileging middle-class experience, with its 'talking head' style having more in common with that of experimental films than popular music videos such as those offered by the cable channel MTV. Champagne does not appear to be aware of his own racial/class biases that inform this assertion. One of his difficulties with *Tongues Untied* is the project itself – the attempt to render visible and give voice to what has been excluded from dominant discourse. He is concerned that '[i]n their eagerness to re-present the formerly undocumented

lives of the Other, such histories necessarily abdicate the project of resisting . . . the very "ideological system" that produces the Other as abject in
the first place' (pp. 71–72). Perhaps his greatest problem with the film is
the way white gay s/m men are represented in one segment of the film:

> The camera lures the spectator with a series of playful, sexy images of
> large white gay men. It peeps like a voyeur on the decadent, carniva-
> lesque atmosphere of the Gay Pride parade, and then juxtaposes these
> 'documentary' images with the 'degrading' images of Black women
> and men, drawing a kind of equivalence between the two sets of images,
> and suggesting a causal connection between the licentious behavior of
> these white men and the representations of Blacks. The suggestion is
> that while Rome burned, these white men in leather were obviously fid-
> dling. (pp. 77–78)

He does not deny that racism exists in the white gay community but contends that it is not the subject of his interrogation of *Tongues Untied*. He is
troubled that Riggs has not challenged straight culture's vilification of
white gay s/m men. In the end, he finds an ideological strand that connects
Hemphill, Riggs, 'antiporn feminists' and even the conservative Right –
that is, their '(middle)-class-inflected sense of disgust related to sexuality –
obviously, not related to all sexuality, but to a particularly culturally problematic kind' (p. 79).

Champagne's 'defence' of Mapplethorpe is in fact a critique of the
class and essentialist 'biases' of Hemphill and Riggs. His stance is determined as well by his disdain for anti-pornography advocates, especially
those who are critical of s/m practices. He chooses to sidestep the issue of
racism in the white gay community and thus evades the question of
whether Mapplethorpe exploited or employed racial stereotypes in his
photographs. The politics of race, sex and subversion, however, are central
to Kobena Mercer's defence of Mapplethorpe in 'Skin Head Sex Thing:
Racial Difference and the Homoerotic Imaginery', which he presented at
a queer film and video conference in 1989. This essay is particularly
intriguing because Mercer 'recanted' publicly his earlier reading of Mapplethorpe's work (1987). Whereas he previously criticized Mapplethorpe's
photos for perpetuating 'racial fetishism', he now assumes a more ambivalent stance and asks such questions as: '[D]o photographs like *Man in a
Polyester Suit* reinscribe the fixed beliefs of racist ideology, or do they problematize them by foregrounding the intersections of difference where race

and gender cut across the representation of sexuality?' (1991, p. 179). While he believes that it is impossible to answer the question unequivocally, he is able to, by situating Mapplethorpe's photographs in the context of contemporary urban gay male culture in the US, make the argument that it is possible to re-read the racial fetishism in Mapplethorpe's work 'not as a repetition of racist fantasies but as a deconstructive strategy that lays bare psychic and social relations of ambivalence in the representation of race and sexuality' (p. 187). Furthermore,

> In social, economic, and political terms, black men in the United States constitute one of the 'lowest' social classes: disenfranchised, disadvantaged, and disempowered as a distinct collective subject in the late capitalist underclass. Yet in Mapplethorpe's photographs, men who in all probability came from this class are elevated onto the pedestal of the transcendental Western aesthetic ideal. Far from reinforcing the fixed beliefs of the white supremacist imaginary, such a deconstructive move begins to undermine the foundational myths of the pedestal itself. (p. 188)

It is impossible to evaluate Mapplethorpe without broaching the question of pornography, but not just because conservative politicians – for example, Senator Jesse Helms – have characterized his work as such and used it as an excuse to cut federal support for the arts. Rather, it is because the centrality of the erotic in lesbian and gay life makes it necessary for us to distinguish between the 'erotic' and 'pornographic', as Audre Lorde has done in 'Uses of the Erotic: The Erotic as Power' (1984c).[4] In this essay, Lorde asserts that the erotic 'offers a well of replenishing and provocative force to the woman who does not fear its revelation, nor succumb to the belief that sensation is enough' (p. 54). However,

> The erotic has often been misnamed by men and used against women. It has been made into the confused, the trivial, the psychotic, the plasticized sensation. For this reason, we have often turned away from the exploration and consideration of the erotic as a source of power and information, confusing it with its opposite, the pornographic. But pornography is a direct denial of the power of the erotic, for it represents the suppression of true feeling. Pornography emphasizes sensation without feeling. (p. 54)

The juxtaposition by the editors of *The Lesbian and Gay Studies Reader* (Routledge, 1993) of Lorde's essay with Kobena Mercer's and Richard Meyer's essays in defence of Robert Mapplethorpe as *not* pornographic is fascinating. The provocative placement invites us to read Mapplethorpe against a Black lesbian feminist exegesis of the uses of the erotic and the difference between the erotic and the pornographic. Using Lorde's criteria, I read Mapplethorpe's photos as racist and pornographic, and this stance is clinched for me by Richard Fung's analysis of gay male pornographic films, in which Asian men are typically depicted as the 'bottom', a position that can be explained by stereotypical assumptions about Asian men as emasculated or undersexed. Alluding to Frantz Fanon's biting comment about representations of African men, Fung notes that in contrast, 'the Asian man is defined by a striking absence down there. And if Asian men have no sexuality, how can we have homosexuality?' (1991, p. 148). Without a penis, Asian men in these films are thus represented as primarily anuses. Fung's conclusion that in commercial gay sexual representation the anti-racist movements have had little impact is critical as we explore and try to understand the intersections of race, sex, and desire (Fung, 1991).

Concluding remarks

Lesbian and Gay Studies is at a critical juncture in our history. We marvel at how far we have come and how much we have grown in just two decades. At the same time, however, we face serious challenges – in particular, from postmodern and queer studies, which in recent years have dominated academic conferences as well as publication lists. In the United States, Lesbian and Gay Studies conferences have become essentially queer studies conferences. At the 1994 annual meeting of National Women's Studies Association in Ames, Iowa, a graduate student asked members of the panel on lesbian studies/queer studies whether, given her discomfort with what she saw as a trend in queer studies to privilege gay perspective over the lesbian, she should study Queer Theory. The unanimous response from the panelists was yes, if she wanted to get a job teaching about lesbians or to have an article published, because the gatekeepers – search committee members or editors – expect the prospective job candidate or author to be well versed in Queer Theory.

My discomfort with Queer Theory is not with the 'return to gender' that eclipses the lesbian that Sheila Jeffreys decries in *The Lesbian Heresy*

(1993) but with Queer Theory's blind spots with respect to issues of race and racism. As I have indicated in this essay, I do not discount the utility of Queer Theory in the study of the lives and struggles of people of colour, especially when the subject matter is the construction of 'identity'. However, I am concerned that when categories such as 'gender' and 'sex' and even 'race' are destabilized, where and how does anti-sexist, anti-racist work fit within the world of theory, in the academy? When the ideas of Essex Hemphill, Marlon Riggs, Audre Lorde, and Barbara Smith can be dismissed as essentialist and therefore theoretically as well as politically flawed, when exposure to Queer Theory can lead to a dramatic re-vision of Mapplethorpe's racist photographs, I fear that there is little room for anti-sexist, anti-racist work in the queer academy.

There are signs that the pendulum may begin to swing in the other direction soon and this is a hopeful development. Paula Moya's criticism of postmodern/queer theorists' appropriation of women of colour is a welcome contribution. So too is Sharon P. Holland's article in *The New Lesbian Studies* in which she examines how the impact of Audre Lorde's work has 'fallen between the cracks of lesbian "culture" and lesbian "studies"' (1996, p. 248). Holland's article appears in a section of the book that is devoted to 'theorizing our future' which includes as well Judith Halberstam's 'Queering Lesbian Studies' and Harriet Malinowitz's 'Lesbian Studies and Postmodern Queer Theory'. Both articles shed light on potential positive outcomes of lesbian/queer cross-pollenation.

For me, the issue is not whether lesbian studies or queer studies emerge as the 'winner' in the academic tug-of-war. Because my involvement in Lesbian and Gay Studies is political as well as academic, and because my politics is informed by my experience as a Chinese American lesbian and is therefore necessarily anti-sexist, anti-racist and anti-homophobic, I am compelled to reclaim the lives of Chinese lesbians, to render them visible, and to dispel stereotypical assumptions about them. I do so in spite of the warning that '[i]n their eagerness to re-present the formerly undocumented lives of the Other, such histories necessarily abdicate the project of resisting . . . the very "ideological system" that produces the Other as abject in the first place' (Champagne, 1995, pp. 71–72).

Notes

1. This musical, set in the closing years of the Vietnam War, is the tragic love story of a Vietnamese bar girl and an American soldier. Often cited as a modern-day version of Puccini's *Madama Butterfly*, it is written by Alain Boubil and Michel Schonberg and produced by Cameron Mackintosh.

2. Letter to Tom Stoddard. I obtained a copy from June Chan of ALOEC.
3. Letter from Tom Stoddard to June Chan, Milyoung Cho, Tsuh Yang Chen and James Haewhom Lee.
4. Originally published in *Sister Outsider* (1984), Lorde's essay is grouped together with Douglas Crimp's 'The Boys in My Bedroom', Kobena Mercer's 'Looking for Trouble (a variation of his 'Skin Head Sex Thing'), Richard Meyer's 'Robert Mapplethorpe and the Discipline of Photography', and Henry Abelove's 'Freud, Male Homosexuality, and the Americans', under the classification 'The Uses of the Erotic' in Henry Abelove, Michéle Aina Barale, and David M. Halperin, (eds), *The Lesbian and Gay Studies Reader.* New York: Routledge, 1993.

References

Butler, Judith, *Gender Trouble: Feminism and the Subversion of Identity.* New York: Routledge, 1990.

Butler, Judith, 'Imitation and Gender Insubordination', in Diana Fuss (ed.), *Inside/Out: Lesbian Theories, Gay Theories.* New York: Routledge, 1991, pp. 13–31.

Champagne, John, *The Ethics of Marginality: A New Approach to Gay Studies.* Minneapolis: University of Minnesota Press, 1995.

Combahee River Collective, 'A Black Feminist Statement', in Cherríe Moraga and Gloria Anzaldùa (eds), *This Bridge Called My Back: Writings by Radical Women of Color.* New York: Kitchen Table/Women of Color Press, 1983, pp. 210–18.

Eaton, Mary, 'Homosexual Unmodified: Speculations on Law's Discourse, Race, and the Construction of Sexual Identity', in Carl Stychin and Didi Herman (eds), *Legal Inversions: Lesbians, Gay Men and the Politics of Law.* Philadelphia: Temple University Press, 1995, pp. 46–73.

Eng, David L., 'In the Shadows of a Diva: Committing Homosexuality in David Henry Hwang's *M. Butterfly*', in Russell Leong (ed.), *Asian American Sexualities: Dimensions of the Gay and Lesbian Experience*, New York: Routledge, 1996, pp. 131–52.

Fanon, Frantz, *Black Skin, White Masks.* London: Paladin, 1970.

Fung, Richard, 'Looking for My Penis: The Eroticized Asian in Gay Video Porn', in Bad Object Choices (ed.), *How Do I Look? Queer Film and Video.* Seattle: Bay Press, 1991, pp. 145–60.

Fuss, Diana, *Essentially Speaking: Feminism, Nature and Difference.* New York: Routledge, 1989.

Hagedorn, Jessica, 'Deja Dread of "Miss Saigon"', in *New York Newday,* 23 January 1991.

Holland, Sharon P., '(White) Lesbian Studies', in Bonnie Zimmerman and Toni A. H. McNaron (eds), *The New Lesbian Studies: Into the Twenty-First Century,* New York: Feminist Press, 1996, pp. 247–55.

Jeffreys, Sheila, *The Lesbian Heresy: A Feminist Perspective on the Lesbian Sexual Revolution*. Melbourne: Spinifex, 1993.

Lorde, Audre, 'Age, Race, Class, and Sex: Women Redefining Difference', in her *Sister Outsider*, Trumansburg, NY: Crossing Press, 1984a, pp. 114–23.

Lorde, Audre, 'The Master's Tools Will Never Dismantle the Master's House', in her *Sister Outsider*, 1984b, pp. 110–13.

Lorde, Audre, 'Uses of the Erotic: The Erotic as Power', in her *Sister Outsider*, 1984c, pp. 53–9.

Malinowitz, Harriet, 'Lesbian Studies and Postmodern Queer Theory', in B. Zimmerman and T. McNaron (eds), *The New Lesbian Studies*, New York: Feminist Press, 1996, pp. 262–8.

Manalansan, Martin F., 'Searching for Community: Filipino Gay Men in New York City', in Russell Leong (ed.), *Asian American Sexualities*. London: Routledge, 1996, pp. 51–64.

Mercer, Kobena, 'Imaging the Black Man's Sex', in Pat Holland, Jo Spence, and Simon Watney (eds), *Photography/Politics: Two*, London: Comedia/Methuen, 1987, pp. 61–9.

Mercer, Kobena, 'Skin Head Sex Thing: Racial Difference and the Homoerotic Imaginery', in Bad Object Choices, *How Do I Look? Queer Film and Video*. Seattle: Bay Press, 1991, pp. 169–210.

Moya, Paula M. L., 'Postmodernism, "Realism", and the Politics of Identity: Cherríe Moraga and Chicana Feminism', in M. Jacqui Alexander and Chandra Talpade Mohanty (eds), *Feminist Genealogies, Colonial Legacies, Democratic Futures*, New York: Routledge, 1997, pp. 125–50.

Suh, Mary, 'The Many Sins of "Miss Saigon"', in *Ms.*, November/December 1990, p. 63.

Takagi, Dana, 'Maiden Voyage: Excursion into Sexuality and Identity Politics in Asian America', in Russell Leong (ed.), *Asian American Sexualities*. London: Routledge,1996, pp. 21–36.

Vaid, Urvashi, *Virtual Equality: The Mainstreaming of Gay and Lesbian Liberation*. New York: Anchor, 1996.

Wat, Eric C., 'Preserving the Paradox: Stories from a Gay-Loh', in *Asian American Sexualities*. London: Routledge, 1996, pp. 71–80.

Yoshikawa, Yoko, 'The Heat is On Miss Saigon Coalition: Organizing Across Race and Sexuality', in Karin Aguilar-San Juan (ed.), *The State of Asian America: Activism and Resistance in the 1990s*. Boston: South End Press, 1994, pp. 275–94.

Further reading

Beemyn, Brett, and Eliason, Mickey (ed.), *Queer Studies: A Lesbian, Gay, Bisexual, and Transgender Anthology*. New York: New York University Press, 1996.

Hemphill, Essex (ed.), *Brother to Brother: New Writings by Black Gay Men*. Boston: Alyson, 1991.

Lim-Hing, Sharon (ed.), *The Very Inside: An Anthology of Writing by Asian and Pacific Islander Lesbian and Bisexual Women*. Toronto: Sister Vision, 1994.

Lorde, Audre, *Zami: A New Spelling of My Name*. Trumansburg, NY: Crossing Press, 1982.

Moraga, Cherríe, *Loving in the War Years: Lo que nunca pasó por sus labios*. Boston: South End Press, 1983.

Ratti, Rakesh (ed.), *A Lotus of Another Color: An Unfolding of the South Asian Gay and Lesbian Experience*. Boston: Alyson, 1993.

Silvera, Makeda (ed.), *A Piece of My Heart: A Lesbian of Colour Anthology*. Toronto: Sister Vision, 1991.

Smith, Barbara (ed.), *Home Girls: A Black Feminist Anthology*. New York: Kitchen Table/Women of Color Press, 1983.

16

Class

Mary McIntosh

CONTEMPORARY LESBIAN AND GAY CULTURE often prides itself on being classless. It is a world separate from family and from workmates, a world in which the markers of class are supposedly irrelevant or reduced to a question of style. According to this idealistic class-blind view, gay people have so much in common that it does not matter what background you come from or what job you do. Lesbian and Gay Studies has been equally blinkered. No one would dream of publishing an anthology on gay or lesbian life without chapters on racial and ethnic oppression, but class is seldom discussed, and then only as an individual experience.[1] There is no counterpart here to the earnest discussions of class that characterized early feminist theory. Yet lesbian and gay activism and the struggle for rights and recognition have often been associated with class politics, or at least with a progressive politics that is opposed to class privilege.

The sex reformers of the late nineteenth century, like Edward Carpenter, took it for granted that 'sex reform would only come as part of a transition to a higher stage of life in socialism' (Weeks, 1977, p. 144).[2] This congruence seemed to have been confirmed by the early moves of the Bolshevik state in Russia in abolishing restrictions on homosexual acts as well as legalizing abortion and contraception and making divorce easier. But the situation became more confused in the 1930s, when although the Nazi state in Germany suppressed Magnus Hirschfeld's Institute for Sexual Science and subjected homosexuals to terror and later to the concentration camps (Grau, 1995), the Soviet state also turned against homosexuality and redefined it as a 'fascist perversion'.

In the recent period of gay activism – over the past twenty-five years – it has tended to be assumed that gay rights will find more support from the left than the right of the political spectrum. The representative of gay Conservatives is usually a lone and embattled voice in meetings around the age of consent or gay partnership rights. Gay liberation emerged in 1970 out of 'the Movement' in America and more specifically out of the student movement and alongside the Women's Liberation movement. Although the Gay Liberation Front *Manifesto* of 1971 saw gay oppression as basically cultural, rooted in pervasive attitudes throughout society, it argued that this culture is in turn related to the oppression of women, which is economic and institutional as well as cultural (Weeks, 1977, p. 197; Reiche, 1970). Sometimes it was argued explicitly (for instance by Milligan, 1973),[3] sometimes just taken for granted, that gay liberation means challenging marriage and the family and challenging gender roles. Marriage was seen as oppressive to women, and the family as the place where children were repressed and trained up for their future. Male domination, the repression of sexuality and a docile workforce were seen as necessary for the smooth functioning of capitalism. So gay liberation was intrinsically anti-capitalist. Later on, during the mid-1970s, Marxist-feminist writers, for instance Kuhn and Wolpe (1978), produced a more elaborate analysis of the relation between marriage, family and capitalism, which focused on the role of women's unpaid child care and housework in reproducing the next generation of workers and servicing the current generation. This evidently placed women's liberation as anti-capitalist, but was much less clear about whether women's interests were identical with those of the male working class.

In the same way, the political implications of gay anti-capitalism were confusing, and were not often spelled out very clearly. Don Milligan, a member of the International Socialist group, argued that liberation is only possible when the capitalist system has been overthrown, but that meanwhile, gay demands should be directed at the organized labour movement, who have the potential to overthrow the capitalist state (1973). More vaguely, most gay theorists saw GLF as being on the side of all oppressed people and did not distinguish class oppression from racial oppression or the oppression of women. In Marxist terms, class oppression *is* different, because class is defined by the relations of production, the part people play in the economic order, whereas other oppressions depend upon socially defined distinctions. So, however deep-seated these distinctions may be, social oppressions are different in kind from class oppression. To make matters more complicated, in very 'class-ridden' societies like ours, where there are distinct class cultures, modes of speech and so on, there are forms of social oppression mapped on to the basic economic oppression of class, so that in some respects class appears as social exclusion as well as economic positioning.

Current political analysis has very different concerns. Political activism tends to adopt a model in which rights are claimed on the analogy of a minority ethnic group (Sinfield, 1996). Meanwhile, Queer Theory shifts attention away from identity and its social origins and towards an idea of queer social practice and subjectivity as a challenge to normativity and essentialism and a vanguard of postmodern self-invention (Morton, 1995). The shelving of the Marxist project has thus turned attention away from questions of class and towards questions of cultural practice, or, as Donald Morton has put it, away from questions of *need* and towards questions of *desire* (Morton, 1995, p. 194). Yet there are a number of sociological and cultural aspects of class that have tended to shift towards the periphery of the field of vision but which it is rewarding to bring back into sharper focus.

Lesbian and gay lifestyles as we know them today are only possible outside normal heterosexual family life. Those men who are husbands and fathers to the world at large yet who have an erotic interest in fleeting or snatched homosexual relations are not usually thought of as gay. Being gay is not just a leisure pursuit, it is a way of life with implications for marriage, family and relationships with women. Similarly, a lesbian is not just a woman who has sex with other women; she is also someone who lives outside marriage and partnerships with men. So modern lesbian and gay lifestyles only emerged at periods in history when it was socially and economically possible for people to live outside the family. There were many other elements as well, of course: not least the shift in the social significance of sex as the procreative imperative declined (D'Emilio, 1983) and its role in defining identities became more salient (Weeks, 1987).

To a certain extent, the lives of Oscar Wilde and other upper-class men at the end of the nineteenth century were precursors of modern gay lives. They used the freedom that their wealth and status – and the relative powerlessness of their wives – gave them to develop something of a homosexual lifestyle without actually forgoing marriage. But for Wilde at least, it turned out that he and his circle were not free enough and family, in the shape of Lord Alfred Douglas's father, was to be his downfall.

Ann Ferguson (1981) has argued that financial independence was a necessary condition for the historical formation of a lesbian identity. It is still true today that lesbians see economic self-sufficiency as highly desirable, and Gillian Dunne (1997, p. 119) has suggested that they see couple relationships between women as ones of 'co-independence', rather than following the primary breadwinner pattern that is so common among heterosexuals. It is useful to bear the historical possibility of independence in mind, but it does not take us very far in explaining when and where a lesbian identity emerges, since a few women have been able to achieve such independence in most periods of European history. But for most women, even in the upper class, there was usually less possibility of an independent life than for men. The 'Ladies of Llangollen', who escaped together from London society to a rural retreat in the depths of Wales towards the end of the eighteenth century (Mavor, 1973), were an exception rather than part of a recognizable way of life. A number of writers have documented the way in which in nineteenth-century America and England bourgeois women were able to have romantic friendships, sometimes expressed in very passionate terms, alongside marriage and motherhood (Faderman, 1982; Smith-Rosenberg, 1975). They seem to have been acceptable and not stigmatized, in fact to have been a part of what Carroll Smith-Rosenberg has called 'the female world of love and ritual'. Such women could not avoid marriage without remaining locked into an even greater dependence, either on their own families or on ones where they were employed as a governess. Independence of a sort would only come, if at all, with the death of their parents. It is interesting to look at the first famous lesbian milieu – that of expatriate American and English women in Paris in the first few decades of this century. Both Gertrude Stein and Alice B. Toklas lost their mothers during their teenage years, while Natalie Barney, Romaine Brooks, Winifred Bryher, Radclyffe Hall, Una Troubridge and Renée Vivien – and also Gertrude Stein – all lost their fathers early in life. Shari Benstock uses this information to help understand the sexual and (often extreme right-wing) political commitments of these women, but at a more material level, she comments that these 'parental deaths often left the daughters rich and free of family constraints' (Benstock, 1990), so it also serves to explain why they were able to create a flourishing lesbian literary and artistic milieu at a period when lesbianism was almost unknown outside medical textbooks.

It was not until the female professions like teaching and nursing developed at the end of the nineteenth century that many middle-class women were able to live an independent life and form self-conscious women's communities (Vicinus, 1985, 1990). The supposed 'surplus of women', those who were unmarried, were seen as redundant in a society that only valued women for their contribution to the comfort of others. These single women were to be among the leaders in the struggle for women's rights; they also set up women's communities: religious houses, nurses' training schools and nurses' homes, women's colleges and girls' schools, settlement houses and residential clubs (Vicinus, 1985). In schools and colleges, in particular, it became possible for lesbian relationships to develop, though the prevailing confusions about sexual feelings, anxiety about the good name of the institution and an overall commitment to public duty rather than to personal life, made these relationships far from straightforward.

For working-class women, independence has been harder to achieve and has taken rather different forms. Throughout the nineteenth century going into service was the commonest way to leave home before marriage. But servants' personal lives were heavily policed and a sexual relationship with a man was likely to lead to dismissal. Servants were often at the mercy of the men and boys of the household or their friends. Little is known about sexual relationships between women fellow-servants; as they often shared a bed, it seems likely that they were quite common, but they would have been a far cry from independent lesbian lifestyles as we know them.

A major alternative, at that period, was prostitution. The more that prostitutes were independent professionals – living away from their parents, unmarried, without children, working without a pimp and possibly in a brothel – the more commentators are likely to remark on the prevalence of lesbian relationships among them. According to Havelock Ellis, for instance,

> Homosexuality . . . is very frequently found among prostitutes – in France, it would seem, more frequently than in England – it may indeed be said that it occurs more often among prostitutes than among any other class of women. It is favoured by an acquired distaste for normal coitus due to professional intercourse with men, which leads homosexual relationships to be regarded as pure and ideal by comparison. It would appear also that in a considerable proportion of cases prostitutes present a congenital condition of sexual inversion, such a condition, with an accompanying indifference to intercourse with men, being a predisposing cause of the adoption of a prostitute's career. (1936, pp. 272–73)

A similar uncertainty about cause and effect exists in a recent study of prostitutes in Oslo: 'There is good reason to believe that, other things being equal, prostitution is a less painful solution for lesbians than for heterosexual women. It's easier for them to keep the necessary emotional distance from customers' (Høigård and Finstad, 1992, p. 73). But one of the prostitutes started a lesbian relationship after she had been working on the street for a while, and she said: 'I don't give a shit. In terms of men, my sex life's ruined. Even though I'm living like a lesbian, I'm not really a lesbian' (p. 109).

It is curious that the explanations that are given are more psychological than sociological, which would point to the fact that prostitutes are relatively independent of family and moral controls and free to take up a lesbian way of life; lesbians who have come out are sexual outcasts for whom the step into prostitution is less problematic. Such sociological approaches would also suggest that the link between the lesbian and the prostitute would be weakened – as it undoubtedly is – in the current period when it is much easier to be a lesbian (and possibly easier to be a prostitute as well).

As gay and lesbian subcultures developed, there was often a close and complex connection between the milieux of prostitutes and those of homosexual men and of lesbians. In the early nineteenth century, it seems possible that the same New York brothels housed both women and 'boys', catering to both straight and homosexual tastes of their male clients (Gilfoyle, 1992, p. 136ff). Male prostitution has often piggy-backed on female prostitution in this way, bringing the two worlds into contact with one another. But there has also been male prostitution closely interwoven with public homosexual life, especially since the eighteenth century. Jeffrey Weeks (1990) has noted that the relatively few 'professionals' were perhaps the only people who lived wholly in the homosexual subculture in the nineteenth and early twentieth centuries; other people dipped into and out of the London scene of 'Molly houses', pubs, fields, walks, squares and lavatories. 'By the 1870s, any sort of homosexual transaction, whether or not money was involved, was described as "trade"' (Weeks, 1990, p. 202). The same interweaving of a 'sodomitical subculture'[4] with 'the delivery of boys and young men to clients on demand' (Boon, 1989) can be found in Paris and the major cities of the Dutch republic from the early eighteenth century.

The overlapping of lesbian and prostitute social worlds has been quite different from this, because the prostitutes' clients are men and outside the lesbian scene. In the few cases where lesbian prostitution has existed, it has not been within a lesbian subculture. Wherever there has been a working-class lesbian bar, pub or club life, prostitutes seem to have been an important part of it. As Joan Nestle, writing about New York, put it, 'In the bars of the late fifties and early sixties where I learnt my Lesbian ways, whores were part of our world. We sat on bar stools next to each other, we partied together, and we made love together' (Nestle, 1987, p. 158). The same was true in my own experience in London in the 1960s: though we middle-class lesbians did not often make love with whores, we certainly went to the same few clubs and to some of the same parties.

Apart from prostitution, the other way in which women from the working class have been able to gain independence and escape heterosexuality has been by cross-dressing and passing as a man. The historical literature is extensive, especially for the eighteenth century, but rather patchy and inconclusive. Martha Vicinus (1989, p. 179) has suggested that most of the accounts of passing women that have survived are of 'working class and peasant women who sought more job opportunities, better pay and greater freedom' (see also d'Emilio and Freedman, 1988, p. 124). There were also examples of women from wealthier backgrounds who passed as men in the military or wore men's clothes either regularly or occasionally (Wheelwright, 1989; Donoghue, 1993; Trumbach, 1991). But many of the cases that came to court (Eriksson, 1981; Friedli, 1987) involved lower-class women, such as the one immortalized in Henry Fielding's pamphlet *The Female Husband* (1746). Such women were often depicted as playing a man's part in order to seduce and defraud other women, or in order to establish themselves in a respectable occupation and escape from poverty. So the sense of outrage against them is partly about class transgression, as well as about gender and sexual morality.

On the other hand, the romantic friendships of the eighteenth and nineteenth century, which are the other precursor of the lesbian relationships we know today, do seem to have been a bourgeois phenomenon. Of course it is possible that this is because the only records that we have are the letters and diaries of these women, who must have been from an educated class in order to write about their feelings. But the quality of these relationships and especially the way in which they were embedded in the women's social world, suggest that they would be unlikely to have flourished in the way that they did outside of the bourgeoisie.

It has also been very difficult to get much historical information about homosexual relations among working-class men. Most of the glimpses that we have come from police records and evidence in criminal trials. For instance, the archives of the Paris police show that in the early eighteenth century there were regular cruising grounds in the city and that undercover agents were used to entrap men who frequented them (Rey, 1989). Although at this period sodomy was commonly thought to be a vice of the nobility (*le beau vice*), it became apparent through these arrests that all classes were involved. By 1749 only 11 per cent of the 244 men arrested were nobles or bourgeois; 53 per cent were small merchants or artisans, 24 per cent domestic servants (with 12 per cent of unknown social class).[5] Indeed, Michel Rey, who has analysed these records, says: 'The greatest danger [the police feared] was the mingling of people of different social status; the aristocratic vice must not be allowed to spread from the Court to the city' (1989, p. 134).

Our knowledge of proletarian homosexuality, then, is scanty and highly dependent upon how vigorously the police pursued it. In Denmark, for instance, it was until 1835 considered unwise to expose sins of sodomy and masturbation to public scrutiny. Although a homosexual network was discovered in 1814-15, it was investigated by a commission of two who recommended to the Chancery that the affair should not be brought to court and the men involved – mainly of the merchant class, including three foreigners – should be dealt with by other means (von Rosen, 1989, p. 198ff). In the Netherlands, through most of the seventeenth century, the authorities tended not to prosecute sodomy unless there were other offences connected with it. After that they prosecuted sodomy itself and in 1730 – and again in 1764 and 1776 – there were waves of persecutions in which large numbers of men of all social classes were tried and executed (Noordam, 1989). But it seems likely that the homosexual subculture had been developing well before these persecutions and the extent of sodomy did not suddenly explode in 1730 (Bray, 1982, p. 81ff).

From the evidence of attempts at repression, we can get some picture of the lives of homosexuals. The London 'molly houses' that were raided in the early eighteenth century by agents of the Society for the Reformation of Manners were evidently much frequented by lower- and lower-middle-class men but also crossing the class spectrum. These men seem to have gone there for mutual pleasure – dancing, cuddling, sex in a back room, effeminate manners and transvestism in some of the clubs – rather than for any element of prostitution. Apart from these houses, there were known cruising grounds like St James's Park. But some men were tried in court for trying to make pickups outside of this homosexual milieu, often by seducing lower-class boys and young men, schoolboys and apprentices (Trumbach, 1989).

A third source of historical evidence, in the form of satirical writing and published polemics, may at first appear to offer insights about social class. In the seventeenth century, such satires tended to portray sodomy as a vice of the gentry, and specifically of the London gentry. But of course the motivation behind such writings was to ridicule London and particularly the Court and its followers. The issue, as Alan Bray has pointed out, was not so much homosexuality as the resentment of the country gentry for an extravagant and parasitic Court (Bray, 1982, p. 37). We have here the beginnings of an association between effeteness and an upper class, seen from below, which identifies the lower class with the solid virtues of masculine activity. Bray goes on to argue that there must be some truth in these satires – 'they were intended to hurt, and without a basis in reality they would have lost their edge' – but that they are probably more useful for their incidental descriptive details than anything else.

What is interesting about these class stereotypes, however, is not only their truth or falsehood but also their social efficacy and the fact that people have to live their lives in relation to them. Alan Sinfield (1994, ch. 6) has a fascinating discussion of the way in which, especially from the Oscar Wilde scandal onwards, the image of the queer is of an effeminate upper-class man. Representations, from writers like Evelyn Waugh and Noel Coward,

> consolidated the queer image, to the point where, unless there were really explicit signs, queers were generally assumed to be leisure-class. And conversely, leisure-class men might fall under suspicion, regardless of their actual preferences. It may still be hard, today, to tell whether certain establishment mannerisms signal queerness, or not. (p. 137)

Many men who had sex with other men did not identify with this image and quite a few, like Quentin Crisp, who came from the lower class 'might affect the Wildean stereotype; for it had come to signal sexuality as much as class' (p. 148). E. M. Forster's *Maurice* (written in 1914, but not published until 1971) and Mary Renault's *The Charioteer* (1953) both describe the problem of a man who encounters the effeminate queer milieu but cannot locate himself in it and aspires, with little cultural support, to a manly ideal. Maurice finds it hard to identify his own sexuality because the only image available to him is 'unspeakables of the Oscar Wilde sort' – effeminate where he is handsome, healthy and masculine, intellectuals and aesthetes where he is an active suburban businessman, upper-class where he is bourgeois. Forster derives this ideal of comradely masculinity from Edward Carpenter,[6] but it was not one that would have been readily available to a man like Maurice as it had been effectively marginalized by the Wildean leisure-class image (Sinfield, 1994, p. 141).

Along with this identification of the queer with effeminacy and the leisure class came the association of men of other classes, but particularly the working class, with masculine heterosexuality. Manual labour and 'rough' manners play a part in hegemonic masculinity that goes beyond the sphere of sexuality,[7] but ridicule of homosexuals and effeminacy is one of the ways in which it is encoded and has long been the common currency of the playground, the barrack room and the factory floor. This made growing up gay more difficult for working-class boys. It also fed into the curious attraction that many upper-class men have felt for working-class men.

Bridging the classes has been an enduring feature of relationships between men; indeed as we have seen, the disruption of class hierarchy was one of the things that the eighteenth-century authorities most feared about homosexuality. Bridging the races has also had great appeal to many white men and, in a very different way, to Black men as Frantz Fanon (1967) has subtly analysed. Not only are the dynamics of masculinity different in different class and race contexts (Tolson, 1977; Connell, 1995), but the dominant culture in terms of both class and race entertains powerful fantasies about the active and uninhibited sexuality of men and women of the subordinated groups. So the upper-class man casts himself as feminine in relation to the raw masculinity of the working-class man – though as Alan Sinfield (1994, p. 149) has pointed out, both Edward Carpenter and John Addington Symonds, advocates of the manly, comradely ideal, also had their major relationships with lower-class men. Often it has been the effeminate man in search of lower-class masculinity, which appears doubly disruptive to a culture that presumes the feminine to be subordinate to the masculine.

The fact that homosexuality has been identified as an upper-class phenomenon has led to an erasure of working-class experience. As Jeffrey Weeks has put it:

> if the idealization of working-class youth was one major theme, the attitude of these working-class men themselves is less easy to trace. They appear in all the major scandals (for example, the Wilde trial, the Cleveland Street scandal) but their self-conceptions are almost impossible to disinter. (1981, p. 105)[8]

Over recent years, oral history has done something to mitigate this situation (Hall-Carpenter archives, 1989; Porter and Weeks, 1991) but sociological work on contemporary life tends to be so class-blind that the specificities of working-class experience never emerge.

Among lesbians the situation has been quite different. The distinction between butch and femme maps on to class in a very different way. It is not that butch is associated with one class and femme with another, but the very butch/femme divide is much more marked in the working-class lesbian scene. Rather than leading to cross-class liaisons, this tends to make middle-class lesbians steer clear of working-class ones, who are perceived as too 'obvious' and attracting too much attention. As Maureen Duffy (1967) wrote about the Gateways Club in London in the 1960s:

> There is less mixing of the levels of society among female than among male homosexuals: teachers talk to other teachers, factory workers and petrol pump attendants clan together with lower-paid office workers and bus conductresses.

Duffy also suggested that at that time professional women tended to go in for select dinner parties or evenings at the theatre:

> They do not want to be regarded as second-class citizens and so avoid contact with people who are obviously this. For the same reason they avoid extremes of dress. (1967, p. 152)

Perhaps these middle-class women had more to lose by coming out of the closet of their restricted circle of friends into the wider world of the lesbian subculture. They had careers to pursue or money to inherit and so a greater investment in maintaining an image of respectability.

What is perhaps surprising is that, if we look at it from the other point of view, it becomes clear that it was working-class lesbians who succeeded in creating something of a community in the decades before gay liberation. The middle-class ones were, if anything, intermittent hangers-on rather than core members of the scene. So some middle-class lesbians will remember a youth spent in the bars where they mixed with tough butches and prostitutes, but they remember it as being hard to gain acceptance: this was less being part of a social melting pot than slumming it in a milieu that was properly working-class.

The oral history study of Buffalo, New York, reveals a flourishing working-class lesbian bar community during the 1940s and 1950s, with the participants marked out by a butch-femme dress code and finding themselves in constant confrontation with the straight world (Davis and Kennedy, 1990; Kennedy and Davis, 1993). Underlying the obvious role-play of the public sphere was a polarization in the private sphere of sexual behaviour. This culminated in the emergence in the 1950s of the 'stone butch' as the ideal butch, the butch who does everything to please her lover, but is herself untouchable.

The issues surrounding butch/femme have been much debated in recent years. The women involved in the Gay Liberation movement of the 1970s were deeply opposed to butch and femme, which they perceived as mimicking forms of male and female behaviour that feminism rejected. Perhaps, in doing so, they were only echoing the criticisms that middle-class lesbians had made throughout the 1950s and 1960s (Nestle, 1988). Towards the end of the 1970s 'lesbian-feminists' gained the ascendancy, with criticisms of butch/femme as being male identified and involving a sexuality that was phallic rather than diffuse and womanly. Curiously, butch and femme were often seen as being middle-class affectations and lesbian-feminists, whatever their real class origins, frequently adopted a working-class accent and style, but one very different from that of the earlier lesbian community. At the same time there was, paradoxically, a romanticization of working-class masculinity; lesbian carpenters, plumbers and car mechanics were idealized, in a strange parallel with the butch Village People styles that were current in some gay male circles.

By the early 1980s, women who had been lesbians from before women's liberation had begun to fight back and to join forces with younger pro-sex feminists. Being a lesbian was not about avoiding men or giving up penetration; it was not about being 'woman-identified'; it was about sex, and an identity that could not be reduced to a political choice (Clark, 1982). Part of this identity was often butch – and towards the end of the 1980s femmes began to be recognized again as well – and so began the slow recuperation of the working-class lesbian culture of the pre-Stonewall era. Butch/femme finally became seen as a form of challenge and resistance to heterosexual norms, rather than as apeing them. So in the lesbian scene today, butch and femme once more play a part. For some, mainly working-class women, this is the traditional butch and femme. For others it is much more ironic and self-conscious than it was thirty years ago. Now butch and femme often represent a conscious politics of disruption and challenge to the gender order, a part of the daily practices of queer politics.

Class has been something of a blind spot for Lesbian and Gay Studies. It appears, if anywhere, in historical work, but rarely in contemporary socio-logical or literary studies.[9] The recognition that sexuality and the social control of sexual behaviour cannot be reduced to a question of class politics has been taken too far. It has been taken to mean that class is irrelevant to understanding the social expressions of sexuality. Just as the gay movement, along with feminism and green politics, were seen as the 'new social forces' that would displace the outworn class politics of the old Left, so it has been assumed that Lesbian and Gay Studies lies somewhere beyond the rigid class analysis of yesteryear. This demotion of class is not, of course, peculiar to Lesbian and Gay Studies. If anything, Lesbian and Gay Studies has been only one of the instruments of a wider campaign against Marxism in academia at large. Postmodernism and the turn to discourse, on the one hand, and the pervasive influence in Britain of American thinking with its empiricist and liberal bent, on the other, have combined to produce a shelving of the Marxist projects of the 1960s and 1970s. Whatever the final judgement on this massive intellectual reversal may be, it seems a pity that all ideas of class have been erased along with Marxism. Even class identities and class cultures, which provide very distinct contexts for people's experience of sexuality, have been ignored in favour of trendier aspects of power and differentiation. Issues of wealth and poverty are deeply unsexy and to talk about them at a queer conference is in poor taste, like talking about money at a social gathering. In this age of the 'pink pound' and a consumerist gay culture, Queer Theory too has taken on bourgeois clothing, with its focus on consumption rather than production, style rather than content. But lesbian and gay historical studies have shown up subtler and more sophisticated ways of looking at class. It is now possible to re-visit those larger structural questions about the class and gender contexts within which we live out our lesbian and gay lives. It is now possible, too, to return to a radical politics that is not narrowly focused on our experiences as lesbians and gay men but that uses an understanding of class and other oppressions to link our demands to a wider radical programme.

Notes

1. A notable exception is Sinfield (1994) which devotes a whole chapter to 'Class Relations'.
2. See also Rowbotham and Weeks (1977).
3. For a discussion of the Trotskyist left and homosexual politics in the 1970s, see Derbyshire (1980).
4. The term comes from Murray and Gerard (1983); see also Rey (1989).

5. Ibid. p. 135:

Table 1: Social Distribution of Sodomy Arrestees

	1723	1737/38	1749
Nobles & Bourgeois	8	17	28
Small Merchants & Artisans	20	63	129
Domestic Servants	12	59	58
Unknown	4	7	29
Totals	**44**	**146**	**244**

6. See Rowbotham and Weeks (1977) Part 1; Carpenter, *Selected Writings* (1984).
7. See for instance Willis (1977).
8. See also Weeks (1990) p. 54ff.
9. Sinfield (1994) and Dunne (1997) are honourable exceptions.

References

Altman, Dennis *et al.*, *Which Homosexuality? Essays From the International Scientific Conference on Lesbian and Gay Studies*. London: Gay Men's Press, 1989.

Benstock, Shari, 'Paris Lesbianism and the Politics of Reaction, 1900–1940', in Duberman, Vicinus and Chauncey, 1990, pp. 332–46.

Boon, L. J., '"Those Damned Sodomites": Public Images of Sodomy in Eighteenth Century Netherlands', in Gerard and Hekma, 1989.

Bray, Alan, *Homosexuality in Renaissance England*. London: Gay Men's Press, 1982.

Caplan, Pat (ed.), *The Cultural Construction of Sexuality*. London: Tavistock, 1987.

Carpenter, Edward. *Selected Writings, Volume 1: Sex* (David Fernbach and Noel Greig eds). London: Gay Men's Press, 1984.

Clark, Wendy, 'The Dyke, The Feminist and The Devil', in *Feminist Review*, No. 11, Summer 1982, pp. 30–9.

Connell, R. W., *Masculinities*. Cambridge: Polity Press, 1995.

Davis, Madeline, and Kennedy, Elizabeth Lapovsky, 'Oral History and the Study of Sexuality in the Lesbian Community: Buffalo, New York, 1940–1960', in Duberman, Vicinus and Chauncey, 1990, pp. 426–40.

D'Emilio, John, 'Capitalism and Gay Identity', in Snitow, Stansell and Thompson, 1983, pp. 100–13.

D'Emilio, John, and Freedman, Estelle B., *Intimate Matters: A History of Sexuality in America*. New York: Harper and Row, 1988.

Derbyshire, Philip, 'Sects and Sexuality: Trotskyism and the Politics of Sexuality', in Gay Left Collective, 1980, pp. 104–15.

Donoghue, Emma, *Passions Between Women: British Lesbian Culture, 1668–1801*. London: Scarlet Press, 1993.

Duberman, Martin. Vicinus, Martha, and Chauncey, George, Jr. (eds), *Hidden From History: Reclaiming the Gay and Lesbian Past*. London: Meridian, 1990.

Duffy, Maureen, 'Lesbian London', in Hunter Davies (ed.), *The New London Spy: An Intimate Guide to the City's Pleasures*. London: Corgi Books, 1967, pp. 249–57.

Dunne, Gillian A., *Lesbian Lifestyles: Women's Work and the Politics of Sexuality*. London: Macmillan, 1997.

Ellis, Havelock, *Studies in the Psychology of Sex*. New York: Modern Library, 1936.

Epstein, Julia, and Straub, Kristina (eds), *Body Guards: The Cultural Politics of Gender Ambiguity*. London: Routledge, 1991.

Eriksson, Brigitte, 'A Lesbian Execution in Germany, 1721: The Trial Records', in Licata and Peterson, 1981, pp. 17–31.

Everard, Myriam, 'Lesbian History: A History of Change and Disparity', in Kehoe, 1986, pp. 123–37.

Faderman, Lillian, *Surpassing the Love of Men: Romantic Friendship and Love Between Women from the Renaissance to the Present*. London: Junction Books, 1982.

Fanon, Frantz, *Black Skin, White Masks*. New York: Grove Press, 1967.

Ferguson, Ann, 'Patriarchy, Sexual Identity, and the Sexual Revolution', in *Signs* Vol. 7, Autumn 1981, pp. 158–72.

Forster, E. M., *Maurice*. London: Penguin, 1972.

Friedli, Lynne, '"Passing Women": A Study of Gender Boundaries in the Eighteenth Century', in Rousseau and Porter, 1987, pp. 234–60.

Gay Left Collective (eds), *Homosexuality: Power and Politics*. London: Allison and Busby, 1980.

Gerard, Kent, and Hekma, Gert (eds), *The Pursuit of Sodomy: Male Homosexuality in Renaissance and Enlightenment Europe*. New York: Harrington Park Press, 1989.

Gilfoyle, Timothy J., *City of Eros: New York City, Prostitution and the Commercialization of Sex, 1790–1920*. New York: W. W. Norton, 1992.

Grau, Günter (ed.), *Hidden Holocaust? Gay and Lesbian Persecution in Germany, 1933–1945*. London: Cassell, 1995.

Hall-Carpenter Archives, *Gay Men's Oral History Group: Walking After Midnight*. London: Routledge, 1989.

Høigård, Cecilie, and Finstad, Liv, *Backstreets: Prostitution, Money and Love*. London: Polity Press, 1992.

Kehoe, Monika (ed.), *Historical, Literary, and Erotic Aspects of Lesbianism*. New York: Harrington Park Press, 1986.

Kennedy, Elizabeth Lapovsky, and Davis, Madeline D., *Boots of Leather, Slippers of Gold: The History of a Lesbian Community*. New York: Routledge, 1993.

Kuhn, Annette, and Wolpe, AnnMarie (eds), *Feminism and Materialism: Women and Modes of Production*. London: Routledge and Kegan Paul, 1978.

Licata, Salvatore J., and Peterson, Robert (eds), *Historical Perspectives on Homosexuality*. New York: Haworth Press, 1981.

Mavor, Elizabeth, *The Ladies of Llangollen: A Study in Romantic Friendship*. Harmondsworth: Penguin Books, 1973.

Milligan, Don, *The Politics of Homosexuality* (pamphlet). 1973.

Morton, Donald, 'Queerity and Ludic Sado-Masochism: Compulsory Consumption and Emerging Post-al Queer', in Zavarzadeh, Ebert and Morton (eds), 1995.

Murray, Stephen O., and Gerard, Kent, 'Renaissance Sodomitical Subcultures?', in *Among Men/Among Women*. Amsterdam: University of Amsterdam, 1983, pp. 183–96.

Nestle, Joan, *A Restricted Country*. London: Sheba Feminist Publishers, 1988.

Noordam, Dirk Jaap, 'Sodomy in the Dutch Republic, 1600–1725', in Gerard and Hekma, 1989, pp. 207–28.

Plummer, Ken (ed.), *The Making of the Modern Homosexual*. London: Hutchinson, 1981.

Porter, Kevin, and Weeks, Jeffrey (eds), *Between the Acts*. London: Routledge, 1991.

Reiche, Reimut, *Sexuality and Class Struggle*. London: New Left Books, 1970.

Renault, Mary, *The Charioteer*. London: Longman, 1953.

Rey, Michel, 'Police and Sodomy in Eighteenth-Century Paris: From Sin to Disorder', in Gerard and Hekma, 1989, pp. 129–46.

Rousseau, G. S., and Porter, Roy (eds), *Sexual Underworlds of the Enlightenment*. Manchester: Manchester University Press, 1987.

Rowbotham, Sheila, and Weeks, Jeffrey, *Socialism and the New Life: The Personal and Sexual Politics of Edward Carpenter and Havelock Ellis*. London: Pluto Press, 1977.

Sinfield, Alan, 'Diaspora and Hybridity: Queer Identities and the Ethnicity Model', in *Textual Practice*, Vol. 10, No. 2, 1996, pp. 271–93.

Sinfield, Alan, *The Wilde Century: Effeminacy, Oscar Wilde and the Queer Moment*. London: Cassell, 1994.

Smith-Rosenberg, Carroll, 'The Female World of Love and Ritual: Relations Between Women in Nineteenth-Century America', in *Signs*, Vol. 1, No. 1, 1975, pp. 1–29.

Snitow, Ann, Stansell, Christine, and Thompson, Sharon (eds), *Powers of Desire: The Politics of Sexuality*. New York: Monthly Review Press, 1983.

Tolson, Andrew, *The Limits of Masculinity*. London: Tavistock, 1977.

Trumbach, Randolph, 'London's Sapphists: From Three Sexes to Four Genders in the Making of Modern Culture', in Epstein and Straub, 1991, pp. 112–41.

Trumbach, Randolph, 'Sodomitical Assaults, Gender Role, and Sexual Development in Eighteenth-Century London', in Gerard and Hekma, 1989, pp. 407–29.

van der Meer, Theo, 'The Persecutions of Sodomites in Eighteenth-Century Amsterdam: Changing Perceptions of Sodomy', in Gerard and Hekma, 1989, pp. 263–307.

Vicinus, Martha, 'Distance and Desire: English Boarding School Friendships, 1870–1920', in Duberman, Vicinus and Chauncey, 1990, pp. 212–29.

Vicinus, Martha, *Independent Women: Work and Community for Single Women, 1850–1920.* London: Virago, 1985.

Vicinus, Martha, '"They Wonder to Which Sex I Belong": The Historical Roots of the Modern Lesbian Identity', in Altman, 1989, pp. 171–98.

von Rosen, Wilhelm, 'Sodomy in Early Modern Denmark: A Crime Without Victims', in Gerard and Hekma, 1989, pp. 177–204.

Weeks, Jeffrey, *Coming Out: Homosexual Politics in Britain from the Nineteenth Century to the Present.* London: Quartet Books, 1977.

Weeks, Jeffrey, 'Discourse, Desire and Sexual Deviance: Some Problems in a History of Homosexuality', in Plummer, 1981, pp. 76–111.

Weeks, Jeffrey, 'Inverts, Perverts, and Mary-Annes: Male Prostitution and the Regulation of Homosexuality in England in the Nineteenth and Early Twentieth Centuries', in Duberman, Vicinus and Chauncey, 1990, pp. 195–211.

Weeks, Jeffrey, 'Questions of Identity', in Caplan, 1987, pp. 31–51.

Wheelwright, Julie, *Amazons and Military Maids: Women who Dressed as Men in Pursuit of Life, Liberty and Happiness.* London: Pandora, 1989.

Willis, Paul, *Learning to Labour.* London: Saxon House, 1977.

Zavarzadeh, Mas'ud, Ebert, Teresa L., and Morton, Donald (eds), *Post-Ality: Marxism and Postmodernism.* Washington, DC: Maisonneuve Press, 1995.

Further reading

Lapovsky Kennedy, Elizabeth, and Davis, Madeline D., *Boots of Leather, Slippers of Gold: The History of a Lesbian Community.* New York: Routledge, 1993.

17

Bisexuality

Jonathan Dollimore

BISEXUALITY HAS BECOME VISIBLE and controversial yet again, only now with its critics and defenders as never before. Recently bisexuals have been variously characterized as promiscuous, immature, undecided, treacherous, cowardly, and carriers of AIDS into the straight community. Conversely, and even more recently, they are being hailed not only as one of the most politically radical of all sexual minorities, but provocatively postmodern as well.

Defended desires

Bisexuality's most perceptive and incisive recent defenders include Sue George, Elisabeth Däumer, Claire Hemmings, Jo Eadie and Nicola Field.[1] Their documentation of the hostility expressed by some gays towards bisexuality makes dismal reading, not least because it suggests that, in relation to bisexuality, some of those gays endorse kinds of discrimination which they themselves experience and loudly protest against. Eadie suggests that the lesbian and gay wish to exclude bisexuals is based on the fear of contamination and miscegenation; he says, contentiously, 'bisexuality is a miscegenate location' (p. 158). Clare Hemmings makes a similar point, paraphrasing the gay hostility to bisexuals like this: 'I'd never sleep with a bisexual because they bring men into the lesbian community/are responsible for the spread of HIV/always leave you for someone of the opposite/same sex/can't be trusted etc.' (p. 130). For both Eadie and Hemmings, the main problem is the current dominance in lesbian and gay culture of identity politics, the objections to which have been put many times but rarely as succinctly as by Susie Bright: 'It's preposterous to ask sexual beings to stuff ourselves into the rapidly imploding social categories of straight or gay or bi, as if we could plot our sexual behaviour on a conscientious, predictable, curve' (cited in Garber, 1995, p. 83).

Given the increasing hostility towards identity politics, it is important to try to be adequately aware of its psychic, social and political investments. Notoriously in human history, those who have made progress have then wanted to deny the same rights to others. To the extent that it sometimes entails this, identity politics becomes the ground of a turf war in which the rhetoric of liberation is a cover for self-empowerment of a politically conservative kind.

An apparent case in point, cited by Eadie and others, concerns the announcement by Brett Anderson, the lead singer with the group Suede, that he was a bisexual who had not so far had any homosexual experience. A writer in the gay *Pink Paper* snarls in response: 'a "bisexual who's never had sex with a man". . . stinks as bad as a white boy blacking up'.[2] Would a gay man who came out without as yet having had any homosexual experience be equally derided? Presumably not. Perhaps the difference is the (questionable) assumption that bisexuality has more *kudos* than homosexuality? In which case we glimpse the increasingly hypocritical policing of the coming-out process in contemporary sexual politics: if you don't come out it's because you're afraid of the stigma; if you do it's only because you want the (supposed) *kudos*. I hasten to add that gays' response to bisexuality is rarely that crass and for the very good reason that other lesbian and gay writers have contributed greatly to developing the libertarian, anti-discriminatory perspective which makes it seem so crass in the first place, and who would be the first to reject its exploitation of anti-racism for new discriminatory purposes of its own.

Another scenario is both more typical and more significant: identity politics are often most invested when the fortunes of a minority have improved, but not securely; in some cases the identity remains precariously dependent upon that improvement, and in a context where hostility not only remains, but has actually intensified, in part as a response to the increased social visibility which the emerging identity entails. Identity politics are inseparable from a consolidation of this ground recently gained and precariously held. Such consolidation is inevitably also a struggle for survival, which includes a struggle for the means of continuing visibility.

In the field of sexuality this overlaps with another, and to me equally significant aspect of this consolidation: such politics are a defensive formation not only against discrimination, but against desire itself. We protect ourselves against those instabilities intrinsic to desire and which threaten to dislocate us psychically and socially, even, or especially, when our sexuality or object choices are relatively settled. An endearing instance of this is given by Sukie de la Croix, a gay man, who meets a straight African-American woman called Troy.

> She was hot, she was raunchy and she scared the shit out of me. Why? Because she raised some heterosexual feelings in me that I thought had disappeared years ago. . . . It took me years to sort out my true sexual identity, and the last thing I need at this point in my life is to do a turn-about.

Four days later he is still sufficiently worried to confide in a friend. The friend laughs and reveals the 'truth': 'Troy is no woman. Troy is a man. And honey . . . I don't mean part-man, I mean all-man!' Sukie exclaims: 'Oh god, the relief, the blessed relief!'.[3] At one level this story illustrates that momentous irony around which so much modern thought revolves: we are defined as much, if not more, by what our identity excludes as what it includes, and our desire, in all its perversity, is drawn to the very exclusions which constitute it. But we shouldn't conclude too quickly that Sukie is just being haunted by his excluded other. Can we confidently say 'who' or what Sukie 'really' desired in this scenario *prior to* the point of his friend's disclosure about Troy? I can't, and I'm not sure he can either. Was this desire really heterosexual, or was it bisexual? Isn't it just possible that he was being other than consciously disturbed by his own homosexuality? And even assuming we could decide, what difference does his friend's disclosure actually make? In short, gay identity (as distinct from homoerotic fantasies of identification), far from being the direct social counterpart of our desires, may in part be a protection against them – including those very desires sanctioned by the identity.

In this respect gay identity may be closer to straight identity than some like to imagine. Isn't Sukie saying as much when he implies that the years-long struggle to achieve what he calls a 'true sexual identity' entailed an organization of desire which was also a policing of it (or, less contentiously, an imposition of restrictions upon it)? If so, then at the heart of a new-found and hard-won gay identity there re-emerges not so much heterosexuality or bisexuality, but an old-fashioned notion of restraint – something to which, at other levels the discourses of sexual liberation have been vociferously opposed.

The problem with identity politics isn't so much its need for restraint and exclusion, but its refusal to develop an adequate political understanding of that need, preferring instead a self-righteous language of self-evident authenticity. And this is one reason why gay hostility to heterosexuality and bisexuality may end up, as Jo Eadie puts it, sustaining a ghetto gay mentality, impeding political alliances. This, he adds, is 'a luxury of those whose oppression is apparently so restricted to sexuality that alliances are not an issue'. Even more to the point is his further contention that the demonizing of heterosexuality polices those within gay spaces as effectively as it keeps the straight identified out of them (p. 155).

Being sexually postmodern

Both Jo Eadie and Claire Hemmings write compellingly about this hostility. From their respective articles one can draw three implications. First and most obviously: the problems that bisexuals experience are mainly a consequence of discrimination by society – straight society, but increasingly also the lesbian and gay community. Second, and relatedly: intrinsically, bisexuality as a form of desire is relatively problem-free. Third: a sexual orientation free of aversion, restraint, and the need to exclude, is the ideal, and bisexuality is the closest there is to it. All three implications have a *prima facie* plausibility, and especially the last: bisexual desire does, after all, cross what is perhaps the most fundamental binary organizing desire as exclusion, namely the homosexual/heterosexual divide.

Even so, I would question all three implications. But perhaps I've oversimplified their argument – it's true after all that both Hemmings and Eadie regard the bisexual as a figure of instability. This is Hemmings:

> The 'I' in 'I am bisexual' is not simply an insubstantial assuption of fixed identity, as in 'I am lesbian' – rather, it signifies transition and movement in itself. To say 'I am bisexual' is to say 'I am not I'. . . . The process of being/becoming bisexual [is] one that is ever re-centring, re-emerging and re-creating the 'I'. (p. 129)

Unstable, yes, but not in a self-threatening way: this is a liberating, dynamic state of unfixity, and one which seems oddly secure in its very instability. This is mainly because the instability is represented as simultaneously a state of freedom for the bisexual and a subversion of the more rigid identities of others. Thus Hemmings' need to prove that bisexuality is 'both politically and theoretically viable' is inseparable from her insistence that 'the bisexual body' is 'a figure of subversion and disruption'.

Actual bisexuals are theorized as 'revolutionary double agents' who can not only *dis*assemble fixed gender relations, but may also have new insights into the tenuous nature of the oppositions which sustain them (pp. 118, 131). To me this sounds like bisexuality passing, if not closeted, as postmodern theory, safely fashioning itself as a suave *doxa*. The main problem isn't these writers' overt political intent; what gives most pause for thought is the assumption that bisexuality, a form of human sexuality with histories and contemporary cross-cultural expressions so extensive as seemingly to implicate us all – even to the point of making the idea that it needs defending seem half-absurd – must be theoretically 'reconfigured' to become, in Hemmings' word, 'politically and theoretically viable'.

Eadie too sees bisexual politics as about 'dismantling the entire apparatus which maintains the heterosexual/homosexual dyad'. Now this was of course a classic ambition of lesbian and gay theory and remains so for some in that tradition. But, not, according to Eadie, for the most influential current advocates of that theory: they, on the contrary, are promoting a 'dominant lesbian and gay sexual epistemology' which now wants to 'cement" rather than dismantle the straight/gay binary (pp. 142, 144). Eadie endorses Donna Haraway's argument against an oppressive homogeneity in favour of difference or what Haraway calls 'infidel heteroglossia' (p. 157), and the imperfect, always partial and perhaps incoherent identity which that seductive phrase implies. If this sounds risky, Eadie exhorts us not to lose our nerve: 'we can profit from that incoherence'; this very uncertainty will enable new communities of difference. Hemmings likewise affirms a bisexual erotics of difference which actively dismantles binary means of identifying difference and which would challenge a Freudian structure of desire, without being left with 'a mass of tangled signifiers' (pp. 136, 135). But what, I wonder in passing, about being left with a mass of tangled desires and identifications?[4] I can't help but feel that the more theoretically sophisticated this celebration of difference becomes, the more experientially unconvincing it also becomes. In that sense it's wishful theory.[5]

Reflect on some of the metaphors for the alleged subversiveness of the bisexual: the revolutionary double agent (Hemmings); the infidel (Eadie, via Harroway), hybridity (Eadie via Bhabha); miscegenation (Eadie). Taking the last first, there may be some who are understandably anxious at such a casual appropriation of racial history for sexual subversiveness. I only want to register that what is excluded in this appropriation is any sense of the psychic difficulty of being in a 'miscegenate location', to use Eadie's phrase. As for the double agent, we might recall that he or she is someone whose political fate has included torture, incarceration and murder (a fate, incidentally, more applicable to the history of the homosexual rather than that of the bisexual). But again my point would be that there is no sense of the manifest psychic dangers inherent in being the double agent, even assuming those real physical dangers have been metaphorically evaded. The physical dangers facing the infidel have if anything been worse, although her chances of maintaining psychic integration somewhat better, assuming she can adhere to a dissident faith which has marked her out as infidel in the first place (unlikely if she's a postmodern infidel since faith and postmodernism don't sit well together).

Earlier I suggested that identity politics might be in part a defence against the instability, the difficulty of desire itself. I'm now suggesting that the new theoretical version of bisexuality presented by Hemmings and Eadie might be a similar kind of defence. But again perhaps I'm misrepresenting the theory. After all, and commendably enough, both Hemmings and Eadie want us to embrace difference. We know of no more intense kinds of desire than those which transgress the borders separating the different. But at a cost: difference is fraught with difficulties for desire which already has difficulties of its own. It's here for example that we discover that our fantasy lives rarely live up to our political ideals. This is not necessarily a cause for guilt or even apology. Arguably, any sexual politics that can't embrace the inevitable political incorrectness of at least some of our desires is useless. And as Majorie Garber suggests, it may above all be bisexuality that compels us to confront the fact that 'eroticism and desire are always to some degree transgressive, politically *in*correct',[6] and even that fantasy, by virtue of its psychic mobility, may also be inescapably bisexual (1995, pp. 31–33). Over and again Garber's remarkable and extensive documentation of bisexual eroticism in 'everyday life' confronts us with the challenges and difficulties of the actual desiring encounter with difference, as distinct from the comfortable theoretical invocation of it.

Desire and identification: two scenarios

In illustration of this consider two sexual scenarios, the one resonant with a partial meaning of what it might mean to be gay, the other with an equally partial meaning of what it might mean to be bisexual. Far from being the proving ground of identity, these scenarios are places where it is compromised so immediately as to suggest this to be the rule of desire rather than its exception.

The gay scenario: the adoration which a self-identified gay man feels for another male as he goes down on him may or may not be implicated in the politically offensive constructions of phallic masculinity in our culture (it depends on the moment, the man, the scenario). But this gay man discovers that gay pride includes not feeling guilty about the fact that it might be, and not feeling the need to apologise for it if it is. Here a political identity conflicts with the very desire it sanctions and pretty quickly too. And I wonder – only in passing – if this kind of conflict isn't the source of relatively new kinds of anxiety inside identity politics; anxieties which are only half allayed by being punitively displaced in the name of 'sexual politics'?

The other scenario: a bisexual male partakes of a threesome in which he watches a man fucking with a woman. His identifications here are multiple: he identifies with the man (he want to be in his position, having sex with her) but he also want to be her. And I mean be her: he doesn't just want to be in her position and have the man fuck him as himself (though he wants that too); no, he wants to he fucked by the man with himself in the position of, which is to say, as, the woman. He knows of no pleasure greater than to be fucked by a man, but in this scenario he also wants to be the woman; he wants to be fucked by him in a way he imagines – fantasizes – only a woman can be. Maybe he desires the man through her. And in this same scenario there may be a further kind of pleasure where desire and identification are inflected by voyeurism: for our bisexual male the sexual attractiveness of the male is heightened by the fact that the latter is apparently desired by the woman; he excites the more because he's desired by her.

If he's a thoughtful kind of bisexual he might have pause to wonder about the relative degree of sexual objectification in this encounter: is the woman more objectified than the man, and should the fact that the history of voyeuristic objectification is different for women than men give him pause for thought – or might he reassure himself with the queer celebration of all desire as objectification? But maybe such considerations are displaced by another, more urgent one: in this scenario, desire circulates between sexual subject positions but not necessarily as a free flow; there may be a tension, a conflict, even an impossibility here. Put simply, this bisexual male may desire to be where he can't be, and desire to become what he cannot become. Here his identity as a coherent sexual subject is very much in question and in a way which suggests that the problems for identity politics are problems for us alll even bisexuals.

It might be said that this makes the bisexual a damaged subject. To which it could be replied that we are all damaged, and life itself, one source of the damage, is also an exercise in damage limitation – whence identity politics. Alternatively we might reflect that although we are all damaged, we aren't all damaged in equally interesting ways. Bisexuals, like homosexuals, are definitely interesting, which is why I want to save them from, rather than for, postmodern theorizing.

Often such theorizing of and by sexual minorities wants to be disturbing, subversive and deviant on the one hand – in a word 'queer' – while also anxious to be seen as essentially healthy, 'together', hip and free on the other. Surprising as it may seem, there is a real sense in which the modern sexual dissident wants to be normal. Even quite a few queers want to be perverts with a normal heart. And you can see why, given how powerfully sexual deviance has been pathologized by medical and psychiatric discourses. But by the very same token, this need to be regarded as healthy, hip and free is itself a need for an identity, and one with a 'straight' history at that.

Nothing I've read in the postmodern defences of bisexuality even hint at the fact that bisexuality may on occasions (contingently, not necessarily) resonate even more acutely than homosexuality or heterosexuality with the difficult, fascinating complexities which ineradicably mark human desire which is vulnerably alive and responsive; on the contrary, its dominant narrative is over-dependent upon the simplistic idea that freedom, stability and completeness lie just the other side of social discrimination.[7]

Eadie does tell us that he encounters, 'with alarming regularity', bisexuals who are anxious about their identity as bisexuals:

> Monogamous [bisexuals] feel they should be having more relationships and [bisexuals] in multiple relationships feel they are perpetuating a stereotype. [Bisexuals] who have had primarily same-sex relationships feel they are expected to have opposite-sex relationships, and [those] in opposite-sex relationships feel they have not proved themselves until they have had a same-sex relationship. (p. 144)

Again, for Eadie, the problem is exclusively socio-political: all these people have been made to feel, socially and politically, that they should be doing something different. And they have been made to feel this by the implicit demands of identity politics, and the straight/gay dyad, both of which lesbians and gays are oppressively endorsing. Eadie is doubtlessly right to some extent: identity politics can be normative and coercive and certainly make people feel anxious about their sexual practices or lack of such practices. But it isn't as simple as that. As so often, a plausible but partial social truth obscures a psychic reality which is inseparable from the social but not reducible to it.[8]

Identity, we know, is formed socially – not only by the here and now but also, and much more so, by the past. So too is desire; to an extent that we can probably never exactly know, desire is constituted by the history of our identifications. Sexual identity is most effectively dislocated by even a preliminary understanding of how it, along with the desire it speaks for, both comprises, and is compromised by, these identifications. History is the outside of desire but also its inside, with the consequence that desire has the potential to be inherently difficult, politically embarrassing and dangerous to all parties concerned. Again, our fantasy life proves as much. I do not mean this in an essentialist, transhistorical way. On the contrary, desire is unpredictable exactly because history, in all its contingency and fixity, its indistinguishable mix of the social and the personal, so radically informs it. I could elaborate this in the abstract for some time, but anyone who has been wrecked by sexual infatuation or unrequited desire knows it. Likewise with anyone who remotely identifies with Tristan or Isolde, Romeo or Juliet, Catherine or Heathcliff. And if that list sounds too straight – and it needn't, depending on who you are and who you're identifying with – then there are homoerotic texts which convey even more acutely what it is to have one's identity wrecked by desire: the Greek lyric poets, including Sappho's famous fragment,[9] James Baldwin's Giovanni, Thomas Mann's Aschenbach and more.

For all its radical affect, there's something predictably safe about the new bisexual politics, not least its apparent reluctance to concede that desire always retains the potential to disturbingly unfix *my* identity, and not only that of my oppressive other (and this is something else it shares with some recent gay/Queer Theory). Hemmings speaks of bisexuality in terms of 'the variety of personal and political positions that a person may *choose* to occupy' (p. 25, my emphasis). But surely desire can also wreck the rational subject presupposed by such choices? Desire can unfix identity in ways which are liberating; it may compel me as a gay person to come out, and to experience that incomparable elation which derives from swapping an inauthetic straight identity for an authetic gay one. Desire can also unfix identity in ways which liberate by destroying an existing identity without replacing it with another. It can wreck us and bring us back to life and maybe both at once. Don't imagine this to be a didactic warning against desire, I'm only remarking on one of its seductive aspects disavowed by much sexual politics. But when identity is destabilized by desire we shouldn't underestimate the potential cost. It is then that we can become flooded by apprehensions of loss endemic to our culture and which it's partly the purpose of identity to protect us against. In this sense too identity can be as much about surviving and evading desire as about expressing it.

Notes

1. Sue George, *Women and Bisexuality*. London: Scarlet Press, 1993; Elisabeth Däumer, 'Queer Ethics; or, the Challenge of Bisexuality to Lesbian Ethics', in *Hypatia*. Vol. 7, No. 4 (Autumn 1992), 91–105; Joseph Bristow and Angelia R. Wilson, (eds), *Activating Theory: Lesbian, Gay and Bisexual Politics*. London: Lawrence and Wishart, 1993; Clare Hemmings, 'Resituating the Bisexual Body', in Bristow and Wilson, pp. 11–138; Jo Eadie, 'Activating Bisexuality: Towards a Bi/Sexual Politics', in Bristow and Wilson, pp. 139–70; see also Eadie's 'We Should Be There Bi Now', in *Rouge*, Vol. 12, 1993, 26–7; Nicola Field, *Over the Rainbow: Money, Class and Homophobia*. London: Pluto Press, 1995. See also *Bisexual Horizons: Politics, Histories, Lives*. Sharon Rose *et al.* (eds). London: Lawrence and Wishart, 1996, and Marjorie Garber, *Vice Versa: Bisexuality and the Eroticism of Everyday Life*. New York: Simon and Schuster, 1995.
2. Cited from Eadie, p. 168, originally appearing in *Pink Paper*, 18 April 1993, p. 14.
3. Sukie de la Croix (*Pink Paper*, 23 July 1993), cited by Field, who finds in his story a fear of bisexuality which 'to some extent . . . mirrors homophobia' (*Over the Rainbow*, pp. 133–34).
4. The ways in which desire may be inflected by identification are multiple. At the very least we might tentatively wonder whether we ever simply desire the person we love, or whether our desire, in part at least, is also an identification with him or her. If so, who are we identifying with – someone completely different from us, or someone obscurely familiar to us: an actual parent or sibling perhaps, or maybe the parent or sibling we wanted but didn't have? And if this sounds too incestuous for those of us with identifications well outside the 'family romance', we might still wonder whether (for example) the person desired might resemble the person we once were; or the person we always wanted to be; or the person others wanted us to be; or the person we would still like to be? My point is that the processes of identification may be most complex in some expressions of bisexuality, conscious or otherwise: 'But bisexuality! You are certainly right about it. I am accustoming myself to regarding every sexual act as a process in which four individuals are involved. We have lots to discuss on this topic. . .' (letter from Freud to Fliess, 1 August 1899, cited from *The*

Complete Letters of Sigmund Freud to Wilhelm Fliess 1887–1904. Translated and edited by Jeffrey Moussaieff Masson, Cambridge, MA: Harvard University Press, 1985.

5. I discuss further the limitations of wishful theory in a different version of this chapter in *Textual Practice*, Vol. 10, No. 3, 1996, pp. 523–39.

6. Garber is giving an account of a conference at which a lesbian 'observed matter-of-factly that one of her most erotic turn-ons was male-male pornography. Many women at the conference, (myself included) nodded agreement; more than a few men, older and younger, looked stunned' (p. 31).

7. In this the postmodern theorists of bisexuality are little different from those 'untheorized' and confessional accounts of bisexual experience that they, the theorists, so often criticise as inadequate.

8. More recently Eadie had found this to be a problem for him to: 'I found it very hard recently to acknowledge that I wanted a monogamous relationship because I was so committed to myself as "a person who has multiple relationships"'. This occurs in a perceptive piece describing Eadie's misgivings about the way the bisexual community, as it becomes stronger, seems to be deploying the same discriminatory tendencies it has hitherto suffered from, especially the tendency to self-define in terms of binary division and exclusion 'Being Who we Are', in *Bisexual Horizons*. pp. 16–20, esp. p. 1. This is where we came in.

9. 'Love, the loosener of limbs shakes me again, an inescapable bittersweet creature' (*The Penguin Book of Greek Verse*. C.A.Trypanis (ed.), Harmondsworth, Penguin, 1971, p. 150). This metaphor of love as loosener of limbs was common in Greek writing about desire and signalled the unwelcome yet irresistible unbinding of the defended self which desire entailed. A fascination with the way desire undermines rather than confirms identity goes back at least this far.

References

Eadie, Joe. 'Activating Bisexuality: Towards a Bisexual Politics', in J. Bristow and A. R. Wilson (eds), *Activating Theory: Lesbian, Gay and Bisexual Politics*. London: Lawrence and Wishart, 1993, pp. 139–70.

Garber Marjorie, *Vice Versa: Bisexuality and the Eroticism of Everyday Life*. New York: Simon and Schuster, 1995.

Hemmings, Clare, 'Resituating the Bisexual Body', in J. Bristow and A. R. Wilson (eds), *Activating Theory: Lesbian, Gay and Bisexual Politics*. London: Lawrence and Wishart, 1993, pp. 11–138.

18

Heterosexuality

Richard Dyer

THE STUDY OF HOMOSEXUALITY entails the study of heterosexuality. I will begin in a moment by saying why. Yet it has not always seemed so, and I'll discuss this next, before showing how developments in Lesbian and Gay Studies made the study of heterosexuality possible. I then offer a thumbnail sketch of the characteristics of this specific sexuality, hetero, before looking at lesbian and gay work on its politics and history. I end by suggesting ways in which the study of heterosexuality opened up by Lesbian and Gay Studies can lead beyond the study of sexuality alone to that of gender and race as well.

The study of homosexuality entails the study of heterosexuality above all because of the latter's apparent naturalness and rightness. It is this that oppresses us and that we have therefore to refute. If we don't do it, it is not likely anyone else will, because it is not really in the interests of heterosexuals to be dislodged from the comfortable and powerful position of being in the right. And perhaps *only* we can do it. Precisely because we are outside heterosexuality, we can see that it is something specific, something identifiable, something straight and narrow.

There is also a broader sense in which Lesbian and Gay Studies has to study heterosexuality. The very idea of there being categories of sexuality – homo, hetero, bi, for starters – is a culturally and historically specific system of classification. Two things distinguish it. First, there is the very fact of classifying, characteristic of Western society's mania for compartmentalization and discrimination. Second, this system of classification does not classify acts but psychologies and forms of desire – heterosexuality is not man-woman coitus but the desire for it and/or the fact of being identified by the desire for it; thus there are 'heterosexuals' as well as man-woman sex acts. This system of classification limits everyone, but Lesbian and Gay Studies has pioneered the perception of it and (probably) lesbians and gay men who can intellectually dismantle it most easily, because we feel so keenly the pressure of its arbitrariness.

That the study of homosexuality entails the study of heterosexuality has however not always been self-evident in Lesbian and Gay Studies.[1] There were at least two good reasons why heterosexuality was not imme- diately on its agenda. Firstly, since homosexuality had been denied, marginalized or denigrated by most scholarship, the prime task for Lesbian and Gay Studies was to discover, promote and celebrate homosexuality. There was far too much to do finding out what gay and lesbian life had been and was like, far too much digging about in archives or under the sur- face of culture to find lesbian and gay traces, to put any energy into a consideration of heterosexuality. Besides, hadn't it had quite enough atten- tion already? Secondly, it was also hard to imagine how you could study heterosexuality without reproducing a pattern damaging to homosexual- ity, a pattern reinforcing heterosexual normativity, thus undermining the very project of Lesbian and Gay Studies. The latter was born into a situa- tion where homosexuality had always figured as the thing to be explained, above all in the reigning enigma: why are some people homo? To think of heterosexuality in this context seemed always to mean thinking of a human norm against which to explain the oddity of homosexuality. It was hard to think what the question about heterosexuality could be except: why are some people not hetero?

Two apparently contradictory things had to happen for there to be the possibility of an epistemological shift in the study of heterosexuality. One fulfilled the ambitions of much lesbian and gay activism this century; the second challenged those ambitions. On the one hand, the lesbian and gay movements built a consciousness that although homosexuality may not be the statistical norm, it is entirely normal for us. Once this is accepted, once homosexuality is *a* normality, then it follows that no sexuality can be *the* norm. Consequently, heterosexuality may be a majority practice, it may be in a position to impose itself as if it is the norm, but it is in fact a particular entity that is both open to and in need of describing and explaining.

On the other hand, there has also always been the sense that homosex- uality is itself not clear-cut and fixed. From the start of lesbian and gay activism, lesbians and gay men instinctively made common cause with many others who were not wholly or at all homosexual: heterosexual trans- vestites, transsexuals who have heterosexual relations, bisexuals and three still more unsettling others. The first are transsexuals who have homosex- ual relations – for is, say, a female-to-male transsexual who has sexual relations with a man therefore homosexual (to themselves they are men having sex with men) or heterosexual (they are 'biologically' women having sex with men)? The second unsettling group is people who change sexuality, who lead long lives as, say, heterosexual and then lead lesbian or gay ones, or of course vice versa (though the latter is probably rarer, given the pressure on people to be straight if they possibly can). Such people's histories can be troubling. For some, it is a case of feeling that they were always really lesbian/gay (or straight) and have now allowed themselves to live and identify thus; such instances reinforce the sense of fixed and definite categories, hetero and homo. Others, though, experience the story of their life differently – that they simply changed, or that they made a decision to change, or that they were really always both but decided to plump for one rather than the other. And they might change again. Here an inner, given identity as hetero, homo or even bi cannot be affirmed, leaving notions of sexual identity fluid and unstable. Thirdly, there is the growing presence of lesbian (and to a lesser extent gay) parents, those who have chosen to parent from within leading a lesbian (or gay) identified life. These unsettle because they definitively unhook procreation from sexuality, undercutting one at least of the definitions of the difference between hetero and homo (in gay chauvinist parlance, between breeders and nonbreeders). It should be stressed that all these groups do not prove that everyone is basically anything and everything, but simply that human sexuality is extraordinarily fluid and diverse, not reducible to the hetero, homo, bi formula.

Confidently embracing the normality of homosexuality robs heterosexuality of its claim to be the norm; muddying the hetero, homo, bi distinction unsettles the confidence with which any group sexual identity can be maintained, thus calling hetero into question just as much as homo. In terms of study, these two moves combined with the growing importance of notions of the historical and cultural construction of sexualities touched on above (and mostly developed by lesbians and gay men) to produce the possibility of addressing heterosexuality as something specific, the possibility of making heterosexuality strange.

To those of us libidinally pretty well utterly outside of heterosexuality, seeing its strangeness may seem a pretty easy move to make (though even we needed the political confidence to make it and say we'd made it), but in fact it was and still is rather difficult. Heterosexuality in the sense of man-woman coitus is normative, even if being heterosexual and having heterosexual desire is culturally and historically limited. It is normative in several senses. It is practised by most adults. It is what we have most evidence of being practised throughout history and the known world. The major world religions and systems of law affirm heterosexuality and proscribe homosexuality. Heterosexuality appears to be the means by which human procreation is achieved, thus making it seem an indispensable and natural part of human existence. All of these make of heterosexuality something that is taken for granted, something assumed to be natural; its normality does not need arguing for, it has the force of 'of course'. We do not stop to think about the grammar we use when speaking or the chemical composition of the air we breathe; similarly, we don't stop to think about the most deeply embedded, routinized norms by which we live. Only a major epistemological jolt can achieve this – like, as I have described above, seeing something abnormal as normal and seeing the edges of both normal and abnormal eroded beyond recognition. Then just what constitutes the normal can come into view – and we need to be able to see this, because the normal defines and oppresses what it designates as abnormal.

What then are the particularities of this strange sexuality, hetero? In order of diminishing indisputability, we might note the following five characteristics:

1. Difference is at the heart of sexual object choice
Heterosexuality always involves attraction and intercourse between two persons who, whatever else may be the case, are primarily differentiated by one category: gender. Evidence suggests that in practice, heterosexuals choose partners who in all respects other than gender (e.g. class, race, nationality, age, ability) are more like them than unlike; yet what is privileged in the understanding of the erotics of the choice is gender difference.

2. Difference is conceptualized as oppositeness
Heterosexuality is posited on the gender difference femininity: masculinity. This is widely conceptualized in terms of opposites: male aggression, strength, hardness, roughness and competitiveness as the opposite of female nurture, weakness, softness, smoothness and co-operativeness. This often then defines male and female sexuality within heterosexuality – masculine active, feminine passive (terms in turn often grafted onto homosexual sex, as when gay men used to ask each other whether they were butch or bitch). Such difference as oppositeness is important for a central tenet of heterosexual ideology, namely, that heterosexual partners are complementary to one another, that penises fit vaginas, that masculinity

balances femininity, that the combination of the two encompasses the range of human qualities and thus constitutes the proper and perfect form of human (sexual) relationships.

3. Difference is in fact power imbalance

Cliff Gorman, the actor who played the flamboyant queen Emory in both the play and the film of The Boys in the Band was interviewed in The New York Times in September 1968. Drinking beer from a can, he insistently protested his heterosexuality, and as if to prove his point, he said that he had recently agreed to play a rapist on television and 'What could be more heterosexual than that?' (see Katz, 1996, p. 109). Radical feminist theory could not have come up with a better definition of the essence of heterosexuality, of heterosexuality taken to its logical conclusion.

This is the position argued by Sheila Jeffreys, who defines 'heterosexual desire [as] eroticised power difference' (1990, p. 299). The ideas of difference and complementarity assume a level playing field between women and men; they do not acknowledge or take into account the socially sanctioned power differences between men and women. This notion of the complementarity of difference, as opposed to its power imbalance, is celebrated as pleasurable in innumerable cultural texts. Romance fiction repeatedly returns to the thrill of the more powerful man for the female heroine, just as pornography returns to the image of the delectability of the vulnerable woman. Both romance and pornography are in fact more complex and varied than this, as are real heterosexual relations, but the romance/porn patterns provide something of a base line for the imagination of heterosexuality.

One can think of heterosexuality's vaunted pleasure in difference as a mere mask for its eroticized power imbalance, and no doubt it often is. However, it is probably the case that the promise and sometimes experience of the former co-exists with the latter, at least some of the time. In a study of heterosexual couple dances in the Hollywood musical (Dyer, 1993), I noted a pattern whereby there was a shift within films from numbers early on where partners either do the same thing or else things that complement each other, to later numbers where the woman is dependent on the man, often to the point where she surrenders control over her body to him. Thus in Top Hat (1935), the archetypal heterosexual couple, Fred Astaire and Ginger Rogers, do identical tap steps side by side in 'Isn't It A Lovely Day?', their first number together in the film, whereas in the climactic 'Cheek to Cheek' he swings her about, drags her back and finally holds her ever closer to the ground, in all cases making her dependent on him and affirming his power over her body. This shift from complementarity to power difference is if anything still more evident in later dance films like *Saturday Night Fever* (1978) or *Dirty Dancing* (1987). In terms of the films' stories, the shift is from numbers expressing initial desire, flirting and courting, to those expressing the full realization of sexual love. Complementarity of differences seems to need to become male domination and female subordination for a relationship to be consummated. Thus it is not that the imagination of heterosexuality cannot genuinely encompass pleasure in difference but that it has difficulty sustaining it, especially at the moment of the supposed affirmation of heterosexual identity, sex itself.

4. Sexuality has something to do with procreation

Most acts of heterosexual penis-vagina intercourse (which does not account for all heterosexual sex acts) do not lead to procreation – but they might. Heterosexual sex is overwhelmingly the most common means of sexual reproduction; for many religious and moral traditions, sexual reproduction (and therefore heterosexuality) is the purpose of sexuality, in the sense of that being the reason why God gave it to humans or that nature developed it; for most heterosexuals, avoidance of conception is a tiresome part of the business of leading a heterosexual life.

5. Sexual practice is an affirmation of one's identity as normal

Heterosexuality, in the sense of man-woman coitus, is still statistically the majority sexual practice and is almost certainly regarded by most people as the norm. The desire to be normal and the pressure on people to conform are both very powerful. At the same time, sexuality is especially privileged by Western society as a ground and explanation of who we are. To feel then that one has the normal sexuality is profoundly affirming of personal identity and social belonging.

The fact that heterosexuality is a majority practice, that it most readily appears natural and the norm, that most of what we know about sex in the past or in other cultures is heterosex, all of this makes it hard not to believe that heterosexuality just is the inevitable and proper sexual order of society. It is was the political challenge to this that marked the first step in the development of a lesbian (and gay) critique of heterosexuality.

I put 'and gay' in brackets in the previous sentence, because it was lesbian theory that led the way in the intellectual and political project of making heterosexuality strange. This can be traced in the early polemical writings of radical feminism, while in academic spheres the most influential texts have probably been two articles published in 1980: Adrienne Rich's 'Compulsory Heterosexuality and Lesbian Existence' and Monique Wittig's 'The Straight Mind'. Though significantly different in many ways (above all in relation to what they have to say about lesbianism), both these texts see heterosexuality as something imposed on women in the interests of men. Thus Rich speaks of 'compulsory heterosexuality' while Wittig speaks of 'the obligatory social relationships between "man" and "woman"'. Rich lists many of the ways that women are coerced into heterosexuality, the sanctions against those that resist or rebel, the remorseless delivery throughout culture of the message of heterosexual inevitability and rightness. For Rich, all this effort is so huge and elaborate that it gives the lie to the idea that heterosexuality is natural – if it were so, why would it be necessary to sell it so hard, to cajole, threaten and punish so insistently those who don't want to practise it? Wittig focuses more on the assumption of heterosexuality built into the foundations of Western thought, and not least the psychoanalysis still fashionable in cultural theory. She argues that 'the straight mind' is founded on universality and difference: it believes that it alone knows how the world is and thus constitutes all difference as difference from straightness.

> To constitute a difference and to control it is an 'act of power, since it is essentially a normative act. Everybody tries to show the other as different. But not everybody succeeds on doing so. One has to be socially dominant to succeed in it'.[2] (Wittig, 1980, p. 108)

Rich relates compulsory heterosexuality to the situation of women; what the former oppresses is the possibility of relations between women, of which lesbianism is perhaps the exemplary form. Thus although it seems to me that compulsory heterosexuality also oppresses gay men, and that there is just as much hysterical social and cultural investment in making sure that the natural form of sexuality develops in men too, Rich's ideas were not designed to make this point. Wittig on the other hand does include gay and even other kinds of men (non-white, for instance) in those oppressed by the straight mind, because this mind does not just oppress those who are not heterosexual but all those who are different from it. In this perspective, heterosexuality is merely the foundational form of all oppression.

> ... the straight mind cannot conceive of a culture, a society where het-
> erosexuality would not order not only all human relationships but also
> its very production of concepts and all the processes which escape con-
> sciousness, as well. (Wittig, 1980, p. 107)

Rich, Wittig and others challenged the naturalness of heterosexuality, by
showing how culture works to enforce it and arguing that it is in the interests of dominant men to have it thought natural (and therefore presumed
to be unchangeable). What they did not point to was any evidence that heterosexuality was not to all intents and purposes natural, in the sense of
being universally practised throughout recorded time. This is tackled by
Jonathan Ned Katz in his book *The Invention of Heterosexuality*. He draws
on the burgeoning work on lesbian and gay history (a field in which his own
work has been profoundly influential), for while this did not initially set out
to deal with heterosexuality, it has inadvertently shed light on it. Lesbian
and gay history has worked predominantly with the model of homosexuality as something experienced in radically different ways in different periods
and different societies, a model that can only be explained by conceiving of
sexuality, all sexuality, as socially and culturally moulded. In tracing such
differences, lesbian and gay historians have inevitably pointed to the
changing ways in which sexuality in general, and therefore heterosexuality,
has been moulded.

In *The Invention of Heterosexuality*, Katz shows that, before the mid-
nineteenth century, the particular concatenation of assumptions given
above that coalesce into heterosexuality did not pertain. Sexual acts
between women and men were understood to be the means for human
reproduction, and in most societies for most of human existence, survival
of the species has been precarious, making it necessary to ensure that such
sexual acts were undertaken. Male-female coitus is not however the same
thing as heterosexual desire or being heterosexual.

Katz looks at a number of historical moments to demonstrate how very
differently (hetero)sexuality has been thought and felt about. The first of
these is ancient Greece, for his account of which Katz draws on the work
of Michel Foucault (itself corroborated, as Katz notes, by many lesbian
and gay classicists). Here the focus is 'free men', and Foucault and Katz
argue that, while a distinction was drawn between such men's 'higher',
'spiritual' love and their 'lower', 'earthly' love, these do not correlate neatly
with heterosexual and homosexual love (or even vice versa, as a certain gay

romanticism about 'Greek love' has sometimes assumed). Rather, high love is focused by free men on other free men, while the baser love is directed at women and boys. The fact that, in the baser love, 'one man's inclinations usually favoured women, another man's, boys' (Katz, 1996, p. 35) was not significant; whether the higher love involved sexual activity has, however, always been controversial.

Katz's second moment draws on his own pioneering research on the New England colonies between 1607 and 1740. Here the fragility of the new settlements put a premium on sexual reproduction, and thus the crucial distinction was between procreative and non-procreative sex acts. All forms of the latter were an abomination, and in law (if not in practice) the punishment for sodomy and adultery was the same (death). We are worlds away from the validation of heterosexuality as a pleasure in difference and power founded in but not limited to procreation. Katz also discusses the organization of sexuality in nineteenth-century America, from about 1820 to 1850, before the invention of the idea of heterosexuality. Here he stresses the distinction between 'the moral character of passionate love and the immoral character of sensual lust', with the former, expressive of one's affective being, just as likely to be directed towards one's own sex as the so-called opposite one.

It is only towards the end of the nineteenth century that the notion of (and term) heterosexuality comes into being. Katz shows how the influential sexologist Richard von Krafft-Ebbing developed a theory of heterosexuality as a form of desire, based upon opposites and especially on the opposition of active (male) and passive (female). This was then elaborated upon by Sigmund Freud to the point that, for him, 'hetero *feeling* defines hetero *being*, whether or not one *acts* heterosexually' (Katz, 1996, p. 66). Through the twentieth century the heterosexual emerged more and more clearly as the sexual norm, until challenged by the lesbian and gay movements.

The idea that heterosexuality is an invention, that it is a culturally and historically produced sexuality, does not dispute that there are everywhere and have always been genital acts between women and men. What it does suggest is that there is nothing natural and inevitable about how those acts are thought and felt about, with what feelings they are performed; it suggests that human beings have control over the construction of human sexualities. This control is not exactly individual. As individuals, we do have some degree of control over how we act, but we do so in the context of what we know about acts, what they mean, how they feel, that is to say, what we have in the broadest cultural sense been taught about acts, meanings and feelings. This cultural sense is also humanly constructed, but collectively, without there being any over-riding consciousness in charge of it, and every individual is born into a situation where the cultural sense of things seems just to be there, a given, unproduced. It is this feeling that makes heterosexuality, as invented really so recently in Western history, feel like something natural.

It is striking that it is overwhelmingly lesbians and gay men who have made a start on denaturalizing heterosexuality. Two anthologies on heterosexuality (Hanscombe and Humphries, 1987; Wilkinson and Kitzinger, 1993) were both produced by lesbians and gay men. The second of these caused consternation, distress and outrage among heterosexual women to whom the editors wrote asking them to contribute pieces reflecting on their heterosexuality. Heterosexual women found themselves named for their sexuality in the way lesbians invariably are and often resented it. Carol Nagy Jacklin comes straight out with it: 'Being asked to contribute . . . as a "heterosexual" is offensive, because to say "I am heterosexual" implies that my sexual preference is an unchanging and essential personal attribute and that "I am traditional"'; she goes on to suggest that heterosexual women 'are at greater risk of having inequitable personal relations' and that while the 'disadvantages [of heterosexuality] are clear, the advantages [are] somewhat less so' (Wilkinson and Kitzinger, 1993, p. 34). Mary Gergen asks 'Why address me so categorically as a heterosexual?' How did Wilkinson and Kitzinger know? 'Because I am married? Or because my husband seems 'straight'?' (p. 62) But at least these women replied and started speculating: one dreads to think with what wounded dignity heterosexual men would have reacted.

Denaturalizing heterosexuality not only unsettles it, it also forms the basis for understanding much else about contemporary culture and society. Many have observed that gender – what we think men and women are and are like – is itself a product of heterosexuality. The latter, as noted, is founded on the notion of the oppositeness of male and female bodies – it requires the notion of gender, or these particular notions of male and female gender, to make sense. Judith Butler speaks of a 'heterosexual matrix', that is

> a hegemonic discursive/epistemic model of gender intelligibility that assumes that *for bodies to make sense* there must be a stable sex expressed through a stable gender (masculine expresses male, feminine expresses

female) that is oppositionally and hierarchically *defined through the compulsory practice of heterosexuality.* (1990, p. 151; my emphasis)

A simplification of the stages in Butler's argument would run something like this: bodies do not of themselves 'make sense'; we, that is the culture, *make* sense of them; the only way our culture can make such sense is by imagining that bodies have stable properties and in particular that bodies engaged in reproductive sex have stable properties that can be captured in a simple binarism (male and female); thus the imperative of heterosexuality requires the notion of different genders. Once you knock away the support of nature to both heterosexuality and gender, you are left only with people obliged to do heterosexual sex. Such doing can then be seen as a performance, a key notion in Butler's work. In one of her most dizzying passages, Butler suggests that the very idea of the naturalness of heterosexuality is itself a product of performance: heterosexuality merely imitates what it has learnt heterosexuality is, but as if this is an imitation of something basic, given by nature:

> . . . the *naturalistic effects* of heterosexualised genders are produced by imitative strategies; *what they imitate is a phantasmatic ideal of heterosexual identity* . . . In this sense, the 'reality' of heterosexual identity is performatively constituted through an imitation that sets itself up as the origin and the ground of all imitations. (Butler, 1991, p. 21; my emphasis)

The implication of Butler's discussion here is not only that heterosexuality is an imitation of something that it takes to be, if you go back far enough, original, natural, something that is not itself an imitation. Because this original never existed, the implication is also that heterosexuality, which is supposed to be the ultimate affirmation of the natural (the normal, the inevitable), constantly fails to achieve this affirmation, because it is only ever an imitation of a fantasy idea of the natural. In short, heterosexuality is a performance that can never pull off what it is supposed to pull off – the fixing of hierarchical gender roles and the suppression of the consciousness of the possibility of all non-heterosexual sexuality. Heterosexuality, and the gender roles it underwrites, in its need to proclaim its own naturalness and normality, can only produce an anxiety at never actually being natural and normal.

This explains much about the images, stories and representations of heterosexuality circulating in our culture: the convoluted stories and relentless repetitions of soap opera, the insane excesses of film melodrama, romance fiction and grand opera, the flight from women as anything but fuck objects in male action fiction and novels of Angst. Cultural representations offer rich pickings for any student of heterosexuality. Why, for example, is there all the running after men in *Pride and Prejudice*, when every instance of actual marriage in the book (or its television adaptation) is absurd and appalling? If cowboys wanted to populate the West, why did they spend so much time galloping away from women? Why is *Sleepless in Seattle* so self-conscious about wanting to present a hetero love story for our times? Why is *Baywatch* so pneumatic? All these perform heterosexuality, but in such remorseless, crazed and alarmed modes that they suggest heterosexuality is indeed on a hiding to nothing in its assertion of its own naturalness and normality.

If denaturalizing heterosexuality casts new light on gender, then it may also do so on race, for the notion of race is profoundly heterosexual. Race is a way of categorizing bodies that reproduce themselves. Notions of pure race and the importance of preserving racial purity require the control of male-female coitus and reproduction, but they do not require notions of heterosexual desire. Once this is invented, however, all hell is let loose for racial purists. For heterosexual desire foregrounds the erotics of difference and power imbalance, the very things that also underpin notions of race. Thus are mobilized the cross-racial desirings that so confuse, alarm and disgust racialist thought. Heterosexuality is in our culture the affective, libidinal means by which people get into man-women sex, and thus into human/racial reproduction. Abandonment of heterosexuality (as opposed to man-woman sex) might also be the means of abandoning racialist obsessions.

It would be rash to claim that only Lesbian and Gay Studies can (or indeed has) looked at the centrality of heterosexuality to the constitution of sexuality, gender and race. Yet not only have lesbians and gay men been at the forefront of naming heterosexuality as something that requires investigation, it is also central to the logic of Lesbian and Gay Studies to carry those investigations forward. We can, after all, only understand how homosexuality is constructed by understanding it as part of a broader, general system of thinking and feeling about sexuality – and a crucial role in that system is played by particular, limited and limiting ideas of heterosexuality. Equally, we can only understand why homosexuality is denigrated or controversial by understanding the construction of heterosexuality as a norm. To understand lesbian and gay existence, we have to understand heterosexuality; in the process, we produce heterosexuality itself as a bizarre object of study.

Notes

1. I take 'Lesbian and Gay Studies' to mean the study of homosexuality by, and openly by, those who identify as homosexual (or by those who study it on our terms). Thus, although homosexuality has long been studied, we can date Lesbian and Gay Studies back to the 1970s – albeit with fabulous precursors.
2. The quotation is from Claude Faugerton and Philippe Robert, *La Justice et les représentations sociales du système pénal*. Paris: Masson, 1978.

References

Butler, Judith, *Gender Trouble: Feminism and the Subversion of Identity*. New York: Routledge, 1990.

Butler, Judith, 'Imitation and Gender Subordination', in Diana Fuss (ed.), *Inside/Out: Lesbian Theories, Gay Theories*, New York: Routledge, 1991, pp. 13–31.

Dyer, Richard, '"I Seem to Find the Happiness I Seek": Heterosexuality and Dance in the Musical', in Helen Thomas (ed.), *Dance, Gender and Culture*, London: Macmillan, 1993.

Hanscombe, Gillian, and Humphries, Martin (eds), *Heterosexuality*. London: GMP, 1987.

Jeffreys, Sheila, *Anticlimax: A Feminist Perspective on the Sexual Revolution*. London: The Women's Press, 1990.

Katz, Jonathan Ned, *The Invention of Heterosexuality*. New York: Plume, 1996.

Rich, Adrienne, 'Compulsory Heterosexuality and Lesbian Existence', in *Signs*, Vol. 5, No. 4, 1980, pp. 631–60.

Wilkinson, Sue, and Kitzinger, Celia (eds), *Heterosexuality: A Feminism and Psychology Reader*. London: Sage, 1993.

Wittig, Monique, 'The Straight Mind', in *Feminist Issues*, Vol. 1, No. 1, 1980, pp. 103–11.

19

Camp

Andy Medhurst

IN THE LATE 1930S, a young white man in Atlanta, Georgia, imprisoned for moral turpitude, was offered the chance of parole and a possible pardon if he agreed to undergo experimental treatment aimed at curing him of his homosexuality. The doctor presiding over this treatment, which involved the use of Metrazol, a chemical which induced convulsive shocks, reported on both the patient's history and the progress of the experiment to the annual meeting of the Southern Psychiatric Association: 'Homosexual experiences began during his fourteenth year and continued thereafter. Feminine mannerisms were evident. Metrazol was administered until fifteen shocks were produced. All homosexual desires had disappeared after the ninth shock, but treatment was continued until all feminine mannerisms had been removed. Normal sex relations were established . . . He was granted a pardon' (Katz, 1976, p.254).

Jonathan Katz's *Gay American History* contains a multitude of stories that catalogue the discrimination, hatred and violence meted out over hundreds of years to sexual nonconformists, but the story of that poor Georgia queen is the one that I have always found the most haunting and enraging. It wasn't apparently enough that his desires were destroyed – no, his effeminacy demanded still more retribution, so his veins were pumped even fuller until he was broken completely, purged of his queening, fit at last to enter the promised land of 'normal sex relations'.

There are, however, happier stories from Georgia:

There was a whole gay subculture in Atlanta and I dived right into it. Within a year I had turned into what was known as a Screaming Queen: wearing make-up, walking down the street screaming at people, screaming at boys, having to run from them. Miss Cocks called it Wrecking. That's what screaming queens would do: go out wrecking people's nerves . . . One of Miss Cocks' favourite wrecks was to park the car near the Greyhound bus station and walk in. She taught me the walk: we'd carry our teasing combs up by our shoulders and just swish around the bus station. The teasing comb was a very important prop; it was just the campest thing you could possibly carry . . . we'd walk into the men's room, and all the men would be standing there peeing, and we'd throw our arms in the air and scream 'Wooooooh!' then we'd run out of the station and jump into the car and drive off screaming and laughing. 'Ooh, we wrecked them, we wrecked them!' (County, 1995, pp. 21–2)

It would be dangerous, although tempting, to over-romanticize Jayne County's glorious account of wrecking the streets of 1960s Atlanta, since such pleasures could only ever be contingent, momentary and fraught with risk. If he (still Wayne then, years before becoming the transgender punk singer Jayne) and his fellow-queen Miss Cocks had been arrested, the contemporary equivalents of Metrazol might have awaited them, in which case the joyful memory of a 'Wooooooh' duet would be scant consolation. Nonetheless, personal recollections like County's are the best, most inspiring antidote I know to the histories of horror like those found in Katz, and this is because camp – before it is anything else, before it gets scrutinized and squabbled over and splayed out on the operating table of theoretical analysis by academics like me – is part of gay men's daily lives, one of the ways in which we have managed to make sense of a world which at best tolerates and at worst exterminates us, a method for negotiating our way through what Jonathan Dollimore has called 'the lived contradictions of subordination' (1991, p. 311). Camp is one of our most fearsome weapons (why else would the paid assassins of heterosexual supremacy be so overwhelmingly determined to eradicate our queening?) and one of our most enriching experiences.

I know this partly because, in my own small way, I used to be a bit of a wrecker myself. While not presuming to put myself in the Jayne County league, I've often savoured the tastes of undisguised screaming. In the early 1980s I spent my days queening it up in the company of Peggy and Flo, Candy and Muriel, Dolly and Bunty, Bet and Arlene – not a woman among them – and, presiding over us all with an unforgivingly regal vindictiveness, La Bellissima Diva Velvetina. Our commitment to feminizing all aspects of everyday discourse was absolute: not only did we bestow female names on each other (when any aspiring queen joined our circle we took considerable care over choosing her new title), and, in the time-honoured way of screamers everywhere, reverse all gender pronouns so men became 'she', but we went further still. If two of our number slept together, this was deemed to be an act of lesbianism ('I saw Peggy and Flo getting Sapphic in the club last night', Velvetina announced), referred to disparagingly as 'bumping pussies', a meagre substitute for the proper fucking from a proper man which we were all ostensibly seeking. I shall curtail such reminiscences before they engulf the whole chapter (and do even more damage to my academic promotion prospects), but they are included here to indicate that my understanding and interpretation of camp do not stem from a stance of dispassionate objectivity. Camp has sustained and nurtured me for many years, giving me an invaluable blade to cut through the throttling tendrils of normative masculinity, and the pages that follow are indelibly marked by that fact. Inevitably, a piece of writing this brief on a topic as notoriously evasive as camp cannot avoid being hideously selective and woefully schematic. My viewpoint is that of one white English queen skidding towards forty – others would have other stories to relate.

Camp, gay men and subcultural politics

Camp, as almost every commentator on the subject has ruefully noted, eludes a single, crisp definition; nonetheless, most of us know it when we see, hear, feel or do it. Camp, above all, is the domain of queens. It is a configuration of taste codes and a declaration of effeminate intent. It flows like gin and poison through subcultural conversations. It revels in exaggeration, theatricality, parody and bitching. It both vigorously undermines and rigorously reinscribes traditional gender roles. Its quicksilver sharpness runs rings around ponderous summarizing. It is why I love Diana Ross, Barbara Stanwyck, 1950s furniture, *The Prime of Miss Jean Brodie* and the Pet Shop Boys. Camp is not an entity but a relationship – a relationship between queens and their circumstances.

Historical accounts of queer subcultures, whether exhaustive academic studies (Chauncey, 1994) or smaller-scale community-based oral histories (Brighton Ourstory Project, 1992), all contain example after example of how gay men used camp as a survival mechanism in a hostile environment. Camp answers heterosexual disapproval through a strategy of defensive offensiveness (camp thrives on paradoxes), incarnating the homophobe's worst fears, confirming that not only do queers dare to exist but they actively flaunt and luxuriate in their queerness. In England in the 1940s, male drag shows toured the country, and the queens performing in them were obliged to use public transport to reach their next engagement:

Sometimes we'd have to wait two hours for a connection, and we'd sit on our suitcases on the platform at Wigan or Crewe, drinking cups of tea and chattering like mynah birds . . . married couples who were going to visit their relations in the country would just stand and stare at us, open-mouthed. They couldn't believe what they saw – a dozen or so men with plucked eyebrows and gaunt white faces and polo-neck sweaters and little white raincoats and suede boots and yellow socks and perhaps a yellow scarf thrown around the neck three times . . . Two or three might be wearing little black berets to mask their bleached hair and there was always one queen who had left on last night's nail polish. And when the train came we'd all bundle on it, giggling and gossiping. (Kirk and Heath, 1984, p. 13)

More wrecking, more scandal, more refusal to conform – and thus more of an embarrassment to homosexuals who sought to live more discreetly, more walled in behind those layers of guilt and denial that the screaming queens had long since minced beyond. The 'homophile' campaigning groups of the post-war era regarded camp queens as a barrier to the wider public tolerance of homosexuality, since while the homophile presented himself as decent, ordinary, different only in the matter of sexual desire, the queen was irredeemably other, a limp-wristed slap in decency's face. Hence the trickle of homosexual-themed novels and gay men's autobiographies from this period depicted camp in derogatory terms, referring to queens as 'creatures who love to make an exhibition of themselves' (Wildeblood, 1957, p. 13) – a charge that was true enough, except that it was meant to be blame, not praise – and 'unintelligent, verbose, neurotic and generally tiresome . . . they resort to plucked eyebrows and an excessive application of the wrong shade of rouge' (Garland, 1961, pp. 47–8). This apparent gulf between responsible homosexuals and outrageous camp queens was, in reality, much less absolute, since they would not only intersect in the few available subcultural venues, but most queers had the agility to switch between codes depending on the demands of the moment. How else would the ostensibly respectable narrator of the second quotation know so much about the quantity and quality of rouge?

Nevertheless, it was the always-obvious queens that the general population saw and goggled at, and because such queens were the only undeniably recognizable homosexual men visible in the public sphere, they came to stand for male homosexuality itself. Consequently, they could hardly be ignored by the younger, politicized gay liberationists of the late

1960s. The liberation generation regarded such camp subcultures with deep ambivalence. Sometimes the response was one of raging hostility: 'we should expose our Princess Floradora Femadonna so that our younger brothers will not fall into the lavender cesspool and be swept down the sewers of fantasyland . . . the princess trip is . . . an artificiality, and an escape from reality' (Hanson, 1972, p. 269). Sometimes it was more sympathetic: 'the queens and the nellies . . . have become our first martyrs. They came out and withstood disapproval before the rest of us did . . . If they suffered from being open, it is straight society whom we must indict, not the queen' (Wittman, 1972, p. 334). Yet even inside such endorsements there was a veiled critique, an implication that camping and queening should be defended but were now being transcended. Martyrs, after all, inhabit the past, their purpose being to inspire but never share in the present, and the present in question was the hippie-inspired, androgynously-dressed counterculture. The pivotal moment for the queen-as-martyr discourse was the Stonewall riot, which in gay popular memory has become indelibly associated with the use of drag and camp to fend off police intimidation and violence. It is impossible to ascertain precisely who did instigate the fightback that sparked the riot (Duberman, 1994), but in gay men's myth of our past we like to think it was some screaming queen. Thus an emblematic camp individual became an enshrined community figurehead, but this queen's starring role was simultaneously her farewell performance – all she did, in the long run, was to usher in the hyper-masculine gay culture of the 1970s, where effeminacy was stigmatized and where the personal ads sternly specified (as so many of them still do today) 'no fems' and 'noncamp'.

In that all-too-brief heyday between Stonewall and AIDS, a small number of gay male critics and theorists attempted to account for the meanings of camp (Babuscio, 1977, Blachford, 1981; Britton, 1978/9; Cohen and Dyer, 1980; Dyer, 1992; White, 1980). Despite disagreements, they reached a relative consensus which paralleled the verdict of the broader gay male community: camp was important once, still offered some incidental pleasures, but lacked political edge when compared to the liberationist agenda of gay rights. The message of camp was 'One makes the best of a bad lot instead of transforming the whole lot' (Blachford, 1981, p. 204). Camp was ameliorative, not transformative.

Beyond gay men's debates, however, something else had already happened to camp. In the mid-1960s it swapped the secret corners of a subcultural ghetto for a much more brightly-lit environment. One text inaugurated that change, Susan Sontag's (in)famous essay 'Notes on Camp', first published in 1964 (Sontag, 1983, pp. 105–120). Sontag's account of camp, her identification of it as a sensibility of apolitical playfulness and ironic detachment, connected to but not dependent on gay men's taste and style codes, marked the crucial point when camp became a word and an idea available to those outside gay male subcultures. The consequent tension, between camp as a product of queers' experiences and perceptions and camp as a discourse available to all, is central to any study of this area.

Sontag's article had a seismic impact – glossy magazines, radio and television discussions, dinner-party chatter, all zoomed in on the phenomenon of camp – because it chose just the right moment to surf a wave, providing a vocabulary for analysing a barrage of texts and images which were emerging in and enlivening Western culture. The mid-1960s were the era of Pop Art, of James Bond, of the Beatles, of TV series like *The Avengers* and *Batman*, and Sontag's beginner's guide to camp seemed to offer a particularly fruitful aesthetic framework for understanding such phenomena. Camp, for Sontag, facilitated the unsettling of hierarchies, it enabled new appreciations of underrated popular forms and advocated an arch scepticism towards established cultural canons; in this respect her version of camp was the perfect aesthetic for its cultural moment, since, as Marc O'Day has said, 'the sixties were a laboratory – or perhaps, rather, a battlefield – in the relativization of all kinds of values' (O'Day, 1994, p. 57). Sontag's take on camp delineated and lionized its qualities of wit, cheek and misbehaviour, she delivered it to a public hungry for its refreshing refusal of staid moralism and thrilled by its effervescent rapture in the play of surfaces. In the process, however, the homosexual specificity of camp was jettisoned. Sontag expertly outlined what camp was like, but downplayed the social and historical reasons which had led to its formulation; she presented its manifestations but evacuated its motives. Shorn of its queer roots, denuded of its origins in gay men's attempt to simultaneously fend off and undermine heterosexual normativity through enacting outrageous inversions of aesthetic and gender codes, camp looked like little more than an amusing diversion. What had been a subculturally specific politics of style was suddenly a commodity in the public domain. As it became clear how much fun camp could be, everybody wanted to join the party – but that left the original hosts unsure how to respond to all the gatecrashers.

Desperately shedding Susan

Academic studies of camp have flourished recently thanks to the fashion-ability of Queer Theory, and if there is one refrain which echoes across all these studies it is this: Sontag got it wrong (Bergman (ed.), 1993; Frank, 1993; Meyer (ed.), 1994; Miller, 1993). 'Notes on Camp' has become a vilified talisman, accused of wrenching camp away from its subcultural origins, depoliticizing it and recasting it as little more than an aesthetic game for jaded sophisticates. There is some truth in these charges; Sontag does indeed foreground a purely aesthetic side of camp and deny it any politics, but then the book she published her essay in was called *Against Interpretation*, conceived as a deliberately provocative rebuff to moral and ideological critiques of culture. She also, in a reflective interview conducted in 1975, reconsidered her views on the politics of camp, suggesting that 'ironizing about the sexes is one small step towards depolarizing them' (Sontag, 1983, p. 339) – a comment that not only cuts the ground from under those who have been so quick to condemn her but also rather remarkably prefig-ures the Queer Theory mantra of performative gender to which those same critics have sworn undying allegiance.

Even if the Queer anti-Sontag lobby could not bring themselves to credit her with any perceptiveness, they could at least have demonstrated some sensitivity to earlier, less dismissive gay responses. 'Sontag's approach proved to be a dead end for other thinkers' (Bergman, 1993, p. 8) may be the brisk, and symptomatically haughty, conclusion of the new Queers, but it sits uneasily with the fact that pioneer gay academics once felt able to call her essay 'brilliant' (Dollimore, 1983, p. 80) and 'marvel-lous' (Dyer, 1992, p. 138). The conflict between these judgements of Sontag is partly a generational one – Queer discourses were characterized by a stridently ungenerous tone and a scorched-earth approach to history – and partly due to the Queer wish to insist on camp as an always-political statement. If your understanding of camp prioritizes its potential politics, then Sontag must be overturned, since for her (at least in the original essay) camp was an antidote to ideological thinking. The gay writers on camp between Sontag and Queer were able to balance their wish to correct her depoliticizing impulses with their realization that camp was indeed partly the matter of taste codes she catalogued; in other words, they thought camp had more political edge than Sontag, but they were not willing to see it as political and nothing else. To take that last step, to purge camp of its aesthetics, would be to strip it of its pleasures – and that is the unfortunate step taken by the most virulently anti-Sontag text of all, Moe Meyer's *The Politics and Poetics of Camp.*

Meyer's grim, mean-spirited, purist brand of camp is established on the first page: 'the un-queer do not have access to the discourses of Camp, only to derivatives constructed through the act of appropriation' (1994, p. 1). Camp, for Meyer, belongs only to the initiated few, which does not mean those belonging to gay male subcultures, but an even fewer few, the elect handful who share his vision of a camp without laughs, a camp that screams only with vanguardist anger and never with giddy delight, a camp that is always on the picket line and never kicks off its slingbacks for a moment's relaxation. Since I too think camp has valuable political possibilities, I can understand Meyer's determination to retrieve camp from its toothless, straightened interpretations. The most culpable of these, Andrew Ross's 'Uses of Camp' (Ross, 1989), deserves all the opprobrium mistakenly heaped on Sontag, and Meyer's demolition of it is long overdue. Yet Meyer's excessive claims for camp as always-and-only-radical cannot convince anyone who has spent time among camp queens, whose turns of phrase and ideological outlook can be frighteningly reactionary, but then Meyer is far more concerned with advancing a rigorous (i.e. inflexible) theoretical model of camp than with recognizing its contentious day-to-day ambivalences.

Queered camp

Though camp may have been displaced in post-Stonewall gay male subcultures, it hardly disappeared. Gay men in London pubs strove to look as macho as possible, but as often as not they stood flannel-shirted-shoulder to leather-jacketed-shoulder watching drag acts on the pub's stage. Earnestly politicized gays hoped that camp codes would fade away in the new dawn of liberated consciousness, but screaming and queening proved hard to banish. Camp, let's not forget, was weaned on surviving disdain – she's a tenacious old tigress of a discourse well versed in defending her corner. If decades of homophobic pressure had failed to defeat camp, what chance did a mere reorganization of subcultural priorities stand?

The temporary nature of that reorganization became apparent in the spaces made available for camp under the umbrella of queer. Perceiving the patient, liberal gradualism of mainstreamed gay campaigning to be wholly inadequate in the context of the AIDS crisis, the righteously furious activists of the queer generation recognized the appropriateness of camp

strategies – an illustrative example might be The Sisters of Perpetual Indul-
gence, the order of gay male nuns – for their confrontational street politics
(Roman, 1993; Lucas, 1994). In doing so, they were following the example of early Gay Liberation protests, which often drew on cross-dressing,
gender-blurring and flagrant theatricality before those elements were sac-
rificed in favour of politer methods. Queer activism sought to re-gay camp,
to reclaim it from the widened-out heterosexualization it had undergone in
the years since Sontag, to imbue its subcultural codes with an overtly ideological edge. This project both informed and was informed by the ways in
which camp had found a new kind of intellectualized legitimacy in the
emerging academic field of Queer Theory. I have already discussed the
Queer Theory texts which sought to intervene in debates specifically about
camp, but there are further, broader ways in which camp discourses were
at the heart of Queer thinking.

In Judith Butler's *Gender Trouble*, for example, a book which has a status in Queer Theory circles comparable to that of Judy Garland's Carnegie
Hall album in pre-Stonewall camp subcultures, the key concept of gender
performativity borrows extensively from camp (Butler, 1990). Although
she largely avoids the word itself, camp seems crucial in Butler's stress on
pastiche and masquerade, in her references to comedy and laughter, and
most of all in her hugely influential choice of drag as a model for how all
gender identities are performed rather than innate. (It may be worth
underlining here that drag and camp are not the synonyms too many of
Butler's followers seem to assume: drag is merely one incarnation of camp,
just one room in camp's mansion.) Butler's theorizing rehabilitated camp
as a radical gesture, relishing how it exposed, through the drag queen's easy
mockery of identity, the fragility of our traditional concepts of gender. This
summary does little justice to the complexity of Butler's arguments, indeed
she became so aghast at simplified interpretations of her thesis that she
devoted a follow-up book to the re-complication of it (Butler, 1993), but
the boiled-down version had already entered broader spheres of debate
and activism.

Paradoxically, this theoreticized vindication of camp threatened to
destroy its specific subcultural vitality. For if we conclude that *all* gender is
play and performance, then camp, which has long held that conclusion as
its cherished secret weapon, no longer has any unique contribution to
make. This is because traditional camp needed a system of rigidly policed
gender roles as a condition of existence; that system both marginalized
those sexual nonconformists who would not or could not fit into it and at

the same time provided in its ridiculous rigidity the raw material for the comic revenge through which they made their marginalization more bearable. At the farthest reaches of the *Gender Trouble* scenario, where a postmodern erasure of certainty has left all positions up for grabs, there is no longer any hierarchy for the disenfranchised to undermine. And if everyone's in drag, then what's the point in a few of us frocking up?

The point, I would argue, is that the performativity theory of gender, seduced by its own conceptual elegance, lost sight of the everyday contexts in which gender is experienced. Sexual inequality did not evaporate simply because an elite phalanx of academics decided that identity was passé. Gender polarities may be considerably less fixed than they once were (after David Bowie, Divine, Boy George, k. d. lang, RuPaul, Madonna, Julian Clary and *The Adventures of Priscilla, Queen of the Desert* how could they not be?), but gender hierarchies still persist, and as long as there are gender hierarchies, camp will remain for some of us a way of questioning and resisting them.

Camp, gender and lesbians

The question of camp's sexual politics is perhaps the most complex topic of all, since it taps into dense and difficult issues about gay men's relation to women, femininity and feminism. At one level, there are the well-known debates over whether camp, in its theatricalized and exaggerated vocabularies of the feminine (changed names and pronouns, drag, diva-worship), is misogynistic – those that claim it is would point to the cruelty of much drag impersonation, or to camp's association of femininity with emotionality and the trivial. Alternatively, camp might be defended on the grounds that it places conventional masculinity just as frequently in the firing line, or that camp gay men's yearning for the feminine, however misplaced and appropriative it may seem, stems from the over-riding wish to be free of the masculine. (Theoretically sophisticated readers may smile at the reductiveness of feminine versus masculine, but for gay men in less comfortable circumstances that binary is often the only starting point available for understanding, and potentially reworking, gender roles.) Certainly the analyses of camp written by liberationist gay men in the 1970s were centrally concerned with the issue of camp's misogyny, a concern originating in the need felt by many gay men of that generation to build strategic alliances between gay and feminist politics.

More recently, different questions have arisen around camp and gender, and the most important of these is whether there has been, is, or could be such a thing as lesbian camp. Given the roots of gay male camp in the pre-liberation subcultures of queens, some lesbian scholars have wondered whether there might be traceable parallels in lesbian butch-femme subcultures, whether participation in such codified gender play might have led lesbians towards developing ironic perspectives on masculinity and femininity analogous to those occupied by gay men. One undoubted parallel that can be seen lies in the mixture of dismay and condescension felt by liberationist lesbians for butch-femme subcultures, who, just as post-Stonewall gay men denigrated their queen predecessors, looked back on butch-femme as some kind of false-consciousness error, unavoidable back then but superfluous in the liberated now. Hence the account of butch-femme in the liberationist classic *Sappho Was A Right-On Woman* is a chapter called 'The Necessity of the Bizarre' within a section entitled 'What It Was Like' (Abbott and Love, 1972). Some lesbian writers of the 1990s have rejected that discourse of dismay, proposing in its place a revised, historically sensitive account of butch-femme that stresses its courage and ingenuity, and demands its recognition as a creative survival strategy that thrived on a 'cunning . . . transformation of gender restrictions into gender rebellion' (Nestle, 1992, p. 18).

Perspectives like that seem to come very close to nominating butch-femme as the lesbian equivalent of camp. Also relevant here is the fact that the mythologized instigator of the Stonewall riot is, in some lesbian accounts, a diesel dyke rather than a flaming queen. On a more theoretical plane, Sue-Ellen Case has rather grandiloquently championed camp for its 'success in ironizing and distancing the regime of realist terror mounted by heterosexist forces' (Case, 1993, p. 298) so that 'a strategy of appearances replaces a claim to truth' (p. 304), before going on to assert that butch-femme offers lesbians a similar opportunity. If subcultural historians like Nestle, widely-circulated lesbian popular memory, and Queer Theorists like Case all support the butch-femme-equals-camp hypothesis, the argument looks watertight.

Until, that is, the factor of gender inequality is reintroduced into the equation. Camp queens and butch dykes do indeed sound like parallel outlaws, each in their own way refusing gender norms by reconfiguring gender polarities, both unswervingly committed to carving out spaces for marginalized desires: but to be parallel is not to be identical. Queens, however scandalously effeminate, were still men, and this, as lesbian historians Kennedy and Davis have argued, makes their rebellion against male power

always different to any rebellion practised by dykes: 'The queen was playing with male privilege. . .For women to confront male authority is to break
all traditional training and roles (1992, p. 76–77). Through their research
into the history of local butch-femme communities, Kennedy and Davis
also point out other telling differences between queens and butches, small
but vital distinctions in style codes, interpersonal behaviour and strategies
of self-presentation. What underpins all these differences is the power-rela-
tion of gender: butches' social and cultural position as women cannot be
lazily equated with queens' social and cultural position as men, and to use
the word 'camp' as a blanket term for both lesbians and gay men conceals
this crucial difference. It is possible to develop this point to the extent
where lesbian butch-femme is awarded a radicalism supposedly unavailable to gay male camp. Kennedy and Davis hint as much in their
opposition of the 'playing' queen and the 'confronting' dyke, while Kate
Davy leaves hints behind to insist firmly that while 'Camp (re)assures its
audience of the ultimate harmlessness of its play, its palatability for bourgeois sensibilities', lesbian butch-femme offers such a profound challenge
that 'phallocratic culture is not reassured' (Davy, 1994, p. 145). While
such 'who's-more-radical' games are far from constructive (and I can't
resist a tiny raise of the eyebrow on noting that Davy expects 'bourgeois
sensibilities' to be smashed by, of all hopelessly bourgeois cultural sites, the
theatre), the important issue here is that once again the over-slick equation
between gay male camp and lesbian gender play is being thought-provok-
ingly called into question.

Writing about media images of sexuality, Tamsin Wilton reaches a similarly sceptical conclusion about the possibility of lesbian camp. The irony
central to camp stems, she contends, from gay men's ambivalent status in
the production and consumption of culture: their gender affords them a
privileged status which their sexuality unsettles. Lesbians are doubly
excluded, on both gender and sexuality grounds, and since camp 'is less a
product of lack of access . . . and more a product of *compromised* access', it
follows that lesbian camp is not feasible (Graham, 1995, p. 145). Paula
Graham has detailed the ways in which contemporary lesbian audiences
find ironic pleasure and subversive potential in appropriating mainstream
Hollywood films, a subcultural practice which at first glance would
unproblematically merit the label 'lesbian camp', but argues that the over-
riding factor problematizing any such label is the way that camp is centred
on femininity: 'A gay man positioning himself in the feminine does disrupt
male authority . . . Lesbians more characteristically experience Western

standards of femininity as unattainable, exclusive and oppressive, and counter-identify' (Graham, 1995, p. 178). So lesbian appropriations of texts can indeed be 'disruptive and gender-destabilizing – but not *camp*' (p. 180).

This seems exactly right: 'camp' is a term with a gender-specific history and which signals a specifically gay male set of cultural strategies, and however similar certain lesbian strategies may initially appear, labelling them camp not only obscures their own particular qualities, subtleties and agendas, but places lesbians in a secondary, dependent position to gay men. The idea of lesbian camp is hugely alluring to those of us, myself included, still committed to maintaining alliances between lesbians and gay men, but it is a mirage, a distraction and a political mistake. Lesbian camp is as impossible as gay male butch-femme, which is not to deny that some gay men now and historically have constructed relationships based on enacted roles of 'masculine' and 'feminine', but to insist that the languages and conceptual frameworks gay men and lesbians have devised to make sense of their lives are not interchangeable across genders. Lesbian subcultures have evolved their own specific methods of reworking dominant gender images into new, more congenial, more sustaining, more women-centred patterns of meaning, and those methods deserve a better fate than being subsumed into a second-hand queens' vocabulary. What's needed is a new terminology. Over to you, girls.

Race, class and camp

While the overwhelming percentage of writing and thinking about camp has centred, quite properly, on its discourses of gender, there are other questions of identity that need to be considered. Issues of race are essential for a full understanding of camp's traditions and controversies, and three points are worth noting here as avenues for further exploration. Firstly, there are the pivotal roles occupied in white gay male diva-worship by women of other ethnicities: what can we learn about the ways ideologies of gender and race cohere and clash on the terrain of camp by deconstructing the adulation bestowed upon black female stars as diverse as Billie Holiday, Jessye Norman and Oprah Winfrey? (Barbra Streisand's Jewishness might also repay study through this framework.) Secondly, a further dimension of the saga of Stonewall, reinforced recently by Nigel Finch's cinematic fictionalization of the roots of the riot, is that the queens at the epicentre of it all were black or Latino. Thirdly, the one text above all that has been endlessly revisited by Queer Theorists in search of the last word on gender performativity is the film *Paris Is Burning*, which (through the eyes of a white Jewish lesbian director) surveys the world of black and Latino drag queens. The heated debates generated by this film's politics of representation have been at the heart of questions over the ethnocentrism of Queer Theory (Butler, 1993, pp.121–42; hooks, 1992, pp. 145–156). The American location of these examples is, I think, telling: the contours of black British camp remain largely uncharted.

Class is similarly vital in considerations of camp. Hostile responses towards camp queens (and, similarly but not identically, to butch-femme lesbians) have often been the product of an unacknowledged class dynamic. When university-educated gay liberationists derided old-style camping as an unfortunate outgrowth of marginalization and oppression, they often did so with a class arrogance that wholly failed to grasp the particularities of working-class queer subcultures. Liberationists in Britain reserved particular scorn for those camp entertainers from working-class backgrounds (Kenneth Williams, Frankie Howerd, Larry Grayson) who had put queening codes at the centre of British popular culture but refused to be open about their sexuality, a scorn which chose to ignore the fact that 'coming out' was usually a far riskier option, or indeed no option at all, beyond the relatively cosy settings of the university or the middle-class professions (Medhurst, forthcoming).

This is not to suggest that queening has ever been a purely working-class phenomenon. Subcultures of middle-class camp have been constant throughout recent gay male history, worlds where the rough-edged tongue of the bitchy bar queen is replaced by the sibilant gossip of the dinner-party, where opera is the soundtrack and chic design the backdrop. Indeed, Alan Sinfield has speculated that, in Britain at least, camp is precisely derived from gay men's aspirations to inhabit the taste and behaviour codes of the aristocracy, a lineage stemming from the repercussions of the Oscar Wilde trial. The image of Wilde, for Sinfield, was formative in shaping a relationship between camp and class which reverberates even today, so that all gay male camp, deliberately or not, contains 'a lurking recollection of the effeminate leisure-class dandy' (Sinfield, 1994, p. 156).

Campus camp

Academic life – with its absurd seriousness about issues of no real importance, its love of erecting gigantic superstructures of meaning on to fragments and minutiae, its fetishes of status and protocol, its aura of being conducted by a marginal subculture who live a life that only tangentially connects to the world lived in by most people – is a site of considerable camp. Those of us who work in Lesbian and Gay Studies cannot escape that fate, but our shrewdly attuned camp antennae might at least equip us to operate with more awareness of it. At the most obvious level, those of us who analyse camp itself are (or should be) only too aware of the potential ludicrousness of the enterprise, the risk, presciently identified by Susan Sontag herself, of producing just another piece of raw material for camp devotees to fall upon with mercilessly shredding claws.

Perhaps the most spectacular instance of camp in Queer Theory can be found in Eve Kosofsky Sedgwick's 'White Glasses', where Sedgwick wonders if all the time she has spent, both professionally and personally, in the company of gay men, if all the intellectual work she has undertaken and supported at the forefront of Lesbian and Gay Studies, have earned her the right to leap into a declaration of 'my – shall I call it my identification? Dare I, after this half-decade, call it . . . my identity? – as a gay man' (Sedgwick, 1993, p. 256). In its yoking together of flagrant preposterousness and swooning conviction, this strikes me as quintessentially camp. On one level Sedgwick's gambit is nothing but a campy daydream (much as I might mime to 'Touch Me In The Morning' in my bathroom mirror and decide to 'be' Diana Ross), but the fact that it invests, in such a recklessly grandiose way, in a structure of feeling which gay men have made their own actually strengthens Sedgwick's logically impossible case. The camp intensity of her yearning very nearly makes her the gay man she pleads to be – until, that is, we snap out of the Queer Theory reverie and remember the material world outside, where little matters like history and biology can't be simply wished away with the requisite number of elaborate footnotes. In that harsher, less cushioned environment, the best Sedgwick could hope for would be a 'What is she *like*?' from some disbelieving queen. Yet there would still be some admiration within that disbelief, a nod to Sedgwick that she is, at least for that one gorgeous moment, about as camp as it gets.

A less admiring response to the intellectual tradition Sedgwick embodies can be found in Donald Morton's *The Material Queer*, a book which starts from the premise that the dominant parameters of Lesbian and Gay Studies have become so enveloped in post-structuralist abstractions that they have ceased to maintain any connection with political commitment (Morton, 1996). There is some validity in Morton's neo-Marxist accusations, particularly in his telling contrast of 'desire', the unchallenged cornerstone of most Lesbian and Gay Studies thinking, with 'need', the material inequalities that have not ceased to exist just because theoretical fashion has turned away from them. Unfortunately, Morton's rhetoric carries him so deep into dour guilt-mongering that he falls into the most embarrassing trap imaginable for a gay man: he becomes camp without realizing it. He begins reasonably by arguing that post-structuralist theories place so much stress on playfulness and pleasure that they ignore concrete material questions of power and privilege, but ends up by lambasting a Queer Theory academic for the unforgivable crime of having a living room. The recipient of this attack is Alexander Doty, who, in the acknowledgements to his book *Making Things Perfectly Queer*, tells a friend how much he's looking forward to sitting down and watching a video with him (Doty, 1993, p. ix). This propels Morton into apoplexy: 'Doty's relaxed social discourse appears to assume unproblematically the availability to all the world of a space like that of the bourgeois living room . . . this is . . . a violently ideological erasure of the historical actuality of spaces available to other subjects in the world' (Morton, 1996, p. 23). Apart from noting the fact that Morton neglects to tell us in which rain-lashed street-corner cardboard box he penned his own book, or that there's nothing like interior design to bring out the stroppiness in a queen, what can one say? As ever, camp is always lurking at the fringes of over-strenuous seriousness, and we queer academics forget this at our peril.

Snapping the elastic

By way of a conclusion (or, as my co-editor of this book suggested I should call it, a conclusionette), I want to think about where camp is now. There's a plausible argument for saying that its codes of mockery, its apparently jaunty rubric of a-scream-a-day-keeps-the-normals-away, should be hideously inappropriate in the era of AIDS. Under the shadow of the pandemic, what have we got to laugh about? Plenty, really, because the camp laugh is often a laugh laced with fury, and there's no better evidence of that than the way in which AIDS funerals have become a new camp space, bittersweet carnivals where celebration mingles with rage.

Another place camp is now is absolutely everywhere. All those fears that camp after Sontag would become blandly open to all have, in some ways, come true. Postmodern culture's swirling soup of signifiers, where TV stations screen kitsch re-runs and there's serious money to be made in selling videocassettes of so-bad-they're-good science fiction films, where irony is compulsory and genuineness virtually illegal, looks from some angles like the triumph of camp. At the beginning of the 1990s I published an article which (camply) concluded by asserting 'postmodernism is only heterosexuals catching up with camp' (Medhurst, 1990, p. 19). But I think I was wrong: postmodern aesthetics can easily be confused with camp, but while camp grows from a specific cultural identity, postmodern discourses peddle the arrogant fiction that specific cultural identities have ceased to exist. Camp has been conceptualized from the historical, palpable, raw material of gay men's cultural experiences – without those experiences there is no camp, only things that resemble it or try to borrow its name.

This is where the most interesting recent book on camp falls apart. Pamela Robertson's *Guilty Pleasures* wants to cut women a slice of the camp cake, to explore 'the exchange between women and gay men as a two-way street' (1996, p. 7). This seems plausible, and women's relationship to gay men's camp would prove a fascinating area of study, but Robertson is greedier than this. Her aim is to insist that there is 'feminist camp', a series of cultural manouevres using irony and masquerade through which women have subversively commented on normative gender roles. These manoeu-vres undoubtedly exist (Robertson cites Mae West as an exemplary practitioner) and can certainly possess a dynamic political potential, but why call them camp? They may live next door to camp, but they don't share the same address, because they, just like lesbian strategies that are like camp but not camp, are not woven from the same specific subcultural experiences.

If the subcultural origin is, as Robertson implies, irrelevant, then why not take the final step and create the category of straight men's camp? The phenomena which might earn such a designation exist in abundance – films like *Wayne's World*, magazines like *Loaded*, sitcoms like *Men Behaving Badly* – all of which encourage heterosexual men to recognize with ironic laughter the excesses of their own gender construction, the ludicrousness of the gender codes they have been socialized into following. But here we reach the limit case, because if straight men's camp is possible then that four-letter word really has lost all meaning. Camp is not an infinitely stretchable piece of elastic, and this is where it snaps. In some ways it's flat-tering that lesbians, heterosexuals, everybody else, are so envious of this gay male cultural strategy that they all want to muscle in on it. It looks like fun, and yes, it can be a screaming great laugh. (It can also be intensely seri-ous, though its straightened variants usually miss this aspect, and at its best it fuses the two.) But it can't be transplanted, because it isn't just any old way of savouring the ironies of gender. It is the way gay men have tried to rationalize, reconcile, ridicule and (in the Jayne County sense) wreck their own specific relationships with masculinity and femininity. It's ours, all ours, just ours, and the time has come to bring it back home.

References

Abbott, Sidney, and Love, Barbara, *Sappho Was a Right-On Woman*. New York: Stein and Day, 1972.

Babuscio, Jack, 'Camp and the Gay Sensibility', in Richard Dyer (ed.), *Gays and Film*, London:BFI, 1977, pp. 40–57.

Bergman, David (ed.), *Camp Grounds: Style and Homosexuality*. Amherst: University of Massachusetts Press, 1993.

Blachford, Gregg, 'Male Dominance and the Gay World', in Kenneth Plummer (ed.), *The Making of the Modern Homosexual*, London: Hutchinson, 1981, pp. 184–210.

Brighton Ourstory Project, *Daring Hearts: Lesbian and Gay Lives in the 50s and 60s*. Brighton: QueenSpark, 1992.

Britton, Andrew, 'For Interpretation: Notes Against Camp', in *Gay Left*, Vol. 7, 1978/79, pp. 11–14.

Butler, Judith, *Bodies That Matter: On the Discursive Limits of 'Sex'*. New York: Routledge, 1993.

Butler, Judith, *Gender Trouble: Feminism and the Subversion of Identity*. New York: Routledge, 1990.

Case, Sue-Ellen, 'Toward a Butch-Femme Aesthetic', in Henry Abelove *et al.* (eds), *The Lesbian and Gay Studies Reader*. London: Routledge, 1993, pp. 294–306.

Chauncey, George, *Gay New York*. New York: Basic, 1994.

Cohen, Derek, and Dyer, Richard, 'The Politics of Gay Culture', in Gay Left Collective (eds), *Homosexuality: Power and Politics,* London: Allison and Busby, 1980, pp. 172–86.

County, Jayne, *Man Enough to be a Woman*. London: Serpent's Tail, 1995.

Davy, Kate, 'Fe/Male Impersonation: The Discourse of Camp', in M. Meyer (ed.), 1994, pp. 130–48.

Dollimore, Jonathan, 'The Challenge of Sexuality', in Alan Sinfield (ed.), *Society and Literature 1945–1970*. London: Methuen, 1983, pp. 51–86.

Dollimore, Jonathan, *Sexual Dissidence: Augustine to Wilde, Freud to Foucault*. Oxford: Oxford Unversity Press, 1991.

Doty, Alexander, *Making Things Perfectly Queer*. Minneapolis: University of Minnesota Press, 1993.

Duberman, Martin, *Stonewall*. New York: Plume, 1994.

Dyer, Richard, 'It's Being So Camp as Keeps Us Going', in *Only Entertainment*, London: Routledge, 1992, (first pub. 1976), pp. 135–48.

Frank, Marcie, 'The Critic as Performance Artist: Susan Sontag's Writing and Gay Cultures', in David Bergman (ed.), 1993.

Garland, Rodney, *The Heart in Exile*. London: Four Square, 1961 (first pub. 1953).

Graham, Paula, 'Girl's Camp? The Politics of Parody', in Tamsin Wilton (ed.), *Immortal, Invisible: Lesbians and the Moving Image*, London: Routledge, 1995, pp. 163–81.

Hanson, Craig Alfred, 'The Fairy Princess Exposed', in Karla Jay and Allen Young (eds), *Out Of The Closets*, New York: Douglas, 1972, pp. 266–71.

hooks, bell, *Black Looks: Race and Representation*. London: Turnaround, 1992.

Katz, Jonathan, *Gay American History: Lesbians and Gay Men in the U.S.A.* New York: Avon, 1976.

Kennedy, Elizabeth Lapovsky, and Davis, Madeline, '"They Was No One To Mess With": The Construction of the Butch Role in the Lesbian Community of the 1940s and 1950s', in Joan Nestle (ed.), *The Persistent Desire: A Femme-Butch Reader*, Boston: Alyson, 1992, pp. 62–80.

Kirk, Kris, and Heath, Ed, *Men In Frocks*. London: GMP, 1984.

Lucas, Ian, *Impertinent Decorum: Gay Theatrical Manoeuvres*. London: Cassell, 1994.

Medhurst, Andy, 'Our Gracious Queens: Effeminacy, Class and Comedy', in *A National Joke: Cultural Identity and English Popular Comedy*. London: Routledge (forthcoming).

Medhurst, Andy, 'Pitching Camp', in *City Limits*, 10–17 May, 1990, pp. 18–19.

Meyer, Moe (ed.), *The Politics and Poetics of Camp*. London: Routledge, 1994.

Miller, D.A., 'Sontag's Urbanity', in Henry Abelove *et al.* (eds), *The Lesbian and Gay Studies Reader*, London: Routledge, 1993, pp. 212–20.

Morton, Donald, 'Changing the Terms: (Virtual) Desire and (Actual) Reality', in D. Morton (ed.), *The Material Queer: A LesBiGay Cultural Studies Reader*, Boulder: Westview, 1996, pp. 1–34.

Nestle, Joan, 'Flamboyance and Fortitude: An Introduction', in Joan Nestle (ed.), *The Persistent Desire: A Femme-Butch Reader*. Boston: Alyson, 1992, pp. 13–22.

O'Day, Marc, '"Mutability is Having a Field Day": The Sixties Aura of Angela Carter's Bristol Trilogy', in Lorna Sage (ed.), *Flesh and the Mirror: Essays on the Art of Angela Carter*, London: Virago, 1994.

Robertson, Pamela, *Guilty Pleasures: Feminist Camp from Mae West to Madonna*. Durham: Duke University Press, 1996.

Roman, David, '"It's My Party and I'll Die If I Want To !": Gay Men, AIDS and the Circulation of Camp in U.S. Theater', in David Bergman (ed.), 1993, pp. 206–33.

Ross, Andrew, *No Respect: Intellectuals and Popular Culture*. New York and London: Routledge, 1989.

Sedgwick, Eve Kosofsky, *Tendencies*. Durham: Duke University Press, 1993.

Sinfield, Alan, *The Wilde Century*. London: Cassell, 1994.

Sontag, Susan, *A Susan Sontag Reader*. Harmondsworth: Penguin, 1983.

White, Edmund, *States of Desire: Travels in Gay America*. London: Deutsch, 1980.

Wildeblood, Peter, *Against the Law*. Harmondsworth: Penguin, 1957.

Wilton, Tamsin (ed.), *Immortal, Invisible: Lesbians and the Moving Image*. London: Routledge, 1995.

Wittman, Carl, 'A Gay Manifesto', in Karla Jay and Allen Young (eds), 1972, pp. 330–41.

Further reading

Bronski, Michael, *Culture Clash: The Making of Gay Sensibility*. Boston: South End Press, 1984.

Core, Philip, *Camp: The Lie That Tells The Truth*. London: Plexus, 1984.

Finch, Mark, 'Sex and Address in Dynasty', in *Screen*, Vol. 27, No. 6, 1986, pp. 24–43.

Medhurst, Andy, 'Batman, Deviance and Camp', in Roberta Pearson and William Uricchio (eds), *The Many Lives of Batman*. London: BFI, 1991, pp. 149–63.

Newton, Esther, *Mother Camp: Female Impersonators in America*. Englewood Cliffs: Prentice Hall , 1972.

Power, Lisa, *No Bath But Plenty of Bubbles: An Oral History of the Gay Liberation Front*. London: Cassell, 1995.

Tyler, Carol-Anne, 'Boys Will Be Girls: The Politics of Gay Drag', in Diana Fuss (ed.), *Inside/Out: Lesbian Theories, Gay Theories*. New York and London: Routledge, 1991, pp. 32–70.

Van Leer, David, *The Queening of America: Gay Culture in Straight Society*. London: Routledge, 1995.

Acknowledgement

This chapter owes plenty to characteristically sisterly insights from Stephen Maddison and to innumerable forms of sustenance from Phil Ulyatt.

20

Gender Performativity

Sarah E. Chinn

IN THE PAST TEN YEARS OR SO, people who theorize gender and sexuality have been talking less and less about 'gender roles' and more about 'gender performativity'. While the concept of gender performances – in a diverse array of shapes such as drag, butch/femme, crossdressing, old fashioned panto Dames and new-look queens like RuPaul – is nothing new, the idea of 'gender performativity' is. The phrase itself, as it is currently used in theories of gender and sexuality, was first applied by Judith Butler in her extremely influential book *Gender Trouble: Feminism and the Subversion of Identity* (1990). In Butler's theory, performativity is something everyone does in order to inhabit a gendered identity, without which one can't be a meaningful subject.

As we'll see, Butler actively (one might even say strenuously) worked, both in *Gender Trouble* and her later book *Bodies that Matter: on the Discursive Limits of 'Sex'* (1993) to disarticulate her theory of performativity from ideas of performance and theatricality. For Butler, the notion of performance entails a desire for a certain level of knowingness and agency, the belief that whatever I'm representing is just playacting, and that I can locate the 'real' me underneath the representation. Rather than set these two ideas in opposition, however, what I want to do in this chapter is let them speak to each other. Many theorists, such as Kate Bornstein, Eve Kosofsky Sedgwick, Sue-Ellen Case and Michael Moon, see a close connection between outrageous, self-conscious theatrics of gender and the too-often unchallenged performances of gendered identity that we go through every day.

Theories of gender performativity have multiple sources, but we can identify two main (although hardly mutually exclusive) threads. The first is more strictly theoretical; its origins are in the philosophy of language, psychoanalysis, and feminist theory. The second has its roots mostly outside academia, in what Kath Weston has called 'street theory', and comes out of the ways queer people have imagined the spaces their own gendered identities – of queen, dyke, butch, transsexual, nelly, femme – occupy. Both of these threads have rich and interlocking histories, but they also have disagreements, mainly about questions of agency and choice. At the bottom of all these theories is a range of interconnected questions: Where does gender come from? How much choice do we have over our genders? Are there inevitable links between sex, gender and sexuality? Could we have a world, or even a person, without gender?

In this chapter I'll be laying out where ideas about gender performativity come from, how they intersect, and how we can use them. This question of 'use' is possibly the most controversial element of performativity theory, and the place where the different camps of theorists get into the most passionate disagreement. Since Queer Theory has its roots in political movements for liberation, we need to ask, how can a theory of performativity help us change currently repressive structures of sexuality, that depend on the assumption and enforcement of binary, heterosexist gender?

In the beginning: performative language

The first person to use the term 'performativity' in a sustained study was the philosopher of language J. L. Austin. In a series of Harvard lectures later collected into the book *How to Do Things With Words* (1962), Austin explored the role of what he called 'performative language'. He initially divided language into two kinds, constative and performative. Constative language is merely descriptive; it tells us about the world around us but doesn't affect the world or the things it describes. Performative language, on the other hand, is language that does something – just by saying something we do something. For Austin the paradigmatic example is 'I pronounce you husband and wife'. This is not a descriptive statement: it's performing an act that can only be performed by words. Before the words were said, the two people they embrace had no more legal relationship than any two people unrelated by blood; afterwards their relationship has changed into 'married couple'. Other kinds of performative language are bets, vows, acts of naming. To say 'I bet' or 'I promise' or 'I name this baby Sarah' or 'I sentence you to five years in prison' is not just saying, it's doing. Certainly, all these acts of performative language might require other proofs – a handshake, a contract, a marriage licence, to name a few – but those texts all require, or at the very least imply, the moment of performativity that brings the act into being.

As a philosopher, Austin was especially concerned with ways in which these 'speech acts', as he called them, could go wrong. Of course, the worst case scenario is that the person saying the performative words doesn't mean them and is offering a false promise. Alternatively, it could be that the person doesn't have the authority to perform the words – there's no money to back up the bet, the baby belongs to someone else or already has a name, the person handing down the sentence is only masquerading as a judge. It's also possible that things go wrong along the way or that there's no one to hear the performance and validate it. Austin called these exceptions 'infelicities', arguing that while constative language can be incorrect ('the earth is flat', 'my bed is floating in mid-air'), performative language can only be misapplied or inappropriate: that is, unhappy.

Austin realized that infelicities happened because speech acts are tied up in social conventions and rituals that seem self-evident but in fact are quite minutely choreographed. A lot of things have to go right in order for a bet to go through, not least of which is that all parties have to agree what a bet means, what the terms are and the obligations a bet entails. But the parties involved rarely have to explain what betting itself means; it's assumed that everyone knows. Since his main concern was *how* performative language worked, he did not stop to ask *why* it worked. What is it that makes us all agree without realizing that we agree that bets are bets, that marriage is a meaningful institution, that parents have the right to name their own children?

This question was partially answered by another philosopher, Jacques Derrida. In his discussion of performativity in *Limited, Inc.* (1972, trans. 1988), Derrida claimed that performatives seem self-evident because speech acts are by nature reiterative. That is, they conform to a pre-existing model that can, in fact must, be cited in order to make sense, and that exists outside of its performers and witnesses. (Derrida claims that this iterable citation is, in fact, the defining characteristic of all language, but that's another story). What Derrida doesn't explain is what these iterable events actually mean in terms of cultural practice: who says them, and about whom, with what results. More important, as a theorist of language, Derrida does not explore where the assumption of the models to be cited comes from, or why people feel so unselfconscious performing them.

Making subjects: Althusser and Foucault

One theorist for whom this was an important question was Louis Althusser. As a Marxist, Althusser wondered what it is that not just keeps people working within the system of capitalism – a system that clearly makes most of their lives harder – but that engenders their loyalty to that system. In part it is fear of the power and violence of the state, which could easily crush resistance. But fear cannot explain people's enthusiasm for the perpetuation of their own oppression. He theorized that there must be social mechanisms that teach everyone to agree to their own domination by capitalism, to consider it not just acceptable or even a virtue, but self-evident and inevitable, something that one would have to be crazy or evil not to accept as true. In fact, those mechanisms provide the ways in which we understand our place in the world and without which we can't function as subjects. Althusser calls these mechanisms Ideological State Apparatuses (ISAs) – they are political structures that are produced by and uphold the state but that feel private and normal.

For Althusser the most important part of Ideological State Apparatuses is that they feel so natural. In fact, he suggests that a defining characteristic of ideology that 'it imposes (without seeming to do so, since these are "obviousnesses") obviousnesses as obviousnesses, which we cannot *fail to recognize* and before which we have the inevitable and natural reaction of crying out . . .: "That's obvious! That's right! That's real!"' (p. 172). He maintained that this happened through a process of 'interpellation' or hailing. Interpellation works like this: through ISAs we understand our world and thereby ourselves. In fact, we can only understand ourselves as subjects in the world through the mediation of ISAs like education, religion, the family, the legal system. Althusser argued that subjects do not create ISAs: quite the opposite. In fact, ISAs interpellate us or call us into being, literally giving us (legal) names, constructing family relationships and so on, even as they make seem self-evident the fact of having a name, or an aunt, or a legal system that has the power to establish both of those facts. In Austin's terms, then, interpellation is the definitive performative speech act: when the doctor says 'It's a girl', or a parent says 'That's my child' or a judge says 'I sentence you' (or 'I marry you') they're all reiterating ideology saying 'You are a subject'.

Part of Althusser's discussion of ideology is an analysis of the punitive and policing elements of interpellation's performativity. There is a constant threat of not being a subject, or of having one's subjectivity severely compromised. As we'll see, this kind of policing is particularly effective in the realm of gender – people who don't conform to expectations of gender are accused of not being 'real women' or 'real men'. Since so much of our sense of self depends upon fitting into the appropriate gender, to fail in being a 'real woman', for example, is to be an incomplete subject. Of course, the worst fate is falling off the ideological map and being a non-person. It's hard to imagine what a non-subject could be; something we don't have a name for or can't recognize as even human, perhaps. Those are the people we call 'unnatural', as though their inability to conform to ideological structures divorces them from the natural order of things.

Althusser's concept of a subject created by ideology was taken up by another French philosopher, Michel Foucault. Central to Foucault's ideas was the notion that systems of power such as the family or the legal system produce subjects, not vice versa. Foucault's work traced the historical development – what he called 'genealogies' – of seemingly unchanging ideas like madness, criminality, justice, sexuality and medicine: ideas that shape the ways in which people understand themselves as subjects.

One of Foucault's most influential works is *The History of Sexuality* (1977), a projected three-volume study that traced the genealogy of 'sexuality' as an identity from the eighteenth century to the current era (Foucault died before completing this project beyond the first introductory volume). Foucault believed that sexual identities as we inhabit them today – 'gay', 'heterosexual', 'bisexual', 'homosexual', 'lesbian', and so on – are not fixed or 'natural', but rather are a product of the interlocking systems of power that form subjectivity. In other words, in order to be a subject one has to 'have' a sexuality, something that makes a specific set of identities out of a collection of sexual practices and partnerings. For, only some practices get attached to identities, mostly in connection to the gender of the partners; other practices are just 'preferences'. Part of the work of these 'discourses' – the interweavings of language, cultural practices and assumptions; Althusser's ISAs without the Marxism – of sexuality is to seem self-evident and natural as well as compulsory.

Discourse is like a menu in a restaurant: there may be a lot of choices, but you can only order from the menu, and you have to pay the price indicated. The menu circumscribes what choices you can make, or even consider making – if you're at a Chinese restaurant, you don't think to order spaghetti. The same goes for sexuality. That is, not only do you have to inhabit a sexuality in order to understand yourself as a subject, you can't imagine not doing so in the terms set up by discourse.

Judith Butler and gender performativity

In the late 1980s, particularly in the US, feminists were grappling with the question of identity. What does it mean to 'be' a woman, for example? Or a lesbian? How do those identities intersect with racial, ethnic and class identities? A lot of feminist organizing had centred around identity, but had not managed to close the gaps between different kinds of women, and had in some cases made those gaps wider. Into this fray strode several feminist theorists (to name a few: Denise Riley, Drucilla Cornell, Elizabeth Grosz, Diana Fuss) trained in the work of Austin, Althusser, Derrida and Foucault as well as of Lorde, Irigaray, and Rich. Of this group, the most influential has been Judith Butler.

A philosopher by training, Butler wanted to use the paradigms developed by the thinkers I've discussed to come to a more satisfying conclusion about where structures of gender and sexuality come from and what we can do to resist coercive models of heterocentrism and misogyny. She saw feminism's downfall in its attachment to identity, since identity requires that we agree on 'a single or abiding ground, which is invariably contested by those identity positions or anti-identity positions that it invariably excludes' (1990, p. 5).

But if gender is not an identity – that is, a set of attributes and behaviours that belong to a certain kind of person, whether by nature or by training – what is it? Drawing on the terms of language philosophy rather than of mainstream feminism, Butler claimed that gender was an act in the same way that performative language is a speech act. Gender is performative.

In *Gender Trouble*, the book in which Butler first lays out her theory of gender performativity, she relies heavily on Foucault and Althusser to pull her argument together. At the foundation of her discussion is the claim that 'there is no gender identity behind the expressions of gender; that identity is performatively constituted by the very "expressions" that are said to be its results' (p. 25). Gender is a discursive structure (in Foucault's words); it is a kind of Ideological State Apparatus (in Althusser's); it is citational and reiterative and has no intrinsic identity of its own (in Derrida's). We are interpellated into gender from birth – the words 'It's a girl', are in fact a command and a threat: 'Be a girl; if you want to be a real subject with a real identity, act out girlness'. Most of the ways to 'be a girl' are implicit within discourse, and others must be explicitly enforced by parents, educational institutions, magazines, and so on. And of course, the most effective way in which gender is enforced is the fact that it just feels natural to behave in certain ways, 'as a girl'.

Butler's central point is that gender performativity is both not optional and not natural. Once a child has been 'girled', for example, with the words 'It's a girl', she is compelled to perform girlness and (or perhaps *because*) she doesn't even recognize this compulsion. Gender is performed reiteratively through an array of 'acts, gestures and desires' (the girl really *wants* to be a girl) that imply an essential gendered self. But for Butler, these 'acts and gestures, articulated and enacted desires create the *illusion* of an interior and organizing gender core' (p. 136, my emphasis). There's no subject underneath the gender, no universal self. Rather, the self is constructed through its strenuous performance of gender.

Of course, the question all this brings us to is 'Why'? Butler's answer is simple: to reproduce normative heterosexuality, which requires that everyone is either male or female, with no gaps and no exceptions. According to the dominant discourse of heterosexuality, everyone is a boy or a girl, and combines accordingly. This is all very well, but as we know there are exceptions: people who desire members of their own sex, people who change gender, people whose physical sexual characteristics (penis, vagina, ovaries) are multiple or partial and can't be easily attached to a gender, and so on. There's also always the fear that one isn't getting it right by being feminine or masculine 'enough'. Surely these exceptions, failures and doubts would weaken the discourse of gender.

Well, says Butler, maybe and maybe not. In many cases, failure and incoherence strengthen the power of discourse, either through a fear that one's subjectivity is being compromised (the embarrassment of being called 'Sir' instead of 'Miss', for instance) or through active punishment of inappropriate behaviours (queerbashing, rape, commitment to a mental institution being among the more violent examples). Too often, subjects blame the inevitable gaps in their successful gender performances on their own inability to live up to the standard; a process that polices the subject through mechanisms of shame and embarrassment.

But there can be times when incoherent gender performativity can expose the constructedness of gender and (hetero)sexuality. Butler lands on drag as a possible place this can happen. Drag is a self-conscious, larger-than-life reiteration of heterosexual normativity. By performing gender in a hyperbolic, stylized way, drag queens don't simply imitate femininity, they reveal how women imitate femininity as well, and what hard work it is. Through parody, drag can expose the seeming naturalness and effortlessness of gender itself; it doesn't imitate an original, but reveals that there is no original, only layers of performance. Drag says, 'If you think my pretending to be a woman is hard, think what an effort it must be for a woman to do'.

This is not to say that drag is inherently subversive. In fact, it can reinforce heteronormativity in several ways. First it can burlesque the idea of successful imitation by the 'inappropriate' gender, by appearing ridiculous. A mainstream reading of stereotype of the swaggering butch or effeminate queen does not expose gender as much as it restates the lines between identity and behaviour: men and women aren't supposed to act that way. Similarly, comedic half-baked drag by 'obvious' men – like Robert Preston in a dress in *Victor/Victoria* – tells us 'real men can't help but be masculine, even in women's clothes'. On the opposite end of the spectrum, drag can also obscure gender's constructedness by focusing on the supposed 'original' and fetishizing it. A man performing 'woman' can romanticize and naturalize 'womanhood' as much as a 'real' women can.

But, says, Butler, drag can get us out of the sense of inevitability that surrounds gender performativity. It can show that even though our gendered options might be limited, we can apply and combine them in a wide variety of ways, attaching behaviours to discordant bodies. Drag is about repeating heterosexual constructs in non- (or anti-) heterosexual contexts, challenging the primacy of the supposed heterosexual 'original'. It can also point out the intimate links between gender, race and class, and that certain gendered performatives require specific racial or class identities to go along with them. But there is a hitch involved. Drag self-consciously denaturalizes gender only if it *is* self-conscious and its agenda, or the agenda of its audience, is antiessentialist.

Performance, performativity, excess and shame

One infelicity that Austin dismissed early on, but that has important applications for the theories of gender performativity that grew out of his work, is the possibility that the performative is being performed for performance's sake, on a stage or as part of a conscious masquerade. An example of infelicity he gives is the 'mockery' in which 'there is no accepted conventional procedure; it is a mockery, like marriage with a monkey' (p. 24). Contemporary lesbians and gay men have performed mockeries of marriage, both as a joke and in earnest, between two or more women or men for a variety of reasons. One has been to highlight the fact that marriage is a convention, not a natural fact: that it is one of the building blocks of heterosexism and enforces specific oppressive positions for women and men. This kind of mockery is aggressive and self-consciously comic, often involving hairy-chested men in elaborate wedding gowns, burlesqued religious rituals, and broad sexual humour. This is somewhat akin to the Yippie nomination of a pig for US President in 1968 – not only did it call into question the whole US political process, it also cast some serious doubts on the calibre of the 'real' candidates and asked how different they were from the admittedly adorable pig nominee.

Not all mockeries are jokes, however. By definition, marriage between two women or two men is 'a mockery'. It falls completely outside the realm of convention; it's a legal impossibility except in those countries in which it is specifically included in the definition of marriage. Austin's example of marriage to a monkey is telling, since within the heterosexual matrix, marriage between two members of the same sex has the same performative values: not simply none, but a negative value. It is not just unhappy, it's ridiculous.

Misperforming gender (that is, being on the receiving end of that ridicule) whether on purpose – in a conscious mockery – or by mistake can be humiliating. In a culture in which heteronormativity rules with stern resolve, being mistaken for the 'wrong' gender is an embarrassment. This is particularly true for men, since to be identified with femaleness is by definition a step down, for women or for men. The words 'sissy', 'nelly', 'effeminate', all have a harsher sting than their equivalents 'butch' or 'mannish'. In many ways, formative learning experiences about gender have shame attached to them: parents or peers saying 'Don't do that, it's not for girls/boys'.

Several theorists of gender performativity see shame as a focal point for understanding how gender works. Eve Kosofsky Sedgwick has speculated that experiencing shame has a foundational role in subject formation. In her essay 'Queer Performativity' (1993) she argues that 'Shame is a bad feeling attached to what one is: one therefore is *something*, in experiencing shame. The place of identity, the structure "identity". . . . may be established and naturalized in the first instance *through shame*' (p. 12). For Sedgwick, then, shame is a constitutive element of all the things that make up identity, most centrally gender and sexuality; it is woven into the parts of ourselves that feel the most personal and the most important. No wonder, Sedgwick argues, that liberation movements are so often about pride, since they represent an attempt to root out that shame.

Sedgwick hardly sentimentalizes shame, but she does see shame as a pivotal tool in the struggle to rethink the coercive power of gender. What if the things we're supposed to be the most ashamed of, the things we're supposed to hide (our failed, or perverse, or incomplete, or mismanaged gender performances) are thrust front and centre? Can there be liberation in shamelessness, which does not mean a neutralization of shame (as pride tries to do), but a celebration of the things we're supposed to be ashamed of? Sedgwick picks up on Butler's suggestion that a way out of gender performativity might be an exaggerated performance of the norm when she picks her ideal gender performer, the drag movie star Divine.

Divine was the alter ego of Baltimore actor Glenn Milstead, brought to life by director John Waters. She was not just enormously fat (over 300 pounds), she was deliciously trashy, starring in films like *Mondo Trasho*, *Female Trouble*, *Pink Flamingos* and, more respectably, *Hairspray*. Divine's characters were invariably tacky in fluffy high-heeled shoes and garish makeup, doing revolting things (things she should have been ashamed of. . . .) like cannibalism, incest, and, less dramatically, like being a big queen, being fat, being vulgar. Divine performs extravagantly all the shameful things about bodies that we're taught to eradicate or at least cover up from sight. Divine is sleazy, trashy, a hyperbole of womanhood even as she's impossible to believe as the way we imagine 'real' women. But Divine's performance is as believable as the gender performances of any woman. On her they're as 'natural' as the performance of normative womanhood (which is to say, not at all) and as seeming moored to her body. As Sedgwick and her co-writer Michael Moon point out, 'Divine's performances forcibly remind us. . .that "drag". . .is inscribed not just in dress and its associated gender codes but in the body itself: in habitual and largely unconscious physical and psychological attitudes, poses, and styles of bodily relation and response'(1993, p. 220).

Here Sedgwick and Moon manage a kind of alliance between the coercive aspects of gender performativity and the extreme theatricality possible in drag. Divine's genius is in bridging the gap. She thinks she's just citing the performative rules of gender, and she acts 'natural' doing it, but to us it's so far from normative gender that it's grotesque (or delightful, depending on your taste). Divine makes a virtue out of her shame, shaking her viewers out of their acceptance of similar feelings. We can't not choose shame, just as we can't not choose our gender, but Divine transforms that coercion into an embrace.

But is it a choice?

In all her work on gender performativity, Judith Butler sounds one chord over and over: gender is not a choice. Gender is not constructed by a single act, but by a *process* that only seems stable, a process of reiteration that produces the effect of identity. As she maintains in *Bodies that Matter* (1993), 'gender performativity cannot be theorized apart from the forcible and reiterative practice of regulatory sexual regimes. . .and in no way presupposes a choosing subject' (p. 15). In part this is because it is so hard to see outside gender performativity. After all, how can we know what alternative options might be if we could choose them? If our subjectivity – our sense of ourselves in every way – is constructed through the process of citing gender norms, and the attendant fears of failure, how could we possibly imagine life outside those norms? But even if we could, it is almost impossible to separate and choose individual gender behaviours from the larger system of gender performativity, or to separate them from an oppressive regime of heteronormativity.

But what about those people who change sex? Wouldn't going through the process of having to unlearn one set of performances and pick up a whole new set provide adequate space in between to see the gaps and fissures in gender? Not to say that such insight is inevitable – plenty of energy has been spent so that transsexuals can feel unself-conscious about performing their new genders, so they can feel like 'real' women and men. But there is a portion of the transsexual/transgender community that has tried to use that in-between space as a place to undo gender.

Kate Bornstein is a major voice in this movement. As a man, and later as a woman, Bornstein was painfully conscious of the coercive elements of gender performativity: 'I was always acting out something that everyone assumed I was' (1995, pp. 8–9). In her discomfort with being a man and identifying as a woman, she underwent genital surgery and hormone treatments, going from Al to Kate. Ironically, under the pressure of having to perform femininity, she went through another profound transformation into a lesbian-identified feminist. Having had to unlearn masculinity and learn femininity, Bornstein embarked on the project of unlearning femininity as a woman. For Bornstein, feminism provided the place to look at gender critically; finally she could recognize the ways in which she had had to exert a huge amount of effort to acquire and maintain her gender identities in order to be a meaningful subject in her own eyes as well as the eyes of others.

In her writing and performance art, Bornstein has tried to imagine ways to reimagine the terms along which we cite gender. Unlike Butler, Bornstein feels quite comfortable with the language of choice and affiliation – she believes it is possible to see outside the binary of heteronormativity, even if we don't know what's there. The metaphors that Bornstein uses for binary gender – a cult and a class system – are telling. While cults enforce membership by a delicate combination of coercion, threats and rewards, they are, at least at the beginning, voluntary. On the other hand, class may be something one is born into, but it is not biologically bounded in the same way we think of gender.

Bornstein asks what it would be like to belong to a gender in the same way one might belong to a sports team, or a religion, or a fan club, or a political party, or a fraternal organization. Each of these modes of 'belonging' bring with them slightly different levels of choice, faith, activity and enjoyment: most people join a religion for a set of reasons quite unlike the reasons others join an amateur soccer club. But all those memberships require a certain set of behaviours and performances that are both conventional *and* at least in part voluntary. After all, joining a sports team requires that you play by the rules, but doesn't force you to carry those rules into all elements of your life – only when you're playing. Bornstein does not deny the conventional and ritual elements of gender. Rather, she wants to refocus gender performativity as pure ritual. In a perfect world, being a woman would be about performing womanness rather than having to accept an ideological package along with it.

And perhaps the central phrase here is 'in a perfect world'. Bornstein is unembarrassed about the utopian quality of her theory. After all, she acknowledges that she still feels coerced by gender to perform her womanhood adequately, to be a convincing 'she'. Like Sedgwick and Moon, she does not underestimate the role of shame in the regime of heterocentric gender. Misperforming or being misperceived in her gender can still humiliate. More importantly, it's not clear from her writing how we could even achieve her goal of 'gender fluidity'. Accepting that gender is an imitation of a copy of an act *ad infinitum* is not necessarily the same as extricating oneself from its regulatory grip. Affiliative gender is a great idea, but her reader is left with a sense of its improbability, if not impossibility.

How to do things with gender

The most pressing question that comes out of gender performativity as a theory is: but what can you *do* with it? That is not to say that all theory has to have an immediate practical application, but gender performativity is so deeply entrenched in our sense of self, and the theories that have arisen to explain it are so rich and suggestive, that it's not surprising that activists have searched for ways to use the theory to help us talk back to the regime of gender.

It can be argued that some people are already playing with gender performatives: butch/femme lesbian couples, for example re-enact the conventions of heterosexual pairing only to turn them on their head. For a femme to perform femininity for the benefit of a woman she must read gender directives against the grain, citing the identity of woman, but citing it out of context. Likewise, the butch plays out masculinity to a tee, even a kind of hypermasculinity, but is under no illusions that she is a man. She is a butch, a very different kind of identity, an identity that – like 'femme' – undoes normative heterosexuality by showing that one can perform the style without embodying the content.

This raises some knotty questions, though. Butch/femme by definition is a relational identity. Without the butch, how can we read the femme beyond the codes of 'woman', for example? One response might be that, given the power of heteronormativity, all gender is assumed relational: to be a woman is to be in sexual relation to men, not to women. Butch/femme explicitly undoes the regulatory link between gender performance and sexual identity, not replacing one identity with another, but reducing (or expanding) identity to another set of carefully constructed rituals.

The power of gender performativity is that you don't even realize you're doing it. It just 'comes naturally'. Butler, Bornstein, Sedgwick and Moon all suggest ways in which we might make gender feel unnatural and strange. This is a huge challenge: even for those people who feel completely alien to their genders (which includes most people at one point or another, however fleeting) it is hard to make the step from feeling distanced from one's gender to actively working for that feeling of distance. While we may recognize that gender is coercive, it is familiar; it is ourselves. The naturalizing effects of gender mean that gender *feels natural* – even the understanding that it is performative, that our subjectivities themselves are constructed through its performance, does not make it *feel* any the less intrinsic. Our identities depend upon successful performance of our genders, and there is an entire cultural arsenal of books, films, television, advertisements, parental injunctions and peer surveillance to make sure those performances are (ideally) unconscious and successful. So suggesting that gender is not an essential part of the self can be experienced as an attack on the integrity of the subject; baldly speaking, it makes people uncomfortable and they don't like it. Moreover, if activists want to focus on gender performativity, they will have to convince others that heterocentrism is neither inevitable nor good: an enormous task given the centrality of the heteronorm in our culture.

Perhaps it is inevitable, then, that the incursions against the regime of gender will almost always be partial, difficult and even dangerous. But they will happen. And change may occur, however fitfully. RuPaul's success was remarkable not just because he made explicit the links between drag and gay male culture, nor because he insisted that RuPaul was both the supermodel and the black gay man (something Glenn Milstead could not manage) but because he made gender liminality so cuddly and appealing. Why wouldn't one want to challenge norms of gender performativity when RuPaul made it look so fun? RuPaul's transformation was not from real man to fake woman, but oscillated between sensitive, political queer to grand blonde diva – explicitly performed identities. And RuPaul's motto, 'You better work!' reminds his viewers that gender is hard work, work that we should give ourselves credit for rather than erasing in shame.

Gender *is* work and, as Butler argues, gender performativity is always on the edge of failure. It takes courage to jump over that edge, and jump with your eyes open. It might be that the best way to do things with gender is to know what gender is doing with us, and then work it.

References

Althusser, Louis, 'Ideology and Ideological State Apparatuses', in *Lenin and Philosophy and Other Essays* (trans. Ben Brewster), London: NLB, 1971, pp. 121–76.

Austin, J. L., *How to Do Things With Words: The William James Lectures Delivered at Harvard University in 1955*. Cambridge, MA: Harvard University Press, 1962.

Bornstein, Kate, *Gender Outlaw: On Men, Women, and the Rest of Us*. New York: Vintage Books, 1995.

Butler, Judith, *Bodies that Matter: On the Discursive Limits of 'Sex'*. New York: Routledge, 1993.

Butler, Judith, 'Critically Queer', *GLQ*, Vol. 1, No. 1, 1993, pp. 17–32.

Butler, Judith, *Gender Trouble: Feminism and the Subversion of Identity*. New York: Routledge, 1990.

Derrida, Jacques, *Limited, Inc.* (trans. Alan Bass). Evanston, IL: Northwestern University Press, 1988. First published 1972.

Sedgwick, Eve Kosofsky, 'Queer Performativity: Henry James's *The Art of the Novel*', *GLQ*, Vol. 1, No. 1, 1993, pp. 1–16.

Sedgwick, Eve Kosofsky, and Moon, Michael, 'Divinity: A Dossier, A Performance Piece, a Little-Understood Emotion', in her *Tendencies*. Durham: Duke University Press, 1993, p. 215–51.

Further reading

Case, Sue-Ellen, 'Toward a Butch-Femme Aesthetic', in Henry Abelove *et al.* (eds), *The Lesbian and Gay Studies Reader*, New York: Routledge, 1993, pp. 294–306.

Foucault, Michel, *The History of Sexuality: An Introduction.* (trans. Alan Hurley). New York: Vintage, 1977.

Garber, Marjorie, *Vested Interests: Cross Dressing and Cultural Anxiety.* New York: Routledge, 1992.

Koestenbaum, Wayne, *The Queen's Throat: Opera, Homosexuality and the Mystery of Desire.* New York: Vintage, 1994.

Newton, Esther, *Mother Camp: Female Impersonators in America.* Chicago: University of Chicago Press, 1972.

Waters, John, *Female Trouble, Multiple Maniacs, Pink Flamingos* and other films (widely available on video).

21

Transgender

Jay Prosser

It is time for us to write as experts on our own histories.
Leslie Feinberg, *Transgender Warriors*

THIS CHAPTER PROVIDES AN HISTORICAL OVERVIEW of the literature on transgender and an introduction to key concepts in the field of transgender studies. I begin by defining transgender and highlighting some tensions in the etymology of the term. In the second section, I examine how these tensions have played out as transgender studies has emerged from three distinguishable arenas: lesbian and gay work on transgender; medical, anthropological, and historical representations of transgender; and transgender political activism. In the third section, I discuss how transgender critics have engaged and reconfigured these arenas. How have their terms come to define transgender studies and how have transgender critics in turn changed the terms of their debates? In the closing section, I examine future possible directions for transgender studies, suggesting a role it might play as a discourse produced at the end of the millennium.

Tense definitions

The term 'transgender' is derived from 'transgenderist': an identity category coined in the late 1980s by males who did not find 'transvestite' or 'crossdresser' adequate to describe their full-time commitment to living as women, nor 'transsexual' accurate, given that their cross-gender living did not entail reconfiguring their bodies with hormones and surgery; transgenderists crossed the lines of gender but not those of sex.[1] Nor, moreover, was the category of drag queen appropriate, for this wrongly connoted the subject's femininity as a performance – something that could be donned and doffed – and this feminine performance as part of a homosexual identity. Transgenderists could be gay or straight; sexuality was not the point.

Trans*gender* described a gender, not a sexual identity. Transgender thus came into being as a specific gender category: one that distinguished subjects from those whose cross-gendered identity was occasional, from those for whom it entailed changing sex, and from those for whom it was a function of their gay sexuality.

Confusingly, however, transgender has since come to have a quite different meaning. It now also functions as a container term which includes, along with transgenderists, those subjects from whom it was originally invented to distinguish transgenderists: transvestites and cross dressers, transsexuals and drag queens, in addition to butches, drag kings, bull dykes, androgynes and intersexuals – any form of what's been dubbed a 'gender outlaw'. One of the first usages of this inclusive sense of transgender appears in a transgender political manifesto by Leslie Feinberg in 1992. Indeed, this collective sense of transgender has been essential to the emergence of a transgender politics, a transgender community, and a transgender studies. It has brought together under a single gender banner individuals who historically have appeared a part of – although often a marginalized part of – sexual communities, straight and gay. Underscoring this unprecedented organization of differently embodied subjects around gender identity, the transgender community is sometimes referred to with the shorthand 'gender community'. Yet while the category of transgender has allowed for political collectivity and affiliation, the two directions of the term "transgender" – with the pull toward gendered specificity and differentiation on the one hand, and comprehensivity and connectivity on the other – remain in some tension within transgender studies.[2]

There is also a tension in the etymology of the term. Literally meaning 'across gender' – and surely coined because of this – the 'trans' in transgender can yet also mean 'beyond'. To cross and to be beyond are quite different topographical states: the one conjures mobility, the other stasis; one, a trajectory in material space, the other a transcendence of it. Like the ambivalence in the development of its range of reference, the etymological ambiguity of transgender provides an index to important questions in transgender studies. Does transgender leave intact the borders of gender or dissolve them? Is the transgendered subject a product of a gender binary or beyond it? What is the significance of the transgendered subject's 'transing' or crossing? What does it reveal about sex and gender – that they are material or immaterial? If the tension in the term's range of reference is pertinent to questions of subject relations, the ambiguity inherent in its etymology can be seen in questions about the conceptual significance of 'trans' for theories of sex, gender and sexuality. As we document the emergence of transgender studies, both sets of questions recur in the form of definitive debates.

The roots of transgender studies

Before the term 'transgender' appeared, transgender identities and dynamics were written about in ways that paved the way for a designated transgender studies. These writings may be grouped into two types: lesbian and gay perspectives which approach transgender as characteristic of lesbian and gay culture; and medical, historical and anthropological studies which treat transgender as a discrete phenomenon.

Transgender in Lesbian and Gay Studies
Because in communities, individual histories and cultural representation, the categories of lesbian/gay and transgender overlap, the study of lesbian and gay subjects has entailed the study of transgendered subjects.[3] Work on the butch lesbian (Newton, 1994; Nestle, 1987, 1992; de Lauretis, 1988; Case, 1989; Devor, 1989; Kennedy and Davis, 1993; Munt, 1997) and on gay drag or camp (Newton, 1979; Bergman, 1993; Meyer, 1994) has evidenced cross-gender identification, behaviour, style, performance, and living in varying degrees among lesbians and gay men. Moreover, given that the most enduring stereotype of homosexuals figures an abject transgendering (lesbians are women who want to be/should have been men; gay men are effeminate; the curious asymmetry perhaps reflects the greater cultural circumscription of male subjectivity), it has been particularly important for Lesbian and Gay Studies to separate out what is real in the cross-gendered experience of lesbians and gays from what is homophobic ideology. This work has also illuminated and challenged the marginalization of transgender subjects *within* lesbian and gay culture, for as those who appear to embody the stereotype of homosexuality, butches and drag queens historically have been subject to stigmatization by other lesbians and gays.

With the development of queer in the late 1980s, transgender moved from the margins to the mainstream, both culturally and academically. Queer might be understood as a collective movement born of crossing identifications (largely between lesbians and gay men), and I argue that cross-gender movement came to be definitive of queer. As Eve Kosofsky Sedgwick has noted '[t]he word "queer" itself means across', and her *Tendencies* (1993) begins with a figure of cross-gender identification – gay men wearing DYKE T-shirts and lesbians wearing FAGGOT T-shirts – to capture queer crossing (p. xii). Queer put transgender to crucial theoretical and political use: to challenge the naturalization of heterosexuality and gender. In the heterosexist binary-gendered world, gender and heterosexuality prop each other up: femininity, female and woman appear to coincide through their difference from masculinity, male and man. What sustains the gender bifurcation is the apparent naturalness of heterosexual desire, that is desire for the *other* (hetero) sex. The feminist recognition of gender and sex as different from each other (with sex standing for biology or the body and gender for socialization or cultural imprinting) may have challenged the naturalness of gender roles but it did little to challenge that of heterosexuality. Transgender by contrast put in question the binary of gender versus sex, *and* that of heterosexuality versus homosexuality, in addition to those of man versus woman, masculine versus feminine, male versus female. In crossing gender, the transgendered queer – the butch or the drag queen – illustrated that in none of these binaries was the 'versus' an essentially dividing space: a man could be feminine, a male could identify and live as a woman, a male who identified as a woman could be for another man a feminine object of desire; and thus queer transgender could *replay* heterosexual gender roles *through* homosexual desire, putting into question what constituted sexuality, gender and sex. Most radically, the transgendered queer displaced sex as the biological base to gender: if a male could live and pass as a woman, then what has femaleness (sex) got to do with what we conceive of as a woman (gender)? The transgendered exemplar suggested that all gender is a case of passing or doing or performing rather than being, that biology is not the grounds for gender: that, as Judith Butler has written, sex is 'gender all along' (1990, p. 8).

Butler's 1990 *Gender Trouble* was the seminal text in presenting the denaturalizing potential of queer transgender (although, again, the term 'transgender' was not yet in theoretical circulation). Other lesbian and gay texts foregrounded cross-gender identifications: before Butler, work on the intersections of race, gender and sexual identities – Anzaldúa, Mercer, and Moraga for instance – showed how categories of otherness are constructed through racist, homophobic and sexist transgendering, and thus transgendering, as in Butler, served as a means to challenge the binaries that produce otherness. Post-Butler, cross-gender dynamics appeared explicitly as deconstructive tropes in work on gender ambiguity and cross-dressing: Garber, Dollimore, Epstein and Straub. In her most recent formulation of queer, Butler writes that, insofar as Lesbian and Gay

Studies limits its subject of discussion to sexuality and 'refuses the domain of gender, it disqualifies itself from the analysis of transgendered sexuality altogether' (1994, p. 11). So enmeshed is transgender in lesbian and gay sexuality that first, transgender has become explicitly a yardstick for measuring the efficacy of Lesbian and Gay Studies; and, second, Butler even terms it a sexuality ('transgendered *sexuality*'). Transgender has come to appear definitively queer.

Queer Theory's embrace of transgender was to prove crucial in the emergence of transgender studies. Without the queer movement beginning in the late 1980s, there would be no transgender movement now, either politically or academically, and I would venture that transgender studies would certainly not have burgeoned as it has without Butler, so influential was *Gender Trouble*'s demonstration of what transgender could do for theory. At the same time, the specification of transgender studies by transgender critics, its naming *as* transgender studies, effects a delimitation of the reach of queer studies. Transgender specifies a methodology, a subjectivity and a community which, while it might overlap, is distinguishable from queer. The relation of transgender to queer is then both a dependent and independent one – derivative and novel – analogous to queer's relation to feminism.

Medical, anthropological and historical approaches:
transgender as object of study
If in Queer Theory transgender was a deconstructive mechanism, in other methodologies transgender has been approached as an object of study in itself. What is transgender? Why, where and when does it exist? Again before transgender became a category of analysis, different disciplines addressed these questions.

The largest body of literature of this kind, medical literature, has focused on aetiology: why do cross-gender identities come into being? Early medical writings emphasized psychological causes; the most recent research explores biological causes, in particular the effects of pre-natal hormones on the brain (Benjamin, 1966; Green and Money, 1969; Green, 1995; Stoller, 1976; Walters and Ross, 1986 and Zhou *et. al.*, 1995). As these texts evidence, the medicalization of transgender has the most implications for transsexuals, for most transsexuals require medical intervention (hormones and surgery) to become in body the gender they feel themselves to be. The medicalization of transgender is epitomized by the entry of 'Gender Identity Disorder' in the *Diagnostic and Statistical Manual of*

Mental Disorders (American Psychiatric Association, 1994). Whereas Queer Theory used transgender to deconstruct a narrative of gender, medical approaches have written out transgendered narratives in order that subjects can be differentiated and diagnosed and receive the treatment they require. The usefulness of this medical narrativization will come into question in a queer-informed transgender politics and transgender studies.

The transsexual deployment of medical technology has given rise to a body of literature critical of transsexuality. In Queer Theory, construction does not have a negative valence: all gender is constructed, a fact that transgendered subjects merely make manifest. In critiques of transsexuality, by contrast, construction has a dehumanizing connotation. The literal (re)construction of transsexual bodies has been used to figure transsexuals as the products of a manipulative medical establishment. Here construction stands for both transsexuals' dependence on medical technology, and the unnaturalness of their sex; to say that transsexuals are constructed men and women is to assert that they are not real men and women. Janice Raymond's lesbian feminist manifesto read male-to-female transsexuals as constructs in this sense: men made by a patriarchal medical empire to colonize women's bodies. *The* definitive text in cultural theory about transsexuals, *The Transsexual Empire* (1979), argued that transsexuality has been brought about by medical technology married to a rigid ideology of gender. According to Raymond, in changing sex to conform to their gender, transsexuals are key in sustaining this ideology: they realign masculinity with maleness, and femininity with femaleness. As a politics committed to changing gender roles, feminism must 'target' transsexuality, and Raymond's did just that; it set up transsexuals as the enemy of feminism and social change. Less vituperatively, sociologists Dwight Billings and Thomas Urban presented transsexuals as consumers or victims of the medical commodification of gender: transsexuals are duped into 'an alluring world of vaginas and penises' (rather like *Cosmo* readers buy make-up) (p. 112). Most recently, gender theorist Bernice Hausman has argued that transsexuals' technological construction is the product of and in turn reproduces a medical invention: gender identity. In emphasizing transsexuals' construction over the ways in which transsexuals have themselves shaped and constructed medical technology to meet their needs, both theories have an effect similar to Raymond's: they undermine the transsexual as a knowing subject; they refuse the possibility of and consequentially moralize sex change. It is not difficult to see why such critiques will become a spur to the development of transgendered politics and theory.

Anthropological and historical studies of transgender provide a welcome counterpoint to such literalist constructionism, and go some way toward reinstating transgendered agency and material experiences. Cross-historical and cross-cultural approaches to transgender show that transgender has existed outside of its medicalization, thereby suggesting that the transsexual is not a medical invention but rather one modern facet of an identity which has been around, in differing forms, at many times and in many places. Anthropological work on the *hijiras* of India (males who choose castration to live as special women), on the *berdache* in Native American cultures (cross-gender living males and females) has uncovered transgender subjects (Williams, 1986; Wieringa, 1989; Nanda, 1994; Roscoe, 1994). Historical work on cross-dressing in individual figures like the fifteenth-century Saint Joan of Arc (Feinberg, 1996), or the seventeenth-century Abbé de Choisy (Bullough and Bullough, 1993), has similarly substantiated the presence of transgender: sometimes as a transhistorical identity or sometimes, as in the case of the mass of literature on cross-dressing on the renaissance stage (Dusinberre, 1975; Clairborne Park, 1980; Shepherd, 1981, Rose, 1984; Levine, 1986; Orgel, 1989; Jardine, 1989) as a period phenomenon.[4] Like Queer Theory's use of transgender, the historical and anthropological documentation of transgender has often put pressure on the gendered binaries, the 'sexual dimorphism' (literally, 'splitting in two shapes-ness' of sex) of modern Western culture. Gilbert Herdt (Introduction, 1994) sees transgender as posing the question: 'Is sexual dimorphism inevitable in human affairs?' (p. 11), and, to be sure, much of this work argues that transgender identities in non-Western cultures or at other periods have been understood as a third or intermediate sex, that two-sexedness is in fact a modern Western invention.[5] Whereas the critiques of transsexual medicalization argued that the transsexual is stuck in and in turn stabilizes constructed gender binaries, anthropological and historical approaches, rather like Queer Theory, have read transgender as destabilizing gender's grounds.

Transgender politics

Like most cultural theories, transgender studies is derived from (and in turn has shaped) a political movement. In addition to the queer movement, certain events can be isolated in contributing to the formation of the transgender movement. Ann Bolin suggests the closure in the 1980s of the gender identity clinics which supervized transsexual transitions in the USA: transsexuals began to assert control over their treatment and diagnoses. The demedicalizing of transgender has continued to be an issue around which transgender politics has mobilized. There is an ongoing campaign to have the diagnosis of Gender Identity Disorder removed from *DSM*, to demedicalize the category altogether.

Transgender politics has also coagulated around legal rights. In Britain, the transsexual activist group, Press for Change, is engaged in a battle against the government to allow transsexuals to change their birth certificates. This is a pivotal issue because without this change, transsexuals cannot marry in their gender, cannot adopt children, have no employment protection, and legally remain in the birth sex that, physically, psychically and socially, they no longer are.[6] While most states in the USA allow a change of birth certificate, transgender subjects still have no protection around their gender identity. For this purpose, an International Bill of Gender Rights was drawn up at the Second International Conference on Transgender Law and Employment Policy in 1993.[7]

A more 'street' interventionist mode of transgender politics, 'transactivism', has arisen around issues of representation and cultural definition. Two events in the USA served as the crucible for transactivism; from them was forged the transactivist group, Transexual Menace (the dropping of an 's' signifying an attempt at redefinition: 'to articulate the concept of an ongoing identity beyond the transition phase' [Warren, 1993, p. 14]). The first event concerned the erasure of transsexual specificity, an erasure both literal and metaphoric. In December 1993, Brandon Teena, a transgendered female-to-male who lived as a man (without hormones or surgery) was raped and murdered in Nebraska when his birth sex was discovered. Transsexuals were enraged not only at Teena's killing but at the representation of Teena as a cross-dressing butch lesbian. Mainstream and gay press alike used female pronouns for Teena, eliding the descriptives transsexual and transgendered, even though Teena lived as a man and had expressed his desire for sex reassignment surgery. A week after lesbian journalist Donna Minkowitz's article ('Love Hurts. Brandon Teena Was a Woman Who Lived and Loved As a Man. She Was Killed For Carrying It Off') appeared in New York's *Village Voice*, Transexual Menace rallied in a high-profile protest outside the newspaper's offices. Teena will probably go down as transgender's Stonewall – the mythical origin of a movement.[8]

The second mobilizing event was the Michigan Womyn's Music Festival, an event from which male-to-female transsexuals had been excluded because of its 'womyn-born-womyn' entrance policy. In the summer of 1994, the newly-formed Transexual Menace rallied together a coalition of transgender activists and set up a transgendered camp – 'Camp Trans' –

directly opposite the festival's land. They challenged the organizers' biologistic definition of woman, and with the overwhelming support of the mainly queer dyke crowd at the festival, transsexual women were allowed onto the land.[9]

Juxtaposed, both events elucidate some of the complex aims of transgender politics. If in the Teena case, transsexual activists insisted on a certain transgender or transsexual specificity, the Michigan case was about the struggle to have transsexual women accepted as ordinary women *not* marked out by their transsexuality. The Teena case brought transsexual difference to attention; the Michigan case sought to de-emphasize it. In addition, each case reveals transsexuals taking a different relation to queerness. While upset by the co-option of Teena's transgenderism as queer, at Michigan, transsexuals won their struggle and challenged the definitions of gender through not only the support of queer women but queer arguments about the inessentiality of gender. Together, the events crystallize a tension around trans specificity and its relation to queer: a tension which will recur in transgender studies.

Experts on our own histories: the emergence of transgender studies

From these three arenas – the queer centralization of transgender, medical, anthropological and historical approaches to transgender, and a focused transgender politics – the new field of transgender studies emerged: sometimes in critique, sometimes in support, but certainly in reference to their debates. What marks the break with previous academic fields – what characterizes transgender studies – is that transgendered subjects began to speak for themselves; as the epigraph to this chapter by Feinberg (1996) suggests, transgender studies began when we started to become experts on our own histories. As transsexual autobiography demonstrates, there is a tradition of transsexuals telling their own stories, and autobiographical narrative has played a very significant role in the historical formation of transsexual subjectivity.[10] Transgender studies has formalized the principle that underlies the autobiographies: transgendered subjectivity depends on speaking as a transgenderist. For those transgendered subjects who have passing as their goal, who seek to erase all traces of their birth sex – that is, transsexuals in particular – this 'speaking as' constitutes a paradox: if the goal of transsexuality is to pass as not transsexual, what does it mean to come out and speak as a transsexual? In the seminal work of transgender theory, Sandy Stone plays this paradox, urging transsexuals to become subjects by 'forgo[ing] passing [and] to be consciously "read",[11] (to read oneself aloud – and by this troubling and productive reading to begin to *write oneself* into the discourses which have been written [about us]' (1991, p. 299). To counteract the representation of the transsexual as object of study (Stone's essay is a clever riposte to Raymond), to begin to ground transsexuality as a subject location rather than a transitional phase to pass through, Stone calls for a reversal of the evaluations of passing and reading.

This call takes its cue from Queer Theory. Indeed it is Stone's harnessing of queer which enables her to write a transsexual subject position. Using Butler's work on gender performativity, Stone conceives of an open, unpassing transsexuality as a way to 'generate new and unpredictable dissonances. . . to map the refigured body onto conventional gender discourse and thereby to disrupt it' (1991, p. 296). As in Queer Theory, transgender is seen to mobilize sex/gender categories. For this queer transsexuality, Stone coins the term 'posttranssexual' because it demands that we move beyond the traditional inscription of transsexuality with its imperative of passing. Stone's reclaiming of transsexual subjectivity as and through a queer model of gender construction has been extended by Kate Bornstein and Susan Stryker whose work literally enacts gendered performativity with a performative autobiographical 'I'.

Other transgender thinkers establish transgender subjectivity through means of narrative rather than performance, emphasizing the trans-historical and trans-cultural reality of transgender identity rather than its queer constructedness. Most recently, Leslie Feinberg's *Transgender Warriors*, in a fashion similar to Bullough and Bullough's work, demonstrates that transgender experience has existed in many cultures and at many periods. Revered by non-Western communalist cultures, transgender was suppressed by Western patriarchal societies which ruled by dividing people against each other into rigid categories (gender, sexuality, race or religion): anyone who didn't fit the categories was stigmatized as an outlaw. Stressing continuity and similarities among transgenderists across time and geographic locations, Feinberg's class-based history of transgender is an attempt to articulate a specifically transgendered community and culture.

Elsewhere I have argued that Feinberg's fictional autobiography *Stone Butch Blues* serves to specify transgender as an identity distinct from, though in important affiliation to, queer. What Feinberg addresses that queer has not is the subjective experience of transgender: the way in which the 'trans' movement may be complex, embodied and painful and not necessarily transgressive – the trouble *for*, not only the trouble caused *by*, the transgendered subject. My own work on transsexual narratives has led me to formulate reasons for sustaining a specifically *transsexual* subjectivity and methodology irreducible to queer. Queer theory's deconstruction of sex – its representation of sex as 'gender all along' – clearly does not hold for those transsexuals who experience a traumatizing split between their sex and gender, whose goal in seeking reassignment is to align their sex to their gender identity. For these subjects, gender and sex may be all too different, sex all too real, that is material, embodied, fleshly. Deconstructing sex does nothing to heal their lives; rather such healing may require the progression of a transsexual trajectory through the very real, very physical routes of hormonal and surgical reassignment. Moreover, for subjects who have been culturally stigmatized as literally constructed monstrous others, constructionism may have a limited usefulness. The power of the appeal to what feels essential, to *what gender feels like*, in effecting changes in cultural representation and legal rights, in continuing to ensure our access to medical treatment, should not be underestimated. Among women and people of colour too – as among lesbians and gays – bodies have had and may continue to have a materiality which cannot be, *which may not always usefully be*, transubstantiated. We need to write theories that reflect rather than erode the materialities of sex as those of race, class and sexuality. Performativity has its political limits.[12]

Perhaps then the split between queer and transsexual identities/methodologies might be rendered as a difference between trans*gender* and trans*sexual*, where transsexuals realize their gender through reconfiguring their sex, and transgenderists de-realize it by living in a gender different from their sex: transsexual could then get to have sex, transgender, gender. Yet such a neat division belies the complex crossings that take place *between* transsexuals and transgenderists. Although some transsexuals might refuse the label 'transgendered' on the basis that they are crossing sex, not a gender divide (if they experience their gender identity – feeling like a man or a woman – as consistent), equally other transsexuals might not believe in a sex divide at all: they might not feel like a man or a woman but perhaps a mixture of both, perhaps simply a transsexual. By the same token, some transgenderists clearly experience their gender as enmeshed with sex. Feinberg is a primary example since s/he used hormones and surgery to reconfigure her body and for a time pursued a female-to-male transsexual trajectory, yet she identifies as a transgendered lesbian, not as transsexual. Clearly then a demarcation between transgendered and transsexual is not sufficient to describe these nuances. I would argue that what we need are more specific subject categories to account for these different identities *within* transgender and transsexual. Having refused a stable demarcation between transgender and transsexual, I maintain, however, that transgender represents a category distinguishable from queer. The very act of transgender identity specification performs a kind of work which queer, in deconstructing the specific identity categories of 'lesbian', 'gay', 'man', and 'woman', has sought to trouble.

If the differences in transgendered narratives are to be foregrounded, the act of speaking as subjects will remain pivotal. Many transgender thinkers agree with Stone on the value of coming out, and undoing our passing. Feinberg writes: 'It is *passing* that is a product of oppression' (1996, p. 89); and Zachary Nataf remarks that the '*necessity* of passing' has now become a key debate in the transgender community (my emphasis, p. 16). While agreeing absolutely with the cruciality of speaking as transgenderists and transsexuals, in advancing it, again I think it crucial that we credit the lure of passing, account for the very human desire to belong, be accepted and be seen for who one feels oneself to be. In this regard also, transgender studies must map out methodological terrain not covered by queer's, perhaps enabled by affiliations to other methodologies: namely, race and feminist studies.

Conclusion: transitioning into the millennium with transgender

To call for specification within the transgender movement is not to shatter its cohesion but, I would argue, citing work by feminists on race and lesbianism as exemplary, to strengthen it. Effective affiliations within and beyond a movement can be made only once differences as well as similarities are recognized. If there are tensions currently in transgender studies, these tensions empower and enrich new work: they are precisely what makes the field so vital.

I have tried to suggest the specification of transgender difference as the cornerstone of this transgender moment. Transgender studies 'happened' because of the need to specify, to differentiate from representations of transgender. In a landmark contribution to transgender studies, Rita Felski (1996) has recently suggested that the transgenderist/transsexual has come to represent our current historical period – postmodernism, discourses of sexual deconstruction at the end of the millennium.[13] The effect of this symbolization is double-edged. Transgender's 'elevation to the status of universal signifier ("we are all transsexuals") subverts established distinctions between male and female, normal and deviant, but at the risk of homogenizing differences that matter politically: the differences between women and men, the difference between those who occasionally play the trope of transsexuality and those others for whom it is a matter of life and death' (p. 347). Transgender studies has certainly been enabled by what 'trans' has come to symbolize in theory, but the proliferation of new and contradictory gender plots within transgender pointedly challenges theory's totalization, its erasure of our embodied specificity. As Felski's essay so rightly suggests, the way to respond to this representation is to work it: to keep on proliferating situated – that is local, but not irresponsibly plural – identity narratives. If it is already engaged in this task to the extent I think it is, transgender studies provides something of a model for other cultural theories: a way to bridge academic theory and real lives as we transition into the next millennium.

Notes

1. Feinberg, *Transgender Warriors,* p. x.
2. For other references to transgender's two meanings, see Bolin 'Transcending' p. 461, Feinberg, *Transgender Warriors* p. x, and Nataf, 'Glossary'. Except when I explicitly address differences between non-transsexual transgenderists and transsexuals in section 3, I use transgender in the second inclusive sense.
3. Feinberg has described the relations between the transgender and the lesbian/gay communities as 'like circles that only partially overlap' (*Transgender Liberation* p. 6).
4. For the most comprehensive trans-cultural and trans-historical study of transgender (its title belies its breadth), see Bullough and Bullough. For a highly readable introduction, see Feinberg, *Transgender Warriors.* Herdt's anthology also spans historical and cultural approaches to transgender. For an excellent illustration that the transsexual existed before the subject's medical 'invention,' see Bullough. For a sympathetic anthropological study of contemporary American male-to-female transsexuals, see Bolin, *In Search of Eve.*
5. For a history of the invention of sexual dimorphism, see Laqueur.
6. Alex Carlisle's Gender Identity (Registration and Civil Status) Bill received slight support among MPs earlier this year, but unfortunately was read before an empty House of Commons. *Hansard.* 2 February 1996, pp. 1282–90.

7. The bill is reprinted in Rothblatt, pp. 167–70, and, in later draft form, in Feinberg, *Transgender Warriors*, pp. 165–68.

8. For transsexual reactions to the representation of Teena as lesbian see *FTM Newsletter* 26, February 1994, and *TNT*, Winter 1994.

9. For accounts of Michigan, see Green and Pratt. For the most detailed description to date of the emergence of the transgender movement, see Nataf, pp. 26–30.

10. On autobiographical narrative and transsexuality subjectivity, see my *Second Skins*.

11. To be read in transsexual lingo is to fail to pass, to be perceived as the sex of one's birth.

12. This is a critique not of Butler's theory of gender performativity *per se* but of the ways in which it has been taken up as an off-the-rack form of gender deconstruction. Butler herself elucidates the limits of transgressive transgender in her 'Gender is Burning: Questions of Appropriation and Subversion' in *Bodies That Matter*. That she does so through a Latina transsexual is a powerful indicator of the conceptual splitting between transsexual and queer.

13. I am grateful to Professor Nancy K. Miller for bringing this essay to my attention.

References

American Psychiatric Association, *Diagnostic and Statistical Manual of Mental Disorders IV*. Washington, DC: American Psychiatric Association, 1994.

Anzaldúa, Gloria, *Borderlands, La Frontera: The New Mestiza*. San Francisco: Aunt Lute, 1987.

Benjamin, Harry, *The Transsexual Phenomenon*. New York: Julian, 1966.

Bergman, David (ed.), *Camp Grounds: Style and Homosexuality*. Amherst: University of Massachusetts Press, 1993.

Billings, Dwight B., and Urban, Thomas, 'The Socio-Medical Construction of Transsexualism: An Interpretation and Critique', in *Social Problems*, Vol. 29, 1982, pp. 266–82. Rpt. R. Ekins and D. King (eds) (1996), pp. 99–118.

Bolin, Ann, *In Search of Eve: Transsexual Rites of Passage*. New York: Bergin and Garvey, 1988.

Bolin, Ann, 'Transcending and Transgendering: Male-to-Female Transsexuals, Dichotomy and Diversity', G. Herdt (ed.) (1994), pp. 447–86.

Bornstein, Kate, *Gender Outlaw: On Men, Women and the Rest of Us*. New York: Routledge, 1994.

Bullough, Vern L., and Bullough, Bonnie, *Cross Dressing, Sex, and Gender*. Philadelphia: University of Pennsylvania Press, 1993.

Bullough, Vern L., 'A Nineteenth-Century Transsexual', in *Archives of Sexual Behavior*, Vol. 16, 1987, pp. 81–4.

Butler, Judith, 'Against Proper Objects', in *differences*, Vol. 6, No. 2/3, 1994, pp. 1–26.

Butler, Judith, *Bodies That Matter: On the Discursive Limits of 'Sex'*. New York: Routledge, 1993.

Butler, Judith, *Gender Trouble: Feminism and the Subversion of Identity*. New York: Routledge, 1990.

Case, Sue-Ellen, 'Towards a Butch-Femme Aesthetic', in Lynda Hart (ed.), *Making a Spectacle: Feminist Essays on Contemporary Women's Theatre*, Ann Arbor: University of Michigan Press, 1989, pp. 282–99.

Clairborne Park, Clara, 'As We Like It: How a Girl Can Be Smart and Still Popular', in Carolyn Ruth Swift Levy, Gayle Green and Carole Thomas Neely (eds), *The Woman's Part: Feminist Criticism of Shakespeare*, Urbana, IL: University of Illinois Press, 1980, pp. 100–16.

de Lauretis, Teresa, 'Sexual Difference and Lesbian Representation', in *Theatre Journal*, Vol. 40, No. 2, 1988, pp. 155–77.

Devor, Holly, *Gender Blending: Confronting the Limits of Duality*. Bloomington: Indiana University Press, 1989.

Dollimore, Jonathan, *Sexual Dissidence: Augustine to Wilde, Freud to Foucault*. Oxford: Oxford University Press, 1991.

Dusinberre, Juliet, 'Disguise and the Boy Actor', in her *Shakespeare and the Nature of Women*, London: MacMillan, 1975, pp. 231–71.

Ekins, Richard, and King, Dave (eds), *Blending Genders: Social Aspects of Cross-dressing and Sex-Changing*. London: Routledge, 1996.

Epstein, Julia, and Straub, Kristina (eds), *BodyGuards: The Cultural Politics of Gender Ambiguity*. New York: Routledge, 1991.

Feinberg, Leslie, *Stone Butch Blues: A Novel*. New York: Firebrand, 1993.

Feinberg, Leslie, *Transgender Liberation: A Movement Whose Time Has Come*. New York: World View, 1992.

Feinberg, Leslie, *Transgender Warriors: Making History From Joan of Arc to RuPaul*. Boston: Beacon Press, 1996.

Felski, Rita, 'Fin de Siècle, Fin de Sexe: Transsexuality, Postmodernism, and the Death of History', in *New Literary History*, Vol. 27, 1996, pp. 337–49.

Garber, Marjorie, *Vested Interests: Cross-Dressing and Cultural Anxiety*. New York and London: Routledge, 1992.

Green, James, 'Camp Trans', in *FTM International Newsletter*, 29 January 1995, p. 11.

Green, Richard, *Sexual Identity Conflict in Children and Adults*. New York: Basic, 1974.

Green, Richard, and Money, John (eds), *Transsexualism and Sex Reassignment*. Baltimore: Johns Hopkins University Press, 1969.

Hausman, Bernice L., *Changing Sex: Transsexualism, Technology, and the Idea of Gender*. Durham: Duke University Press, 1995.

Herdt, Gilbert, 'Introduction: Third Sexes and Third Genders', in G. Herdt (ed.), 1994, pp. 21–84.

Herdt, Gilbert (ed.), *Third Sex, Third Gender: Beyond Sexual Dimorphism in Culture and History*. New York: Zone, 1994.

Jardine, Lisa, '"Make Thy Doublet of Changeable Taffeta": Dress Codes, Sumptuary Law and "Natural" Order', in *Still Harping on Daughters: Women and Drama in the Age of Shakespeare*, New York: Columbia University Press, 1989, pp. 141–68.

Kennedy, Elizabeth Lapovsky, and Davis, Madeline D., *Boots of Leather, Slippers of Gold: The History of a Lesbian Community*. New York: Routledge, 1993.

Laqueur, Thomas, *Making Sex: Body and Gender from the Greeks to Freud*. Cambridge, MA: Harvard University Press, 1990.

Levine, Laura, 'Men in Women's Clothing: Antitheatricality and Effeminization from 1579–1642', in *Criticism*, Vol. 28, 1986, pp. 121–45.

Mercer, Kobena, 'Reading Racial Fetishism: The Photographs of Robert Mapplethorpe', in Emily Apter and William Pietz (eds), *Fetishism as Cultural Discourse*, Ithaca: Cornell University Press, 1993, pp. 307–30

Meyer, Moe (ed.), *The Politics and Poetics of Camp*. London: Routledge, 1994.

Minkowitz, Donna, 'Love Hurts. Brandon Teena Was a Woman Who Lived and Loved As a Man. She Was Killed For Carrying It Off', in *Village Voice*, 19 April 1994, pp. 466–82.

Moraga, Cherríe, *Loving in the War Years*. New York: South End, 1983.

Munt, Sally R. (ed.), *Butch/Femme: Inside Lesbian Gender*. London: Cassell, 1997.

Nanda, Serena, 'Hijiras: An Alternative Sex and Gender Role in India', in G. Herdt (ed.), 1994, pp. 373–418.

Nanda, Serena, *Neither Woman Nor Man: The Hijiras of India*. Bellmont, CA: Wadsworth, 1990.

Nataf, Zachary I., *Lesbians Talk Transgender*. London: Scarlet, 1996.

Nestle, Joan, *A Restricted Country*. Ithaca, NY: Firebrand, 1987.

Nestle, Joan (ed.), *The Persistent Desire: A Femme-Butch Reader*. New York: Alyson, 1992.

Newton, Esther, *Mother Camp: Female Impersonators in America*. Chicago: University of Chicago Press, 1979.

Newton, Esther, 'The Mythic Mannish Lesbian: Radclyffe Hall and the New Woman', in *Signs*, Vol. 9, No. 4, 1984, pp. 557–75. Rpt. in Estelle B. Freedman, Barbara C. Gelpi, Susan L. Johnson, and Kathleen M. Weston (eds), *The Lesbian Issue: Essays from Signs*, Chicago: University of Chicago Press, 1985, pp. 7–26.

Orgel, Stephen, 'Nobody's Perfect, or, Why Did the English Stage Take Boys for Women?', *South Atlantic Quarterly*, Vol. 88, No. 1, 1989, pp. 7–29.

Pratt, Minnie Bruce, 'Border', in her *S/he*, New York: Firebrand, 1995, pp. 181–4.

Prosser, Jay, 'No Place Like Home: The Transgendered Narrative of Leslie Feinberg's Stone Butch Blues', in *Modern Fiction Studies*, Vol. 41, No. 3/4, 1995, pp. 483–514.

Prosser, Jay, *Second Skins: The Body Narratives of Transsexual Autobiography*. Forthcoming, Columbia University Press.

Raymond, Janice, *The Transsexual Empire: The Making of the She-Male* (1979). Reissued with a new introduction on transgender. New York: Teacher's College Press, 1994.

Roscoe, Will, 'How to Become a Berdache: Toward a Unified Analysis of Gender Diversity', in G. Herdt (ed.), 1994, pp. 329–72.

Roscoe, Will, *The Zuni Man-Woman*. Albuquerque: University of New Mexico Press, 1991.

Rose, Mary Beth, 'Women in Men's Clothing: Apparel and Social Stability in the Roaring Girl', *ELR*, Vol. 14, No. 3, 1984, pp. 367–91.

Rothblatt, Martine, *The Apartheid of Sex: A Manifesto on the Freedom of Gender*. London: Pandora, 1996.

Sedgwick, Eve Kosofsky, *Tendencies*. Durham: Duke University Press, 1993.

Shepherd, Simon, 'Roaring Girls', in *Amazons and Warrior Women: Varieties of Feminism in Seventeenth-Century Drama*. New York: St. Martin's Press, 1981, pp. 67–92.

Stoller, Robert J., *The Transsexual Experiment*. New York: Aronson, 1976.

Stone, Sandy, 'The "Empire" Strikes Back: A Posttranssexual Manifesto', in J. Epstein and K. Straub, 1991, pp. 280–304.

Stryker, Susan, 'My Words to Victor Frankenstein Above the Village of Chamounix: Performing Transgender Rage', in *GLQ: A Journal of Lesbian and Gay Studies*, Vol. 1, No. 3, 1994, pp. 237–54.

Walters, William A. W., and Ross, Michael, W. (eds), *Transsexualism and Sex Reassignment*. Oxford: Oxford University Press, 1986.

Warren, Barbara E., 'Transexuality, Identity and Empowerment: A View from the Front Lines', *SIECUS Report*, Feb./Mar. 1993, pp. 14–16.

Wieringa, Saskia, 'An Anthropological Critique of Constructionism: Berdaches and Butches', in Dennis Altman, Carole Vance, Martha Vicinus and Jeffrey Weeks (eds), *Homosexuality, Which Homosexuality?* London: GMP, 1989, pp. 215–38.

Williams, Walter, *The Spirit and the Flesh: Sexual Diversity in American Indian Culture*. Boston: Beacon Press, 1986.

Zhou, Jiang-Ning, Hofman, Michael A., Gooren, Louis J. G., and Swaab, Dick F., 'A Sex Difference in the Human Brain and its Relation to Transsexuality', in *Nature*, No. 378, 1995, pp. 68–70.

Further reading

Thompson, Raymond, with Sewell, Kitty, *What Took You So Long? A Girl's Journey to Manhood*. London: Penguin, 1995.

22

Sex Debates

Judith Halberstam

THE INSTITUTIONALIZATION OF QUEER THEORY has raised questions about its political affiliations and its increasing distance from queer cultures; as we begin to break down the pros and cons of institutional recognition, we should also attempt to account for what happens within the academy to discussions of the actual practices of queer sex. Surprisingly, we talk about sex – sexual practices and erotic variation – much less than we might imagine and this is at least partly because we talk a great deal about categories like 'lesbian' and 'gay'. We almost seem to assume that particular practices attend upon particular sexual identities even as we object to the naturalization of the homo-hetero binary. In actual fact, knowing that someone is gay or lesbian tells you nothing or, at least, very little about their sexual practices; and yet, we still seem to think that anal sex between men and oral sex between women provide paradigms for gay and lesbian sexual behaviour in much the same way that intercourse might for heterosexuals. Perhaps in our frenzy to de-essentialize gender and sexual identity, we omitted to de-essentialize sex.

'Sex,' Gayle Rubin has claimed, 'is always political'; but, she went on to show, there is no linear or cause and effect relationship between sex and politics and to posit such a relation is to mimic the religious fundamentalists who believe in a congruence between perverse sexual identity and moral corruption (Rubin, 1984, p. 267). Of course, if we want to argue that sexual perversity has no essential relation to criminality, we must also concede that sexual transgression does not feed directly into radical politics. The relationship between sex and politics remains contestatory and contradictory and continues to defy attempts to force organic links between sexual and other forms of behaviour. Discussions of sex in queer contexts more and more come to focus upon fantasy, pleasure and acts. Furthermore, the more we talk explicitly and in intellectually responsible ways about sex, the more we learn about the damage that can be done in the name of sexual morality. As Gayle Rubin's pioneering work has shown repeatedly, 'there is a hierarchy based on sexual behavior'; this hierarchy does not simply place heterosexuality at the top of the scale and homosexuality at the bottom, it accounts for all kinds of sexual difference from sex work to sado-masochism. In 1981 Rubin wrote: 'It is time that radicals and progressives, feminists and leftists, recognize this hierarchy for the oppressive structure that it is instead of reproducing it within their own ideologies' (p. 226). I think the challenge to recognize sexual hierarchies has still not been met, but there are some strands within contemporary Queer Theory which have been influenced by the history of a sex radical discourse and which are dedicated to finally producing appropriate languages and discourses for the dissemination of sexual information and towards the depathologization of perverse sex practices.

Historical constructions of sex

In order to understand the role of 'sex' in queer studies, it is important to historicize sexuality. The monumental effect of Michel Foucault's study, *The History of Sexuality, Volume One: An Introduction* (1980), has been to make scholars question their assumptions about the transhistorical nature of sex. By arguing that sex has a history and that the history of sex is in some respects the history of modern notions of the self, Foucault effectively rewrites the relations between sex and power, sex and politics, sex and history. Foucault's history shows that since 1870 with the invention of modern homosexuality, medicine, the law, sexology, psychology and other disciplines have produced elaborate discourses of sex which culminate in or participate in the 'implantation of perversions': according to such a theory, sexual identity emerges as the culmination of a set of desires. In other words, one no longer merely participates in particular sex acts, those sex acts coalesce into the specifications of individuality itself. So, rather than being a man who engages in sodomy with other males, the sodomite becomes a 'homosexual'.

This enormously useful model of the very recent invention of sex has changed completely the study of sexuality in the last decade. It is no longer standard practice to engage in the historical recovery of homosexual figures from different historical periods; instead queer scholars have tried to understand how sex may have worked in other time periods, what its relation has been to class identity, racial identities and gender identity and kinship forms, and historians are less apt to assume that same-sex activity wherever and whenever it emerges means the same thing. By the same token, historians of sexuality are less likely to assume that we even know what we mean by sex in a contemporary sense. Eve Sedgwick, for example, offers a critique of Foucault's work by suggesting that the project of defamiliarizing sexuality within history has inadvertently 'counterpoise(d) against the alterity of the past a relatively unified homosexuality that "we" do "know today"' (1990, p. 45). I think about all 'we' do 'know today' is that the categories and models that we have developed to describe, contain and manage desire, in no way exhaust the possibilities of erotic variation.

As Sedgwick's work has so clearly shown, furthermore, these models are ruthlessly arbitrary and oddly weighted towards defining sexual identity in terms of gender of object choice (homo-hetero). Sedgwick's wildly creative and humorous list of other possible ways of organizing sexual variation underscores, indeed, the absurdity of our current sexual system. Her list points to the obvious: 'even identical genital acts mean very different things to different people'; the banal: 'some people like to have a lot of sex, others little or none'; the phantasmatic: 'many people have their richest mental/emotional involvement with sexual acts they don't do, or even don't want to do'; and the aversive: 'for some people the possibility of bad sex is aversive enough that their lives are strongly marked by its avoidance; for others, it isn't' (Sedgwick, 1990, p. 25). The list, in other words, reveals how many ways people already organize their desires in terms that far exceed the homo-hetero binary.

If we accept that Foucault's work has shown us how little contemporary sexual systems have in common with earlier sexual systems and that Sedgwick's work questions whether we even know much about contemporary sexual systems, what effect does such unknowing have upon work being done on the history of sexuality? For one thing, these forms of uncertainty have resulted in productive and energetic debates about the meanings of early forms of same-sex desire. Scholars have tended in recent years to resist labelling pre-nineteenth-century same-sex eroticism as homosexual and such forms of desire have been read as part of a class system or a gender system rather than part of a sexual system (Halperin, 1989). Lesbian historians in particular have had furious debates about the meaning of close bonds between women at different historical junctures. For example, Carroll Smith-Rosenberg's and Lillian Faderman's models of 'romantic friendship' bracketed the question of genital activity between women from definitions of lesbianism and defined lesbianism in relation to a largely asexual and romanticized notion of intimacy fostered within a culture of separate spheres for men and women (Smith-Rosenberg, 1975; Faderman, 1981). Both Smith-Rosenberg and Faderman have been criticized by a subsequent generation of lesbian historians for separating lesbianism from overt sexual activity and for reproducing rather stereotypical notions of the moral and pure nature of nineteenth-century true womanhood (Moore, 1992).

More recently, queer theorists have proposed models of cross-identifying and passing women and their more feminine (often married) lovers as paradigmatic of nineteenth-century same-sex relations between women. Esther Newton's classic essay, 'The Mythic Mannish Lesbian' insisted that the mannish woman eventually dominated discourses about female homosexuality because the butch embodied an 'active lust' at a time when 'sexual desire was not considered inherent in women', and also because 'gender reversal became a powerful symbol of feminist aspirations' (1984, p. 566). In other words, the mannish lesbian makes desire between women visible and potent and rescues lesbianism from the asexual pit of romantic friendship. Lisa Duggan's work on turn of the century American lesbians has also noted the dependence of lesbianism upon a model of sexual difference. In an essay on the sensational trial of Alice Mitchell for the murder of her young female lover, Duggan notes that the press commented upon 'Alice's "masculine" characteristics and Freda's "feminine" manner' (1993, p. 798). She also shows how cross-gender identification and cross-dressing are main elements in this case and in others like it from the same period. Duggan summarizes the motivations and effects of cross-identifications for young women: 'Through masculine identification they separated themselves from the family-based female world, defined their desire for other women as erotic, and declared their unyielding commitment to a new way of life' (p. 809).

But strains of an ahistorical approach to lesbian history do still make appearances within contemporary lesbian scholarship. Terry Castle's rather successful book, *The Apparitional Lesbian* (1993), strenuously objects to recent currents in queer history. Castle argues that the constructivist approach to lesbian definition has needlessly obscured the meanings, the realities and the history of lesbian desire. She argues that while women may not have used the word 'lesbian' prior to the late nineteenth century, nonetheless other vernacular words like 'tommy' and 'fricatrice' did exist, and, furthermore, 'where there are words. . .there is identity' (p. 10). Castle goes on to claim that 'lesbian' is far from the unstable and incoherent signifier that Queer Theory makes it out to be; on the contrary, she claims, 'I believe we live in a world in which the word lesbian still makes sense, and that it is possible to use the word frequently, even lyrically, and still be understood' (p. 14). This approach to lesbian definition has the appeal of a commonsense attempt to cut through the theory and attend to the actualities of lesbian life; however, something definitely is lost in Castle's polemic. Having dropped the historicized notion of pre-identitarian sexual practices between women and having insisted upon the stability of the term 'lesbian' and all its colloquial synonyms, Castle proceeds to blot out crucial differences between tribades in the Renaissance,[1] cross-identifying women in the early nineteenth century like diarist Ann Lister, women identified women of the late twentieth century and non-lesbian identifying women like Greta Garbo who may appear as lesbian within elaborate representational homoerotic sexual codes. How can all of these different versions of desire be comfortably accommodated under one definitional term? And, furthermore, what are the effects of insisting that they all be labelled 'lesbian'?

I am arguing here for specificity and detail in relation to sex in history. There are very good and clear reasons why theorists resist the temptation to stretch terms like 'lesbian' across a vast array of sexual phenomena. Valerie Traub, for example, in her work on early discourses on tribadism from the seventeenth century, emphasizes that 'tribades were not lesbians' (Traub, 1995, p. 99), rather, she astutely points out, associations made in this early literature between tribadism and enlarged clitorises 'provide the raw material out of which the social categories 'lesbian' and 'heterosexual' would begin to be constructed' (p. 98).

Castle, on the other hand, allows for no such historical reckoning of the production of the category 'lesbian'. She willingly unites under this heading people who may identify as men, as transgender, as heterosexual. Some historical figures like Anne Lister did not even identify with the terms of the day for same-sex erotic behaviour. Lister, in fact, rejected the label 'sapphic' for herself and continuously refers to her masculinity throughout her diaries: on the topic of 'saffic regard', Lister remarks: 'I said there was artifice in it. It was very different from mine and would be no pleasure to me' (Lister, 1824, p. 49). Lister, a Halifax gentlewoman who kept explicit diaries of her sexual adventures for ten years, articulates here her pleasure and not her identity. She says that she is not 'saffic' because that mode of lovemaking affords her no pleasure; clearly then 'saffic' refers to some sexual practices between biological women but not to others. Lister's lovers furthermore are very different from her; they are mostly married feminine women who are unsatisfied by their husbands. What does it mean then to call both Anne Lister and her lovers 'lesbian' and to make lesbian signify some commonsensical notion of regular sexual practices between women? Lister's explicit descriptions of the sex she engages in with her various lovers completely underscores the absurdity of such definitional attempts. Lister often fantasizes about having a penis and while she energetically makes love to her partners, she does not allow them to touch her sexually in the same way: she writes, 'I do what I like but never permit them to do so' (p. 48). Lister was clearly tribadic and engaged in a kind of masculine sexual aesthetic. We might ask, therefore, how is this 'lesbian', or even how 'lesbian' is this form of sexual practice?

Queer discourses about the history of sexuality stress the contingent nature of sexual practices, sexual acts and their meanings and sexual identities. They stress, furthermore, the very different histories of sexuality and sexual trajectories marked out by class and race. An upper-class woman in Victorian England could cross-dress with some impunity; a working-class woman might have to pass successfully as a man when she cross-dressed; a black woman in nineteenth-century America might consider it too dangerous to cross-dress: anyway, an act like cross-dressing means very different things to different people at different historical moments, and, predictably, the sexuality inferred by the act of cross-dressing cannot be considered 'lesbian' in any uncomplicated way. The project for queer historians, then, is no longer to find and document and record the presence of gay men and lesbians throughout history; rather it is to judge the meaning of sex in any given historical location and to trace the development of notions of identity and sexual selves from within discourses of acts and pleasures. The effect of the production of the homo-hetero binary at the turn of the twentieth century was to commit a representational violence upon the multiplicity of sexual practices in existence: the homo-hetero binary still continues to clamp down upon sexual excess and insists upon clear sexual distinctions between perverse and normal sexual behaviour and between male and female sexualities.

Against feminist sex

The kinds of debate which currently preoccupy queer theorists in relation to sex relate clearly to the debates about the historical meaning of sex, but also they have their own specificities. In this next section, I present the questions about sex which have been raised by two decades of political organizing around the categories gay and lesbian, and I show that politics and sex have much more complicated and contradictory relations than we would like to think. For example, while people may well invest in values like equality and reciprocality in their political lives, they may not want those same values dominating their sexual lives. The rise of lesbian feminism in the 1970s presented women with some very thorny questions about the non-continuities between sex and politics and resulted ultimately in internal sex wars within dyke communities. These debates produced both sexual morality and sex radicalism and ultimately led to the overturning of a strongly sex-negative strain within lesbian politics.

Within present-day cultural stereotyping, gay men tend to be associated with excessive sexuality while white lesbians are still linked to frigidity and spectrality. White lesbian desire becomes entwined with suffusive eroticism rather than overwhelming sex drives. Lesbians of colour tend to be stereotyped along racial as well as sexual lines: the black lesbian, for example, is often stereotyped as the butch bulldagger or as sexually voracious and so it makes no sense to talk about such a construction in terms of invisibility and spectrality. As Anna Marie Smith has pointed out: 'It is simply not true that all lesbians are equally 'invisible'. Black lesbians, working class butches, and lesbian prison inmates pay a very high price for their extraordinary visibility' (Smith, 1995, p. 175). For this reason, when white lesbians continue to invest exclusively in this construction of lesbian sex as elusive and intangible, other hyper-visible lesbian sexualities are totally discounted. Lesbian feminist Marilyn Frye makes explicit this argument about lesbian invisibility in an essay on 'Lesbian Sex' where she claims that in comparison to gay men and heterosexuals, lesbians seem not to articulate their desires. She has a lesbian feminist reading of this problem which blames the patriarchy for silencing us and then suggests that patriarchal language cannot account for our specialized and unique lesbian love (Frye, 1991). Frye writes: 'Lesbian "sex" as I have known it most of the time I have known it is utterly inarticulate. Most of my lifetime, most of my experience in the realms commonly designated as "sexual" has been prelinguistic, noncognitive' (p. 6). All that Frye's comments on lesbian sex reveal is that some white women of a certain generation and class lacked a sexual vocabulary. No general theory of lesbian desire can be inferred from this fact despite the tone of the essay which tends to universalize.

While the mannish lesbian presented a counter-image to the romantic friend at the turn of the century, in the second half of the twentieth century it has been the butch-femme couple which has signified active and complex desire between women. Joan Nestle's work on femme desire and Elizabeth Kennedy and Madeline Davis's oral histories of butch-fem communities in Buffalo, New York in the 1940s and 1950s both provide detailed portraits of how lesbian life was organized and how it thrived prior to gay/lesbian liberation and the so-called sexual revolution (Nestle, 1987; Kennedy and Davis, 1993). As many social histories of lesbianism have now shown, the rise of lesbian feminism in the 1970s rejected butch-fem and its forms of sexual role-playing as a gross mimicry of heterosexuality. The rejection of the butch as a repulsive stereotype by some lesbian feminists also had the unfortunate effect of pathologizing the only visible signifier of queer dyke desire; the rejection of the fem produced limits for lesbian feminine expression and grounded middle-class white feminism within an androgynous aesthetic. The suppression of role-playing therefore by lesbian feminists in the 1970s and 1980s further erased an elaborate and carefully scripted language of desire that butch fem dykes had produced in response to dominant culture's attempts to wipe them out.

Chicana writer Cherríe Moraga in *Loving in the War Years* points out that the attack on butch-fem role-playing made by white feminists also erased cultural and ethnic differences between women (Moraga, 1983). Moraga details her own sexuality and sexual consciousness in relation to her hybrid ethnic identity: she discusses growing up the daughter of a Mexican mother and a white father and she attempts to account for both her whiteness and her sense of herself as Chicana. Alongside her open and courageous critique of sexism within communities of colour, Moraga carefully describes the various forms of feminist racism which she is forced to experience. One particular form has to do with feminist sex. Moraga comments upon the presumption within lesbian feminism that 'lesbian sexuality was *naturally* different from heterosexual sexuality' (Moraga, 1983, p. 125). She struggles with the notion that power should automatically vanish from sexual relations between women and wonders about the charge of 'male-identification' against those women who retain desires for sexual power. Moraga concludes that her sense of her sexuality may well be structured as much by Mexican cultural norms as by lesbian standards and therefore it may bear closer relation to what men and women of color do sexually than what white lesbians prescibed. She writes:

What I need to explore will not be found in the feminist lesbian bedroom, but more likely in the mostly heterosexual bedrooms of South Texas, L.A., or even Sonora, Mexico. Further, I have come to realize

that the boundaries white feminists confine themselves to in describing
sexuality are based in white-rooted interpretations of dominance, submission, power-exchange etc. (p. 126)

If 'chingon' and 'chingada' describe the commonly understood gender
roles within Mexican culture, Moraga says, then Chicana lesbians cannot
suddenly be expected to cast off these sex roles in favour of a lesbian feminist egalitarianism. Prescribed sexual behaviour along lesbian feminist
lines enacts a form of cultural imperialism and ignores the specificities of
different sexual cultures.

One complaint that butches and fems in general have lodged against
middle-class lesbian feminist versions of sex culture is that the dominant
strands at least of cultural lesbian feminism never replaced the erotic codes
and practices of the butch-fem bar culture from the 1950s and 1960s with
anything but negative sex recommendations. In their history of butch fem
community, Kennedy and Davis report on and celebrate the diverse sexual
culture that blazed a trail for later lesbian communities. They document
and record the social organizations, courtship rituals, class and race divisions and sexual practices of a group of self-identified butches and fems.
Despite severe oppression in the form of homophobia at work and at home,
economic hardship and social ostracism, this group of lesbians was creative
and daring in its sexual and social experiments. Since lesbian feminists of
the 1970s, as Kennedy and Davis put it, 'defined these butch-fem communities as an anathema to feminism', we must assume that lesbian
feminists had conceived of some social and sexual codes and systems to
replace what they saw as anachronistic and derivative self-presentations
(1993, p. 11). It is interesting therefore to find that the lesbian feminist
journals of the late 1970s and early 1980s seem to lack a sexual language
for lesbianism.

It is quite common nowadays to claim that we have overdone the critique of this brand of lesbian feminism and that in fact just as many women
in the 1970s and the 1980s were sexually adventurous as they may be
today. This may be so: we have few ways of measuring such things; but I
would claim that women in the early 1980s tended not to represent their
sexual practices, in lesbian feminist venues at least, as anything other than
thoroughly proper, romantic, mutual and loving. At the risk of reifying a
history that is of course complex and multifaceted, I want to argue here
that the cultural feminist strand of lesbianism is not a myth or a convenient
bogy created by queers in order to make their own sexual politics appear

all the more transgressive. Cultural feminism, as Alice Echols and other feminist historians have shown, has had a long-lasting effect upon lesbian self-definition and at the time that the sex wars raged, cultural feminists seemed to be in the majority (Echols, 1984). It is worth examining some of the history and some of the dominant ideals of cultural feminism if only to show how thoroughly contemporary queer dyke communities have rejected such models of sexual culture.

Some of the positions within white lesbian feminist circles around sexuality tended towards a conservative essentialism. Even radical and fringe feminists like Valerie Solanas tended to cede sex to men, equate femininity with intimacy rather than sexuality and argue for the purity of lesbian sex as a full expression of feminism, egalitarianism and the joys of mutual desire untainted by the power dynamics inherent in patriarchal heterosexuality (Solanas, 1970). The anti-pornography movement solidified the notion that sexuality within patriarchy tended to further the oppression of women (Lederer, 1980). Feminists felt that pornography was an expression of patriarchal attitudes towards women and towards the female body and that pornography both represented and produced sexism, or worse, violence against women and rape (Dworkin, 1989). Instead of the anti-pornography position developing into a call for sex education or for the fostering of sexual diversity, as Carole Vance's work has shown, it actually fed into moralist fears about perversity and a religious right-wing effort to legislate against certain forms of sexual expression (Vance, 1992). As had happened at the beginning of the century in relation to first-wave feminism, sexual purity and moralism became a feature of lesbian feminism.[2]

In case readers think that this is all speculation, I would like to turn briefly to one account of lesbian desire that appeared in the pages of a well-known lesbian feminist publication. It is not clear how representative this piece is but it is certainly worth remarking upon how cloying, sterile and generally unappealing it is by way of making a case against what we might call 'feminist sex'. In their attempts to avoid sexist or pornographic language, some lesbian feminist writers who wanted to depict loving sex scenes were reduced to talking about 'vaginas' and 'digital manipulations' in tones that sounded highly clinical. Here is one particularly asexual piece of lesbian erotica from *Common Lives, Lesbian Lives* (1983). In this story, called 'Making Adjustments' by Teresa Lilliandaughter, the narrator and her lover are having trouble agreeing on when to have sex and how to co-ordinate their desires around their schedules. The lover has less desire than the narrator so the narrator attempts to find creative solutions to the dilemma. One involves talking it out and trying to find out why her lover does not desire her: she tells her lover: 'I guess I feel like we should always feel the same, so if I'm horny, you should be horny' (Lilliandaughter, 1983, p. 35). Another solution that the lovers hit upon is that the narrator should masturbate more but, she says, she doesn't want to because she really wanted her lover. The lover responds: 'maybe we can work out a joint effort. . .Why don't you masturbate while I stroke you or something?' (p. 37). Finally, they decide to do it, the lover doesn't mind, she says, 'because you come fast'. To the sex scene:

> She begins to massage my breasts and tickle the side of my neck. Then she starts to nibble and chew on my ear lobe. I start using the vibrator. Ummmm. Her hands feel so good.
> 'Can I just have a little finger in my vagina?'
> 'You want a little finger? How about a regular size finger'
> 'Yeah gimme a regular size finger in the vagina. To go.' Like ordering in a fast food place. (p. 39)

After she comes, the narrator notes with satisfaction 'it only took a few minutes, six to be precise'. The scene continues in this way and now the lover takes a turn with the vibrator and the narrator tickles her neck, nibbles her ear and inserts fingers into vagina, being careful never to give the impression of fucking and never to lose control in such a way that the scene would degenerate into something pornographic.

This sex scene has more in common with a Kinsey report than a porno story. And yet this is an example of the kind of feminist sex that was supposed to avoid the patriarchal pitfalls of fucking, sucking, rubbing, biting, dildo wearing and role-playing. The absence of all gender and sex play from this scene and its assumption of sameness and equality as the basis for desire can only really produce this particular narrative over and over again: in other words the narrative of waning desire and the attempts of the participants to revive or inspire sexual reawakenings. The scene is asexual in fact, if a sex scene can be asexual, because it de-eroticizes sex. Furthermore, the adjustments that the title refers to involve adjusting expectations in order to accommodate the non-desire of one's partner. There is an overwhelming sense of sexual defeat in the story and one feels that many lesbians paid a high price for this kind of adjustment in this process of lesbian culture changing from a working class butch-fem role-playing community to a politicized middle-class woman-loving-woman community.

Conclusion

It is not surprising therefore that what we call 'The Sex Wars' emerged within some lesbian feminist communities as women struggled with the discrepancies between their own desires and their political goals: feminists dealt with questions about how to reconcile rape fantasies with anti-pornography politics or sado-masochistic sexual practices with a fight against patriarchal domination. Unfortunately, in general, women felt some obligation to become the moral guardians of culture and sex *per se* seemed to be patriarchal, while feminists claimed eroticism. As women grew more and more conflicted about the relations between reality and fantasy, the personal and the political, ethics and desire, communities began huge debates about sexuality which were constantly criss-crossed by other debates about race and class and role-playing. The histories of sex, and of lesbian sex in particular, which I have reproduced in this essay are most obviously class histories: a rejection of bar culture has been a mostly middle-class rejection of what was perceived as a stigmatized form of lesbian community.

The so-called 'sex wars' (Duggan and Hunter, 1996) of the 1980s erupted at least in part on account of a sex-positive reaction to what was perceived as a suffocating lesbian morality: this reaction was motivated by the revelation that feminist sex negativity sprang from only one small group of lesbians and that many other lesbian communities had and continue to cultivate thriving sex cultures in bars, play parties and private homes. In the last fifteen years, the lesbian feminist tendencies that we tend to call 'cultural feminism' have been almost completely replaced by sex-positive lesbian feminism. Some strains of sex negativity do linger (particularly among academic lesbian and Women's Studies) but on the whole lesbian sexual morality has been replaced by an invigorated butch-fem culture and an elaborate bar culture with its attendant sexual subcultures. Furthermore, the appearance in particular of vocal and activist transsexual communities has made visible the presence of other sexual minorities and their relative autonomy from the more respectable and assimilated mainstream gay and lesbian populations. A new wave of transgender scholarship currently promises to shake up the comfortable identity categories which gay and lesbian scholarship has depended upon, and clearly the next decade promises new sexual revolutions.

Notes

1. 'Tribade' is a word of Greek origin and it refers to a woman who rubs sexually upon another person. It refers to the pleasurable friction of rubbing a clitoris on another person's thigh, pubic bone, hip, buttocks or any other fleshly surface. Early accounts of the tribade connected her with some form of hermaphroditism and the possession of a giant clitoris (Traub, 1996).
2. For more on radical lesbian sex culture see Califia (1994) and Caught Looking (1992).

References

Califia, Pat, *Public Sex: The Culture of Radical Sex*. Pittsburgh, PA: Cleis Press, 1994.

Castle, Terry, *The Apparitional Lesbian: Female Homosexuality and Modern Culture*. New York: Columbia University Press, 1993.

Caught Looking, Inc., *Caught Looking: Feminism, Pornography, Censorship*. East Haven, CT: Long River, 1992.

Duggan, Lisa, 'The Trials of Alice Mitchell: Sensationalism, Sexology, and the Lesbian Subject in Turn-of-the-Century America', in *Signs*, Vol. 18, No. 4, Summer, 1993, pp. 791–814.

Duggan, Lisa, and Hunter, Nan D., *Sex Wars: Sexual Dissent and Political Culture*. New York: Routledge, 1996.

Dworkin, Andrea, *Pornography: Men Possessing Women*. New York: Dutton, 1989.

Echols, Alice, 'The Taming of the Id: Feminist Sexual Politics 1968–1983', in Carole Vance (ed.), *Pleasure and Danger: Exploring Female Sexuality*, New York: Routledge, Kegan & Paul, 1984, pp. 50–72.

Faderman, Lillian, *Surpassing the Love of Men: Romantic Friendship and Love Between Women from the Renaissance to the Present*. New York: William Morrow, 1981.

Foucault, Michel, *The History of Sexuality, Volume 1: An Introduction*, (trans. Robert Hurley). New York: Vintage, 1980.

Frye, Marilyn, 'Lesbian Sex', in Judith Barrington (ed.), *An Intimate Wilderness: Lesbian Writers on Sexuality*, Portland, OR: Eighth Mountain, 1991, pp. 1–8.

Halperin, David, *One Hundred Years of Homosexuality*. New York: Routledge, 1989.

Kennedy, Elizabeth, and Davis, Madeline, *Boots of Leather, Slippers of Gold: The History of A Lesbian Community*. New York: Routledge, 1993.

Lederer, Laura, *Take Back the Night: Women on Pornography*. New York: Morrow, 1980.

Lilliandaughter, Teresa, 'Making Adjustments', in *Common Lives, Lesbian Lives: A Lesbian Quarterly*, No. 7, Spring, 1983, p. 35.

Lister, Anne, *No Priest But Love: The Diaries of Ann Lister from 1824–1826*. Helena Whitbread (ed.). New York: New York University Press, 1992.

Moore, Lisa, '"Something More Tender Still than Friendship": Romantic Friendship in Early Nineteenth Century England', in *Feminist Studies*. Vol. 18, No. 3, Autumn, 1992, pp. 499–520.

Moraga, Cherríe, *Loving in the War Years*. Boston: South End Press, 1983.

Nestle, Joan, *A Restricted Country*. Ithaca, NY: Firebrand, 1987.

Newton, Esther, 'The Mythic Mannish Lesbian: Radclyffe Hall and the New Woman', in *Signs*, Vol. 9, No. 4, 1984, pp. 557–75.

Rubin, Gayle, 'The Leather Menace: Comments on Politics and S/M', in Samois (ed.), *Coming to Power*, Boston: Alyson Press, 1981, pp. 194–229.

Rubin, Gayle, 'Thinking Sex: Notes for a Radical Theory of the Politics of Sexuality', in Carole Vance (ed.), *Pleasure and Danger: Exploring Female Sexuality*, New York: Routledge, Kegan & Paul, 1984, pp. 267–312.

Sedgwick, Eve Kosofsky, *Epistemology of the Closet*. Berkeley and Los Angeles: University of California Press, 1990.

Smith, Anna Marie, 'The Regulation of Lesbian Sexuality Through Erasure: The Case of Jennifer Saunders', in Karla Jay (ed.), *Lesbian Erotics*, New York: New York University Press, 1995, pp. 164–82.

Smith-Rosenberg, Carroll, 'The Female World of Love and Ritual: Relations Between Women in Nineteenth Century America', in *Signs*, Vol. 1, No. 1, Autumn, 1975, pp. 1–29.

Solanas, Valerie, *S.C.U.M. Manifesto*. New York: Olympia Press, 1970.

Traub, Valerie, 'The Psychomorphology of the Clitoris', *GLQ*, Vol. 2, No. 1/2, 1995, pp. 81–114.

Vance, Carole S., 'Negotiating Sex and Gender in the Attomey General's Commission on Pornography', in Lynne Segal and Mary McIntosh (eds), *Sex Exposed: Sexuality and the Pornography Debate*, London: Virago, 1992, pp. 29–49.

Vance, Carole S. (ed.), *Pleasure and Danger: Exploring Female Sexuality*. New York: Routledge & Kegan Paul, 1984.

Further reading

Edwards, Tim, *Erotics and Politics: Gay Male Sexuality, Masculinity and Feminism*. London: Routledge, 1994.

Wilton, Tamsin, *Finger-Licking Good: The Ins and Outs of Lesbian Sex*. London: Cassell, 1996.

23

Sadomasochism

Lynda Hart and Joshua Dale

WHAT HAS COME TO BE KNOWN as sadomasochistic sexuality has affinities with sexual and spiritual practices that are recorded in writing and visual art throughout history. The term itself, however, is etymologically connected to the names of the Marquis de Sade and Leopold von Sacher-Masoch. As Gilles Deleuze points out, 'the names of Sade and Masoch have been used to denote two basic perversions, and as such they are outstanding examples of the efficiency of literature' (Deleuze, 1989, p. 15). In the context of Lesbian and Gay Studies, sadomasochistic sexual practices have become particularly highly charged and controversial. While heterosexual s/m sexuality has thrived rather quietly and uneventfully throughout the centuries, gay, and particularly lesbian, s/m has generated heated debates both between the dominant culture and gay and lesbian subcultures, as well as within gay and lesbian subcultures. This is due, in large part, to a legacy that has pathologized and/or criminalized homosexuality *per se*.[1] Hence, the assumption held by many people that s/m is a 'violent' eroticism, is aided and abetted by this historical convergence.

This chapter aims to provide readers with a sketch of s/m within recent gay and lesbian studies, highlight certain key concepts that inform understandings of s/m sexuality, outline some of the forms that debates about s/m have taken within gay and lesbian studies, and point out research in the field that leads to clearer understandings of what s/m means to its practitioners and how it has been received and conceptualized by both proponents and opponents. We do not, however, pretend to write an objective or comprehensive historical account. Both writers of this chapter seek to begin a discussion that will explain and dispel some of the negativity that circulates in relationship to gay and lesbian s/m. We have divided the writing of this chapter into two parts: Joshua Dale has written the first section that focuses on gay s/m; Lynda Hart has written the section on lesbian s/m. We are aware, however, of the problems of such a division, based as it is on a presumed gender dualism. It is particularly pertinent to be reminded of this since s/m sexual subcultures have been one of the sites where gender dichotomies have been most broken down. Nevertheless, there has been an evident difference between gay and lesbian s/m.

Gay s/m: history, practice, theories

It is impossible to know how many men, or women, were involved in s/m before it became a (relatively) open part of gay life.[2] The earliest signs of visibility began with the post-World War I motorcycle clubs made up of 'outlaw bikers'. These, whether gay, straight, or mixed, supported the leather lifestyle in which s/m people made their connections and found acceptance. But s/m practitioners were underground within this underground, which made for a doubly closed society.

Outside the tight-knit s/m fraternity however, gay style was changing. Straight society's stereotypes of gay men in the harshly anti-gay climate of the 1950s remained relentlessly focused on the image of the effeminate, lisping 'Nelly', limp-wristed in a fuzzy sweater. But these weren't the only men buying 'body-building' magazines like *Physique Pictorial* and *Grecian Guild Pictorial*, whose photos of posing musclemen (often in Greco-Roman settings to establish themselves as 'art' instead of pornography) increasingly dared to cater to a gay readership (Hooven, 1993, pp. 84–88). While American illustrators such as George Quaintance began to push the envelope of bodybuilding pictures into more overt gay themes, it was Tom of Finland's late 1950s publication of his drawings of masculine loggers, military and motorcycle men that helped to build a homoeroticism that was proudly gay in its depictions of desire. Finland's drawings of men in leather jackets, boots, and caps began to offer an alternative to the gay style of high camp and ushered in the 'homomasculine' style of gay macho. 24 June 1964 saw the publication of *Life Magazine*'s issue on 'Homosexuality in America', which depicted not camp and drag, but the Chuck Arnett mural of leather-jacketed men that presided over San Francisco's most famous leather bar, the Tool Box. The photo also captured the leathermen milling around beneath the mural, the effect was to issue an open invitation for gay men to join the leather life.

But although this gay macho style went fist-in-glove with the s/m subculture's erotic rituals for testing the 'manly' virtues of endurance and toughness, wearing a leather jacket was no entry into the highly secretive s/m society of the time, even if one did roar up to the local bar on a Harley.

Leather had become the new gay fashion, but whilst the dark rituals of s/m thrilled the hearts of many and leather bars proliferated, making initial contact with the leather world remained intimidating. Writer Don V. reports that he spent nearly every Saturday night of 1976 parked across from the Ramrod trying to muster the courage to go inside (p. 2). But getting through the door was only the beginning, for in the leather-trendy 1960s and 1970s the hopeful initiate's first shaky step into the Gold Coast in Chicago or Hellfire in New York was often an anticlimax. Horrified at the influx of tourists invading their sacred haunts, s/m leathermen retreated further during this period – to private parties and exclusive playrooms. (Stein, 1992, p. 148). While the rituals one could see enacted at the Minesha became legends in their own time, much of the serious s/m was for invited guests only. The bar etiquette was not quite as impenetrable as it had been in the 1950s, when tops (masters) signalled their availability to bottoms (slaves) by exposing their left shoulders while standing at the bar (Magister, 1992, p. 100). But some things had not changed: to ask questions in the s/m bars of the 1970s was still to admit ignorance and invite rejection. Young and beautiful bottoms were easily accepted; those in other categories were not.

S/m organizations

All this began to change in the 1980s, when leatherfolk began to organize. There had been organizations before, like the small, closed, early bike clubs, and individual leathermen like Larry Townsend and John Preston were visible in the early gay liberation movement. But for the most part, the s/m community, which constituted itself through networks of personal connections, was a marginalized segment of the gay population. Gays and lesbians concerned with the straight world's perception of 'perverted' homosexuals were not sympathetic to doubly bent s/m people. Two groups founded in the early 1980s, Gay Male S/M Activists (GMSMA) and the Lesbian Sex Mafia (LSM) sought to change this. From the beginning their agendas included asserting the rights of people with s/m lifestyles to be part of gay liberation; in effect to promote the equality of leatherpeople within the gay community as a whole. This desire for visibility and acceptance ran parallel to the efforts made by ethnic minorities to secure equality within the movement; indeed it mirrored the agenda of gay organizations vis à vis straight society. As they worked through the 1980s towards this goal, gradually their efforts were rewarded: from 1987 on, Gay Pride marches have included large gay and lesbian s/m contingents (Stein, 1992, p. 145).[3]

Along with this new visibility of s/m practitioners in the lesbian and gay community came the rise of academic dialogues which attempted to disconnect s/m from the mechanisms of social oppression – torture, violence, etc. – which it seemingly embraced and glorified. In several interviews, Michel Foucault defended s/m along the line taken by leatherpeople, defining s/m as a game which creates a new organization of the body's pleasures. Leo Bersani contests that this stance merely confirms the eroticism inherent in the master/slave relationship, and therefore s/m 'may not survive an antifascist rethinking of power structures' (Bersani, 1987, p. 90). But if s/m practices do not seriously question the relationship between eroticism and power, leatherpeople have always been aware that it is their recognition of this linkage which constitutes their identity as radical outlaws, on the margins of both gay and straight societies. Their agitation for 'leather rights' and visibility in the gay community was a call for general awareness of this connection; to achieve this goal, the new s/m organizations adopted two crucial platforms: a policy of open membership and an emphasis on education.[4]

Open doors

From the beginning, GMSMA and LSM (as well as the many s/m groups that followed) declared their organizations open to all gay men and lesbians who were interested in the leather life (Stein, 1992, p. 151). Education came up in large part because of the need to 'teach these newcomers the ropes'. This has continued to be a priority for GMSMA in particular, which currently holds educational events several times a month in New York. Their seminars include sessions on s/m techniques such as bondage, abrasion, shaving, genitorture, flogging, boot blacking, rubber fetishism, temporary and permanent piercing, electrical torture, and workshops for novice tops and bottoms. Other groups such as S/M Gays in London hold similar activities. Their efforts in making the world of s/m accessible for first-timers have succeeded so well that GMSMA reports getting new members who are coming out as gay and into s/m simultaneously.

One element common to all of the s/m organizations of the 1980s and 1990s, whether gay, lesbian, straight, or pansexual, is the tripartite mantra which informs their activities: 'safe, sane, and consensual'. The first two elements of this coda were in place prior to the new wave of s/m organizations. When novice tops learned by apprenticeship to a more experienced master, safety was emphasized in their instruction (Magister, p. 99). As for 'sanity', the closed nature of leatherspace at that time aided the identification of dangerous players.[5] The third term, 'consensuality', has received a new emphasis in the s/m organizations. To ascertain what will constitute consensual behaviour, s/m organizations emphasize the importance of negotiation. The 1970s saw the development of handkerchief codes, which established immediately the likes and dislikes of potential partners.[6] In addition, the new organizations recommend in their training seminars lists of questions to ask before starting a scene. These include items such as whether the bottom wears contact lenses, has back problems, or is taking medication, and also encompass a new regime of multiple safewords, which enables a bottom to stop a scene any time he or she has something to talk over. S/m thus has become less a polarized expression of a master's power over a slave than a mutual exchange of power. This idea of mutuality also appears in *Urban Aboriginals*, Geoff Mains's unique anthropological study of the s/m scene from an insider's viewpoint. Mains mentions that the master/slave roles, traditionally more long-termed and invariant, had by the early 1980s become more fluid, so that the 'mutualists' had 'become a predominant element of the leather community' (1984, p. 33).

Previously, in Larry Townsend's 1972 underground classic, *The Leatherman's Handbook* negotiation was treated with definite ambivalence. 'Prolonged discussion can often break the relationship of the respective future roles', he wrote (1993, p. 137). Though there are obvious benefits to negotiation, it lessens the illusion of the top's total control over the bottom, which is integral to s/m. John Preston, whose fame during his three decades in the leathersex world was guaranteed by the phenomenal popularity of his novel, *Mr Benson*, comments: 'Now, there's a group in New York that has a Slave School and a Master School. Don't drool, these are the most anti-sexual things you can imagine' (1996, p. 184). Preston also objects to what he calls the 'over-codification' of the leathersex scene: for example, exclusionary dress codes at club events or 'the endless patter of silly bottoms talking about the "right way to do things"' (1992, pp. 215–216). Taken together, the increased emphasis on negotiation, the fluidity of the roles and the burgeoning opportunities to find out about all aspects of s/m have combined to form a new emphasis on techniques of inflicting pain and pleasure, which eschews the former desires for edging toward the depths of submission and mastery. This is what Preston finds unsexy: that the theme of *Mr Benson*, total domination by an all-knowing master of a willing slave whose trust runs beyond the need for verbal communication is less a part of the s/m scene than before.[7] The importance of communication notwithstanding, it would seem that when it comes to s/m, less negotiation may equal hotter role-play.

Submission or spirituality?

The s/m community has fanned the flames of its passion through a redirection of its energies: from submission to spirituality. We can see this in two attempted renamings of the very phrase sado/masochism: in the 1970s, some practitioners began to refer to s/m as 'sensuality and mutuality', while the late 1980s saw the phrase 'sex magic' coined (Thompson, 1992, p. xiv). Increasingly s/m people are using new-age terminology like 'personal transformation and growth' and 'healing' to describe their activities: 'Through erotic enactment and the emotional catharsis it provides, radical sexuality can be an empowering, soul making process' (Thompson, 1992, p. xviii). Some of the more extreme ideas of s/m spirituality connect s/m to the body modification and purification rituals of traditional and/or tribal societies.[8]

How may we contrast this new spiritual focus to the earlier s/m principle of total, willing submission? In his influential essay, 'Is the Rectum a Grave?' Leo Bersani argues that sexuality (as we now constitute it) is identical to masochism. He argues that sexual pleasure involves a 'shattering of the psychic structures themselves that are the precondition for the very establishment of a relation to others' (1987, p. 217). Fear of this occurrence leads people to attempt to constitute sex as a nurturing, loving event rather than one that is intrinsically 'violent' to the human organism. The leatherpeople who follow the former trend attempt to educate an ignorant public about the non-violent nature of s/m practices. This approach has yet to bear fruit: witness the controversy sparked in 1989 by the retrospective of Robert Mapplethorpe's photographs, which included some s/m images. Obscenity charges were filed against the Cincinnati Contemporary Arts Center. Senator from North Carolina Jesse Helms agitated to deny funding to 'obscene' works of art; and the debates quickly escalated from s/m to all art that called attention to socially marginalized groups and lifestyles.[9]

Mapplethorpe's photography has been criticized on grounds of racism[10] as well as obscenity. In addition, his photographs have been decried by detractors in the art world as lifeless, cold, and static (Morrisroe, 1995, p. 193). Even Nick, a well-known s/m top who was the subject of several photographs said 'Robert's pictures always struck me as an art-sified version of S/M. They're not like photographs snapped during a scene at all' (Morrisroe, 1995, p. 191). Mapplethorpe's photographs certainly have little relation to those who would connect s/m to new-age concepts like self-healing or growth, but they do have a distinct connection to sub-mission-based s/m, for his view of sex and the act of photographing strongly echo Bersani: 'When I have sex with someone I forget who I am. For a minute I even forget I'm human. It's the same thing when I'm behind a camera. I forget I exist' (Morrisroe, 1995, p. 193).

According to French theorist Jean-François Lyotard, the project of avant-garde art is to disturb and shock our consciousness, 'undoing the presumption of the mind with respect to time', to the point of dismantling it in a way similar to Bersani's characterization of sexuality (1989, p. 211). The shock of seeing Mapplethorpe's photographs then, has something in common with the effect s/m can have, in which the self willingly submits to an experience that undoes its organization. According to Lyotard, in view-ing avant-garde art the 'will is defeated'. The sublime pleasure which results stems from this privation. This is the potential which submission – whether to avant-garde art or s/m play – has for the human subject. The journey which Lyotard describes is not a return ticket to greater health and sanity, but an 'agitation' which sustains in a timeless moment conscious-ness undone. During s/m, the onslaught of intense pain, which can trigger the sublime pleasure of self-dissolution, might indeed result in feelings of well-being or even 'empowerment', but this is an irony that lies deep at the heart of s/m. It may well, indeed, be a paradox that constitutes it.

Lesbian-feminism and s/m

Simone de Beauvoir wrote a feminist critique of misinterpretations of the life and work of the Marquis de Sade in 1966 ('Must We Burn Sade?'), but it was not until the early 1970s that essays on lesbian s/m by practitioners began to appear in such publications as *Echo of Sappho* and *Gay Commu-nity News*. The first book on lesbian s/m was *What Colour is Your Handkerchief?* But it was the publication of the book, *Coming to Power: Writings and Graphics on Lesbian S/M*, in 1982 that introduced a lexicon of lesbian sadomasochism to a wider audience and into a feminist context. This pro-s/m anthology was followed shortly by the anthology *Against Sadomasochism: A Radical Feminist Analysis* (1982). Together, these publications encapsulated a debate that has continued into the present. Many radical feminists and some lesbians denounced s/m sexuality as 'male-identified', arguing that women who advocated or participated in such practices had internalized the misogyny of the dominant hetero-patri-archal culture and were not only abusing themselves but also reinstating a sexual ethic that degraded all women. Proponents of lesbian sado-masochism rebutted this argument in a number of ways, often referring to the 'theatrical' nature of s/m (an argument that goes back at least as far as Theodor Reik's massive study *Masochism in Modern Man*, published in 1941), or appealing for tolerance from other feminists by arguing that it was a sexual practice that engaged in a process of healing the wounds left over from prior abuses. Other proponents took a libertarian approach, appealing to the rights of individuals to engage in any behaviour as long as it was 'safe, sane, and consensual'.

Historical background

The contentiousness of this issue might be traced back to the beginnings of the contemporary feminist movement. As lesbians became more open and vocal members of feminist communities, the mainstream, liberal fem-inist movement, represented by such organizations as the American National Organization of Women (NOW) began to yield a bit in their posi-tion that lesbians were a threat to feminism. After failing to make lesbians, especially butch lesbians, conform to the liberal standards of appearance and behaviour that liberal feminists thought necessary to gain political and economic power, there began to be a shift toward marking lesbians as the 'sign' of the 'true feminist'. Katie King wrote about this phenomenon in which lesbians became feminism's 'magical sign', and radical feminists began to reify lesbians as *the* quintessential feminist. The legendary slogan, attributed to Ti-Grace Atkinson, who wrote openly against lesbian s/m, *feminism is the theory, lesbianism is the practice*, generated even more contro-versy. Heterosexual feminists felt excluded from the practice of feminism (conflated with the *real* of feminism) and lesbians became burdened with the responsibility of upholding feminism's ethical high ground. Radical les-bians, who did not experience the latter as a burden, invented the concept of the *realesbian*, an entity that was made within these debates *as if* it were *already* born. Early radical feminists such as Susan Griffin were particu-larly outspoken in making an alliance between women and nature, which other feminists objected to on the grounds that this left women allied with primary matter and processes and implicitly incapable of making the secondary revisions necessary for the construction of culture. Because lesbian was then becoming the sign that signified women's 'essence' in radical feminist discourse, depictions of lesbian sexuality tended toward equations between sexual practices and 'natural' acts – such as blossoming flowers, waterfalls, or drifting clouds. A history of pathologizing lesbians for their sexual proclivities, largely inherited from late nineteenth and early twentieth-century sexological discourse, led many lesbian-feminists to downplay or deny that sex, as such, was a very important part of what gave lesbians a particular identity. Hence lesbian identity became more important than lesbian sexual practices, at least in mainstream feminist accounts. This legacy has left a very powerful trace up to the present day, not only on popular notions of what lesbians do sexually but also on lesbians themselves, many of whom have to a large degree continued to labour under the ways in which these historical identities have constrained what they can say about their sexual desires and practices.

Some pro-s/m pioneers

The two most prominent and consistent American spokespeople for lesbian s/m have been Pat Califia and Gayle Rubin, whose numerous books and articles have created a canon of lesbian s/m work in their own right. Califia's fiction, in addition to her book, *The Lesbian S/M Safety Manual*, have given lesbian s/m a high profile within and outside American feminist circles. Rubin's article 'The Leather Menace: Comments on Politics and S/M', shied the discourse away from what had primarily been personal testimony towards a nuanced critical/intellectual/political analysis of the lesbian s/m controversy. Her article led the way for other American and British writers to defend lesbian s/m. Carole S. Vance's edited anthology, *Pleasure and Danger: Exploring Female Sexuality* and issue No. 3 of the journal *Heresies* (1981) added considerable knowledge to lesbian sexual practices that had remained partially secret or hidden. *Out the Other Side*, an anthology published in 1989, contained an article by Susan Ardill and Sue O'Sullivan, 'Upsetting the Applecart: Difference, Desire, and Lesbian Sado-Masochism', that discussed the s/m debates in Great Britain. In America s/m was beginning to get picked up as a hot issue for the new Fundamentalist Christian Right to add to their growing list of activities that contradicted the notion of 'family values'.

S/m and academic discourse

As Lesbian and Gay Studies and Queer Theory have begun to gain some ground in academic circles, lesbian scholars have begun to publish a wide array of articles discussing this history and how it was made. However, within this new, more open and prolific discourse, the older battlelines to a large extent remain drawn. In 1993, for example, a book entitled *Unleashing Feminism* was published, which was a second collection of essays arguing that there was no place for lesbian s/m within the 'gay nineties'. Most of these articles made analogies between lesbian s/m and historical incidents that created massive global trauma – such as the Holocaust – or more recent incidents that were guaranteed to win the sympathies of almost anyone who was even vaguely aligned with what is loosely thought of as 'leftist' or progressive politics in America. Feminists have had a very difficult time making the simple and obvious argument that when a woman says 'No' she means 'No'. In a hetero-patriarchal culture that has, in what is often the *best* case scenario, configured 'women' as people who do not or cannot always know what they desire or even *if* they desire certain sexual activities, while at worst, a culture that has simply disregarded what women desire in favour of men's desires, one can see how lesbian s/m could appear as very threatening since it allows for such fantasies in which sexual activities take place over and against a woman's vocalized negative response.

However, one of the things that has created such confusion about lesbian s/m is the assumption that fantasy and reality are consonant. At the same time, to argue that they are entirely disjunctive also fails to account for the subtleties of their relationship. What lesbian s/m sexuality strives to achieve, among other things, is the power of women to act out their sexual fantasies, however they may have been constructed, within the confines of an exchange that is negotiated in advance and allows for each partner to trust that her psychic, emotional, and physical boundaries will be respected within the sexual scene without restricting them in advance on the basis of any ideological system, including liberal or radical feminism.

Within academic gay and lesbian studies, a number of articles have been written in the last few years that address these issues more openly. However, they tend to shy away from discussing actual sexual practices between women, focusing instead on identity constructions and on the need to think gender and sexuality as separate though intersecting discourses. There remains then a rather large gap between publications such as Califia's *The Second Coming*, and other anthologies that contain a mixture of s/m fantasies and personal testimonies, or collections of lesbian photography, notably the recent Cassell anthology *Nothing But The Girl: The Blatant Lesbian Image*, and academic feminist discussions of s/m sexuality, which usually appear as chapters in books or articles in scholarly journals. Such separation is often articulated as a practice/theory split. It is due, in large part I think, to a prohibition (even if unspoken) against discussing sexuality in graphic terms within the 'genteel' space of academia. In America, this is fuelled even more so by the heatedness of the sexuality and pornography debates and the threats against academia that have come from the New Right for allowing the discourse of *any* sexualities to have entered the pristine walls of higher education.

Racial and ethnic differences: problems in nomination

No discussion of s/m, however brief and cursory, can overlook the ways in which racial and ethnic differences also make this topic a site of contention. The language of s/m sexuality sometimes uses expressions such as 'master' or 'mistress' and 'slave', which has obvious negative connotations, particularly within North American culture. In addition, some s/m practitioners use imagery and emblems that are considered to be fascist or neo-fascist, and thus allude to the Holocaust. This is probably the most vexed area of concern both outside and inside s/m subcultures. Many practitioners within s/m subcultures disassociate themselves from such iconography; others argue that *resemblance* is mistaken here for mimesis, or reproduction, and that such imagery is not a recollection of a historical past, but a reworking without forgetting an historical present.

Switching: object or practice?

Finally, s/m is often a site of contestation because it tends to disrupt gender differences. Some lesbians and gay men engage in sexual play with members of the 'opposite' gender, while at the same time refusing to relinquish their identity claims as lesbian and gay. S/m, then, shifts the context of the gender/sexuality debates at large from a discourse that has been primarily *object*-oriented to one that is *practice*-oriented. The recently-published volume of fiction, *Switchhitters* (Queen and Schimel, 1996), in which gay men write their lesbian fantasies and *vice versa* typifies this trend. Perhaps even more volatilely, especially among women, lesbians have recently become more vocal about 'daddy',[11] and to a lesser extent, 'mommy' fantasies, which brings up the spectre of incest, an issue that has received a great deal of play in the debates about trauma and memory and reawakens the feminist struggle to counter Freud's renunciation of the reality of incest.

Because of its 'underground' history, lesbian and gay s/m has become circulated in the dominant discourse as a 'secret', and has thus become a lightning rod for projective identifications and disidentifications. As more writings and graphics of lesbian and gay s/m become available, controversies about its place in lesbian and gay liberation movements multiply. While some feminists are now arguing that s/m is trendy, others continue to argue vehemently that it is a virtually apocalyptic practice that could bring down the whole foundation of feminist movements. Much is left to be said about why and how s/m has come to occupy this peculiar place in cultural consciousness. Much more, perhaps, is to be said about how the unconscious of both cultures and individuals is at once arrestingly drawn to s/m sexuality while rather obsessively denouncing it.[12] Meanwhile, lesbian and gay s/m practitioners continue to develop its possibilities, build networks for communication, theorize these practices, and enjoy its pleasures.

Notes

1. See Hart's *Fatal Women* (1994) for a theory of the ways in which lesbian sexuality has been historically constructed as criminal *a priori*.
2. In the 1970s when he was researching *States of Desire*, Edmund White was reportedly amazed at the amount of s/m he found in rural America (Preston, 'What You Learn', 1996, p. 186).
3. This was not without considerable difficulties. In the early 1980s, s/m gays were blamed for AIDS by some within the gay community in a parallel to straight society's scapegoating of homosexuals in general (Rojes, 1992, p. 182).
4. Testimony to the difficulties newcomers had in entering the closed s/m world of the time is the fact that GMSMA was founded by outsiders to the s/m scene (Stein, 1992, p. 149).
5. It may be a bit more difficult to do so now: the publication in *The Village Voice* of an article entitled 'Dangerous Top' hopefully marked the end of a decade-long reign of abuse by a nonconsensual s/m top. Flyers circulated in areas near leather bars and postings to Internet s/m newsgroups were crucial to building community awareness of his activities.
6. A safe word is a previously agreed upon code used (by the bottom usually) to

temporarily stop the action of an s/m scene. Location and colours of handkerchiefs worn in various positions signify the precise desires of the wearer.

7. Other writers in the scene support his view. Pat Califia (1992) says about *Mr Benson*: 'I am curious about why so few of us even come close to living that fantasy' (*Leatherfolk*, p. 222).

8. For example, re-enactments of the Native American Sun Dance or 'ball dancing', which is taken from Hindu Sadhu religious rituals (Thompson, 'Black Leather', 1992, pp. 162–65).

9. For historical accounts of the Mapplethorpe controversy see Wendy Steiner, *The Scandal of Pleasure: Art in the Age of Fundamentalism*. Chicago: University of Chicago Press, 1995; and Lisa Duggan and Nan Hunter, *Sex Wars: Sexual Dissent and Political Culture*. New York: Routledge, 1995.

10. See Kobena Mercer, 'Skin Head, Sex Thing', in Bad Object Choices (ed.), *How Do I Look? Queer Film and Video*. Seattle: Bay Press, 1991, pp. 169–210.

11. See Pat Califia's anthology of s/m fiction, *Doing It For Daddy* (1994), for an example of these fantasy formations.

12. I have discussed all of the above issues at greater length in my book, *Between the Body and the Flesh: Performing Sadomasochism*. New York: Columbia University Press, 1997.

References

Ardill, Susan, and O'Sullivan, Sue, 'Upsetting the Applecart: Difference, Desire, and Lesbian Sadomasochism', in Christian McEwan and Sue O'Sullivan (eds), *Out the Other Side*, Freedom, CA: Crossing Press, 1989, pp. 122–44.

Atkinson, Ti-Grace, 'Why I'm Against SM Liberation', in *Majority Report*. 1976, pp. 90–92.

Bersani, Leo, 'Is the Rectum a Grave?', in Douglas Crimp (ed.), *AIDS: Cultural Analysis, Cultural Activism*, Cambridge, Massachusetts and London: The MIT Press, 1991, pp. 197–222.

Bright, Susie, and Posener, Jill, *Nothing But the Girl: The Blatant Lesbian Image*. New York: Freedom Editions, 1996.

Califia, Pat, *Doing It for Daddy: Short and Sexy Fiction About a Very Forbidden Fantasy*. Boston: Alyson, 1994.

Califia, Pat, *The Lesbian S/M Safety Manual*. Boston: Lace Publications, 1988.

Califia, Pat, 'The Limits of the S/M Relationship, or Mr Benson Doesn't Live Here Anymore', in Mark Thompson (ed.), *Leatherfolk: Radical Sex, People, Politics and Practice*, Boston: Alyson, 1992, pp. 221–33.

de Beauvoir, Simone de, 'Must We Burn Sade?', introduction to *The Marquis de Sade: The 120 Days of Sodom and Other Writings*, (eds and trans. Austryn Wainhouse and Richard Seaver). New York: Grove Weidenfeld, 1966, pp. 3–64.

Deleuze, Gilles, 'The Language of Sade and Masoch', in *Coldness and Cruelty*, New York: ZoneBooks, 1989, p. 15.

Hart, Lynda, *Between the Body and the Flesh: Performing Sadomasochism*. New York: Columbia University Press, 1997.

Hart, Lynda, *Fatal Women: Lesbian Sexuality and the Mark of Aggression*. Princeton: Princeton University Press and Routledge, 1994.

Heresies. 'The Sex Issue', Vol. 12, No. 3, 1981.

Hooven, F. Valentine III, *Tom of Finland: His Life and Times*. New York: St Martin's Press, 1993.

King, Katie, 'The Situation of Lesbianism as Feminism's Magical Sign: Contests for Meaning and the U.S. Women's Movement, 1968–1972', in *Communication*, Vol. 9, 1986, pp. 65–91.

Lyotard, Jean-François, *The Lyotard Reader* (Andrew Benjamin ed.). Oxford: Basil Blackwell, 1989.

Magister, Thom, 'One Among Many: The Seduction and Training of a Leatherman', in Mark Thompson (ed.), *Leatherfolk*, Boston: Alyson, 1992, pp. 91–106.

Mains, Geoff, *Urban Aboriginals: A Celebration of Leathersexuality*. San Francisco: Gay Sunshine Press, 1984.

Morrisroe, Patricia, *Mapplethorpe: A Biography*. New York: Random House, 1995.

Preston, John, 'What Happened?', in Mark Thompson (ed.), *Leatherfolk*, Boston: Alyson, 1992, pp. 210–21.

Preston, John, 'What You Learn After 30 Years of S/M', in Michael Bronski, *Taking Liberties: Gay Men's Essays on Politics, Culture and Sex*, New York: Masquerade Books, 1996, pp. 175–87.

Queen, Carol, and Schimel, Lawrence, *Switchhitters*. Pittsburgh, Pennsylvania: Cleis Press, 1996.

Reik, Theodor, *Masochism in Modern Man*, (trans. Margaret H. Beigel). New York: Farrar, Strauss, 1941.

Reti, Irene (ed.), *Unleashing Feminism: Critiquing Lesbian Sadomasochism in the Gay Nineties*. Santa Cruz: Her Books, 1993.

Rubin, Gayle, 'The Leather Menace: Comments on Politics and S/M', in *Coming to Power*. Boston: Alyson, 1981, pp. 192–227.

Samois (eds), *Coming to Power: Writings and Graphics on Lesbian S/M*. Boston: Alyson, 1982.

Samois, *What Color is Your Handkerchief?* Berkeley, CA., 1976.

Stein, David, 'S/M's Copernican Revolution: From a Closed World to an Infinite Universe', in Mark Thompson (ed.), *Leatherfolk*, Boston: Alyson, 1992, pp. 142–57.

Thompson, Mark (ed.), *Leatherfolk: Radical Sex, People, Politics and Practice*. Boston: Alyson, 1992.

Townsend, Larry, *The Original Leatherman's Handbook*. Introduction by John Preston. Los Angeles: LT Publications, 1993.

V. Don, 'Old S/M New York', Online. Newslink. Internet: Gay Male S/M Activists, 1996. http:// www.ability,net/gmsma/walking_tour.html

Vance, Carole S. (ed.), *Pleasure and Danger: Exploring Female Sexuality*. Boston: Routledge, 1982.

Further reading

Bataille, Georges, *Eroticism: Death and Sensuality*. (trans. Mary Dalwood). San Francisco: City Lights Books, 1986.

Bersani, Leo, *Homos*. Cambridge, MA: Harvard University Press, 1996.

Califia, Pat, and Sweeney, Robin (eds), *The Second Coming: A Leatherdyke Reader*. Los Angeles, CA.: Alyson, 1996.

Linden, Robin *et al.*, *Against Sadomasochism: A Radical Feminist Analysis*. East Palo Alto: Frog in the Well Press, 1982.

Peraldi, François, 'Polysexuality', in *Semitotext(e)*, Vol. 10, 1981. New York: Semiotext(e), 1995.

Preston, John, *Mr Benson*. New York: Badboy, 1992.

Ricardo, Jack, (ed.) *Leathermen Speak Out: An Anthology on Leathersex*. San Francisco: Leyland Publications 1991.

Sedgwick, Eve Kosofsky, 'A Poem is Being Written', in her *Tendencies*, Durham, N.C.: Duke University Press, 1993.

Silverman, Kaja, *Male Subjectivity at the Margins*. New York: Routledge, 1992.

Thompson, Bill, *Sadomasochism: Painful Pleasure or Pleasurable Play?* New York: Cassell, 1995.

Townsend, Larry, *The Leatherman's Handbook II*. 2nd edn. New York: Carlyle Communications, 1989.

Weinberg, Thomas and Levi Kamel, G. W. (eds), *S and M: Studies in Sadomasochism*. New York: Prometheus Books, 1983.

24

Pathologizing Sexual Bodies

Cath Sharrock

THE AIDS EPIDEMIC has unleashed another epidemic: the patholo-gizing of the male homosexual as both site and carrier of disease. In this chapter I am going to review the work of some recent gay theorists, who have analysed the ways in which AIDS has led to a homophobic iden-tification between disease and homosexuality. I want also to give a history to this identification in order to explore two key issues. First, I will be con-sidering how representations of AIDS seem to be reactivating earlier homophobic paradigms, specifically, eighteenth-century paramedical accounts of homosexualities – both male and female. Secondly, by insert-ing the historical representation of lesbianism into this equation, I want to broaden our historical understanding of this pathologizing process. As I move between the past and the present I am not trying to argue for a trans-historical patterning, but to point, instead, to moments of historical similarities that make it all the more important that we disrupt, by interro-gating, the pathologizing of homosexualities.

I need to begin by focusing upon a politically significant, and popularly used misnomer. Simon Watney argues that it is 'singularly misleading and inappropriate' to speak of AIDS as a disease and to invoke, as many have done, plague metaphors, 'for the simple reason that HIV is *not* contagious' (Watney, 1996, p. 238). Unlike earlier plagues, such as cholera and the Black Death, there are, he argues, preventative methods available to limit the spread of the HIV virus and AIDS and we do not find quarantine actu-ally being used in these cases, as they had been before. It is the popular misconception of AIDS as a 'contagious disease' that is responsible, in part, for the metaphor of homosexuality *as* a contagious disease to which I want now to draw attention. The very phrase, 'gay plague', which first became current in the early 1980s, identifies AIDS as if it were somehow intrinsic to homosexuality. Metaphorically this phrase allows for an identi-fication of homosexuality as itself a 'plague', against which the 'healthy' (heterosexual) must be protected. In thinking in terms of illness as metaphor, I am invoking Susan Sontag's work and, specifically, her understanding of plague as 'the principal metaphor by which the AIDS epidemic is understood' (Sontag, 1988, p. 44). Sontag is herself drawing upon the social anthropologist, Mary Douglas' structuralist reading of concepts of pollution in *Purity and Danger* (1966). Douglas' observation that a polluting person is always thought of as being wrong is inverted by Sontag to produce the following equation: 'a person judged to be wrong is regarded as, at least potentially, a source of pollution' (Sontag, 1988, p. 48). The person who is in the 'wrong' therefore threatens both to pollute the person who is in the 'right' and to disavow their claims to such propriety. If we translate these ideas back into the metaphorical terrain of the 'gay plague' we can begin to understand the political investment at stake in representing homosexuality as a polluting illness.

Leo Bersani offers a suggestive mode of analysing the politically encoded discourse that frames HIV and AIDS:

> The persecuting of children or of heterosexuals with AIDS (or who have tested positive for HIV) is particularly striking in view of the popular description of such people as 'innocent victims'. It is as if gay men's 'guilt' were the real agent of infection. (Bersani, 1991, pp. 209–10)

The 'innocent victims' here have become the 'wronged' party, as it were, their 'innocence' (or 'right') corrupted by the 'guilty' infection of homosexuality into them. This passage witnesses both a clinical breaking down of boundaries and a symbolic and defensive reconstruction of them. On a clinical level, the physical bodies of those who are presumed not to be sexually active – children – and of those who are thought to be immune to the improprieties of homosexual behaviour – heterosexuals – have become infected with the illness that supposedly links them with homosexuals. Symbolically, however, their status as 'innocent victims' protects them from the assumed 'guilt' of those people who are deemed the willing agents of their own infection: homosexuals. The dual process at play in this passage alerts us to an anxious desire to distance the non-homosexual community from an illness that is seen to be symptomatic of the 'guilt', the culpability of being gay. As Jan Zita Grover observes: 'AIDS is not simply a physical malady; it is also an artifact of social and sexual transgression, violated taboo, fractured identity – political and personal projections'

(Grover, 1991, p. 18). The moral distinction between 'innocent victims' and 'guilty' agents of infection legitimizes homophobia as an ethical imperative. Socially unacceptable forms of sexual behaviour are semantically refashioned as socially destructive modes of being. According to this semantic logic the state has a duty to its 'healthy' (heterosexual) subjects to protect them from the contagious impact of those 'unhealthy' (homosexual) non-subjects who threaten the body-politic with disease.

If the body of the 'innocent victim' can metaphorically displace the 'guilt' for his/her own illness upon the homosexual, the body of the gay man, on the other hand, is forced to bear the mark, indeed the stigmata, of his own transgressive and sinful actions. Even though AIDS is not, of course, exclusive to the gay community, this way of ethically interpreting it suggests that it is still thought of as being somehow peculiarly the *fault* of gay people. Although the earliest, 1981, acronym used to label this illness, GRID (Gay-related immunodeficiency), was replaced a year later by AIDS (acquired immune deficiency syndrome) when research found non-gay people falling ill with the same symptoms, it is as if the 'emergent' moment of GRID cannot avoid framing subsequent understandings of AIDS. I am here drawing upon Simon Watney's interpretation of the way in which homosexuality has been caught within what we might term a contagious discourse of blame, which 'resolutely insists that the point of emergence of the virus should be identified as its *cause*'. He continues:

> Epidemiology is thus replaced by a moral etiology of disease that can only conceive homosexual desire within a medicalized metaphor of contagion. Reading AIDS as the outward and visible sign of an imagined depravity of will, AIDS commentary duly returns us to a premodern vision of the body, according to which heresy and sin are held to be scored in the features of their voluntary subjects by punitive and admonitory manifestations of disease. (Watney, 1993, p. 204)

Here we find the conflation of homosexuality with contagion and the rhetoric of sinfulness surrounding it being given a specifically premodern inflection. Watney's sense of the impropriety of imposing historically anachronistic plague metaphors upon AIDS is reinforced by his understanding that such a representation leads, inevitably, to the equally inaccurate and politically problematic framing of homosexual desire as contagion.

According to Watney, one way of reading the representation of people with AIDS from an historicized perspective is by comparison with the treatment of nineteenth-century female prostitutes who contracted syphilis (Watney, 1987, pp. 33–4). Such a model renders one alert to the process by which a person with a sexually transmitted disease is held responsible for their own malaise, with the body breaking out into the symptoms which brand them sexually transgressive. Leo Bersani, (1991) Dennis Altman (1986) and Sander L. Gilman (1991) also discuss the historical parallels between the discourse around AIDS and syphilis, with Gilman stressing the defensive strategy that comes into play in response to the invasive threat posed by a perceived infectious disease: 'The desire to locate the origin of a disease is the desire to be assured that we are not at fault, that we have been invaded from without, polluted by some external agent' (Gilman, 1991, p. 100). So, within the nineteenth-century British context of colonial expansion and black slavery, the 'origin' of syphilis is conveniently construed as the 'other', the African. Gilman updates this pattern by arguing that within the 1980s AIDS was construed as an 'African' or 'Haitian' disease (Gilman, 1991, p. 100).[1]

We have seen how the defensive structuring of 'healthy' self and 'infectious' other also lends itself to the heterosexist paradigm which seeks to displace both the cause and the 'guilty' manifestation of AIDS onto the homosexual. I want now to engage with the playing out of this homophobic paradigm at an earlier period of British history: the eighteenth century. In so doing I am, in part, challenging Watney's argument that the identification of AIDS with plague and contagion takes us back to a 'premodern' perspective. I agree with him that the rhetoric of sinfulness invoked by plague mentalities is distinctly premodern, as it articulates a moral schema dominated by religious notions of sin and retribution. However, both the condemnatory linking of 'emergence' and 'cause' and the identification of homosexuality as a contagious disease, through which the bodily malaise of the victim is deemed to mark his (and her) socio-sexual transgression are not peculiarly premodern. In this section of the essay I want to show how paramedical and moral discourses on both male and female homosexuality in the eighteenth century frame the homosexual as a source of contagion. This form of representation is, in many ways, strikingly akin to that of both female prostitutes with syphilis in the nineteenth century and people with HIV and/or AIDS from the 1980s onwards.

When talking of homosexuality, however, one must be careful not to impose a later model of sexuality upon an earlier one. Both the terms, homosexual and lesbian, only began to be used in the late nineteenth century. This does not mean, of course, that same-sex desire came into being only when the label was invented to define it. Instead, it draws our attention to the different ways in which sexuality – be it hetero, bi, or homo – are figured according to the historical moment. Sexuality, as Michel Foucault understands it, is not 'a natural given' that remains the same throughout history and in all cultures, but 'a historical construct', discursively produced according to what any historical period understood, and, indeed, wanted to be understood of sexuality (Foucault, 1978, p. 105). With this in mind, we need to approach the eighteenth century with its own discursive formulations of sexuality in mind.

A number of historians of sexuality understand the eighteenth century to mark a transitional period in the conceptualization of what we now term homosexuality. According to Randolph Trumbach, it is at this point that the homosexual as a distinct identity-type began to emerge. The idea that a man might have sex exclusively with other men, rather than moving between male and female partners, is what distinguishes these 'mollies', as they were called, from their Renaissance precursors.[2] 'Mollies' were thought of as being effeminate, whereas their female counterparts, 'Tommies' or 'Sapphists', were, unsurprisingly, understood to be rather masculine in their physique and deportment.[3] Trumbach maintains that their sexual orientation tended not to be explained away as much as it had been before by recourse to physiological theories (hermaphroditism, for example), but according to more modern criteria: 'the result of the corruption of an individual's mind that had occurred in early experience' (Trumbach, 1991, p. 112). My understanding of this period, on the other hand, suggests a coming together of these two diagnostic readings: physiological predeterminism joins with the 'corruption' of experience to produce a threatening image of contagious sexual deviance.

Paramedical treatises on venereal disease in the eighteenth century are littered with condemnatory descriptions of the mal-effects of both male and female homosexuality. Humphrey Nettle's poetic satire, *Sodom and Onan* (1772) wishes upon 'B——rs' (those shamefully, nameless men) the 'rank poison' of venereal disease (p. 22). Later his polite refusal to sanction an act by specifically naming it, leads to his defining male homosexuality as 'this growing ill' (p. 23). Such a circumlocution has the effect of textually producing the thing that he wishes to be realized: the association of that dreadful thing with contagion. The text invites the venereal punishment both literally to impede sexual activity and metaphorically to disavow the propriety of the activity itself. Significantly, Nettle's wishes had, in fact already come true, as earlier key texts, such as John Marten's *A Treatise of all the Degrees and Symptoms of the Venereal Disease* (1708), confidently pronounce that 'B——ry' (again!) results in venereal infection. Here the refusal to write the word is justified in terms that doubly banish the sexually transgressive subject from the terrain of socio-textual approval. As 'it's not fit to be named', so 'one would think, [it] would not be practis'd in a Christian Country. . .' (p. 68). The reference to Christianity does not call upon the rhetoric of 'sinfulness', but is, instead relying upon a hierarchical binary of good and healthy Christian versus bad and diseased non-Christian. The text produces the contagious identification of homosexuality in order to relegate it to the realms of the undesirable 'Other'.

Such a pattern of displacement is regularly repeated in treatises concerned specifically with perceived sexually deviant practices. Here we find a double play upon the idea of infection. Sodomy is always presented as a foreign infection; an imported 'unnatural vice' that threatens to corrupt those upright English subjects who would not otherwise have thought of doing such a thing. Like infected merchandize and cargo, the known means of spreading plague (again, an unhealthy, because foreign import), the 'emergence' and 'cause' of homosexuality is the non-Englishman, whose physical malaise symptomatically registers his own 'guilty' sexual practice. In the anonymous *Plain Reasons for the Growth of Sodomy in England* (1728), homosexuality is specifically defined as a 'Contagion' imported from Italy: 'the *Mother* and *Nurse* of Sodomy' (p. 12). English aristocrats are said to have learned sodomitical behaviour from the Italians and this is held, in part, responsible for their physiological deterioration into 'enervated effeminate Animal[s]'.[4] A textual digression into the far reaches of history then, analogously, expands the threat that effeminate homosexuality poses: '*Rome* . . . sank in Honour and Success, as it rose in *luxury* and *Effeminacy*, they had Women Singers and Eunuchs from *Asia*, at a vast Price: which so softened their Youth, they quite lost the Spirit of Man-hood, and with it their Empire' (p. 18). Given that by 1728, when this text was written, England was busy establishing itself as the dominant colonial power in Europe, it is difficult not to read this passage as expressing an encoded anxiety about the possible collapse of its colonial strength into the weakness of its effeminate subjects. What is also striking about this passage is that can be read as invoking, by inversion, the classic colonial fear of 'going native'. The state takes into itself those attributes that it perceives to be the hall mark of the 'Other'. Obviously, I am not suggesting that the text is primarily concerned with colonialism, but rather that it appropriates a fear of contagion from the colonialist paradigm in order to register an anxiety about the emasculation of the nation-state.[5] By adopting effeminate foreign characteristics the self-identification of England as a masculinist and thus powerful state is disrupted. The mimetic expression of homosexuality in England textually figures the debilitating effects of a spreading and infectious sexual disease as if it were also the cause of national malaise. These displacement tactics, at once locating the source of infection outside the 'healthy' (heterosexual) functioning of the state and yet also textually tracing the invasive movement of the 'unhealthy' (homosexual) into itself resonate with the fear of the 'polluting' homosexual later discursively constructed in relation to HIV and AIDS.

The textual identification between what we now term lesbianism and contagion are often more indirect than those just explored in relation to gay men. Paramedical representations of lesbianism are most frequently to be found in treatises on hermaphroditism in the eighteenth century.[6] The female hermaphrodite is defined as one who has an unusually large clitoris. It is because the woman is endowed with an extended clitoris that she is said both to desire another women and thought capable of having sexual intercourse with her. In this way, the texts are trying to explain away such sexual practices as being symptomatic of physiological abnormality. As the physique of the woman is perceived to be monstrous, so too is her sexual desire. Medical discourse steps in to legitimize the heterosexist values of the society. The rhetoric of contagion is not to be found in these texts. However, we can trace an intertextual movement between discourses on hermaphroditism and masturbation, in particular, which transforms the hermaphroditic lesbian body into the abused product of her own illicit sexual desire. It is here that we can also find the identification of lesbianism with contagion.

An early anti-masturbation treatise, *Onania* (1708/9) interlinks masturbatory and hermaphroditic theories:

> It is certain that in some Women, especially those who are very salacious, and have much abused themselves with SELF-Pollution, the *Clitoris* is so vastly extended, that, upon its thrusting out of the passage, it is mistaken for a *Penis*; such have been called . . . *Tribades* and accounted *Hermaphrodites*, because . . . they have been able to perform the Actions of Men with other Women. (p. 195)

This passage is open to many different readings. Within an intertextual frame, as we shall see, it both constructs the lesbian as one whose sexuality can become infectious and betrays the reasons why such a contagious effect is feared and so discursively 'policed', to use Foucault's phrase (Foucault, 1978). The infectious potential of 'SELF-Pollution', or masturbation, is discussed both in this text and others on the same subject. *Onania* warns that masturbation is often a form of taught behaviour that is most frequently to be practised in the close community of schools. Such activity, spreading between the girls, symptomatically produces lesbianism as its contagious effect: the abused clitoris is unnaturally elongated and leads to the women's 'perform[ing] the Actions of Men with other Women'. A later French treatise against masturbation, Tissot's *Onanism* (1766), which was to run into numerous translated English editions in the eighteenth century alone, similarly refigures the masturbatory as the lesbian act. The so called '*Clitorical*' women in this text are said to be traceable back to Sappho of Lesbos. These women, upon whom 'Nature has been pleased to bestow a semi-resemblance to men' are found to have 'seized upon the functions of virility' in their sexual relations with each other (p. 46). Again they were initiated into 'this Habit' through the mimetic and, in this way, contagious example of servant maids in their households; a cross-class pollution adding further anxieties to this transaction. The anti-social habit of masturbation infectiously gives rise to the socially unacceptable practice of lesbianism.

The representation of lesbian sex as a simulation of heterosexual intercourse in these texts is the moment at which we can locate an anxiety about the possible import of lesbianism itself, which renders its contagious nature so worrying to the paramedical writers. The women 'perform the Actions of Men with other Women' and 'seize the functions of virility'. On the one hand, the idea of 'performance', in particular, suggests the classic (and persistent) understanding of lesbian sex as an apeing of the real thing: heterosexual intercourse. On the other hand, if one can 'perform' this act, what might this suggest about the distinction between the real (heterosexual) and the performed (lesbian) act? I am thinking here about Judith Butler's understanding of the 'performative' and of her analysis of the production of both heterosexualized gender difference and heterosexuality itself. Her interpretation of drag is helpful:

> it seems there is no original or primary gender that drag imitates, but *gender is a kind of imitation for which there is no original*; in fact it is a kind of imitation that produces the very notion of the original as an *effect* and

consequence of the imitation itself. In other words, the naturalistic effects of heterosexualized genders are produced through imitative strategies; what they imitate is a phantasmatic ideal of heterosexual identity, one that is produced by the imitation as its effect. In this sense the 'reality' of heterosexual identities is performatively constituted through an imitation that sets itself up as the origin and the ground of all imitations. In other words, heterosexuality is always in the process of imitating and approximating its own phantasmatic idealization of itself – *and failing*. (Butler, 1991, p. 21)

According to Butler, then, the 'original' heterosexual practice is itself only an apeing of an original; a theoretically unviable attempt to assert the primacy of heterosexuality as the stable, authoritative origin. The 'performative' practice of the lesbians in the antimasturbatory treatises challenges the authoritative distinctions between the implied natural (heterosexual) and unnatural (lesbian) sexual behaviour that the medical men seek to establish. Significantly, the same challenge is posed to the diagnostic reading of lesbianism in John Marten's treatise on venereal disease. Here the 'vastly extended clitoris', produced by too 'Lustful' (masturbatory) activity and warranting the women's being categorized as 'Hermaphrodites', lead again to the 'performative' conclusion: 'such have been able to perform the Actions of a Man, in accompanying with other women' (Marten, 1708, p. 374). The inscription of lesbian practice into a textual account of venereal diseases makes explicit the links between female homosexuality and contagion that have been intertextually traced.

The discursive attempts to construct lesbianism as an unnatural and infectious mode of sexuality in fact betray the ideological investment in representing it in this way; the legitimizing of heterosexuality as the natural, non-infectious and healthy mode of sexual relations. Such a self-legitimizing exercise, that relies upon the construction of the undesirable 'Other' as that which one is not – or rather wishes not to be – writes us back into the defensive posturings of the 'plague' mentality that still pervades the discourses around HIV and AIDS. Earlier in this chapter, I discussed both the contemporary identification of male homosexuality as a contagious disease and its historical precursors. We can now see that, historically, lesbians have been figured in the same way. Given that lesbians are categorized as a 'low-risk' group in relation to HIV and AIDS, one might not expect the equation of lesbianism and contagion to be current. However, in the late 1980s, the National Blood Transfusion Service distributed leaflets listing the types of people deemed insufficiently healthy to give blood safely; both gay men and lesbians were included within these groupings. What this linking of gay men and lesbians reveals is another twist in the narratives of contagion: it is merely by being a homosexual, male or female, that one is 'plague-ridden'.

Notes

1. See also Cindy Patton (1994), 'Black Bodies/White Trials' in Jonathan Goldberg, (ed.), *Reclaiming Sodom*, New York and London: Routledge, pp. 106–16.
2. The Renaissance 'Molly' is discussed in Alan Bray's (1982) *Homosexuality in Renaissance England*. London: Gay Men's Press, pp. 81–114.
3. For studies of the eighteenth century 'Molly' and sodomitical subcultures, see Rictor Norton (1992), *Mother Clap's Molly House: The Gay Subculture in England 1700–1830*, London: Gay Men's Press; Randolph Trumbach (1987), 'Sodomitical Subcultures, Sodomitical Roles, and the Gender Revolution of the Eighteenth Century: The Recent Historiography', in Robert Purks Maccubbin, (ed.), *'Tis Nature's Fault. Unauthorized Sexuality during the Enlightenment*, Cambridge: Cambridge University Press, pp. 109–21. See also Alan Sinfield's (1994) suggestive reading of effeminacy in eighteenth- and nineteenth-century England, in *The Wilde Century. Effeminacy: Oscar Wilde and the Queer Moment*, London: Cassell, pp. 25–51. For lesbianism in the eighteenth century, see Emma Donoghue (1993), *Passions Between Women: British Lesbian Culture 1668–1801*, London: Scarlet Press.
4. It is important to note that *Plain Reasons* is discussing an aristocratic, homosexual type that is different from that of 'Mollies', who, as Norton (1992) substantially documents, tended to be artisans. For further readings of *Plain Reasons*, see Ed Cohen (1993), *Talk on the Wilde Side: Toward a Genealogy of a Discourse on Male Sexualities*, London: Routledge, pp. 113–14; Sinfield (1994), pp. 39–40.
5. For the relationship between theories of masculinity and national identity, see Michele Cohen (1996), *Fashioning Masculinity: National Identity and Language in the Eighteenth Century*, London: Routledge; Cohen (1993), pp. 15–34.
6. Paramedical representations of lesbians as hermaphrodites in eighteenth-century England are discussed in Emma Donoghue (1993), pp. 25–58 and Cath Sharrock (March 1994), 'Hermaphroditism, or, "The Erection of a New Doctrine": Theories of Female Sexuality in Eighteenth-century England', *Paragraph*, Vol. 1, No. 17, pp. 38–48.

References

Altman, Dennis, *AIDS and the New Puritanism*. London: Pluto Press, 1986.

Bersani, Leo, 'Is the Rectum a Grave?', in Douglas Crimp (ed.), *AIDS: Cultural Analysis, Cultural Activism*, Cambridge, Massachusetts and London: The MIT Press, 1991, pp. 197–222.

Bray, Alan, *Homosexuality in Renaissance England*. London: Gay Men's Press.

Butler, Judith, 'Imitation and Gender Insubordination', in Diana Fuss (ed.), *Inside/Out: Lesbian Theories, Gay Theories*, New York and London: Routledge, 1991, pp. 13–32.

Cohen, Ed, *Talk on the Wilde Side: Toward a Genealogy of a Discourse on Male Sexualities*. London: Routledge, 1993.

Cohen, Michele, *Fashioning Masculinity: National Identity and Language in the Eighteenth Century*. London: Routledge, 1996.

Donoghue, Emma, *Passions Between Women: British Lesbian Culture 1668–1801*. London: Scarlet Press, 1993.

Douglas, Mary, *Purity and Danger: An Analysis of the Concepts of Pollution and Taboo*. London and New York: Ark, 1996.

Foucault, Michel, *The History of Sexuality. An Introduction* (Vol. 1), (trans. Robert Hurley). Harmondsworth: Penguin, 1978.

Gilman, Sander L., 'AIDS and Syphilis: The Iconography of Disease', in Douglas Crimp (ed.), *AIDS: Cultural Analysis, Cultural Activism*, Cambridge, Massachusetts and London: The MIT Presss, 1991, pp. 87–107.

Grover, Jan Zita, 'AIDS: Keywords', in Douglas Crimp (ed.), *AIDS: Cultural Analysis, Cultural Activism*, Cambridge, Massachusetts and London: The MIT Press, 1991, pp. 17–30.

Marten, John, *A Treatise of all the Degrees and Symptoms of the Venereal Disease, In both Sexes*. London, 1708.

Nettle, Humphrey, *Sodom and Onan: A Satire*. London, 1772.

Onania, or, The Heinous Sin of Self-Pollution, and all its Frightful Consequences (in Both Sexes) Considered. (1708/9; 1752 edition), London.

Patton, Cindy, 'Black Bodies/White Trials', in Jonathan Goldberg (ed.), *Reclaiming Sodom*. New York and London: Routledge, 1994, pp. 106–16.

Plain Reasons for the Growth of Sodomy in England. London, 1728.

Sharrock, Cath, 'Hermaphroditism, or, "The Erection of a New Doctrine": Theories of Female Sexuality in Eighteenth-century England', in *Paragraph*, Vol. 1, No. 17, March 1994, pp. 38–48.

Sinfield, Alan, *The Wilde Century: Effeminacy, Oscar Wilde and the Queer Moment*. London: Cassell, 1994.

Sontag, Susan, *AIDS and its Metaphors*. Harmondsworth: Penguin, 1988.

Tissot, 'M.' (Samuel) (1766; 3rd edition), *Onanism: Or, A Treatise Upon the Disorders Produced by MASTURBATION: Or, The Dangerous EFFECTS of Secret and Excessive Venery, by M. Tissot*. (trans. A. Hume). London.

Trumbach, Randolph, 'London's Sapphists: From Three Sexes to Four Genders in the Making of Modern Culture', in Julia Epstein and Kristina Straub (eds), *Body Guards: The Cultural Politics of Gender Ambiguity*, New York and London: Routledge, 1991, pp. 112–41.

Trumbach, Randolph, 'Powers of Observation: AIDS and the Writing of History', in Donald Morton (ed.), *The Material Queer. A LesBiGay Cultural Studies Reader*, Boulder, Colorado and Oxford: Westview Press, 1996, pp. 236–42.

Trumbach, Randolph, 'Sodomitical Subcultures, Sodomitical Roles, and the Gender Revolution of the Eighteenth Century: The Recent Historiography', in Robert Purks Maccubbin (ed.), *'Tis Nature 's Fault: Unauthorized Sexuality during the Enlightenment*, Cambridge: Cambridge University Press, 1987, pp. 109–21.

Trumbach, Randolph, 'The Spectacle of AIDS', in Henry Abelove, Michele Aina Barale and David M. Halperin (eds), *The Lesbian and Gay Studies Reader*, New York and London: Routledge, 1993, pp. 202–11.

Watney, Simon, *Policing Desire: AIDS, Pornography, and the Media*. Minneapolis: Minnesota Press, 1987.

Further reading

Butler, Judith, *Bodies that Matter: On the Discursive Limits of 'Sex'*. New York and London: Routledge, 1993.

Crimp, Douglas (ed.), *AIDS: Cultural Analysis, Cultural Activism*. Cambridge, Massachusetts and London, 1991.

Epstein, Julia, and Straub, Kristina (eds), *Body Guards: The Cultural Politics of Gender Ambiguity*. New York and London: Routledge, 1991.

Foucault, Michel, (1987-1990), *The History of Sexuality*, Vols. 1–3, (trans. Robert Hurley). Harmondsworth: Penguin.

Goldberg, Jonathan (ed.), *Reclaiming Sodom*. New York and London: Routledge, 1994.

Patton, Cindy, *Inventing AIDS*. New York and London: Routledge, 1990.

Singer, Linda, *Erotic Welfare: Sexual Theory and Politics in the Age of Epidemic*. London: Routledge.

Acknowledgement

I wish to thank Simon Watney for his helpful comments.

25

Lesbian and Gay Studies in the Age of AIDS

Simon Watney

> Being blithe about transgression quickly becomes a way of forgetting
> that people actually suffer, and so of putting the (moral) emphasis in
> the wrong place. Prometheus didn't think that transgression was a
> good idea: he thought that elitist knowledge was unjust.
>
> Adam Phillips, *On Flirtation*

> There are two central goals of an undergraduate college education in
> the liberal arts: to produce students who can reason and argue for
> themselves, conducting a Socratically 'examined life', and also to pro-
> duce students who are, to use the old Stoic term, 'citizens of the entire
> world'.   Martha Nussbaum, 'The Softness of Reason'

Introduction

I'd like to begin with a couple of anecdotes, and some basic research.

On a trip to a major US city a friend of mine who is a full-time AIDS
worker met a graduate student studying at a leading local university. They
struck up a friendship, and had sex a few times. The American talked a lot
about current Queer Theory – the 'tyranny of identity', the 'shattering of
the self', and so on. My friend was puzzled that the American, who is of
Hispanic origins, dismissed all aspects of social identity as fictions which
are merely 'performative'. Six months later my friend was back in the
United States, and looked up the student. It was 1995. Sadly his news was
not good. He had been recently diagnosed HIV-positive, and his health was
poor. This well educated young man, attending one of the most prestigious
universities in the developed world, living at the epicentre of the AIDS crisis, could talk the night away about Lacan and Derrida, but he knew
absolutely nothing about any single aspect of AIDS medical science or
related social science. He knew *nothing whatsoever* about treatment issues.

A few months ago I had a bit of a panic about an article I'd agreed to write for a book. Since agreeing to do it I'd been ill myself and had to convalesce for many months. The article was to be about mass media responses to AIDS, and it suddenly occurred to me that if I phoned around a few academic departments with credentials in the field of Lesbian and Gay Studies I would probably find somebody doing interesting work which might be published in my place. I gave up after about half a dozen calls, all reporting back more or less the same message: 'Sorry, nobody studying AIDS here'. In fairness, I was directed to some excellent work by young art historians, but this was not what I was after.

Thinking about this article, I decided to undertake a fast quantitative survey of the literature. I took down from my shelves twelve available anthologies of Lesbian and Gay Studies materials, six British and six American, all published in the 1990s. In all, I counted a total of 233 articles, of which twenty-five were about some aspect of HIV/AIDS. In three recent special 'queer' issues of respected academic journals there was a total of thirty-nine articles, of which three were about HIV/AIDS. Moreover, out of a total of ninety items broadcast in the British lesbian and gay TV series *Out On Tuesday/Out* between 1989 and 1992, only six dealt with the epidemic.[1] This was widely regarded at the time as the 'cutting edge' of contemporary British queer culture.

In this article I want to explore some of the implications of these and other anecdotes and evidence. It is by now clearly apparent that throughout the Anglophone world there are distinct institutional and discursive historical barriers between the separate (if often overlapping) domains of lesbian and gay politics, the lesbian and gay press (where it survives), lesbian and gay community-based HIV/AIDS work, and Lesbian and Gay Studies. This is by no means necessarily a bad thing. With limited resources and varying goals, it may well be the case that territorial specialization and targetting is inevitable. Yet it is surely strange that all the combined energies and enthusiasm of the emergent field of Lesbian and Gay Studies has so far had so little to say about our intimate lived experience of the epidemic. For example, many lesbian and gay AIDS specialists feel abandoned by much of contemporary lesbian and gay politics, as well as by the Lesbian and Gay Studies movement, which often seems to prefer to view the epidemic through the binoculars of arcane literary theory, rather than from the perspective of establishing and fulfilling urgent, practical research needs.

This article is written in the belief that it is important that we sometimes pause to consider both the quality and quantity of the dialogue and interaction between the different sectors of our wider movement. It is vital that we should be able to meaningfully articulate together the various changing aims and strategies of these different sectors, and the many different currents and undercurrents of thought that inform them. Furthermore, it would of course be unwise and naïve to imagine that AIDS is only present in the curriculum by direct, named reference. Indeed, we should by now have come to expect complex displacements and dissociations related to AIDS in the lives of individuals and entire generations of lesbians and gay men, in relation to a catastrophe to which Lesbian and Gay Studies has responded with great caution.

None of the above is perhaps especially surprising, not least because so many of our responses to AIDS are in effect 'private'. Yet what does this tell us about working assumptions concerning the relations between 'private' and 'professional' life? How have we drifted into a situation in which almost everyone working in HIV/AIDS education argues the need to develop and evaluate appropriate Safer Sex materials for gay men rooted in our collective experience, whilst many within the Academy seem increasingly hostile to the very idea of community-based lesbian and gay identities, as if these were an embarrassing form of philosophical error, rather than a most remarkable political and cultural *achievement*? From the constantly beleaguered sector of community-based HIV/AIDS education and service provision, it does seem hard to understand why the queer Academy has found it so seemingly difficult to engage constructively and supportively with much the worst catastrophe in the (albeit brief) history of our common movement.

This in turn raises questions concerning the commonality of international Lesbian and Gay Studies. Whilst with notable exceptions the epidemic is largely invisible in terms of research or writings about it in Lesbian and Gay Studies departments in Britain, Australia and the United States, this doubtless reflects many different local circumstances, and should not be taken as simply an invariant international phenomenon. Nor is the current situation explicable in terms of a lack of potential research funding. Thus in Britain for example, far fewer undergraduate or graduate students have had much direct experience of illness or death in their immediate social circles than in Australia or the USA, though this would not necessarily guarantee a lack of interest in the subject of AIDS within UK-based Lesbian and Gay Studies. There may also be complex intergenerational issues at stake. Certainly there are major differences between the curriculum and the teaching of Lesbian and Gay Studies in Britain and the US, not least at the level of actual lived identities. For example, in Britain academics working in the field describe themselves as lesbians or gay men, whilst in the United States the nomenclature of queer is far more widespread as a term denoting individual and collective identity.

AIDS has been extensively studied under the rubric of many well-established academic disciplines including most noticeably medicine, psychology, and sociology, but in the domain of Lesbian and Gay Studies it usually undergoes a strange sea-change, like so much else besides, and becomes curiously abstracted and transformed into a largely theoretical issue, which may enter the curriculum as an example of other wider debates concerning 'abjection', or 'otherness', or whatever. Yet it remains significant that most lesbians or gay men working on questions of sexuality and AIDS do so either outside Lesbian and Gay Studies, or outside the Academy altogether.

The historical background

The greatest single social and political achievement of the international Gay Liberation Front (GLF) movement of the early 1970s was to usher in a vast range of new possibilities concerning how lesbians and gay men might live lives free of legal and other forms of acute discrimination. Rejecting the older, pre-Wolfenden homosexual culture of concealment and fear which had been so much a product of the legalized persecution of homosexuality, GLF celebrated sexual diversity and insisted on the equal validity of all forms of consensual sexual behaviour. Throughout the Anglophone world, very large numbers of lesbians and gay men worked to establish the first lesbian and gay newspapers and magazines, 24-hour switchboards, housing agencies, support groups, and so on, as well as professional organizations for doctors, teachers and so on, together with Trade Union groups and sections within established political parties, churches, and so on. At the same time there was a slow but steady growth of commercial clubs, bars, restaurants and so on, together with the emergence of an entire culture produced by and for lesbians and gay men in the form of theatre, film and dance companies, independent publishing houses, etc. Indeed, it is extremely difficult for younger lesbians and gay men to comprehend that almost none of the everyday institutions that we take for granted today were available twenty-five years ago.

Alas, very little scholarly historical research has been undertaken concerning the emergence and development of either 'the gay movement' or 'the gay scene' in the 1970s. Subsequent commentators have accused GLF of promoting a supposedly 'universalizing discourse of identity and rights'.[2] Yet such accusations remain unsubstantiated assertions for the obvious reason that there is no evidence whatsoever that would support the proposition that lesbian and gay identities were imagined or experienced in the 1970s as two invariant, monolithic constructions, accepted willy-nilly by *all* 'out' lesbians and gay men. For the many hundreds of thousands of lesbians and gay men who were deeply involved in the social and political struggles of the 1970s and 1980s, it is frequently galling in the extreme to be glibly informed that academics (usually American) somehow invented the critique of sexually grounded identities in the late 1980s and 1990s.[3]

In other words, the modern world of lesbian and gay culture is still very much in its infancy. For example, we have not yet lived to see a generation of confident 'out' lesbian and gay pensioners, though that day is not now far off. Inevitably, the relations between the different generations of a recently emergent social movement are likely to be subject to considerable strain and stress, as younger women and men frame new demands and react against the perceived authority of their predecessors. This situation is further complicated by the contingent history of the wider, changing relations between women and men. Yet what we have gained far outweighs anything we might have lost. The widely felt sense of commonality between substantial numbers of lesbians and gay men in their teens and twenties in the 1990s could hardly have been imagined two decades ago, just as 1950s 'homosexuals' could not have imagined the sense of collectivity developed by the first generations of 'out' lesbians and gay men in the 1970s and 1980s, reflected in the tremendous range of social groups listed in the back pages in any regular lesbian and/or gay male newspaper or news magazine.

However, the development of the modern lesbian and gay movement has been deeply fractured and fragmented by other contingent political and social factors. Of these, the three most conspicuous are, first, the political impact of feminism and gender-based politics and culture; second, the often contradictory impact of the larger political disposition of Reagan-Thatcherism; and third, AIDS. Lesbian and gay and post-gay identities grounded in homosexual desire and behaviour have all been profoundly shaped by these huge influences, in an enormous variety of ways. Thus campaigns against sexual censorship have united some women and men together, and divided others, on both sides of the debate. Similarly, AIDS has united many lesbians and gay men, and divided others. So much for the fantasy of a supposedly uniform lesbian or gay identity, imposed on all!

The proliferation of lesbian-only, and gay, and mixed initiatives has led to a wide variety of different and sometimes conflicting perceptions across the wider arena of lesbian and gay culture and activism. AIDS workers have frequently found fault with the lesbian and gay press, and lesbian and gay politics, just as some lesbian and gay activists have complained that 'too much' attention is paid to AIDS. Meanwhile, it is sometimes asserted that the emergence of the thriving commercial gay scene of the 1990s is nothing more than a reflection of negative and essentially exploitative commercial interests. Such a crude verdict stands in a long tradition of ultra-leftism within the lesbian and gay 'movement', substantial sections of which were always more of the old self-styled Marxist revolutionary left, than of sexual politics. In the main however, the lesbian and gay political movements after GLF were remarkably practical in their demands and their strategies. Lesbian and gay sexual politics were never only concerned with lesbians and gay men: always there was also a wider critique of the organization and power relations of sexuality as a whole, with all its constantly changing forms and identities. Some prominent lesbian and gay politicos may have disliked and even despised the commercial gay scene of the 1970s, but every large-scale political movement contains its share of puritans, and it is simply untrue to assert, as one contemporary British critic who was not around at the time claims, that: '. . . there was a complete split between the politicos and the 'scene queens', a split dating back almost 30 years' (Woods, 1995, p. 15).

Apart from the far left, there was always a constant to-and-fro traffic between the 'movement' and the 'scene' in the lives of most politically active lesbians and gay men in the twenty years after Stonewall. Besides, such totalizing criticisms of the gay scene in the 1970s or today are usually based on the naïve supposition that lesbian and gay culture should somehow be immune to the impact of wider ongoing social changes – as if lesbian and gay culture, unlike the rest of society, should somehow have remained totally free and unpolluted by any of the influences of Reagan-Thatcherism which we would expect to find at work in relation to the constant process of the making and remaking of all contemporary social groups and formations. It is certainly important not to over-emphasize the size or the impact of either the most conservative wing of 'assimilationist' politics within the wider historical lesbian and gay movement, or its opposite revolutionary socialist wing. In reality, few have ever argued against targetted political campaigns designed to reduce or end anti-gay legal discrimination, whilst at the same time few 'out' lesbians or gay men have ever believed that issues of sexual politics begin and end in Westminster, or Washington, or Sydney, or Ottawa. The great majority of those who have ever been heavily involved in lesbian and gay politics or culture have also been extensively involved in a multitude of ways with the gay scene, and this is as true of OutRage or Queer Nation or ACT UP as it was of GLF.

It is against this complex, little-understood historical backdrop that the Lesbian and Gay Studies movement (LGSM) was painstakingly established, in different countries, in relation to different local conditions and local histories. The origins of this movement, in relation to the field of further and higher education, lay in a convergence of many different social forces, ranging from the work of earlier community-based 'independent scholars' to the production of community archives in many cities, and the role of 'out' lesbian and gay academics working within the university system in the wake of GLF. The Women's Movement provided a powerful model for a political movement that aimed as far as possible to be non-sexist in principle and in practice. Feminist academics had also successfully established the validity of Women's Studies within the academic curriculum, though not of course without considerable resistance and continuing contestation. In Britain there was a close relationship between the emergent terrain of Lesbian and Gay Studies and the emergent terrain of cultural studies. For example, it is worth recalling that the first issue of *Working Papers in Cultural Studies* from the University of Birmingham, which launched the Cultural Studies movement, appeared in Britain in 1971, at the height of GLF activism (Dyer, 1971, pp. 53–64). Moreover, that first issue of WPCS contained an article by Richard Dyer about Tom Jones, the popular Welsh singer and symbol of glamorous working-class male heterosexual masculinity, alongside articles by Stuart Hall, Roland Barthes, and others. In the face of later claims that GLF initiated some kind of unitary gay identity, which was believed to be based on some timeless trans-cultural subjective 'essence' of homosexuality, it is well worth pausing to reflect on the sophisticated and prophetic questions with which Dyer concluded his article:

> Rather than seeking to explain why Tom Jones is popular, in itself rather a trivial question, one is saying, given that Jones *is* popular . . .

what does this tell us about the kind of society we live in? Given that he is like *this* what can we suppose (and set up for further research) about contemporary culture and consciousness? (p. 64)

In Britain, one powerful and influential strand of Lesbian and Gay Studies has long been concerned with posing such questions in relation to the position of lesbians and gay men within British culture, and in relation to the cultural forms developed by lesbians and gay men ourselves. This tendency has also been strongly shaped by the historical and theoretical work of Jeffrey Week, Stuart Hall, Michel Foucault and others. Profoundly informed by psychoanalysis (but not necessarily Lacanian), this style of Lesbian and Gay Studies proceeded in the course of the 1970s and 1980s to develop the implications of Dyer's originating and immensely invigorating questions. It provided the central political and intellectual ground of Lesbian and Gay Studies in Britain and Australia, and remains influential throughout the international LGSM diaspora.[4]

How then have we moved from the open-minded eclecticism of the early LGSM, with its involvement in questions of anthropology, historiography, sociology and so on, to the present arid domain of compulsory theoretical abstraction, with its rigid orthodoxies and its remorseless anti-idealism? This tendency is far more marked in the United States than in Britain, and a full historical analysis of the international LGSM would doubtless need to be sensitive to the many ways in which local national political and cultural circumstances have been introjected into the heart of different national LGSM traditions. Certainly the widespread nihilism of much American Queer Theory reveals a deeper sense of exclusion from any ordinary (heterosexual) opportunities for involvement in democratic politics. Moreover, the scale of catastrophic loss from AIDS in the USA is also doubtless reflected in a host of complex ways in Queer Theory and queer studies, in ways which are significantly different to the situations obtaining in countries such as Britain, where the size of the epidemic has been proportionately smaller, or in countries where homosexual transmission has accounted for a smaller percentage of overall cases.

Lesbian and Gay Studies in the age of AIDS

At the end of a lengthy and sometimes illuminating recent analysis of theories of spectatorship in film studies, Caroline Evans and Lorrains Gamman launch what I take to be a currently fashionable assault on the very notion of sexual identities. Apparently unaware of any of the actual, complex history involved, they cite as if it were evidence, the unsubstantiated claims of film critic Alan McKee, writing in the journal *Screen* in 1993, of: '. . . the identity politics of (the) 1970s . . . where a transcendental and essential 'gay identity' stabilized homosexual projects'(p. 38). From here it is only a skip and a jump to the familiar ritual denunciation of lesbian and gay identities as an illusion, a deception, a false ontology – followed by much excited gushing about the supposed virtues of 'multiple, shifting and changeable' sexual subject-positions, which is apparently how many bright young contemporary queers think about themselves.[5]

In effect, the struggles in the 1970s to establish 'theory' as an important element within our understanding of sexuality has ironically led to a narrow stranglehold in much of the Academy by forces which are overtly hostile to lesbian and gay identity politics of any kind. This is especially marked in the United States, where even more than in Britain, contemporary university education consists increasingly of learning by rote, with little reward for intellectual curiosity, or scepticism concerning received wisdoms. Indeed, there can be few more transparent examples of discursive 'regulatory regimes' than American Queer Studies, in which students are herded through a curriculum that in effect often denies the validity or authenticity of any kind of communitarian or collective lesbian and gay culture or politics. I happen to think that this is a very regrettable situation, and that furthermore it explains much about the troubled relations between Lesbian and Gay Studies and the epidemic.

Sadly, much of contemporary Lesbian and Gay Studies seems always to know in advance what it is going to discover. Thus the lives of actual lesbians and gay men are neatly evacuated from the intellectual range of enquiries, and are replaced by fetishized 'texts', which have to stand in for real people. For those of us who worked hard in the 1970s to establish the idea of a 'politics of representation', it is often an unhappy and astonishing experience to witness the extent to which such an approach has come to obscure any clear representations of politics. Much of the current confusion seems to derive from the theoretical assumption that language is the *only* mode of consciousness. Yet what after all is sex, if not a mode of primary communication concerning meanings and feelings that exceed and are not necessarily available to language, save in a *post hoc* mode? What concerns me most in all of this is that constant attacks on the very notion of lesbian and gay male identities developed within the privileged, hothouse world of academia, are grossly irresponsible in the immediate context of the AIDS crisis, and the types of necessary, communitarian identity politics which provide the most reliable forms of resistance and mutual protection.

From the outside, much of the current Lesbian and Gay Studies movement often looks not unlike any other self-congratulatory academic tea-party, with the highest stockades and the most daunting ditches all around it, aggresively refusing access to all but the queerest of the queer (as defined from within). From the outside, nothing could be more remarkable than an academic tendency which has been debating sexual identity and identities for more than a decade, as if this has no connection whatsoever with AIDS! In retrospect, it would appear that there have thus been two simultaneous yet almost entirely unrelated sets of academic and intellectual debates being conducted about (homo)sexual identities since the early 1980s, and it is to these that I now turn.

First, there has been a long debate, grounded above all in a philosophical critique of 'essentialism', which has interpreted lesbian and gay identities as if they are nothing more than responses to oppressive (heterosexual) power, as if all sexual identities were primarily products of 'regulatory regimes'. We are thus urged to combat 'naïve' notions about fixed, or even stable sexual identities. From this perspective, human sexuality is always and everywhere polymorphously perverse, and if you think you are exclusively attracted to either the opposite or the same sex, then you are no more than a helpless and deluded victim, and most certainly not a happy, liberated queer. In this view, identities are always known in advance, in order to be denied. The mutable and inevitably deeply contingent historical forms and dispositions of human sexuality are read as if 'gay identity' somehow involved denying the *ultimate* provisionality of sexual identities. I emphasize the word 'ultimate' because it seems to me that there is all the difference in the world between the insistence on the provisionality and contingency of sexual identities in the longer historical duration, and a certain style of deconstructionist denial of the validity of the category of sexual identity itself on the grounds that such identities are 'merely' provisional, and of their nature 'essentialist'.

It is as if the category of 'the subject', especially the sexual subject, has taken the place within the liberal academic imagination formerly held by 'the ruling class' and its many avatars within the thought-structures of the old far left. Such an approach to sexuality can only take place if the identities under attack are highly abstract and generalized, and largely projective. This can only happen if the whole debate has, in advance, been effectively disconnected from any direct involvement with ordinary human lives, in all their grinding confusion and perplexity. In place of the (always provisional, always to-be-constructed) collectivity of lesbian and gay political and social identities, we are offered only the spectacle of heroically 'transgressive' queers, bravely seeing off dragons of essentialist error, and other thought-crimes – whilst all around them the world in which they live is constantly changing, not least in response to an epidemic which so manifestly disproportionately affects those involved in such debates. This relentless denial of the (always provisional, always to-be-constructed) validity of lesbian and gay identities is frequently evinced with much the same bracing intellectual self-confidence that I well remember being used in the 1970s by those who were then dismissing our identities as merely a froth of 'false-consciousness' in Britain and the United States. These days however in Britain, the more fanatical anti-gay deconstructionist position is more widely espoused by journalists than by academics, and feeds back into the Academy via the publishing explosion associated with the LGSM.[6] 'Anti-gay' politics in Britain amongst men who formerly defined themselves as gay is what happened to queer politics in Britain. It delights in a blatantly snobbish contempt for 'ordinary' lesbians and gay men, who are frequently portayed as more or less uniformly stupid, mindless 'consumers', unable to think or care about anything except body-building, tattoos, body-piercing, designer-clothes, house music and drugs. When the epidemic is mentioned, it is as personal tragedy, but never as a political issue. For example, it is noticeable that the 'anti-gay' tendency in British sexual politics has never had any involvement or shown public concern over HIV/AIDS treatment issues. In fact many leading 'anti-gay' politicos have consistently belittled the work of already beleaguered AIDS service organizations, which provide much-needed and reliable treatment information. This is not the place, but work needs to be done in relation to the historical, cultural mapping of the self-styled 'AIDS dissident' movement, and queer and 'anti-gay' politics and the constituencies they may represent.

The other major debate about lesbian and gay identities has taken place within and outside the university system, but almost entirely outside the academic field of Lesbian and Gay Studies. This other debate has been overwhelmingly concerned with HIV/AIDS prevention and education – work which could not be trusted to be undertaken with any sense of urgency by most heterosexual academic sociologists and psychologists. It has been a debate about the relations between gay male identity, and sexual behaviour – above all, with the adoption and maintenance of safer sex.

It has therefore also been closely connected to the development and evaluation of safer sex education, which is likely to need to change over time, as the epidemic changes, not least in relation to the availability of adequate resources for prevention work, and appropriate campaigns.[7] This second debate about lesbian and gay identities has taken place in the gay press, in books and journals and conferences and magazine articles, and has frequently drawn upon the insights and arguments of the LGSM.[8] It has also been undertaken in academic departments of sociology and education studies.[9] Statistics play an especially important role in the AIDS crisis, not least in relation to our abililty to detect changing trends and patterns or new infections, and their possible relations to other determining factors.[10] At the same time however there have been important and sometimes heated debates about the methods and values of conventional mainstream 'behavioural' studies within academic departments undertaking HIV/AIDS related research. For example, some researchers regard sexual behaviour as if it were just like any other, with little or no sense of what the study of sexuality tells us about the great complexity of human sexual behaviour, not least in relation to the role of the unconscious.[11] Yet as far as I can tell, little of any of this has been considered under the rubric of the LGSM on either side of the Atlantic or Pacific.

To take one example, there was an immensely important international debate focused on the values and beliefs associated with the use of the term 'relapse' in relation to gay men's sexual behaviour for several years from 1989 until about 1992. This was not merely a semantic squabble about the use of words. Rather, it drew attention to a previously unacknowledged division between those who thought of safer sex simply as an 'event', and those who recognized it as a *process*.[12] This in turn reflected profoundly conflicting attitudes towards unsafe sex. Yet this debate never 'crossed over' into the mainstream of the LGSM, and like other such debates it went largely unheard beyond the immediate environment in which contestation had taken place, such as AIDS service organizations around the world producing gay men's health education campaigns, and the social studies tracks of the annual International AIDS Conferences, and in specialist publications. Throughout the early 1990s there has also been a heated international debate about sexual identities in relation to 'negotiated risk', and the potential danger of developing so-called 'AIDS education' campaigns which might have the effect of increasing risks.[13] It is surely in retrospect significant that little if any of the above has been of much interest to the LGSM, with the significant exception of questions concerning lesbians and safer sex. The 're-gaying' of AIDS in the 1990s has not taken place with the support of either the mainstream world of lesbian and gay politics, or the LGSM, yet the 'de-gaying' of AIDS was arguably the most important social and political issue facing gay men all around the world from the late 1980s until today. In Britain it remains significant that much 'anti-gay' opinion has also criticized the 're-gaying' of the epidemic, and cheerfully advises us not to trust wicked scientists.[14] This in turn reflects a wider ignorance of and/or hostility to scientific method in its entirety as one of the many regrettable symptoms of postmodernism. The recognition that science is neither neutral nor necessarily benign is used to justify a wholesale rejection of all things scientific, and this is particularly tragic at a time when it has been so important for us to engage with scientists in the development of potential treatment drugs, or prevention campaigns. Indeed, it is precisely because activists have understood that science is *not* neutral that we have been involved in the biopolitics of AIDS all along.[15]

Conclusion

What, if any, conclusions can be drawn from the above? We may perhaps detect a few trends. Certainly there is an air of unpleasant snobbishness in some academic pronouncements concerning 'ordinary' (e.g., non-academic) lesbian and gay lives, as if having read Judith Butler and Jacques Derrida placed one far above the unsophisticated masses, with their quaint and amusing beliefs about themselves and one another. Ultimately this probably doesn't matter very much, because it affects so very few people, and is part and parcel of the nature of the institutions of further and higher education these days. Yet identity politics do matter, not least because they continue to provoke so much hostility from those who would seek to return us to a largely imaginary past in which 'politics' were unpolluted by such vulgar issues as gender or sexuality or race. They also matter *personally*: for whilst all sexual identities may be (or may become) restrictive to some people, it is equally important to emphasize that they may also provide refuge and stability, whilst providing us with our most intimate sense of psychic and social belonging in the world. Needless to say, much of the lesbian and gay cultural agenda of the 1970s and 1980s looks narrow and didactic ten or twenty years on, yet this hardly justifies a total rejection of the history of the wider social movement of which we are all, willingly or unwillingly, a part. The challenge is not to denounce such identifications, but to explore them, and their significance in the complex process of the forging and

reforging of identities. It is terribly easy to pose as a romantic Outsider, forever 'transgressing' against the evil norms of liberal humanism, or 'crude
essentialism', or 'bourgeois society' – it is rather more difficult to understand the real world, and the possibilities it provides both for growth and
fulfilment and for misery.

It would undoubtedly be a sad day if an over-intellectualized Lesbian
and Gay Studies movement drifted into a cynical politics which threatens
to end up in direct conflict with the lives of most lesbians and gay men, getting along as best we can, involved with our communities at every level,
from our 'families of friends'[16] to our involvement with all the institutions
that frame our lives. 'Coming out' is most decidedly not just 'another'
closet, if you've ever been in or come from the closet. To pretend otherwise
is to disengage oneself from issues of the most immediate and pressing relevance to most lesbians and gay men, not least in relation to AIDS. It also
signifies a certain loss of short-term historical memory, which I have no
doubt is also intimately associated with the epidemic, if in ways we have
barely yet begun to understand.[17]

Hence the importance of insisting that our identities are never only
negative responses to 'regulatory regimes' – they are also and always
shaped by the forces of life-affirming pleasure and sexual love. We need to
be able to understand the constant interaction between these two sets of
processes at work in the forging of individual and collective sexual identities. It is only in a banal and unhelpful sense that they can be dismissed as
fictions since, as Jeffrey Weeks observes, without them: 'We would have no
basis to explain our individual needs and desires, nor a sense of collective
belonging that provides the agency and means for change' (1995, p. 99).
The British psychoanalyst Adam Philips has felicitously described: '. . . the
new pieties of the contemporary sexual enlightenment – that it is more
truthful and better not to know who you are, that it is preferable to shift and
float than to know, stop or stay' (1994, p. 124). Far from having been no
more than an 'essentialist error', the emergence of lesbian and gay identity
politics around the world has been one of the most remarkable social
advances in the post-War period. Frankly, you either accept the validity of
gay and lesbian identities, or you oppose them. There is no half-way house
on this particular road. Nobody begged us to go out and have Gay Liberation, or OutRage or Queer Nation or ACT UP. Nobody forced us at
gun-point to form the modern lesbian and gay press, or the many national
and international organizations which represent many different aspects of
our lives as 'out' lesbians and gay men. Shame and concealment may be a

modish stance for some daring 1990s dandies, but for most they remain involuntary sources of pain and unhappiness. Gay Pride may be a rather rough-and-ready old idea, but at least the sexual politics of the 1970s and 1980s didn't spend *all* its time and energy in misplaced anger and campaigns against ourselves, unlike many of today's queer and 'anti-gay' moralists, who pour out of the gyms to denounce supposedly brain-dead 'muscle-Mary's'. Can anyone seriously believe that 'coming out' merely delivers one into the hands of new systems of oppressive power? What exactly are these terrible 'regulatory regimes' we are warned about, and to which the dreadful illusion of sexual identity makes us so vulnerable? How does any if this relate to the pressing and constantly changing demands of the epidemic in our midst? How are we to study AIDS?

Notes

1. See Colin Richardson, 'TVOD: The Never-Bending Story', in P. Burston and C. Richardson (eds) *A Queer Romance: Lesbians, Gay Men and Popular Culture*, London: Routledge, 1995, pp. 241–44.

2. Steven Seidman, 'Identity and Politics in a "Postmodern" Gay Culture: Some Historical and Conceptual Notes', in Michael Warner (ed.) *Fear Of A Queer Planet: Queer Politics and Social Theory*, Minneapolis: University Of Minnesota Press, 1993, pp. 105–143. See also in much the same vein and reaching similar conclusions, Kenneth Mackinnon, 'Gay's The Word – Or Is It?', in V. Harwood *et al.* (eds) *Pleasure Principles: Politics, Sexuality and Ethics*, London: Lawrence & Wishart, 1993, pp. 109–24.

3. For example, see Paul Burston and Colin Richardson, 'Introduction', in *A Queer Romance*, op. cit. See also Simon Watney, 'Emergent Sexual Identities and HIV/AIDS', in P. Aggleton *et al.* (eds), *AIDS: Facing The Second Decade*, London: Falmer Press, 1993, pp. 13–29.

4. The history of this international movement remains in urgent need of analysis.

5. Such attitudes are closely connected to the influential writings of, amongst others, the US academics Judith Butler and Leo Bersani.

6. For example, the various books and many articles by British journalists Paul Burston and Mark Simpson and other publications from Cassell and Routledge.

7. For an overview of the vast literature on this subject it is most helpful to start with Edward King's *Safety In Numbers: Safer Sex and Gay Men*. London: Cassell, 1993 and New York: Routledge, 1994.

8. See Dennis Altman, *Power and Community: Organizational and Cultural Responses to AIDS*. London: Falmer Press, 1994. See also Simon Watney, *Prac-*

tices Of Freedom: Selected Writings On HIV/AIDS. London: Rivers Oram Press, 1994 and Durham NC: Duke University Press, 1994; and Jeffrey Weeks, *Invented Moralities: Sexual Values In An Age Of Uncertainty*. London: Polity Press, 1995.

9. For example, in Britain, the Institute of Education at the University of London, or the School of Behavioural Sciences at Macquarie University, Sydney, Australia.

10. See Simon Watney, 'The Political Significance of Statistics in the AIDS Crisis: Epidemiology, Representation and Re-Gaying', in Helena Reckitts and Joshua Oppenheimer (eds), *Acting on AIDS*. London: Serpent's Tail Press, 1997; (available on the internet: eking@dircon.co.uk)

11. See Simon Watney, 'AIDS and Social Science: Taking The Scenic Route Through An Emergency', in *Practices Of Freedom*. op. cit.

12. See Peter Davis and Project SIGMA, 'On Relapse: Recidivism or Rational Response?' in P. Aggleton *et al.*(eds), *AIDS: Rights, Risks And Reason*, London: Falmer Press, pp. 133–42. See also Michael Rooney and Peter Scott, 'Working Where The Risks Are', in B. Evans *et al.* (eds), *Working Where The Risks Are: Issues In HIV Prevention*, London: Health Education Authority, 1992, pp. 13–65.

13. See Susan Kippax, R. W. Connell, G. W. Dowsett and June Crawford, *AIDS: Sustaining Safer Sex: Gay Communities Respond To AIDS*. London: Falmer Press, 1993.

14. For example, see Mark Simpson, 'Unholy Trinity', *Time Out*, 8–15 February, 1995, p. 90.

15. See contributions by Edward King, Peter Scott and Mark Harrington in Helena Reckitts and Joshua Oppenheimer (eds), *Acting On AIDS*, op. cit.

16. I heard Armistead Maupin use this phrase in a British television interview some years ago.

17. See Walt Odets, *In The Shadow Of The Epidemic: Being HIV Negative In The Age Of AIDS*. Durham NC: Duke University Press, 1995. See also Simon Watney, 'These Waves of Dying Friends: Gay Men, AIDS and Multiple Loss', in Peter Horne and Reina Lewis (eds), *Outlooks: Lesbian and Gay Sexualities and Visual Cultures*, London: Routledge, 1996, pp. 159–70.

References and Further Reading

Bronski, Michael, 'Sex in the '60s, Sex in the '90s: The Problems Of Pleasure', in *Steam*, Vol. 2, No. 2, Summer 1994, pp. 132–4.

Dyer, Richard, 'The Meaning Of Tom Jones', in *Working Papers In Cultural Studies*. Issue One, University of Birmingham (UK), Spring 1971, pp. 53–64.

Escoffier, Jeffrey, 'Inside the Ivory Closet: The Challenges Facing Lesbian and Gay Studies', *OUT/LOOK*. No. 10, San Francisco, Autumn 1990, pp. 40–50.

Evans, Caroline, and Gamman, Lorraine, 'The Gaze Revisited, or Reviewing Queer Viewing', in Paul Burston and Colin Richardson (eds), *A Queer Romance*, London: Routledge, 1995, pp. 13–56.

Gevisser, Mark, 'Lesbian and Gay Students Choose', in *The Nation*, 26 March 1988, pp. 413–14.

King, Edward, *Safety In Numbers: Safer Sex And Gay Men*. London: Cassell, 1993; New York: Routledge, 1994.

Nussbaum, Martha, 'The Softness Of Reason: A Classical Case For Gay Studies', in *The New Republic*, 13 and 20 July 1992, pp. 26–35.

Phillips, Adam, *On Flirtation*. London: Faber and Faber, 1994.

Rofes, Eric, 'Gay Groups vs. AIDS Groups: Averting Civil War in the 1990s', in *OUT/LOOK*, No.8, San Francisco, Spring 1990, pp. 8–17.

Schulman, Sarah, *My American History: Lesbian And Gay Life During The Reagan/Bush Years*. London: Cassell, 1994.

Sedgwick, Eve Kosofsky (ed.), *Gary In Your Pocket: Stories and Notebooks of Gary Fisher*. Durham NC: Duke University Press, 1996.

Sedgwick, Eve Kosofsky, 'Socratic Raptures, Socratic Ruptures: Notes Toward Queer Performativity', in Susan Gubar and Jonathan Kamholtz (eds), *English Inside and Out*, New York: Routledge, 1993, pp. 122–37.

Vance, Carol S., 'Anthroplogy Rediscovers Sexuality: A Theoretical Comment', in *Social Science and Medicine*, Vol. 33, No. 8, 1991, pp. 875–84.

Watney, Simon, 'AIDS and the Politics of Queer Diaspora', in Monica Dorenkamp and Richard Henke (eds), *Negotiating Lesbian and Gay Subjects*, New York: Routledge, 1995, pp. 53–71.

Weeks, Jeffrey, *Invented Moralities: Sexual Values In An Age Of Uncertainty*. London: Polity Press, 1995.

Woods, Chris, *State Of The Queer Nation: A Critique of Gay and Lesbian Politics in 1990's Britain*. London: Cassell, 1995.

Acknowledgement

The author would like to thank Sally Munt, Andy Medhurst, and Daniel Monk for their helpful comments on an earlier draft of this chapter.

Name Index